Workshop on Lexical and Grammatical Resources for Language Processing

(LG-LP 2014)

Held at COLING 2014

Dublin, Ireland
24 August 2014

ISBN: 978-1-63439-226-6

Printed from e-media with permission by:

Curran Associates, Inc.
57 Morehouse Lane
Red Hook, NY 12571

Some format issues inherent in the e-media version may also appear in this print version.

Printed by Curran Associates, Inc. (2014)

For permission requests, please contact the Association for Computational Linguistics
at the address below.

Association for Computational Linguistics
209 N. Eighth Street
Stroudsburg, Pennsylvania 18360

Phone: 1-570-476-8006
Fax: 1-570-476-0860

acl@aclweb.org

Additional copies of this publication are available from:

Curran Associates, Inc.
57 Morehouse Lane
Red Hook, NY 12571 USA
Phone: 845-758-0400
Fax: 845-758-2634
Email: curran@proceedings.com
Web: www.proceedings.com

Introduction

The first instance of the Workshop on Lexical and Grammatical Resources for Language Processing (LG-LP 2014) took place on August 24th in Dublin, in conjunction with COLING 2014. It was co-sponsored by ASIALEX and endorsed by SIGLEX

The workshop aimed to bring together members of the language-resource (LR) landscape, focusing on complex linguistic knowledge that requires linguistic expertise, e.g. on dictionaries, ontologies and grammars. Such manually-built resources are key to the development of natural language processing (NLP) tools and applications. We intended to strengthen the cohesion of the scientific 'production chain' spanning from the construction of LRs to their exploitation in hybrid or symbolic NLP. It is necessary to increase mutual awareness between researchers along this production chain, regarding their activities, skills and needs, in view of improving the building processes of the resources, their validation and their exploitation.

Many linguists are comfortable with descriptive tasks such as checking lexical entries for a given feature, even if each entry requires analysing or pondering. On the other hand, computer scientists are familiar with formalization and, usually, with notions such as falsifiability or reproducibility, which are fundamental to sciences. Combining all these skills is likely to stimulate innovation. The workshop offered an opportunity of interaction which is required to overcome the compartmentalization between humanities and sciences, and to intensify co-operation between the two ends of the chain. Researchers were encouraged to exchange about how they manage to face several challenges:

- the context of this production chain requires that they not be content with understanding phenomena, but also achieve actual production of formalized results;
- resulting resources should reach a reasonable level of verifiability, e.g. by finding formal or syntactic bases as a support to semantic description;
- methods which are able to cover the most diverse languages are to be preferred;
- the format of manual construction of complex LRs must be highly readable, so that errors can be easily detected and corrected;
- conceptual models are not easy to assign to large amounts of language data; due to idiosyncratic behaviour of lexical entries, it is often required to manually examine them individually as regards syntax or semantics;
- many multiword expressions, including support-verb constructions, are somewhere halfway between compositional and non-compositional constructs;
- actual implementation of NLP systems and real-world applications may provide feedback on complex lexical and grammatical LRs used in them, but experimentation is required to accurately relate features of the LRs with features of results obtained in NLP.

We received 31 submissions and accepted 19: an acceptance rate of 61%. We scheduled 10 papers for oral presentation and 9 as posters. The workshop closed with a general discussion.

We would like to thank the members of the Program Committee for their timely reviews. We would also like to thank the authors for their valuable contributions.

Jorge Baptista, Pushpak Bhattacharyya, Christiane Fellbaum, Mikel Forcada, Chu-Ren Huang, Svetla Koeva, Cvetana Krstev, Éric Laporte
Co-Organizers

Organizers:

Jorge Baptista, University of Algarve, Portugal
Pushpak Bhattacharyya, Indian Institute of Technology Bombay, India
Christiane Fellbaum, Princeton University, USA
Mikel Forcada, Universitat d'Alacant, Spain
Chu-Ren Huang, The Hong Kong Polytechnic University, Hong-Kong
Svetla Koeva, Bulgarian Academy of Sciences, Bulgaria
Cvetana Krstev, University of Belgrade, Serbia
Éric Laporte, Université Paris-Est Marne-la-Vallée, France

Program Committee:

Wirote Arunmanakun, Chulalongkorn University, Thailand
Jorge Baptista, University of Algarve, Portugal
Núria Bel, Universitat Pompeu Fabra, Spain
Pushpak Bhattacharyya, Indian Institute of Technology Bombay, India
Dunstan Brown, University of York, UK
Rebecca Dridan, University of Oslo, Norway
Christiane Fellbaum, Princeton University, US
Mikel Forcada, University of Alicante, Spain
Chu-Ren Huang, Polytechnic University, Hong-Kong
Svetla Koeva, Bulgarian Academy of Sciences, Bulgaria
Cvetana Krstev, University of Belgrade, Serbia
Éric Laporte, Université Paris-Est Marne-la-Vallée, France
Nuno Mamede, IST-UL, Portugal
Ruli Manurung, University of Indonesia, Indonesia
Denis Maurel, Université de Tours, France
Nurit Melnik, Open University, Israel
Adam Meyers, New York University, US
Jee-sun Nam, Hankuk University of Foreign Studies, Korea
Maria das Graças Volpe Nunes, Universidade de São Paulo, Brazil
Kemal Oflazer, Carnegie-Mellon University, Qatar
Thiago Pardo, Universidade de São Paulo, Brazil
Adam Pease, Articulate Software and the Hong Kong Polytechnic University, US & Hong Kong
Miriam Petruck, International Computer Science Institute, Berkeley, US
Adam Przepiórkowski, Polish Academy of Sciences, Poland
Laurent Romary, Humboldt University of Berlin, Germany
Rachel E. Roxas, De LaSalle University, the Philippines
Agata Savary, Université de Tours, France
Carlos Subirats, Universidad Autonoma de Barcelona, Spain
Yukio Tono, Tokyo University of Foreign Studies, Japan
Francis M. Tyers, Noregs Arktiske Universitet, Tromsø, Norway
Aline Villavicencio, Universidade Federal do Rio Gande do Sul, Brazil

Revision of the proceedings:

Takuya Nakamura, LIGM, CNRS, France

Table of Contents

Paraphrasing of Italian Support Verb Constructions based on Lexical and Grammatical Resources

Konstantinos Chatzitheodorou
Aristotle University of Thessaloniki
University Campus, 54124, Thessaloniki, Greece
chatzik@itl.auth.gr

Abstract

Support verb constructions (SVC), are verb-noun complexes which play a role in many natural language processing (NLP) tasks, such as Machine Translation (MT). They can be paraphrased with a full verb, preserving its meaning, improving at the same time the MT raw output. In this paper, we discuss the creation of linguistic resources namely a set of dictionaries and rules that can identify and paraphrase Italian SVCs. We propose a paraphrasing computational method that is based on open-source tools and data such as NooJ linguistic environment and OpenLogos MT system. We focus on pre-processing the data that will be machine translated, but our methodology can also be applied in other fields in NLP. Our results show that linguistic knowledge constitutes a 95.5% precision rate in identifying SVC and an 88.8% precision rate in paraphrasing SVCs into full verbs.

1 Introduction

NLP systems, particularly statistical MT (Brown et al., 1993) need very large corpora in order to produce high quality results. In less-resourced language pairs, many words may occur infrequently, so the estimation of the word alignments can be inaccurate. Furthermore, multiword expressions are still a *hot potato* area for an MT system either statistical or rule-based (Bannard and Callison-Burch, 2005).

A possible technique to resolve all those problems is to generate paraphrases. Paraphrases are alternative ways of expressing the same information within one or more languages (Callison-burch, 2007). The benefits of paraphrasing are multiple: the unknown words will be reduced, the MT output will be better understandable, the accuracy of the meaning will be the same etc.

In MT, paraphrases help to create a more fluent translation and are valuable in the evaluation of MT results (Zhou et al., 2006). Additionally, paraphrases encourage the end user to understand better the main idea of a given text and improve the linguistic level of the text in general, because it is better to express an idea using a full verb than a support verb that has no meaning and a noun.

In this paper, we focus our discussion on paraphrasing Italian SVCs and we propose a computational model for producing monolingual paraphrases. The sentence (1) is an example of a SVC, while the sentence (2) is its paraphrase. The sentence (1) consists of a support verb (*fare*) "make" and a noun (*viaggio*) "trip" that is the head of the sentence. In sentence (2) we observe that the SVC is replaced by a verb, which is the verbal form of the noun. Hence, the SVC of the sentence (1) semantically corresponds to the full verb of the sentence (2).

1. *Mario* ***fa un viaggio*** *negli Stati Uniti d'America.* "Mario **makes a trip** in the United States of America."

2. *Mario* ***viaggia*** *negli Stati Uniti d'America.* "Mario **travels** in the United States of America."

To generate this type of paraphrases, we use semi-automatic methods. On the one hand, the result will be improved and the whole procedure does not take long time to create the linguistic resources. On the

Proceedings of the Workshop on Lexical and Grammatical Resources for Language Processing, pages 1–7,
Coling 2014, Dublin, Ireland, August 24 2014.

other hand, it is not as simple as it may seem, taking into account many both decisions depend on the features of both the support verb and the nominalised verb.

The paper is organised as follows. Section 2 represents the past related work on paraphrasing. Section 3 describes the theoretical background on SVC and Section 4 the linguistic resources and tools used for creating the module. In Section 5, we state our method, explaining step-by-step how the SVC are identified and paraphrased, as well as the obtained results in Section 6. Finally, Section 7 concludes and discusses our work.

2 Related work

In literature, there are many published studies about paraphrasing SVCs. Research methods range from manual linguistic and lexicographic work to automatic NLP-oriented studies. Related work on paraphrasing includes MT, Question Answering, Information Extraction and Text Mining, Summarisation etc.

On the automatic side Bannard and Callison-Burch (2005) use statistical methods in order to acquire paraphrases that will improve the MT output. They use bilingual corpora for extracting the monolingual paraphrases by pivoting through phrases among the two languages. According to their method, if the X is an English phrase and Y its Italian paraphrase and T another possible paraphrase of Y, then, T is equal to X, so it is the paraphrase of X. Other studies (Barzilay and McKeown, 2001; Pang et al., 2003) have used monolingual parallel corpora, such as translations of classic novels in order to automatically generate the paraphrases.

Dictionary and ruled-based paraphrasing is less popular because it requires linguistic knowledge and time. However, Bareiro and Cabral (2009) present ReEscreve, a system that generates monolingual (in Portuguese) paraphrases using resources from OpenLogos MT system. Even if OpenLogos is an old MT system its lexical resources, grammatical rules and syntactic-semantic ontology (SAL) (Scott and Barreiro, 2009) can be applied in many fields in NLP. Other dictionary approaches that can be also used for paraphrasing are WordNet (Fellbaum, 1998; Green et al., 2001) and NOMLEX (Macleod et al., 1997).

3 Support verb constructions

SVCs are predicate noun complexes where the main verb has not a strong value (Gross, 1975). SVCs occur in many languages, such as Italian. For instance, in the Italian phrase *fare un viaggio* the verb *fare* is semantically reduced. In Italian, SVC include verbs like *dare* "give", *avere* "have", *prendere* "take", *essere* "be" etc.

A semantically weak verb is called support verb (Vsup) (Gross, 1975) or light verb (Polenz, 1963). One of its characteristics is that the predicative noun (Npred) is realised as head of a noun phrase. Identifying a SVC is not an easy task and several factors should be taken into consideration. Firstly, they are not frozen expressions because they can be syntactically splitted by a determiner, an adjective or an adverb. For example, *fare un lungo viaggio* "make a long trip". Secondly, there are constructions with the same structure but they are fake (pseudo SVCs). For example, *fare una banca* "make a bank" looks like a SVC but in that case *fare*'s semantic is not reduced.

Given that the meaning of the SVCs is mainly reflected by the nominal predicate, we paraphrase them by replacing the Vsup with a related full verb generated from the predicate noun. For instance, the phrase *faccio una telefonata a Maria* "make a call to Maria" can be simply paraphrased as *telefono a Maria* "I call Maria". The idea behind this methodology is to pre-process a text that will then be translated by a MT Engine so a better MT output will be archived.

4 Linguistic resources and tools

4.1 OpenLogos

OpenLogos is an open source program that machine translates from English and German into French, Italian, Spanish and Portuguese. The system was created by Scott in 1970 but then has been extended by the German Research Centre for Artificial Intelligence (DFKI). It is an old rule-based system MT, but its resources, such as the electronic dictionary, the rules and the SAL which is embedded in the dictionaries, are valuable (Barreiro et al., 2011).

In our work we use only the electronic dictionaries including the SAL, in order to implement a module that will identify and automatically paraphrase SVCs.

4.2 NooJ

As mentioned above, our goal is to implement linguistic resources, tools and methodologies that can be used in automatic processing of SVC and in exporting paraphrases. In this paper, we are presenting only SVCs that consist of the Vsup *fare*.

The main linguistic tool for recognising and paraphrasing SVCs is NooJ (Silberztein, 2003). NooJ is a freeware, linguistic-engineering development environment implemented for formalising various types of textual phenomena such as orthography, lexical and productive morphology, local, structural and transformational syntax. It contains several modules that include large coverage lexical resources such as dictionaries for specific purposes and local grammars that are represented by finite-state transducers for many different languages. Its electronic dictionaries contain the lemmas with a set of information, such as:

$$\text{lemma,(1)+(2)+(3)+}\ldots\text{(4)+}\ldots$$

where (1) corresponds to the category/part-of-speech (e.g. "Ver"), (2) to one or more inflectional and/or derivational paradigms (e.g. how to conjugate verbs, how to nominalise them etc.), (3) to one or more syntactic properties (e.g. "+transitive" or "+PREPin") and finally, (4) to one or more semantic properties (e.g. distributional classes such as "+Human", domain classes such as "+Politics").

Our module consists of specific local grammars and electronic dictionaries in order to recognise paraphrase and translate SVCs, such as *fare una presentazione* "make a presentation" → *presentare* "present". In order to process SVCs, we first converted the OpenLogos dictionary into NooJ format. Each lemma is associated with the category, the inflectional paradigm, the equivalent in English and attributes from SAL ontology. There are also some lemmas containing the Greek equivalent that will help for further research.

Figure 1 illustrates a sample of the electronic dictionariy that consists of 75509 entries. 20501 of them are nouns (2335 of them are proper names and toponyms), 10910 are verbs, 22193 are adjectives, 4621 are adverbs, 151 are conjunctions, 5 are determinatives, 295 are prepositions and 118 are pronouns. 14380 over 75509 lemmas are multiword expressions.

```
ora,N+FLX=N50+ME+dur+ID=59726+EN="hour"+EL="ώρα"
numero intero,N+IN+symb+ID=64248+EN="integer"+EL="ακέραιος αριθμός"+UNAMB
sala da ballo,N+PL+encl+ID=9936+EN="ballroom"+EL="αίθουσα χορού"+UNAMB
entro,PREP+IN+ID=133986+EN="within"+EL="μεταξύ"
bello,A+FLX=A10+AV+state+ID=10871+EN="beautiful"+EL="όμορφος"
ciascuno,PRO+FLX=DET3+ID=0+EN="each"+EL="καθένας"
cinquantasette,A+FLX=A240+NUM+thirtytwo-ninetynine+ID=49175+EN="fifty seven"+EL="πενήντα επτά"
```

Figure 1: NooJ electronic dictionary entries.

Additionally, for the verbs that can be nominalised we created manually its derivational paradigm and the Greek equivalent. Applying a derivational paradigm to a given word is possible to change its syntactic category but not its semantic value. In total, 78 derivational paradigms were created for 289 verbs. For instance, the affix *–zione* changes the verb *presentare* into the noun *presentazione* and the affix *–ata* change the verb *telefonare* to the noun *telefonata*. This is extremely important, in order to generate the paraphrases. Figure 2 illustrates dictionary verb and noun entries that are linked to SVC with the support verb *fare*.

Moreover, it was needed to create from scratch inflectional grammars and other syntactic grammars in NooJ format in order to disambiguate the Italian language.

```
abbreviazione,N+FLX=N51+PNT+ID=1663+EN="abbreviation"+EL="συντόμευση"+Vsup=Fare
abbreviare,V+FLX=V107+OBTR+prep+Aux=avere+ID=1652+EN="abbreviate"+EL="συντομεύω"+DRV=DRV06:N51+Nom+Vsup=Fare
accenno,N+FLX=N10+PNT+ID=3573+EN="adumbration"+EL="υπαινιγμός"+Vsup=Fare
accennare,V+FLX=V100+INOP+Aux=avere+ID=58946+EN="hint"+EL="υπαινίσσομαι"+DRV=DRV52:N10+Nom+Vsup=Fare
accensione,N+FLX=N51+PNT+ID=60828+EN="ignition"+EL="ανάφλεξη"+Vsup=Fare
accendere,V+FLX=V258+OBTR+prep+Aux=avere+ID=67379+EN="kindle"+EL="αναφλέγω"+DRV=DRV05:N51+Nom+Vsup=Fare
accorciamento,N+FLX=N10+ID=0+EN="no-trans"+EL="σύμπτυξη"+Vsup=Fare
```

Figure 2: NooJ electronic dictionary entries.

5 Automated processing of SVCs

5.1 Identification of SVCs

To identify and extract paraphrases for SVCs, we updated OpenLogos dictionaries with morfo-syntactic-semantic information and with derivational and distributional properties as well. This was necessary due to new words that were added in the Italian vocabulary in the last years. We have also created local grammars that are combined with the electronic dictionaries.

We firstly focused on identifying the SVC and updating the existing dictionaries. We obtained that by designing a simple local grammar, that recognises and annotates SVCs and their predicate nouns (see Figure 3). The grammar checks for a verb *fare* followed optionally by a determiner <DET>, adjective <A> or adverb <ADV> and a noun <N>, and annotates it as a SVC (<**SVC=+Pred=$N_**>).

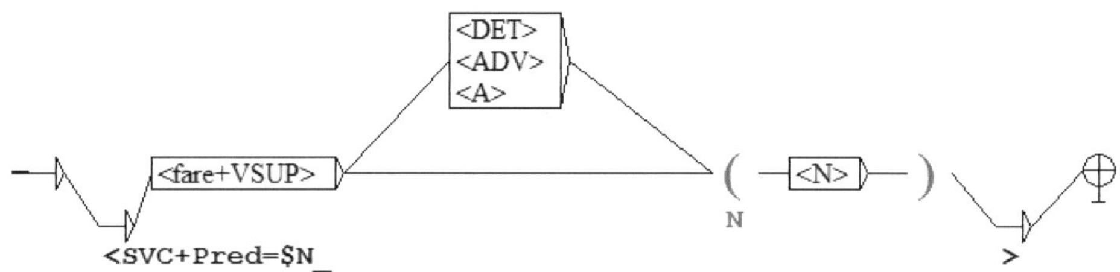

Figure 3: NooJ local grammar for recognizing and annotating SVCs and their predicates.

We applied that grammar to the Italian monolingual Europarl corpus (Koehn, 2005) in order to extract the lemmas of the predicate noun (**$N_**). Then, we updated manually the electronic dictionary by adding the new predicate nouns. We also associated every new predicate to a corresponding lexical full verb and every verb with a derivational paradigm (see Figure 4).

domanda... 2082522 Sua zia mi ha	fatto una maledizione/<SVC+Pred=maledizione>	, e mi sono caduti tutti
tutti i capelli. 2090119 Samuel Colt	fece una pistola/<SVC+Pred=pistola>	. 2095570 - Un tizio ha fatto una
una pistola. 2095570 - Un tizio ha	fatto una carneficina/<SVC+Pred=carneficina>	giu' al conservificio. 2096597 Devo fare
carneficina giu' al conservificio. 2096597 Devo	fare una vaccinazione/<SVC+Pred=vaccinazione>	di richiamo. 2102068 Senti, ho bisogno
Senti, ho bisogno che tu	faccia una preghiera/<SVC+Pred=preghiera>	ai tuoi amici angeli e
del diavolo. 2115421 Cosa pensi che	faccia Morte/<SVC+Pred=morte>	a chi gli spiattella in
a chi gli spiattella in	faccia una bugia/<SVC+Pred=bugia>	? 2120134 Quindi facciamo una lista ecominciamo
in faccia una bugia? 2120134 Quindi	facciamo una lista/<SVC+Pred=lista>	ecominciamo ad escludere qualcosa. 2122399 Facciamo
fermata sul Monte Fato? 2129074 - Allora	faremo una lista/<SVC+Pred=lista>	. 2130125 Ricevi coordinate misteriose da un
Ma una volta che ti	fai una famiglia/<SVC+Pred=famiglia>	, le cose si complicano. 2153649 Una
cose si complicano. 2153649 Una volta	feci uno special/<SVC+Pred=special>	sui programmi notturni. 2156466 Domani faremo
faremo una ricerca. 2158767 Non può	fare certe prodezze/<SVC+Pred=prodezza>	come questa, senza che ci
chiudere il becco, allora mi	farò una dose/<SVC+Pred=dose>	. 2163722 Ci sono dei lavori nella
Se potessi avere quelle lettere,	farei una fortuna/<SVC+Pred=fortuna>	. 2170008 Avevo idea di fare una

Figure 4: NooJ concordance after annotation of SVCs and identification of the lemma of the predicate nouns.

5.2 Paraphrasing

After updating the electronic dictionaries, more monolingual paraphrases can be obtained easily. Figure 5 represents a local grammar used to recognise, generate SVCs and transform them into their verbal paraphrases. The grammar checks for the verb *fare* in present indicative tense followed by a <DET>, an <A> or an <ADV> and a noun, and generates the verbal paraphrases in the same tense. Furthermore, we restrict our research to Vsup *fare* but the same methodology can be apply to other SVCs. The same structure follow the grammars created for the other grammatical tenses and moods. The elements **<$V=:fare+PR+1+s>**, and **$N_PR+1+s** represent lexical constraints that are displayed in the output, such as specification of the support verb that belongs to a specific SVC. The predicate noun is identified, mapped to its deriver and displayed as a full verb while the other elements of the phrase are eliminated. Figure 6 shows a NooJ concordance were Italian SVCs are identified and paraphrased as full verbs.

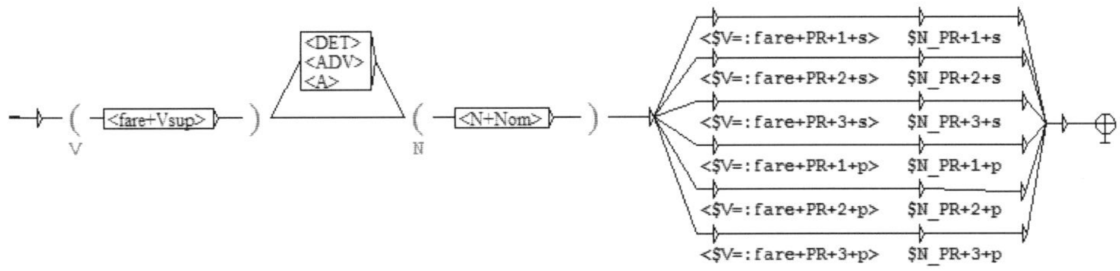

Figure 5: NooJ local grammar for paraphrasing SVCs.

lista ecominciamo ad escludere qualcosa. 2122399	Facciamo una visita/visitiamo	alla sorella? 2126016 Che ne dici
alla sorella? 2126016 Che ne dici,	facciamo una fermata/fermiamo	sul Monte Fato? 2129074 - Allora faremo
citta' misteriosa e non ti	fai nessuna domanda/domandi	? 2130357 Ma una volta che ti
per me. 2159218 Quindi esattamente alle 4:15,	fai una chiamata/chiami	anonima alla polizia. 2159261 Se ti
sono dei lavori nella strada,	facciamo una deviazione/deviamo	. 2165350 Se potessi avere quelle lettere
Ce ne faremmo uno doppio. 2327766	Facciamo una festa/festeggiamo	! 2327773 Beh, me ne fai una
E' l'ultima volta che	faccio una favore/favorisco	a te e ai tuoi
tantoin tanto faccio una scommessa. 2395233	Faccio una corsa/corro	verso l'aeroporto di San
una multa a Batman? 2411766 Voi	fate una controllo/controllate	approfondito sul fascicolo personale di

Figure 6: NooJ concordance for paraphrasing.

6 Evaluation

We performed a manual evaluation by judging the precision and the recall of 100 phrases that include the *fare*. We should notice that only 95 of them were containing SVCs while the other 5 contain the verb *fare* followed by a non predicate noun, hence they cannot be paraphrased. This test set was extracted radomly from the Italian OpenSubtitles corpus (Tiedemann, 2004). Table 1 details the evaluation results of recognition and paraphrasing of SVCs. We calculated the results for recognising and paraphrasing given that a recognised SVC is not always paraphrased correctly. We observe that our module can recognise 86 over 90 SVC that means a precision rate of 95.5%. Regarding recall, 86 over 95 SVCs were recognised so, an 90.5% rate was obtained. On the other hand, a precision rate of 88.8% (80/90) and a recall rate of 84.2% (80/95) were obtained for the generated paraphrases. The F-measure for recognising is 92.93 while for paraphrashing is 86.43.

According to Bareiro and Cabral (2009), MT performs better when translating full verbs over SVCs. We translated in Google Translate[1] the same test set both with SVC and its paraphrases and then we calculated the BLEU score (Papineni et al., 2002) having as reference the English version (with a single reference translation). Even if the test set is small for an automatic evaluation, results show an improvement of 0.6 BLEU points when we pre-process the data paraphrasing. In more detail, the obtained BLEU score for the original test set is 42.76 while for the paraphrased is 43.36.

	Precision	Recall
Identifing	86/90	86/95
Paraphrasing	80/90	80/95

Table 1: Human evaluation results.

[1] `https://translate.google.com/`.

The evaluation results clearly show that paraphrasing can improve the quality of MT. We expect that the low recall scores could be higher upon the improvement of the electronic dictionaries and local grammars.

7 Conclusions and Outlook

In this paper, we present a SVC-based paraphrasing framework that uses existing tools and technologies and hand crafted additions for purposes of increasing translation accuracy. Our methodology archived a precision of 95.5% and a recall of 90.5% in identifying and a precision of 88.8% and a recall of 84.2% in paraphrasing. We also applied our method in a freely available MT system and results show a significant improvement.

To make our paraphrasing methodology more accurate, further analysis and work on electronic dictionaries is needed. Especially, we need to work on the pseudo *fare* SVCs. Furthermore, our work should focus on paraphrasing SVC with full verb that is not associated to the predicate noun such as *fare una sigaretta* "make a cigarette" $\rightarrow$ *fumare* "smoke". Last but not least, the graphs should be extended in order to not discard the adverbs and adjectives that are included in the SVCs. In that case, the MT quality will be more accurate.

In future research, we are also willing to extend the local grammars and dictionaries in order to generate bilingual paraphrases in other languages such as Greek and English. For instance, *fare una presentazione* $\rightarrow$ *to present* in English or *fare una presentazione* $\rightarrow$ $\pi\alpha\rho o\upsilon\sigma\iota\alpha\zeta\omega$ in Greek.

References

Colin Bannard and Chris Callison-Burch. 2005. *Paraphrasing with bilingual parallel corpora.* In ACL-2005.

Anabela Barreiro, Bernard Scott, Walter Kasper and Bernd Kiefer. 2011. *OpenLogos Rule-Based Machine Translation: Philosophy, Model, Resources and Customization.* Machine Translation, volume 25 number 2, Pages 107-126, Springer, Heidelberg, 2011. ISSN: 0922-6567. DOI: 10.1007/s10590-011-9091-z.

Anabela Barreiro and Lus Miguel Cabral. 2009. *ReEscreve: a translator-friendly multi-pupose paraphrasing software tool.* MT Summit XII - Workshop: Beyond Translation Memories: New Tools for Translators MT, August 29, 2009, Ottawa, Ontario, Canada.

Regina Barzilay and Kathleen McKeown. 2001. *Extracting paraphrases from a parallel corpus.* In ACL-2001.

Peter F. Brown and Vincent J.Della Pietra and Stephen A. Della Pietra and Robert. L. Mercer. 1993. *The Mathematics of Statistical Machine Translation: Parameter Estimation.* In Computational Linguistics.

Chris Callison-burch. 2007. *Paraphrasing and Translation.* PhD Thesis, University of Edinburgh.

Christiane Fellbaum. 1998. *WordNet: An Electronic Lexical Database.* Cambridge, MA: MIT Press.

Rebecca Green, Lisa Pearl and Bonnie J. Dorr. 2001. *Mapping WordNet Senses to a Lexical Database of Verbs.* In Proceedings of the 39th Annual Meeting of the Association for Computational Linguistics, pages 244251, Toulouse, France.

Maurice Gross. 1975. *Mthodes en Syntaxe.* Paris: Hermann.

Philipp Koehn. 2005. *A Europarl: Parallel Corpus for Statistical Machine Translation.* MT Summit.

Catherine Macleod, Adam Meyers, Ralph Grishman, Leslie Barrett, Ruth Reeves. 1997. *Designing a Dictionary of Derived Nominals.* Proceedings of Recent Advances in Natural Language Processing, Tzigov Chark, Bulgaria, September, 1997.

Bo Pang, Kevin Knight, and Daniel Marcu. 2003. *Syntax-based alignment of multiple translations: Extracting paraphrases and generating new sentences.* In Proceedings of HLT/NAACL.

Kishore Papineni, Salim Roukos, Todd Ward, and Wei-Jing Zhu. 2002. *BLEU: a method for automatic evaluation of machine translation.* In ACL-2002: 40th Annual meeting of the Association for Computational Linguistics.

Peter von Polenz. 1963. *Funktionsverben im heutigen Deutsch.* Sprache in der rationalisierten Welt, Dsseldorf, Schwann.

Bernard Scott and Anabela Barreiro. 2009. *OpenLogos MT and the SAL representation language.* In Proceedings of the First International Workshop on Free/Open-Source Rule-Based Machine Translation / Edited by Juan Antonio Prez-Ortiz, Felipe Snchez-Martnez, Francis M. Tyers. Alicante, Spain: Universidad de Alicante. Departamento de Lenguajes y Sistemas Informticos. 23 November 2009, pp. 1926.

Max Silberztein. 2003. *NooJ Manual.* Available for download at: `www.nooj4nlp.net`.

Jorg Tiedemann and Lars Nygaard. 2004. *The OPUS corpus – parallel & free.* In Proceedings of the Fourth International Conference on Language Resources and Evaluation (LREC'04). Lisbon, Portugal, May 26-28.

Liang Zhou, Chin-Yew Lin, Dragos Stefan Munteanu, and Eduard Hovy. 2006. *Paraeval: Using paraphrases to evaluate summaries automatically.* In Proceedings of HLT/NAACL.

Using language technology resources and tools to construct Swedish FrameNet

Dana Dannélls **Karin Friberg Heppin** **Anna Ehrlemark**

Department of Swedish
University of Gothenburg
firstname.lastname@svenska.gu.se

Abstract

Having access to large lexical and grammatical resources when creating a new language resource is essential for its enhancement and enrichment. This paper describes the interplay and interactive utilization of different language technology tools and resources, in particular the Swedish lexicon SALDO and Swedish Constructicon, in the creation of Swedish FrameNet. We show how integrating resources in a larger infrastructure is much more than the sum of the parts.

1 Introduction

This paper describes how Swedish language technology resources are exploited to construct Swedish FrameNet (SweFN),[1] a lexical-semantic resource that has been expanded from and constructed in line with Berkeley FrameNet (BFN). The resource has been developed within the framework of the theory of Frame Semantics (Fillmore, 1985). According to this theory, semantic frames including their participants represent cognitive scenarios as schematic representations of events, objects, situations, or states of affairs. The participants are called frame elements (FEs) and are described in terms of semantic roles such as AGENT, LOCATION, or MANNER. Frames are evoked by lexical units (LUs) which are pairings of lemmas and meanings.

To get a visualization of the notion of semantic frames consider the frame `Vehicle_landing`. It has the following definition in BFN: "A flying VEHICLE comes to the ground at a GOAL in a controlled fashion, typically (but not necessarily) operated by an operator." VEHICLE and GOAL are the *core elements* that together with the description uniquely characterize the frame. Their semantic types are *Physical_object* and *Location*. The *non-core elements* of the frame are: CIRCUMSTANCES, COTHEME, DEGREE, DEPICTIVE, EVENT_DESCRIPTION, FREQUENCY, GOAL_CONDITIONS, MANNER, MEANS, MODE_OF_TRANSPORTATION, PATH, PERIOD_OF_ITERATIONS, PLACE, PURPOSE, RE_ENCODING, SOURCE, and TIME. The lexical units evoking the frame are: *land.v*, *set_down.v*, and *touch_down.v*. In addition, the frame contains a number of example sentences which are annotated in terms of LUs and FEs. These sentences carry valence information about different syntactic realizations of the FEs and about their semantic characteristics.

Currently SweFN contains around 1,150 frames with over 29,000 lexical units of which 5,000 are verbs, and also 8,300 semantically and syntactically annotated sentences, selected from a corpus.

SweFN has mainly been created manually, but as a response to an ever increasing complexity, volume, and specialization of textual evidence, the creation of SweFN is enhanced with automated Natural Language Processing (NLP) techniques. In contrast to the construction of English resources, as well as the construction of framenets for other languages, the resources used to construct SweFN are all linked in a unique infrastructure of language resources.

2 The development of framenets in other languages

FrameNet-like resources have been developed in several languages and have been exploited in a range of NLP applications such as semantic parsing (Das et al., 2014), information extraction (Moschitti et

[1] http://spraakbanken.gu.se/eng/resource/swefn

Proceedings of the Workshop on Lexical and Grammatical Resources for Language Processing, pages 8–17,
Coling 2014, Dublin, Ireland, August 24 2014.

al., 2003), natural language generation (Roth and Frank, 2009), and semi-automatic disambiguation of polysemous words (Alonso et al., 2013).

Currently the most active framenet research teams are working on Swedish FrameNet (SweFN) (Borin et al., 2010; Heppin and Gronostaj, 2014), Japanese FrameNet (JFN) covering 565 frames, 8,500 LUs, and 60,000 annotated example sentences (Ohara, 2013) and FrameNet Brazil (Br-FN) for Brazilian Portuguese (Torrent, 2013) covering 179 frames, 196 LUs, and 12,100 annotated sentences.[2]

Even though the point of departure for all FrameNet-like resources is BFN, they differ in a number of important aspects. SweFN has focused on transferring frames and populating them with LUs. For each frame there are annotated example sentences extracted from corpora. Sentences illustrate the instantiation of a number of LUs and FEs with regard to the frame, but many LUs do not yet have associated example sentences. BFN and Spanish FrameNet (Subirats, 2009) also use isolated corpus sentences for annotation while the SALSA project for German (Burchardt et al., 2009) has the aim of creating full-text annotation of a German corpus. JFN, Spanish FrameNet, and FN-Br all use BFN software to construct frames, while SweFN uses its own software and tools. Even though JFN uses BFN software and annotations tools for as much compatibility with BFN as possible, the Japanese writing system differs considerably from that of English, and several modifications have been necessary to handle the different character systems and word boundary issues.

Most framenets have the intention of covering general language. However, there are domain specific resources such as, the Copa 2014 FrameNet Brasil, a multilingual resource for the language of soccer and tourism (Torrent et al., 2014) covering Portuguese, English and Spanish. Bertoldi and de Oliveira Chishman (2011) describe work buiding a FrameNet-like ontology for the language of criminal justice contrasting the differences between English and Portuguese languages and legal cultures.

3 Lexical and grammatical resources and tools for Swedish

Swedish FrameNet is part of SweFN++, a larger project with the goal to create a multifaceted panchronic lexical macro-structure for Swedish to be used as an infrastructure component for Swedish language technology and development of NLP applications and annotated corpora. One goal of SweFN++ is to re-use and enhance existing in-house and external lexical resources and harmonize them into a single macro-structure for processing both modern and historic Swedish text (Borin et al., 2010). Another goal is to release all SweFN++ resources under an open content license.

3.1 SALDO – association lexicon

SALDO (Borin et al., 2013a)[3] is a Swedish association lexicon which contains morphological and lexical-semantic information for more than 131,000 entries, of which around 10% are verbs. SALDO entries are arranged in a hierarchical structure capturing semantic closeness between lexemes. Each lexical entry of SALDO has a unique identifier. Each lexical entry, except 41 top nodes, also has a main descriptor, which may be complemented with a second determinative descriptor. These descriptors are other, more central, entries from SALDO. The SALDO entry for the noun *flaska* 'bottle', with its descriptors, is shown in figure 1.

SALDO is the pivot of all the Swedish lexical language technology resources maintained at Språkbanken. Having one pivot resource makes it possible for all Språkbanken resources to be compatible with each other (Borin and Forsberg, 2014).

3.2 Swedish Constructicon

The Swedish Constructicon (SweCcn)[4] is an electronic database of Swedish constructions (Lyngfelt et al., 2012; Sköldberg et al., 2013). Just as it is precursor the Berkeley Constructicon,[5] it builds on experiences from Construction Grammar and is historically, methodologically and theoretically closely related to Frame Semantics and FrameNet (Fillmore et al., 2012). While framenets map single lexical

[2] `http://www.framenetbr.ufjf.br`
[3] `http://spraakbanken.gu.se/saldo`
[4] `http://spraakbanken.gu.se/swe/swecxn`
[5] `http://www1.icsi.berkeley.edu/~hsato/cxn00/21colorTag/index.html`

Figure 1: A search for the noun *flaska* 'bottle' in SALDO shows that it only has one sense. We are also shown the lemma, the part of speech, the primary descriptor *förvara* 'store.v', the secondary descriptor *hälla* 'pour.v', and finally primary and secondary children, that is entries which have *flaska* as primary or secondary descriptor.

units to the frames they evoke, a constructicon deals with the pairing of form and meaning in more complex linguistic units, typically (partially) schematic multiword units that cannot easily be referred to by either grammatical or lexicographic descriptions alone.

In SweCcn each construction is described individually in a construction entry, defined by its specific characteristics in form, meaning, function, and distribution. Each entry includes a free text definition, schematic structural description, definitions of construction elements (CEs) and annotated example sentences. Since the constructicon must account for both form and meaning, the construction elements can be both semantic roles and syntactic constituents. For example, the construction `reflexiv_resultativ`, instantiated in *äta sig mätt* 'eat oneself full', is defined as a verb phrase where somebody (ACTOR) or something (THEME) performs an action (ACTIVITY) that leads to a result which affects the ACTOR/THEME, expressed with a reflexive particle. The construction roughly means "achieve something by V-ing", and can be applied to both transitive and intransitive verbs, altering the verbs' inherent valence restrictions. The syntactic structure of the construction is [V refl AP], and the construction elements are defined as the semantic roles ACTOR, THEME, ACTIVITY and RESULT, as well as the reflexive particle. Example sentences like *dricka sig full* 'drink oneself drunk' and *springa sig varm* 'run oneself warm' are added to the entry, while an example like *känna sig trött* 'feel tired' does not fit since one doesn't get tired by feeling.

Swedish Constructicon is developed as an extension of Swedish FrameNet and forms a part of the SweFN++ infrastructure. Swedish Constructicon currently consists of about 300 construction entries, ranging from general linguistic patterns to partially fixed expressions, of which a significant part are constructions in the borderland between grammar and lexicon, commonly neglected from both perspectives.

3.3 Karp – open lexical infrastructure

Karp is an open lexical infrastructure with three main functions: (1) support the creation, curation, and mutual integration of the lexical resources of SweFN++; (2) publish all lexical resources at Språkbanken, making them searchable and downloadable in various formats such as Lexical Markup Framework (LMF) (Francopoulo et al., 2006), and Resource Description Framework (RDF) (Lassila and Swick, 1999); (3) offer advanced editing functionalities with support for exploitation of corpora resources (Borin et al., 2013b).

There are 21 resources with over 700,000 lexical entries available in Karp. Since all resources utilize the lexical entries of SALDO, a large amount of information becomes accessible when performing simple searches. For example when we look up the SALDO entry *flaska..1* 'bottle', we find information about the synset from Swesaurus,[6] a WordNet-like Swedish resource, as well as synset and sense from Princeton WordNet,[7] syntactic valence from PAROLE,[8] identifier from Loan Typology Wordlist (LWT),[9]

[6] `http://spraakbanken.gu.se/eng/resource/swesaurus`
[7] `http://wordnet.princeton.edu/`
[8] `http://spraakdata.gu.se/parole/lexikon/swedish.parole.lexikon.html`
[9] `http://lingweb.eva.mpg.de/cgi-bin/ids/ids.pl?com=simple_browse&lg_id=187`

the lexical ID from Lexin,[10] etc. Each of these resources is in turn linked to mono- and multi-lingual information that can be exploited by any other resource or application.

3.4 Korp – Swedish corpora

Korp is a Swedish corpus search interface developed at Språkbanken. It provides access to over 1.6 billion tokens from both modern and historic Swedish texts (Borin et al., 2012; Ahlberg et al., 2013). The interface allows advanced searches and comparisons between different corpora, all automatically annotated with dependency structure using MaltParser (Nivre et al., 2007).

One functionality provided by Korp is *Related Words*. This shows a list of words fetched from SALDO which are semantically related to the search term. Only words that actually occur in the corpora are retrieved by this function. By clicking on one of these, a new corpus search is done with this word as search term (Borin et al., 2012). Another functionality in Korp is *Word Picture* which uses statistical data to select typical examples illustrating collocational semantic relations for chosen expressions. This query system extracts frequent collocations of the word in question along with an analysis of the parts-of-speech of the collocating words.

4 The development of SweFN

As described by the BFN research team, manual construction of a framenet resource involves several steps, including defining frames and frame elements, collecting appropriate lexical units for the frames, comparing the findings with printed dictionaries, extracting syntactic and collocational contexts to illustrate the frame, and analyzing sentences to explore the use of LUs (Fillmore et al., 2003).

The work procedure of SweFN is based on transfer of information from BFN. To a large extent we follow the BFN development process, but the development of SweFN differs in three crucial aspects: (1) when we transfer frames from BFN to Swedish, there is usually no need to re-define them. However, the frames are checked for compatibility with Swedish language and culture; (2) our inventory of LUs is derived from the SALDO lexicon; (3) we utilize in-house resources, all linked in the Swedish infrastructure for language technology, SweFN++.

Taking BFN as a starting point saves time and effort in developing frames. Most of the effort goes to figure out what SALDO entries evoke which frames and to find suitable example sentences. In order to find appropriate LUs evoking a particular frame we consult: (1) the lexical resources in Karp (see section 4.3); (2) printed dictionaries; (3) the corpus infrastructure Korp for concordance search in order to investigate additional uses of the words. This process occasionally results in new frames or modification of the frames of BFN (see section 4.4).

4.1 SALDO

The manual process of constructing a SweFN frame begins with choosing a frame from BFN or word of interest. When we create a frame equivalent to one which already exists in BFN, we transfer the frame features which are more or less language independent from the BFN frame to the SweFN frame. These features include frame description, frame-to-frame relations, and FEs. We then search for appropriate SALDO entries evoking the frame as well as example sentences for annotation. If suitable entries exist in SALDO they are chosen for use as LUs. Otherwise we suggest entries to be added to SALDO (Borin et al., 2013a). Each SALDO sense is allowed to populate only one SweFN frame except in a few cases where some inflectional forms evoke one frame and other forms another frame.

When we instead use a word or expression as a starting point we look up all senses in SALDO and systematically add each sense to the frame it evokes. The selection of LUs from SALDO to populate the frames of SweFN is done in different ways. One method is to determine which of the English LUs of BFN frames have suitable equivalents in Swedish. Thereafter different types of searches are made in SALDO. For example, working on the frame `Containers`, having introduced the noun LU *flaska* 'bottle' one can search for entries ending with *flaska*, thus finding a number of compounds such as *champagneflaska* 'champagne bottle', *droppflaska* 'dropper bottle (med.)', *engångsflaska* (one+time+bottle)

[10] `http://lexin2.nada.kth.se/lexin/`

'non-returnable bottle', *glasflaska* 'glass bottle', *halvflaska* (half+bottle) '375ml bottle', *miniatyrflaska* 'miniature bottle', *nappflaska* (pacifier+bottle) 'baby bottle', *sprayflaska* (spray+bottle) 'spray can', *tomflaska* 'empty bottle', *vattenflaska* 'water bottle', *värmeflaska* (heat+bottle) 'warm water bottle', to name a few. Another method is searching for entries having the LU in question as one of the determiners. For example, working on the `Animal` frame, a search may be done on the determiner *djur* 'animal' resulting in a long list of lexical entries for different species of animals, which may be entered into the frame.

The possibility of doing searches in SALDO as described above, in combination with compounding being very productive in Swedish, is one reason for the relatively large number of LUs in SweFN.

4.2 Swedish Constructicon

Constructions are more complex linguistic units than words, they are common in use and difficult to ignore when working with authentic text. One way to enrich SweFN with more representative examples of how to express meaning in language is to include constructions as frame-evoking units in the database. Currently work is being done on systematically linking constructions in SweCcn with frames in SweFN (Ehrlemark, 2014), but the task is not as straight-forward as identifying which frame is evoked by a certain LU. First, not all constructions evoke frames, carrying little meaning from a semantic point of view. This includes such general patterns as constructions for modification, predication, passive voice or filler-gap constructions. Second, constructions that potentially correspond with frames do not always fit the distribution pattern of frame elements described in the target frame. This group includes figurative constructions or constructions that are more, or less, general than the target frame in SweFN. Constructions which do correspond with frames may be called frame-bearing constructions (Fillmore et al., 2012). A frame-bearing construction evokes a target frame in the same manner as an LU, with matching construction elements and frame elements.

The linking of constructions with frames is carried out through manual analysis of constructions and their semantic valence patterns. The work includes paraphrasing the meaning of a construction to identify which frame or frames it may evoke, and thereafter comparing the construction elements with the FEs of the target frame. For example, SweCcn includes three constructions for comparisons: `jämförelse` 'comparison', which has the two subordinate constructions `jämförelse.likhet` 'comparison.similarity' and `jämförelse.olikhet` 'comparison.difference' – all three are Swedish equivalents of corresponding constructions in the Berkeley Constructicon (Bäckström et al., 2014). In all three cases the CEs in the construction entries correspond to the FEs in the `Evaluative_comparison` frame which has the following definition: a PROFILED_ITEM is compared to a STANDARD_ITEM with respect to some ATTRIBUTE. By establishing a link between, in this case the `comparison` constructions and the `Evaluative_comparison` frame, we may enrich the frame with typical example sentences such as *Hennes cykel är bättre än min* 'Her bicycle is better than mine' and *Popband är lika arga som rockband* 'Popbands are as angry as rockbands'.

Another example is the pair of constructions `proportion_i_om` and `proportion_per`, which distinguish different syntactic patterns for expressing proportion in Swedish. In both cases, the construction combines two entities, a numerator and a denominator, joined by a preposition. However, they differ regarding domain of use, preposition used, and definiteness of the second noun phrase. The construction `proportion_i_om` describes time, and therefore corresponds to frames that express proportion in relation to time units, such as `Frequency` and `Speed_description`. The construction `proportion_per` is a more general construction that expresses `Frequency` and `Speed_description` as well as other ratio relations as described in the frames `Relational_quantity`, `Rate_quantification`, `Proportion`, and `Price_per_unit`. Thus, a link between SweFN and SweCcn may refer the user to correct Swedish constructions for ratio relations from the frames they evoke.

At the time of writing, about half of the entries in SweCcn are linked to frames in SweFN. The continuing work with comparing and linking the two resources does not aim to link all constructions with frames, but rather to distinguish frame-bearing from non-frame-bearing constructions. The linking allows the user to easily go between a construction and the frame or frames it evokes and correspondingly from a frame to constructions evoking the frame. In this way, both SweCcn and SweFN become more representative of the language they set out to describe and better incorporated for future pedagogical and language technological uses.

4.3 Karp

As well as being the editing tool used to build SweFN and other resources, Karp is an important tool for accessing information. Searching on any expression, word form or lemma results in a display of every occurrence in all SweFN++ resources, except instances in the corpus. This gives, for example, an overview of different senses of polysemous words, in which resources they have been entered and how. Thus, we can see which SweFN frames are evoked by different senses of a word, we can see synonymous words in Swesaurus (Borin and Forsberg, 2014), the morphology of the word as well as multiword units containing this word in SALDO, samples of sentences from Korp where the chosen word occurs, and constructions in Swedish Constructicon which use this word (Lyngfelt et al., 2012).

SweFN developers use Karp to find SALDO entries that evoke a particular frame, SweCcn developers use Karp to find frames evoked by constructions, or constructions that evoke frames. Figure 2 shows an example of a view in Karp. In this particular view SweFN and SweCcn resources were selected, but other choices are also possible. The combination of searches shown here are in turn for a certain construction or frame (two first boxes), for constructions that match a certain frame (third box). This particular search is for constructions that match `Similarity`, which here resulted in 14 different constructions, each of which contained potential patterns which in turn could be used to perform new searches in Korp. Finally, in the fourth box the search is for a particular SALDO sense, and in the fifth box for a certain LU. Searches for other types of units such as frame elements, etc. are also possible.

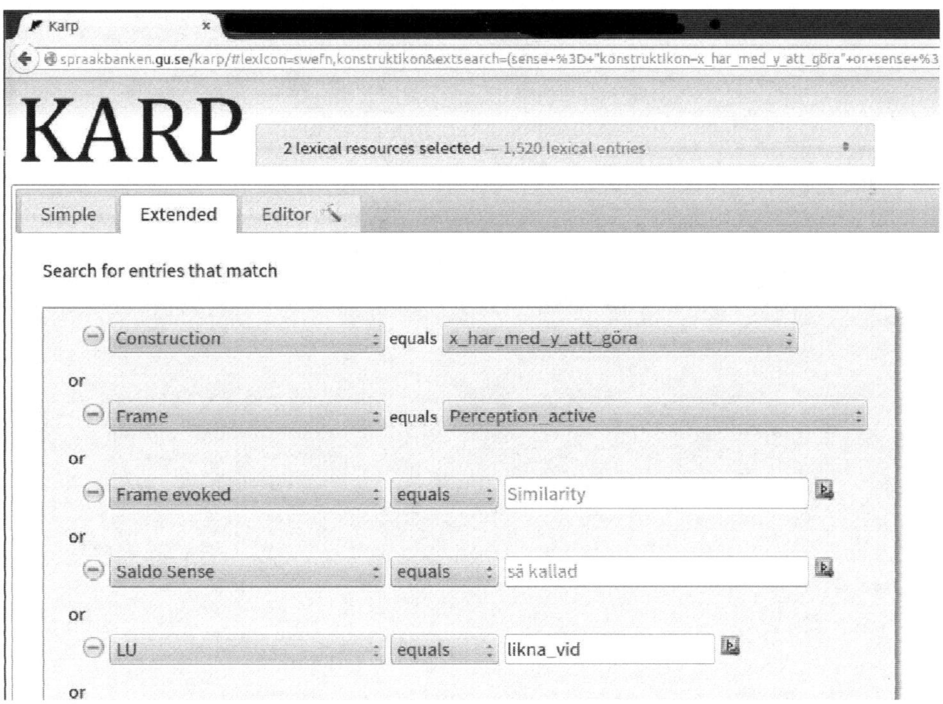

Figure 2: The Karp editing tool provides various functionalities to extract information from a number of different lexical resources. The combination of searches above is selected to illustrate the variety of possibilities in Karp.

4.4 Korp

The Korp corpora and search interface serve several purposes in the creation of SweFN. The coverage of lexical variation found in corpora is much larger than the variation we find in a lexicon and this helps in defining senses of polysemous words. From the corpora, example sentences are extracted to illustrate valence structures of LUs evoking frames. Korp extended search allows searches that combine SweFN LUs and syntactic structures of SweCcn constructions. The Related Words function provides a method of easily expanding the set of LUs populating a frame and giving easy access to example sentences where lexical variations are observed. Word Picture offers guidance in disambiguation as of LUs well as in analyzing semantic and syntactic structures.

Korp is a useful tool to check for compatibility with Swedish language and culture. Extended searches help us modify BFN frames and create new frames. There are two situations when BFN frames have been modified for SweFN (Heppin and Gronostaj, 2014): (1) the BFN frames are not suitable because of linguistic or cultural differences. For example the BFN frame `Jury_deliberation` has been redefined to `Deliberation` in SweFN. In `Deliberation` the FE corresponding to the FE JURY in BFN is changed to DELIBERATION_GROUP seeing that there is no jury in the Swedish legal process and a more general frame is appropriate as it covers deliberations in different kinds of legal systems; (2) the BFN frames are too general for our purposes, for example `Sound_makers` in BFN corresponds to two more specific frames in SweFN: `Noise_makers` and `Musical_instruments`. Completely new frames have also been created when there is a need for a frame not yet created for BFN. SweFN, for example, has a greater emphasis on nominal LUs than framenets for other languages. Therefore, frames such as `Animals`, `Countries`, and `Plants` have been created.

After determining the appropriate pairing of SALDO units and SweFN frames, searches are made for example sentences manifesting these LUs in the Korp corpora. The sentences we aim to find should have a variation of valence structure to give a broad overall picture of the LU patterns.

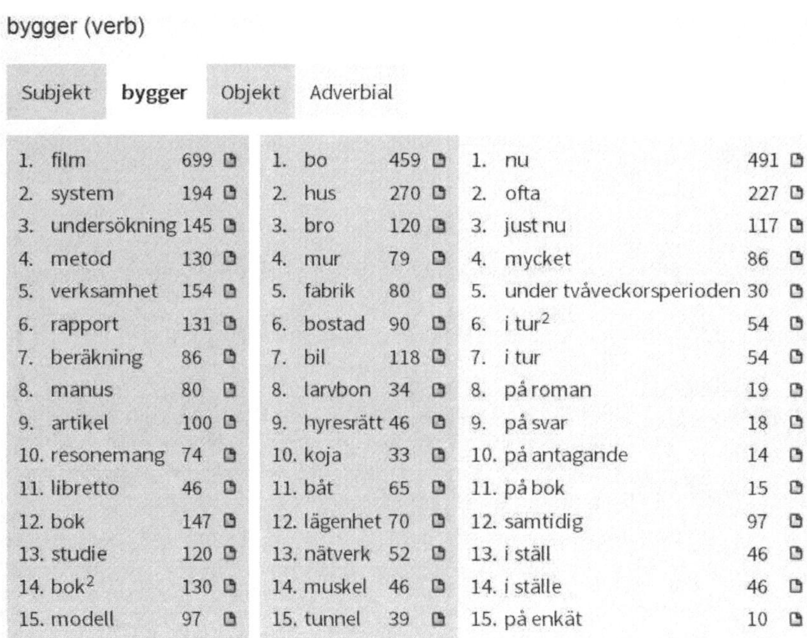
bygger (verb)

Subjekt		Objekt		Adverbial	
1. film	699	1. bo	459	1. nu	491
2. system	194	2. hus	270	2. ofta	227
3. undersökning	145	3. bro	120	3. just nu	117
4. metod	130	4. mur	79	4. mycket	86
5. verksamhet	154	5. fabrik	80	5. under tvåveckorsperioden	30
6. rapport	131	6. bostad	90	6. i tur^2	54
7. beräkning	86	7. bil	118	7. i tur	54
8. manus	80	8. larvbon	34	8. på roman	19
9. artikel	100	9. hyresrätt	46	9. på svar	18
10. resonemang	74	10. koja	33	10. på antagande	14
11. libretto	46	11. båt	65	11. på bok	15
12. bok	147	12. lägenhet	70	12. samtidig	97
13. studie	120	13. nätverk	52	13. i ställ	46
14. bok^2	130	14. muskel	46	14. i ställe	46
15. modell	97	15. tunnel	39	15. på enkät	10

Figure 3: Word picture from Korp of the verb bygga 'build' in present tense, e.g. *bygger*. The columns display from left to right subjects, objects, and adverbials. The number to the right in each column is the frequency of the collocation in Korp.

Word Picture is useful when taking a starting point in individual, polysemous words, to determine which frames are evoked by the different senses. In figure 3 items, which are listed in subject and object positions respectively, highlight two different senses of the verb *bygga* 'build', one abstract and one concrete sense. The nouns found in subject position, such as *film* 'film', *system* 'system', *undersökning* 'examination', *metod* 'method', *rapport* 'report', etc., occur with the sense of *bygga* 'build' which is typically found in an abstract intransitive construction with the preposition *på* 'on' as in 'founded on', 'built on', or 'based on'. This sense evokes the `Use_as_a_starting_point` frame. The nouns in the object position, such as *hus* 'house' and *bro* 'bridge', collocate with the agentive verb *bygga* 'build' in the concrete sense of 'construct' or 'erect', which evokes the `Building` frame (Heppin and Gronostaj, 2014).

5 Consistency checks and automatic extension of the data

There is no gold standard to evaluate the quality of SweFN against as there is no other comparable resource. FrameNet-like resources for other languages are constructed with different foci and under different conditions. However, there is a constant assessment of the correctness of the resources built into the workflow and ongoing consistency checks to avoid inconsistency between resources. The Karp tool gives error messages, for example when SALDO entries are listed in more than one frame. Other types of checks are run with certain intervals, for example to see if there are annotation tags which do not follow the standard format. Confronted with different types of error messages the developers go back to the frames in question to revise the contents of the frame, such as which LUs are said to evoke the frame, or the choice of and annotation of example sentences.

One part of the work is directed towards developing computational methods to facilitate the manual construction of SweFN. We have so far focused on three tasks: (1) semantic role labeling (SRL) (Johansson et al., 2012); (2) automatic sentence extraction, i.e. finding example sentences with varied syntactic and semantic complexities (Pilán et al., 2013); (3) automatic expansion of the SweFN lexicon to determine which frame is evoked by a given word by combining statistical and rule-based methods based on SALDO descriptors and extracted information from Korp (Johansson, 2014).

6 Conclusions

The building of one big macro-resource for Swedish language technology, where the individual resources interact with and enhance each other, provides a unique overview of the Swedish language. One search on a lexical expression results in a list of descriptions from all of the separate resources. The information derived is not only useful for the end user, but also for the continuing work on all parts of the linguistic macro-structure.

We have here focused on how two language technology resources, SALDO and SweCcn, are exploited in the development of SweFN, but also on how these resources enhance each other and other resources. We mainly address the manual perspectives of the workflow, illustrating what data may derive from the different resources, how this data may be used to facilitate work, and how the contents of one resource may reappear in the contents of another. We have given a sketch of the language technology tools with the aim to reveal their potential importance in the development of SweFN.

The construction of SweFN, and even more so the construction of a macro-resource such as SweFN++, will continue to develop in the foreseeable future. New insights as well as new problems will continue to give rise to changes.

Acknowledgements

The authors would like to thank the Department of Swedish at the University of Gothenburg and the three anonymous reviewers. The research presented here was supported by the Swedish Research Council (grant agreement 2010-6013), the Bank of Sweden Tercentenary Foundation (grant agreement P120076:1), and by the University of Gothenburg through its support of the Centre for Language Technology and of Språkbanken.

References

Malin Ahlberg, Lars Borin, Markus Forsberg, Martin Hammarstedt, Leif-Jöran Olsson, Olof Olsson, Johan Roxendal, and Jonatan Uppström. 2013. Korp and Karp a bestiary of language resources: the research infrastructure of Språkbanken. In *Proceedings of the 19th Nordic Conference of Computational Linguistics (NODALIDA 2013), Oslo University, Norway. NEALT Proceedings Series 16*, number 16, pages 429–433.

Héctor Martínez Alonso, Bolette Sandford Pedersen, and Núria Bel. 2013. Annotation of regular polysemy and underspecification. In *ACL (2)*, pages 725–730. The Association for Computer Linguistics.

Linnéa Bäckström, Benjamin Lyngfelt, and Emma Sköldberg. 2014. Towards interlingual constructicography. on correspondence between constructicon resources for English and Swedish. *Constructions and Frames*, 6(1):9–32. John Benjamins Publishing Company.

Anderson Bertoldi and Rove Luiza de Oliveira Chishman. 2011. The limits of using FrameNet frames to build a legal ontology. In *CEUR Workshop Proceedings*, volume 776, pages 207–212.

Lars Borin and Markus Forsberg. 2014. Swesaurus; or, The Frankenstein approach to Wordnet construction. In *Proceedings of the Seventh Global WordNet Conference (GWC 2014)*.

Lars Borin, Dana Dannélls, Markus Forsberg, Maria Toporowska Gronostaj, and Dimitrios Kokkinakis. 2010. The past meets the present in Swedish FrameNet++. In *Proceedings of the 14th EURALEX International Congress*, pages 269–281.

Lars Borin, Markus Forsberg, and Johan Roxendal. 2012. Korp the corpus infrastructure of Språkbanken. In *Proceedings of LREC 2012*. Istanbul: ELRA.

Lars Borin, Markus Forsberg, and Lennart Lönngren. 2013a. SALDO: a touch of yin to WordNet's yang. *Language Resources and Evaluation*, 47(4):1191–1211.

Lars Borin, Markus Forsberg, Leif-Jöran Olsson, Olof Olsson, and Jonatan Uppström. 2013b. The lexical editing system of Karp. In *Proceedings of the eLex 2013 conference*, pages 503–516, Tallin.

Aljoscha Burchardt, Katrin Erk, Anette Frank, Andrea Kowalski, Sebastian Padó, and Manfred Pinkal, 2009. *Multilingual FrameNets in computational lexicography*, chapter Using FrameNet for the semantic analysis of German annotation, representation, and annotation. Berlin: Mouton de Gryter.

Dipanjan Das, Desai Chen, André F. T. Martins, Nathan Schneider, and Noah A. Smith. 2014. Frame semantic parsing. *Computational Linguistics*, 40(1):9–56.

Anna Ehrlemark. 2014. Ramar och konstruktioner – en kärlekshistoria [Frames and constructions – a love story]. Department of Swedish, University of Gothenburg. GU-ISS 2014-01.

Charles J. Fillmore, Miriam R.L. Petruck, Josef Ruppenhofer, and Abby Wright. 2003. FrameNet in Action: The Case of Attaching. *IJL*, 16(3):297–332, September.

Charles J. Fillmore, Russell Lee-Goldman, and Russell Rhomieux, 2012. *Sign-based construction grammar*, chapter The FrameNet constructicon. Stanford: CSLI.

Charles J. Fillmore. 1985. Frames and the semantics of understanding. *Quaderni di Semantica*, 6(2):222–254.

Gil Francopoulo, Monte George, Nicoletta Calzolari, Monica Monachini, Nuria Bel, Mandy Pet, and Claudia Soria. 2006. LMF for Multilingual, Specialized Lexicons. In *Proceedings of the 5th International Conference on Language Resources and Evaluation (LREC)*, pages 233–236.

Karin Friberg Heppin and Maria Toporowska Gronostaj. 2014. Exploiting FrameNet for Swedish: Mismatch? *Constructions and Frames*, 6(1):51–71. John Benjamins Publishing Company.

Richard Johansson, Karin Friberg Heppin, and Dimitrios Kokkinakis. 2012. Semantic role labeling with the Swedish FrameNet. In *Proceedings of the 8th Conference on International Language Resources and Evaluation (LREC)*, pages 3697–3700, Istanbul, Turkey.

Richard Johansson. 2014. Automatic expansion of the Swedish FrameNet lexicon – Comparing and combining lexicon-based and corpus-based methods. *Constructions and Frames*, 6(1):91–112. John Benjamins Publishing Company.

Ora Lassila and Ralph Swick. 1999. Resource Description Framework (RDF). Model and Syntax Specification. Technical report, W3C. `http://www.w3.org/TR/REC-rdf-syntax`.

Benjamin Lyngfelt, Lars Borin, Markus Forsberg, Julia Prentice, Rudolf Rydstedt, Emma Sköldberg, and Sofia Tingsell. 2012. Adding a Constructicon to the Swedish resource network of Språkbanken. In *Proceedings of KONVENS 2012*, Vienna. LexSem workshop.

Alessandro Moschitti, Paul Morarescu, and Sanda M. Harabagiu. 2003. Open domain information extraction via automatic semantic labeling. In *Proceedings of the 16th International FLAIRS Conference*, pages 397–401.

Joakim Nivre, Johan Hall, Jens Nilsson, Atanas Chanev, Glsen Eryigit, Sandra Kbler, Svetoslav Marinov, and Erwin Marsi. 2007. MaltParser: A language-independent system for data-driven dependency parsing. *Natural Language Engineering*, 13(2):95–135.

Kyoko Hirose Ohara. 2013. Toward constructicon building for Japanese in Japanese FrameNet. *Veredas: Frame Semantics and Its Technological Applications*, 17(1):11–28.

Ildikó Pilán, Elena Volodina, and Richard Johansson. 2013. Automatic selection of suitable sentences for language learning exercises. In *20 Years of EUROCALL: Learning from the Past, Looking to the Future. 2013 EUROCALL Conference, 11th to 14th September 2013 Evora, Portugal, Proceedings.*, pages 218–225.

Michael Roth and Anette Frank. 2009. A NLG-based application for walking directions. In *Proceedings of the 47th ACL and the 4th IJCNLP Conference (Software Demonstrations)*, pages 37–40.

Emma Sköldberg, Linnéa Bäckström, Lars Borin, Markus Forsberg, Benjamin Lyngfelt, Leif-Jöran Olsson, Julia Prentice, Rudolf Rydstedt, Sofia Tingsell, and Jonatan Uppström. 2013. Between grammars and dictionaries: a Swedish Constructicon. In *Proceedings of the eLex 2013 conference*, pages 310–327, Tallin.

Carlos Subirats, 2009. *Multilingual FrameNets in Computational Lexicography*, chapter Spanish FrameNet: a frame-semantic analysis of the Spanish lexicon. Berlin: Mouton de Gryter.

Tiago Timponi Torrent, Maria Margarida Martins Salomão, Ely Edison da Silva Matos, Maucha Andrade Ganomal, Júlia Gonçalves, Bruno Pereira de Souza, Daniela Simões, and Simone Rodrigues Peron-Corrêa. 2014. Multilingual lexicographic annotation for domain-specific electronic dictionaries: the Copa 2014 FrameNet Brasil project. *Constructions and Frames*, 6(1):72–90. John Benjamins Publishing Company.

Tiago Timpioni Torrent. 2013. Behind the labels: Criteria for defining analytical categories in FrameNet Brasil. *Veredas: Frame Semantics and Its Technological Applications*, 17(1):44–65.

Harmonizing Lexical Data for their Linking to Knowledge Objects in the Linked Data Framework

Thierry Declerck
DFKI GmbH,
Language Technology Lab
Stuhlsatzenhausweg, 3
D-66123 Saarbrücken,
Germany
declerck@dfki.de

Abstract

In this position paper we discuss some of the experiences we made in describing lexical data using representation formalisms that are compatible for the publication of such data in the Linked Data framework. While we see a huge potential in the emerging Linguistic Linked Open Data, also supporting the publication of less-resourced language data on the same platform as for mainstream languages, we are wondering if, parallel to the widening of linking language data to both other language data and encyclopaedic knowledge present in the Linked Data cloud, it would not be beneficial to give more focus more on harmonization and merging of RDF encoded lexical data, instead of establishing links between such resources in the Linked Data.

1 Introduction

In recent years a lot of initiatives have emerged towards the RDF based representation of language data and the hereby opened possibility to publish those data in the Linked Open Data (LOD) cloud[1]. This development has been leading to the establishment of a specialized Linked Data (LD) cloud for language data. The actual diagram of this rapidly growing Linguistic Linked Open Data (LLOD) framework[2] reflects the distinct types of language data that already exist in LOD compliant formats, supporting their publication in the cloud and enabling their cross-linking and their linking to other knowledge objects available in the LOD context.

And to further stress the importance of this development, the main conference in the field of language resources, LREC, has declared the LOD as one of the hot topics of its 2014 edition[3] and we can observe from the list of accepted papers and workshops/tutorials that indeed this is really a hot topic for the description of language resources.

Some projects and initiatives have been very active in this field, and we want to mention here only a few, like the LOD2 project[4], which released among others the NIF (**N**LP **I**nterchange **F**ormat)[5] specifications, or the Monnet project[6], which delivered the *lemon* model for the representation of lexical

[1] See http://linkeddata.org/
[2] See http://linguistics.okfn.org/resources/llod/
[3] http://lrec2014.lrec-conf.org/en/calls-for-papers/lrec-2014-hot-topics/
[4] See http://lod2.eu/Welcome.html
[5] See http://nlp2rdf.org/nif-1-0
[6] http://cordis.europa.eu/fp7/ict/language-technologies/project-monnet_en.html

Proceedings of the Workshop on Lexical and Grammatical Resources for Language Processing, pages 18–23,
Coling 2014, Dublin, Ireland, August 24 2014.

data in ontologies[7], and the current project LIDER, which is aiming at providing "the basis for the creation of a Linguistic Linked Data cloud that can support content analytics tasks of unstructured multilingual cross-media content"[8]. Participants of those projects and many other researchers joined in standardization activities, mainly in the context of W3C, like the Ontolex community group[9].

We are also aware of works porting dialectal dictionaries (Wandl-Vogt and Declerck, 2013) or polarity lexicons (Buitelaar et al., 2013) onto LOD compliant representation formalisms. A benefit of such approaches is the fact that lexical data can be linked to meanings encoded in knowledge sources that are accessible via a URI, such as senses encoded in the DBpedia instantiation of Wiktioanry, and from there one can navigate to multilingual lexical equivalents, if those are available.

As a concrete example, working on historical German text, we could link the old word form "Fegfeur" (*purgatory*) via its modern German lemma "Fegefeuer" not only to a lexical sense in the DBpedia instantiation of Wiktionary: http://wiktionary.dbpedia.org/page/Fegefeuer-German-Noun-1de, also with access to 7 translations of this sense, but also leading to the DBpedia page for "purgatory", one get additional semantic information, so for example that the word is related to the categories "Christian_eschatology", "Christianity_and_death" etc.[10] And, in fact, the recent release of BabelNet 2.5 is summarizing this information in one page[11] for the reader, integrating information from WordNet, Wiktionary and Wikipedia. This example alone gives a very strong argument on why it is worth to encode language data using the same type of representation formalism as for knowledge objects available in the Linked Data cloud.

2 Representation Formalisms used

Based on the Resource Description Framework (RDF)[12], SKOS (Simple Knowledge Organization System)[13] "provides a model for expressing the basic structure and content of concept schemes such as thesauri, classification schemes, subject heading lists, taxonomies, folksonomies, and other similar types of controlled vocabulary."[14] This representation language is being widely used, since SKOS concepts can be (1) "semantically related to each other in informal hierarchies and association networks", (2) "the SKOS vocabulary itself can be extended to suit the needs of particular communities of practice" and finally, because it (3) "can also be seen as a bridging technology, providing the missing link between the rigorous logical formalism of ontology languages such as OWL and the chaotic, informal and weakly-structured world of Web-based collaboration tools."[15] With the use of SKOS (and RDF), we are also in the position to make language resources compatible with other language resource available in the LOD cloud, as we could see with our examples above with the DBpedia instantiation of Wiktionary16 or the very recent release of BabelNet. Since, contrary to most knowledge objects described in the LOD, we do not considers strings (encoding lemma and word forms as part of a language) as being just literals, but in also knowledge objects, we considered the use of SKOS-XL and of the lemon model, which was developed in the context of the Monnet project[17]. *lemon* is also available as an ontology[18].

3 A concrete Exercise with (German) polarity Lexicons

Inspired by (Buitelaar et al., 2013) we aimed at porting German polarity lexicons to a Linked Data compliant format, and so publish our data directly in the cloud. Our starting points are the following resources:

---

[7] See http://lemon-model.net/
[8] See http://www.lider-project.eu/
[9] http://www.w3.org/community/ontolex/wiki/Main_Page
[10] Details of this work is decribed in (Resch et al., 2014)
[11] See http://babelnet.org/search.jsp?word=Fegefeuer&lang=DE
[12] http://www.w3.org/RDF/
[13] http://www.w3.org/2004/02/skos/
[14] http://www.w3.org/TR/2009/NOTE-skos-primer-20090818/
[15] Ibid.
[16] See http://dbpedia.org/Wiktionary. There, *lemon* is also used for the description of certain lexical properties.
[17] See http://lemon-model.net/
[18] See http://www.monnet-project.eu/lemon

- A polarity lexicon for German[19] (Clematide and Klenner, 2010)
- GermanPolarityClues[20] (Waltinger, 2010)
- GermanSentiSpin[21]
- SentiWS[22] (Remus et al., 2010)

3.1 Pre-Processing of the lexical Data: Harmonization

As the reader can imagine, all those resources were available in distinct formats and containing distinct types of features. Therefore, we first had first to define a pre-processing of the different lexical data for the purpose of their harmonisation. This point leads us to a general remark: It is by far not enough to transform the representation of the lexical data onto RDF and related languages for ensuring their semantic interoperability in the LOD cloud, but preliminary work has to be performed. Just to give an example of the outcome of this work, we present a harmonized entry in Figure 1 below:

```
"fehler" => {                                                    # lemma
            "prov::GermanPC.lex" => {                            # provenance info
                    "pos::N" => {                                # PoS info
                            "pol_rank" => "0.783019",            # ranking in the orginal source
                            "pol_val" => "NEG",                  # polarity feature in the orig souce
                    },
            },
            "prov::GermanSentiSpin.lex" => {
                    "pos::N" => {
                            "pol_rank" => "0.0087112",
                            "pol_val" => "NEG",
                    },
            },
            "prov::GermanSentiWS.lex" => {
                    "pos::N" => {
                            "pol_rank" => "0.6752",
                            "pol_val" => "NEG",
                    },
            },
            "prov::german.lex" => {
                    "pos::N" => {
                            "pol_rank" => "0.7",
                            "pol_val" => "NEG",
                    },
            },
    },
```

Figure 1: The harmonized entry "fehler" (*error*) . The remaining differences in this polarity lexicon can be only in the value of the features "pos", "pol_val" and "pol_rank".

Only on the base of this harmonized lexicon, we started to model the lexical resource for publication on the LOD framework. But before getting onto the presentation of the model, we should note that the harmonized lexicon also contributed to a reduction of the lexical data: instead of originally 4 (lemma) entries, we have now only one.

[19] Downloadable at http://sentimental.li/german.lex
[20] Downloadable at http://www.ulliwaltinger.de/sentiment/
[21] SentiSpin is originally an English resource (Takamura eta., 2005), tranlsated to German by (Waltinger, 2010b).
[22] Downloadable at http://asv.informatik.uni-leipzig.de/download/sentiws.html

3.2 The LOD compliant Representation of the harmonized polarity Lexicon

Our work consisted in providing a representation of the lexical data using as much as possible information that is available in external resources, like the ISOcat registry[23], and an ontological model for the representation of polarity data, which is a slight extension of the MARL model, described in (Westerski et al., 2013). In below, we just display an excerpt of the description of the entry "fehler":

```
:LexicalSense_Fehler
      rdf:type lemon:LexicalSense ;
      rdfs:label "fehler"@de ;
      lemon:reference <http://wiktionary.dbpedia.org/page/Fehler-German-Noun-1de> .

:Opinion_Fehler
      rdf:type skosxl:Label , :lemma ;
      rdfs:label "Fehler"@de ;
      hasOpinionObject :Opinion_Fehler_2 , :Opinion_Fehler_3 , :Opinion_Fehler_4 ,
:Opinion_Fehler_1 ;
      :hasPoS <http://www.isocat.org/rest/dc/1333> ;
      skosxl:literalForm "fehler"@de .

:Opinion_Fehler_1
      rdf:type :Opinion_Object ;
      rdfs:label "Fehler"^^xsd:string ;
      op:assessedBy <http://tutorial-topbraid.com/lex_tm#german.lex> ;
      op:hasPolarity op:Negative ;
      op:maxPolarityValue "1.0"^^xsd:double ;
      op:minPolarityValue "-1.0"^^xsd:double ;
      op:polarityValue "-0.7"^^xsd:double .

  ......
```

Figure 2: The RDF, SKOS-XL and lemon representation of the entry, with a link to an ontological framework representing polarity information. The various polarities given by the various sources are represented as "OpinionObjects".

As the reader can see, such representation can link the lexical information to a wide range of related information, and what in the context of former infrastructures for language resources was represented by a set of external metadata can be incorporated here directly in the choice of classes and properties. In fact, we do not need to encode the information that the entry has PoS Noun, since this information is encoded in the details of the reference in Wiktionary/DBpedia we are pointing to.

4 Some "philosophical" Comments

The work we described briefly in this position paper, as well as work performed by researchers for porting for example dialectal dictionaries onto the LOD compliant formats (see Wandl-Vogt & Declerck, 2013) show a real potential for publishing distinct types of lexical data in the cloud, and to make this data accessible for both humans and machine in a very principled way. As noted, the use of carefully selected (widely accepted) classes and properties in the representation of the lexical data can also replace the use of complex metadata sets: parts of those metadata sets being implicitly encoded in the semantic representation the lexical data.

This positive aspect should not hide the fact that, at least in our opinion, the community is not thinking enough in providing for harmonization of the original lexical data. In many cases the data sets in the Linguistic Linked Open Data are redundant, repeating for example many times the lemmas of lexical entries in the different types of data set. We think that similar to the ISOcat data category we could aim at having a "centralized" repository for lemmas of one language, so that this lemma is not repeated for example in Wiktionary, Lexvo[24] and many other data sets in the LLOD. We are wondering if, in

[23] See for example http://www.isocat.org/rest/dc/1333 for our selected ISOcat entry for the pos "noun".

[24] See http://www.lexvo.org/

the precise context of the LOD – linking lexical data to other data sets in the cloud – it would not be possible to have exactly one lexical data set for reach language. Figure **3** below sketches our intended model, taking as example terminology in the field of financial reporting.

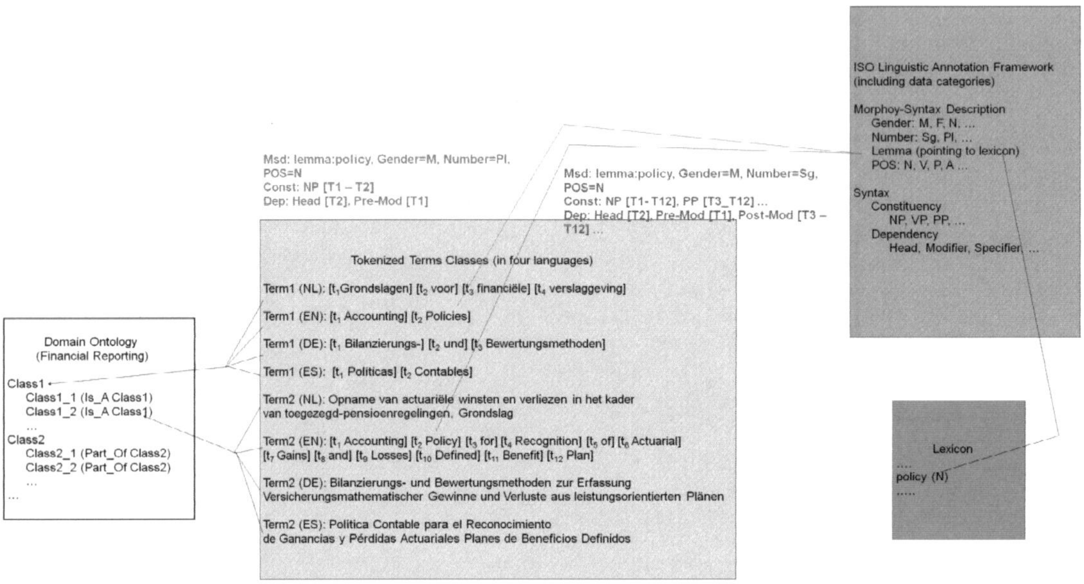

Figure 3: An example instantiation of the model we are aiming at: a unique (lemma) lexicon for one language (bottom right). Getting the full forms from a repository of such forms, including feature structures describing their morpho-syntactic information. Those are linking to occurrences of terms or labels that are used in knowledge objects (domain ontologies, taxonomies etc.). This model allows to precisely linking information from the lexicon, the morpho-syntactic descriptions and potential grammatical patterns as those are used in labels, comments or definitions in the context of knowledge objects in the LOD data sets. This model for representing lexical and linguistic data would be specialized for establishing linking between language data and representation of world knowledge. We expect from this approach an improvement in fields like domain specific machine translation and ontology-.based multilingual information extraction.

5 Conclusions

In this short position paper, we presented some experiences done in the context of the emerging Linguistic Linked Open Data framework. This lead us to make some comments on the way we could go for a much more "compressed" distribution of semantically (using LOD compliant representation languages) encoded language data, which could be more easily re-used in the context of knowledge-based NLP applications. The result would be a set of language specific "centralised" repositories of lemmas and related full forms, all equipped with URIs, that are used in the context of knowledge objects present in the Linked Data framework.

Acknowledgments

The research described in this paper is partly supported by the European Lider project. LIDER: "Linked Data as an enabler of cross-media and multilingual content analytics for enterprises across Europe" is a FP7 project with reference number 610782.

References

Buitelaar, P., Mihael Arcan, Carlos A. Iglesias, J. Fernando Sánchez, Carlo Strapparava (2013) Linguistic Linked Data for Sentiment Analysis. In: 2nd Workshop on Linked Data in Linguistics (LDL 2013): Representing and linking lexicons, terminologies and other language data. Collocated with the Conference on Generative Approaches to the Lexicon, Pisa, Italy

Clematide, S, Klenner, M. (2010). "Evaluation and extension of a polarity lexicon for German". In: Workshop on Computational Approaches to Subjectivity and Sentiment Analysis (WASSA); Held in conjunction to ECAI 2010 Portugal, Lisbon, Portugal, 17 August 2010 - 17 August 2010, 7-13.

Clematide, S., Gindl, S., Klenner, M., Petrakis, S., Remus, R., Ruppenhofer, J., Waltinger, U. and Wiegand, M. (2012). MLSA ? A Multi-layered Reference Corpus for German Sentiment Analysis." In: Proceedings of the Eight International Conference on Language Resources and Evaluation (LREC'12), Istanbul, 23 May 2012 - 25 May 2012.

Hellmann, S., Lehmann, J., Auer, A. and Brümmer, M.: *Integrating NLP using Linked Data* In: 12th International Semantic Web Conference, 21-25 October 2013, Sydney, Australia.

Klenner, M., Clematide, S., Petrakis, S., Luder, M. (2012). "Compositional syntax-based phrase-level polarity annotation for German". In: The 10th International Workshop on Treebanks and Linguistic Theories (TLT 2012), Heidelberg, 06 January 2012 - 07 January 2012,

McCrae,J., Aguado-de-Cea, G., P. Buitelaar, P. Cimiano, T. Declerck, A. Gómez-Pérez, J. Gracia, L. Hollink, E. Montiel-Ponsoda, D. Spohr, T. Wunner.(2012) Interchanging lexical resources on the Semantic Web.*Language Resources and Evaluation.*

Remus, R., Quasthoff, U. and Heyer, G. (2010). "SentiWS - a Publicly Available German-language Resource for Sentiment Analysis." In: Proceedings of the 7th International Language Ressources and Evaluation (LREC'10), 2010

Resch, C., Declerck, T., Mörth, K, and Czeitschner, U. (2014) Linguistic and Semantic Annotation in Religious Memento Mori Literature. In *Proceedings of the 2nd Workshop on Language Ressources and Evaluation for Religious Texts.*

Hiroya Takamura, Takashi Inui, and Manabu Okumura. (2005). Extracting semantic orientations of words using spin model. In *Proceedings of the 43rd Annual Meeting of the Association for Computational Linguistics. Association for Computational Linguistics.*

Waltinger, U. (2010b). "Sentiment Analysis Reloaded: A Comparative Study On Sentiment Polarity Identification Combining Machine Learning And Subjectivity Features". In: Proceedings of the 6th International Conference on Web Information Systems and Technologies (WEBIST '10).

Wandl-Vogt, E., Declerck, T. (2013). Mapping a Traditional Dialectal Dictionary with Linked Open Data. In. Kosem, I., Kallas, J., Gantar, P., Krek, S., Langemets, M., Tuulik, M. (eds.) 2013. *Electronic lexicography in the 21st century: thinking outside the paper. Proceedings of the eLex 2013 conference, 17-19 October 2013, Tallinn, Estonia.* Ljubljana/Tallinn: Trojina, Institute for Applied Slovene Studies/Eesti Keele Instituut.

Westerski, Adam and Sánchez-Rada, J. Fernando, Marl Ontology Specification, V1.0 May 2013, available at http://www.gsi.dit.upm.es/ontologies/marl

Terminology and Knowledge Representation Italian Linguistic Resources for the Archaeological Domain

Maria Pia di Buono **Mario Monteleone** **Annibale Elia**
Dept. of Political, Social and Communication Sciences
University of Salerno
Fisciano (SA), Italy
{mdibuono, mmonteleone, elia}@unisa.it

Abstract

Knowledge representation is heavily based on using terminology, due to the fact that many terms have precise meanings in a specific domain but not in others. As a consequence, terms becomes unambiguous and clear, and at last, being useful for conceptualizations, are used as a starting point for formalizations. Starting from an analysis of problems in existing dictionaries, in this paper we present formalized Italian Linguistic Resources (LRs) for the Archaeological domain, in which we integrate/couple formal ontology classes and properties into/to electronic dictionary entries, using a standardized conceptual reference model. We also add Linguistic Linked Open Data (LLOD) references in order to guarantee the interoperability between linguistic and language resources, and therefore to represent knowledge.

1 Introduction

Knowledge representation is heavily based on using terminology, due to the fact that many terms have precise meanings in a specific domain but not in others. As a consequence, terms becomes unambiguous and clear, and at last, being useful for conceptualizations, are used as a starting point for formalizations. Sowa (2000) notes that "most fields of science, engineering, business, and law have evolved systems of terminology or nomenclature for naming, classifying, and standardizing their concepts". As well, Parts Of Speech (POS) present two levels of representation, which are separated but interlinked: a conceptual-semantic level, pertaining to ontologies, and a syntactic-semantic level, pertaining to sentence production. Starting from an analysis of problems in existing dictionaries, in this paper we present formalized Italian Linguistic Resources (LRs) for the Archaeological domain, in which we integrate/couple formal ontology classes and properties into/to electronic dictionary entries, using a standardized conceptual reference model. We also add Linguistic Linked Open Data (LLOD) references in order to guarantee the interoperability between linguistic and language resources, and therefore to represent knowledge.

2 Related Works

Different models/mechanisms have been developed to overcome knowledge representation issues deriving from increasing complexity and diversity of linguistic resources.

WordNet, one of the most widespread resource, is based on is-a, part-of and member-of relations between synsets, which are used to represent concepts. At any rate, WordNet relations are not used in a consistent way, inasmuch sometimes they are broken or present redundancy (Martin, 2003).

Rule based systems are usually founded on logical rules (Bender, 1996) and fuzzy rules (Zadeh, 1965, 2004; Surmann, 2000).

Generally speaking, the ontology-based approach deals with knowledge representation issues processing a set of words and their semantic relations in a certain domain (Gruber, 1993; Cocchiarella, 1996; Brewster et al., 2004; Tijerino et al., 2005; Sanchez, 2010; Hao, 2010; Wang et al., 2011).

We intend to develop a linguistic knowledge base, i.e. a lexical database, in which the ontology schema will be integrated to process language on the basis of syntactic relations, i.e. formal grammars.

Proceedings of the Workshop on Lexical and Grammatical Resources for Language Processing, pages 24–29, Coling 2014, Dublin, Ireland, August 24 2014.

3 Italian Linguistic Resources for the Archaeological Domain

In order to develop our LRs, we apply Lexicon-Grammar (LG) theoretical and practical framework, which describes the mechanisms of word combinations and gives an exhaustive description of natural language lexical and syntactic structures. LG was set up by the French linguist Maurice Gross, during the '60s, and subsequently applied to Italian by Annibale Elia, Maurizio Martinelli and Emilio D'Agostino. All electronic dictionaries, built according to LG descriptive method, form the DELA[1] System, which works as a linguistic engine embedded in automatic textual analysis software systems and parsers[2]. Our LRs also include information taken from the Thesauri and Guidelines of the Italian Central Institute for the Catalogue and Documentation (ICCD)[3].

ICCD resources are organized in:

- Object definition dictionary
- Marble sculptures
- Metal containers
- Marble sculptures – Sarcophagi and reliefs
- Vocabulary of Metals
- Vocabulary of Glasses
- Vocabulary of Materials
- Vocabulary of Mosaic Pavement Works
- Vocabulary of non-figurative mosaics
- Vocabulary of Mosaics
- Vocabulary of Coroplastics.

Only the Object definition dictionary provides, for each entry, the following different and structured information: Broader Term [BT], Broader Term Partitive [BTP1], Broader Term Partitive [BTP2], Narrower Term [NT], Narrower Term Partitive [NTP], Use [USE], Use For [UF].

	BT	BTP1	BTP2	NT	NTP	USE	UF
amuleto	Strumenti Utensili e oggetti d'uso	Amuleti e oggetti per uso cerimoniale, magico e votivo			a forma di anatra a forma di ariete a forma di colonna ...		cornetto

Table 1. An example of lemma categorization from ICCD dictionary

Broader term fields indicate the taxonomy classification, so *amuleto* (amulet) is an element of *Strumenti, Utensili e Oggetti d'uso* (Tools), which is a general category, and *Amuleti e oggetti per uso cerimoniale, magico e votivo* (Magic & Votive Supplies), which is a specific category.

The NTP field specifies the lemma, and this helps us to infer that *amuleto* occurs in different compound entries, for instance: *amuleto a forma di anatra* (duck amulet), *amuleto a forma di ariete* (ram amulet) and so on. UF is a no-preferential lemma (i.e. a variant); this implies that *cornetto* (horn amulet) can stand for *amuleto* (and its specific types), but ICCD guidelines suggest to use the first one. According to our approach, it is necessary to lemmatize all possible variants, including those having even a low-frequency use.

Our electronic dictionary[4], which represents an additional resource to the ICCD ones listed above, is composed by ca. 11000 entries, with both simple and compound words, including spelling variants, i.e.: *(dinos+dynos+dèinos) con anse ad anello* (ringed-handle (dinos+dynos+dèinos)), and synonyms, generally extracted from the UF field, i.e. *kylix a labbro risparmiato* (spared-lip kylix), which stands for lip cup or *cratere* (crater)which stands for *vaso* (vase).

1Dictionnaires Électroniques du LADL (Laboratoire d'Automatique Documentaire et Linguistique).
2DELA electronic dictionaries are of two types: of simple words and of Multi-Word Expressions (MWE).
3http://www.iccd.beniculturali.it/index.php?it/240/vocabolari.
4In 4 we give an excerpt of the Italian Archaeological Electronic Dictionary.

Besides, our additional resource has been created extracting terms from existing literature. Also, from ICCD unstructured data (i.e. the vocabulary of Coroplastics) Proper and Place Names have been retrieved, which are now entries of our dictionary.

3.1 Formal, syntactic and semantic features

The main formal structures recorded in our electronic dictionary are:

- Noun+Preposition+Noun+Preposition+Noun (NPNPN), i.e. *fibula ad arco a coste* (ribbed-arch fibula);
- Noun+Preposition+Noun+Adjective (NPNA), i.e. *anello a capi ritorti* (twisted-heads ring);
- Noun+Preposition+Noun+Adjective+Adjective (NPNAA), i.e. *punta a foglia larga ovale* (oval broadleaf point).

We also notice the presence of open series compounds. Open series compounds are multi-words in which we can identify one or more fixed elements co-occurring with one or more variable ones, i.e. *palmetta a (cinque+sei+sette+*DNUM*) petali* (little plam with (five+six+seven+DNUM) petals).

As for semantics, we observe the presence of compounds in which the head does not occur in the first position; for instance, the open series *frammenti di (terracotta+anfora+laterizi+*N*)* (fragments of (clay+anphora+bricks+N)), places the heads at the end of the compounds, being *frammenti* (fragments) used to explicit the notion "N0 is a part of N1".

As far as syntactic aspects are concerned, some open series compounds, especially referred to coroplastic description, are sentence reductions[5] in which it is used a present participle construction. For instance *statua raffigurante Sileno* (Silenus statue) is a reduction of the sentence:

	Questa statua raffigura Sileno (This statue represents Silenus)
[relative]	→ *Questa è una statua che raffigura Sileno* (This is a statue which represents Silenus)
[pr. part.]	→ *Questa è una statua raffigurante Sileno* (This is a statue representing Silenus).

In compounds containing present participle forms, semantic features can be identified using local grammars built on specific verb classes (semantic predicate sets); in such cases, co-occurrence restrictions can be described in terms of lexical forms and syntactic structures.

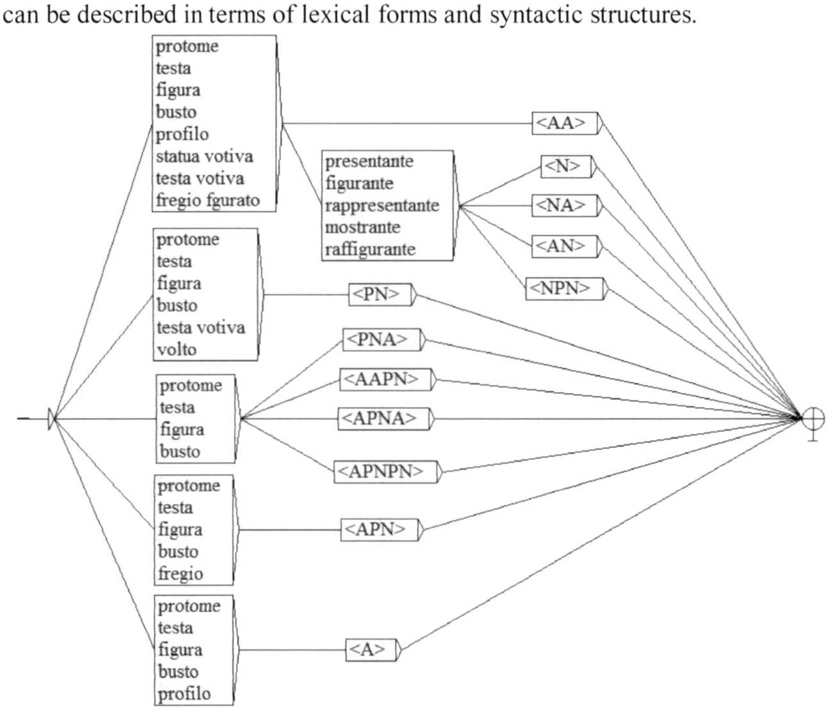

Figure 1. An example of Finite State Automaton to recognize open series compounds.

[5] Here the notation "sentence reduction" is to be intended in Z. S. Harris' sense.

4 Ontology-Based Electronic Dictionary

An ontology-based electronic dictionary is likely to incorporate more information than thesauri. This comes from the fact that with reference to a thesaurus, an ontology also stores language-independent information and semantic relations. Therefore, the use of ontology in the upgrading of LG electronic dictionaries may ensure knowledge sharing, maintenance of semantic constraints, semantic ambiguities solving, and inferencing on the basis of ontology concept networks.

As far as our ontology schema is concerned, we refer to ICOM International Committee for Documentation (CIDOC) Conceptual Reference Model (CRM), an ISO standard since 2006, compatible with the Resource Description Framework (RDF). It provides definitions and a formal structure for describing the implicit and explicit concepts and relationships used in Cultural Heritage documentation.

In our dictionary, for each entry we indicate:

- its POS (Category), internal structure and inflectional code[6] (FLX);
- its variants (VAR) and synonyms (SYN), if any;
- the type of link (LINK) (RDF and/or HTML);
- with reference to our taxonomy, the pertaining knowledge domain[7] (DOM);
- the CIDOC CRM Class (CCL).

Entry	Category	Internal Structure	FLX	VAR	SYN	LINK	DOM	CCL
dinos con anse ad anello	N	NPNPN	C610	dynos con anse ad anello/déinos con anse ad anello		RDF	RA1SUOCR	E22
kylix a labbro risparmiato	N	NPNA	C611		lip cup	RDF	RA1SUOCR	E22

Table 2. An extract of our ontology-based electronic dictionary.

5 Linguistic Linked Open Data (LLOD) Integration

The LLOD is a project developed by the Open Linguistics Working Group (OLWG). It aims to create a representation formalism for corpora in Resource Description Framework/Web Ontology Language (RDF/OWL). The initiative intends to link LRs, represented in RDF, with the resources available in the Linked Open Data (LOD)[8] cloud. The LLOD goal is not only to provide LRs in an interoperable way, but also to use an open license and link LRs with other resources in order to combine information from different knowledge sources. According to the LOD paradigm (Berners-Lee, 2006), Web resources have to present a Uniform Resource Identifier (URI) for entities to which they refer to, and to include links to other resources. According to Chiarcos et al. (2013a), "linking to central terminology repositories facilitates conceptual interoperability".

Benefits of LLOD are also identified in linking through URIs, federation, dynamic linking between resources (Chiarcos et al., 2013b).

Besides, data structured in RDF format can be queried by means of the SPARQL language. Indeed, if RDF triples represent a set of relationship among resources, than SPARQL queries are the patterns for these relationships.

One of the most relevant LLOD resources are stored in and presented by DBpedia (www.dbpedia.org). DBPedia is a sample of large Linked Datasets, which offers Wikipedia information in RDF format and incorporate other Web datasets.

Therefore, we have referred and will refer to DBPedia Italian[9] datasets to integrate our LRs with LLOD. DBPedia Italian is an open project developed and maintained by the Web of Data[10] research unit of Fondazione Bruno Kessler[11].

6All inflectional codes are built by means of local grammars in the form of Finite State Automata/Transducers.

7The taxonomy we use is structured on the basis of the indications given by the ICCD guidelines. Therefore, the tags RA1SUORC stands for Archaeological Remains/Tools/Receptacles and Containers.

8http://www.w3.org/standards/semanticweb/data.

9http://it.dbpedia.org/?lang=en.

According to Linked Data prescriptions, URI schema is structured as

http://it.dbpedia.org/resource/ordine_dorico	Resource URI
http://it.dbpedia.org/page/ordine_dorico	HTML representation
http://it.dbpedia.org/data/ordine_dorico.{ rdf | n3 | json | ntriples }	Machine-readable resource representation

Table 3. Sample of URI schema for the resource *ordine dorico* (doric order).

In order to reuse such prescriptions, we adopt a Finite State Transducer-based system which merge specific matching URIs with electronic dictionary entries.

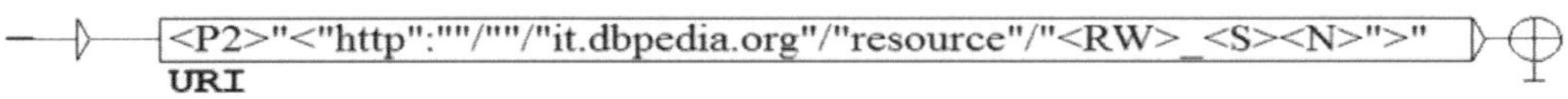

Figure 2. An example of Finite State Transducer for LLOD integration.

When we apply the transducer to dictionary entries tagged with "LINK=RDF", NooJ[12] generates a new string in which the resource URI is placed before the original entry. In this way, the transducer enriches all entries of our electronic dictionary with DBPedia resources. For instance, the result given by the transducer for the compound *Ordine dorico* is the following string:

<http://it.dbpedia.org/resource/ordine_dorico>,Ordine dorico,N+NA+FLX=C509+LINK=RDF++DOM=RA1ED++CCI=E26+URI

Resulting strings may be used to automatically read text by means of Web browsers and/or RDF environments/routines. When the generated string is processed by a Web Browser, it will generate a link to the HTML representation. Otherwise, when the header "HTTP *Accept:*" of the query is produced by a RDF-based application, it will produce a link to the machine-readable representation.

6 Future work

Our future goal is to develop an application useful for both retrieve and process RDF data from LLOD resources. We intend to implement an environment structured into two workflows: the first one (based on SPARQL language) to query online repositories and create a system of Question-Answering, the second one to retrieve natural language strings, in particular those contained in the fields "rdfs: comment" and "dbpedia-owl: abstract". Such data will constitute the basis for the development of a supervised machine-learning algorithm that, through the matching with existing dictionaries and grammars local, will further upgrade the LRs.

Note

Maria Pia di Buono is author of section 3.1, 4, 5 and 6, Mario Monteleone is author of sections 3 and 3.1, Annibale Elia is author of sections 1 and 2.

References

Edward A. Bender. 1996. *Mathematical methods in artificial intelligence*. Los Alamitos, CA: IEEE Press.

Tim Berners-Lee. 2006. *Design issues: Linked Data.* http://www.w3.org/DesignIssues/LinkedData.html.

Christopher Brewster, Kieron O'Hara, Steve Fuller, Yorick Wilks, Enrico Franconi, Mark A. Musen, Jeremy Ellman, Simon Buckingham Shum. 2004. Knowledge representation with ontologies: The present and future. *IEEE Intelligent Systems*, *19*(1):72–81.

Christian Chiarcos, Phillip Cimiano, Thierry Declerck, John Mc Crae. 2013a. Linguistic Linked Open Data (LLOD). Introduction and Overview. *Proceedings of LDL 2013*, Pisa, Italy.

Christian Chiarcos, John McCrae, Phillip Cimiano, Christiane Fellbaum. 2013b. Towards Open data for Linguistica: Linguistic linked data. In Oltramari A., Vossen P., Quin L., Hovy E. (eds.). *New Trends of Research in Ontologies and Lexical Resources.* Springer, Heidelberg.

[10]http://wed.fbk.eu/.
[11]http://www.fbk.eu/.
[12]NooJ is a linguistic development environment. For more information http://www.nooj-association.org/.

Nino Cocchiarella. 1996. Conceptual realism as a formal ontology. In Poli, R., & Simons, P. (Eds.). *Formal ontology*. Kluwer Academic, London, UK:27-60.

Nick Crofts, Martin Doerr, Tony Gill, Stephen Stead, Matthew Stiff. 2010. *Definition of the CIDOC Conceptual Reference Model. ICOM/CIDOC Documentation Standards Group*. CIDOC CRM Special Interest Group. 5.02 ed.

Maria Pia di Buono, Mario Monteleone (in press) Knowledge Management and Extraction for Cultural Heritage Repositories. In Silberztein M., Monti J., Monteleone M., di Buono M.P. (eds.). *Proceedings of International NooJ 2014 Conference.* Cambridge Scholars Publishing.

Annibale Elia, Maurizio Martinelli, Emilio D'Agostino. 1981. *Lessico e strutture sintattiche. Introduzione alla sintassi del verbo italiano*. Liguori Editore, Napoli.

Lee Gillam, Mariam Tariq and Khurshid Ahmad. 2007. *Terminology and the construction of ontology*. 11 (1):55-81.

Maurice Gross. 1968. *Grammaire transformationnelle du français: syntaxe du verbe.* Larousse, Paris.

Tom Gruber. 1993. *A translation approach to portable ontology specifications. Knowledge Acquisition*, *5*(2):199–220.

Zellig S. Harris. 1970. *Papers in Structural and Transformational Linguistics.* Reidel, Dordrecht.

Zellig S. Harris. 1976. (translation by Maurice Gross), *Notes du Cours de Syntaxe*, Éditions du Seuil, Paris.

Hao Liang. 2010. Ontology based automatic attributes extracting and queries translating for deep web. *Journal of Software, 5:713–720.*

Philippe Martin. 2003. Correction and Extension of WordNet 1.7. *ICCS 2003, 11th International Conference on Conceptual Structures.* Springer, Verlag, LNAI 2746:160-173.

David Sanchez. 2010. A methodology to learn ontological attributes from the web. *Data & Knowledge Engineering*, *69*(6), 573–597.

John Florian Sowa. 2000. *Knowledge Representation: Logical, Philosophical, and Computational Foundations*. Brooks Cole Publishing Co., Pacific Grove, CA.

Hartmut Surmann. 2000. Learning a fuzzy rule based knowledge representation. In *Proceedings of the ICSC Symposium on Neural Computation*, Berlin, Germany:349-355.

Yuri A. Tijerino, David W. Embley, Deryle Lonsdale, Yihong Ding, & George Nagy. 2005. Towards ontology generation from tables. *WWW: Internet and Information Systems*, *8*(3):261–285.

Antonio Vaquero, Francisco Álvarez, Fernando Sáenz. 2006. Control and Verification of Relations in the Creation of Ontology- Based Electronic Dictionaries for Language Learning. In *Proceedings of the SIIE 2006 8th International Symposium on Computers in Education*, Vol. 1:166-173

Yingxu Wang, Yousheng Tian, & Kendal Hu. 2011. Semantic manipulations and formal ontology for machine learning based on concept algebra. *International Journal of Cognitive Informatics and Natural Intelligence*, 5(3):1–29.

Lotfi A. Zadeh. 2004. Precisiated Natural Language (PNL). *AI Magazine,* 25(3):74–91.

SentiMerge: Combining Sentiment Lexicons in a Bayesian Framework

Guy Emerson and Thierry Declerck
DFKI GmbH
Universität Campus
66123 Saarbrücken
{guy.emerson, thierry.declerck}@dfki.de

Abstract

Many approaches to sentiment analysis rely on a lexicon that labels words with a prior polarity. This is particularly true for languages other than English, where labelled training data is not easily available. Existing efforts to produce such lexicons exist, and to avoid duplicated effort, a principled way to combine multiple resources is required. In this paper, we introduce a Bayesian probabilistic model, which can simultaneously combine polarity scores from several data sources and estimate the quality of each source. We apply this algorithm to a set of four German sentiment lexicons, to produce the SentiMerge lexicon, which we make publically available. In a simple classification task, we show that this lexicon outperforms each of the underlying resources, as well as a majority vote model.

1 Introduction

Wiegand (2011) describes sentiment analysis as the task of identifying and classifying opinionated content in natural language text. There are a number of subtasks within this field, such as identifying the holder of the opinion, and the target of the opinion.

In this paper, however, we are concerned with the more specific task of identifying *polar* language - that is, expressing either *positive* or *negative* opinions. Throughout the rest of this paper, we will use the terms *sentiment* and *polarity* more or less interchangeably.

As Pang and Lee (2008) explain, sentiment analysis has become a major area of research within natural language processing (NLP), with many established techniques, and a range of potential applications. Indeed, in recent years there has been increasing interest in sentiment analysis for commercial purposes.

Despite the rapid growth of this area, there is a lack of gold-standard corpora which can be used to train supervised models, particularly for languages other than English. Consequently, many algorithms rely on sentiment lexicons, which provide prior knowledge about which lexical items might indicate opinionated language. Such lexicons can be used directly to define features in a classifier, or can be combined with a bootstrapping approach.

However, when presented with a number of overlapping and potentially contradictory sentiment lexicons, many machine learning techniques break down, and we therefore require a way to merge them into a single resource - or else a researcher must choose between resources, and we are left with a leaky pipeline between resource creation and application. We review methods for combining sources of information in section 2, and then describe four German sentiment lexicons in section 3.

To merge these resources, we first want to make them match as closely as possible, and then deal with the differences that remain. We deal with the first step in section 4, describing how to align the polarity scores in different lexicons so that they can be directly compared. Then in section 5, we describe how to combine these scores together.

We report results in section 6, including evaluation against a small annotated corpus, where our merged resource outperforms both the original resources and also a majority vote baseline. Finally, we discuss distribution of our resource in section 7, future work in section 8, and conclude in section 9.

Proceedings of the Workshop on Lexical and Grammatical Resources for Language Processing, pages 30–38, Coling 2014, Dublin, Ireland, August 24 2014.

Lexicon	# Entries
C&K	8714
PolarityClues	9228
SentiWS	1896
SentiSpin	95572
SentiMerge	96918

Table 1: Comparison of lexicon sizes

2 Related Work

A general problem is how to deal with missing data - in our case, we cannot expect every word to appear in every lexicon. Schafer and Graham (2002) review techniques to deal with missing data, and recommend two approaches: maximum likelihood estimation and Bayesian multiple imputation. The latter is a Monte Carlo method, helpful when the marginal probability distribution cannot be calculated analytically. The probabilistic model presented in section 5.1 is straightforward enough for marginal probabilities to be calculated directly, and we employ maximum likelihood estimation for this reason.

A second problem is how to combine multiple sources of information, which possibly conflict, and where some sources are more reliable than others. This becomes particularly challenging in the case when no gold-standard data exists, and so the sources can not be evaluated directly. Raykar et al. (2010) discusses this problem from the point of view of crowdsourcing, where there are multiple expert views and no certain ground truth - but we can equally apply this in the context of sentiment analysis, viewing each source as an expert. However, unlike their approach, our algorithm does not directly produce a classifier, but rather a newly labelled resource.

Confronted with a multiplicity of data sources, some researchers have opted to link resources together (Eckle-Kohler and Gurevych, 2013). Indeed, the lexicons we consider in section 3 have already been compiled into a common format by Declerck and Krieger (2014). However, while linking resources makes it easier to access a larger amount of data, it does not solve the problem of how best to process it.

To the best of our knowledge, there has not been a previous attempt to use a probabilistic model to merge a number of sentiment lexicons into a single resource.

3 Data Sources

In the following subsections, we first describe four existing sentiment lexicons for German. These four lexicons represent the data we have merged into a single resource, with a size comparison given in table 1, where we count the number of distinct lemmas, not considering parts of speech. Finally, in section 3.5, we describe the manually annotated MLSA corpus, which we use for evaluation.

3.1 Clematide and Klenner

Clematide and Klenner (2010) manually curated a lexicon[1] of around 8000 words, based on the synsets in *GermaNet*, a *WordNet*-like database (Hamp and Feldweg, 1997). A semi-automatic approach was used to extend the lexicon, first generating candidate polar words by searching in a corpus for coordination with known polar words, and then presenting these words to human annotators. We will refer to this resource as the C&K lexicon.

3.2 SentimentWortschatz

Remus et al. (2010) compiled a sentiment lexicon[2] from three data sources: a German translation of Stone et al. (1966)'s *General Inquirer* lexicon, a set of rated product reviews, and a German collocation dictionary. At this stage, words have binary polarity: positive or negative. To assign polarity weights, they use a corpus to calculate the mutual information of a target word with a small set of seed words.

[1] `http://bics.sentimental.li/index.php/downloads`
[2] `http://asv.informatik.uni-leipzig.de/download/sentiws.html`

3.3 GermanSentiSpin

Takamura et al. (2005) produced SentiSpin, a sentiment lexicon for English. It is so named becaused it applies the Ising Model of electron spins. The lexicon is modelled as an undirected graph, with each word type represented by a single node. A dictionary is used to define edges: two nodes are connected if one word appears in the other's definition. Each word is modelled as having either positive or negative sentiment, analogous to electrons being spin up or spin down. An energy function is defined across the whole graph, which prefers words to have the same sentiment if they are linked together. By using a small seed set of words which are manually assigned positive or negative sentiment, this energy function allows us to propagate sentiment across the entire graph, assigning each word a real-valued sentiment score in the interval $[-1, 1]$.

Waltinger (2010b) translated the SentiSpin resource into German[3] using an online dictionary, taking at most three translations of each English word.

3.4 GermanPolarityClues

Waltinger (2010a) utilised automatic translations of two English resources: the SentiSpin lexicon, described in section 3.3 above; and the Subjectivity Clues lexicon, a manually annotated lexicon produced by Wilson et al. (2005). The sentiment orientations of the German translations were then manually assessed and corrected where necessary, to produce a new resource.[4]

3.5 MLSA

To evaluate a sentiment lexicon, separately from the general task of judging the sentiment of an entire sentence, we relied on the MLSA (Multi-Layered reference corpus for German Sentiment Analysis). This corpus was produced by Clematide et al. (2012), independently of the above four lexicons, and consists of 270 sentences annotated at three levels of granularity. In the first layer, annotators judged the sentiment of whole sentences; in the second layer, the sentiment of words and phrases; and finally in the third layer, they produced a FrameNet-like analysis of each sentence. The third layer also includes lemmas, parts of speech, and a syntactic parse.

We extracted the sentiment judgements of individual words from the second layer, using the majority judgement of the three annotators. Each token was mapped to its lemmatised form and part of speech, using the information in the third layer. In some cases, the lemma was listed as ambiguous or unknown, and in these cases, we manually added the correct lemma. Additionally, we changed the annotation of nominalised verbs from nouns to verbs, to match the lexical entries. Finally, we kept all content words (nouns, verbs, and adjectives) to form a set of test data. In total, there were 1001 distinct lemma types, and 1424 tokens. Of these, 378 tokens were annotated as having positive polarity, and 399 as negative.

4 Normalising Scores

By considering positive polarity as a positive real number, and negative polarity as a negative real number, all of the four data sources give polarity scores between -1 and 1. However, we cannot assume that the values directly correspond to one another. For example, does a 0.5 in one source mean the same thing in another? An example of the kind of data we are trying to combine is given in table 2, and we can see that the polarity strengths vary wildly between the sources.

The simplest model is to rescale scores linearly, i.e. for each source, we multiply all of its scores by a constant factor. Intuitively, the factors should be chosen to harmonise the values - a source with large scores should have them made smaller, and a source with small scores should have them made larger.

4.1 Linear Rescaling for Two Sources

To exemplify our method, we first restrict ourselves to the simpler case of only dealing with two lexicons. Note that when trying to determine the normalisation factors, we only consider words in the overlap between the two; otherwise, we would introduce a bias according to what words are considered in each

[3] `http://www.ulliwaltinger.de/sentiment`

[4] `http://www.ulliwaltinger.de/sentiment`

Lemma, POS	vergöttern, *V*
C&K	1.000
PolarityClues	0.333
SentiWS	0.004
SentiSpin	0.245

Table 2: An example lemma, labelled with polarity strengths from each data source

source - it is only in the overlap that we can compare them. However, once these factors have been determined, we can use them to rescale the scores across the entire lexicon, including items that only appear in one source.

We consider lemmas with their parts of speech, so that the same orthographic word with two possible parts of speech is treated as two independent lexical entries, in all of the following calculations. However, we do not distinguish homophonous or polysemous lemmas within the same part of speech, since none of our data sources provided different sentiment scores for distinct senses.

For each word i, let u_i and v_i be the polarity scores for the two sources. We would like to find positive real values λ and μ to rescale these to λu_i and μv_i respectively, minimising the loss function $\sum_i (\lambda u_i - \mu v_i)^2$. Intuitively, we are trying to rescale the sources so that the scores are as similar as possible. The loss function is trivially minimised when $\lambda = \mu = 0$, since reducing the sizes of the scores also reduces their difference. Hence, we can introduce the constraint that $\lambda\mu = 1$, so that we cannot simultaneously make the values smaller in both sources. We would then like to minimise:

$$\sum_i \left(\lambda u_i - \frac{1}{\lambda} v_i\right)^2 = |u|^2 \lambda^2 - 2u.v + |v|^2 \lambda^{-2}$$

Note that we use vector notation, so that $|u|^2 = \Sigma_i u_i^2$. Differentiating this with respect to λ, we get:

$$2\lambda |u|^2 - 2|v|^2 \lambda^{-3} = 0 \qquad \Rightarrow \qquad \lambda = \frac{\sqrt{|v|}}{\sqrt{|u|}}$$

However, observe that we are free to multiply both λ and μ by a constant factor, since this doesn't affect the relationship between the two sources, only the overall size of the polarity values. By dividing by $\sqrt{|u|\,|v|}$, we derive the simpler expressions $\lambda = |u|^{-1}$ and $\mu = |v|^{-1}$, i.e. we should divide by the root mean square. In other words, after normalising, the average squared polarity value is 1 for both sources.[5]

4.2 Rescaling for Multiple Sources

For multiple sources, the above method needs tweaking. Although we could use the overlap between all sources, this could potentially be much smaller than the overlap between any two sources, introducing data sparsity and making the method susceptible to noise. In the given data, 10749 lexical items appear in at least two sources, but only 1205 appear in all four. We would like to exploit this extra information, but the missing data means that methods such as linear regression cannot be applied.

A simple solution is to calculate the root mean square values for each pair of sources, and then average these values for each source. These averaged values define normalisation factors, as a compromise between the various sources.

4.3 Unspecified scores

Some lexical items in the PolarityClues dataset were not assigned a numerical score, only a polarity direction. In these cases, the task is not to normalise the score, but to assign one. To do this, we can first normalise the scores of all other words, as described above. Then, we can consider the words without scores, and calculate the root mean square polarity of these words in the other sources, and assign them this value, either positive or negative.

[5] In most sentiment lexicons, polarity strengths are at most 1. This will no longer be true after this normalisation.

5 Combining Scores

Now that we have normalised scores, we need to calculate a combined value. Here, we take a Bayesian approach, where we assume that there is a latent "true" polarity value, and each source is an observation of this value, plus some noise.

5.1 Gaussian Model

A simple model is to assume that we have a prior distribution of polarity values across the vocabulary, distributed normally. If we further assume that a language is on average neither positive nor negative, then this distribution has mean 0. We denote the variance as σ^2. Each source independently introduces a linear error term, which we also model with a normal distribution: errors from source a are distributed with mean 0 and standard deviation σ_a^2, which varies according to the source.[6]

5.2 Hyperparameter Selection

If we observe a subset $S = \{a_1, \ldots, a_n\}$ of the sources, the marginal distribution of the observations will be normally distributed, with mean 0 and covariance matrix as shown below. If the error variances σ_a^2 are small compared to the background variance σ^2, then this implies a strong correlation between the observations.

$$\begin{pmatrix} \sigma^2 + \sigma_{a_1}^2 & \sigma^2 & \cdots & \sigma^2 \\ \sigma^2 & \sigma^2 + \sigma_{a_2}^2 & \cdots & \sigma^2 \\ \vdots & \vdots & \ddots & \vdots \\ \sigma^2 & \sigma^2 & \cdots & \sigma^2 + \sigma_{a_n}^2 \end{pmatrix}$$

To choose the values for σ^2 and σ_a^2, we can aim to maximise the likelihood of the observations, i.e. maximise the value of the above marginal distributions at the observed points. This is in line with Schafer and Graham (2002)'s recommendations. Such an optimisation problem can be dealt with using existing software, such as included in the SciPy[7] package for Python.

5.3 Inference

Given a model as above (whether or not the hyperparameters have been optimised), we can calculate the posterior distribution of polarity values, given the observations x_{a_i}. This again turns out to be normally distributed, with mean $\hat{\mu}$ and variance $\hat{\sigma}^2$ given by:

$$\hat{\mu} = \frac{\sum \sigma_{a_i}^{-2} x_{a_i}}{\sigma^{-2} + \sum \sigma_{a_i}^{-2}}$$

$$\hat{\sigma}^{-2} = \sigma^{-2} + \sum \sigma_{a_i}^{-2}$$

The mean is almost a weighted average of the observed polarity values, where each source has weight σ_a^{-2}. However, there is an additional term σ^{-2} in the denominator - this means we can interpret this as a weighted average if we add an additional polarity value 0, with weight σ^{-2}. This additional term corresponds to the prior.

The weights for each source intuitively mean that we trust sources more if they have less noise. The extra 0 term from the prior means that we interpret the observations conservatively, skewing values towards 0 when there are fewer observations. For example, if all sources give a large positive polarity value, we can be reasonably certain that the true value is also large and positive, but if we only have data from one source, then we are less certain if this is true - our estimate $\hat{\mu}$ is correspondingly smaller, and the posterior variance $\hat{\sigma}^2$ correspondingly larger.

[6]Because of the independence assumptions, this model can alternatively be viewed as a Markov Network, where we have one node to represent the latent true polarity strengths, four nodes to represent observations from each source, and five nodes to represent the hyperparameters (variances)

[7]`http://www.scipy.org`

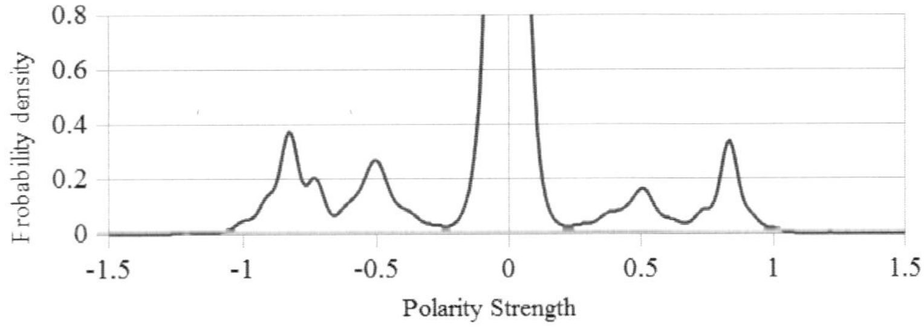

Figure 1: Gaussian kernel density estimate

6 Experiments and Results

6.1 Parameter Values

The root mean square sentiment values for the sources were: C&K 0.845; PolarityClues 0.608; SentiWS 0.267; and SentiSpin 0.560. We can see that there is a large discrepancy between the sizes of the scores used, with SentiWS having the smallest of all. It is precisely for this reason that we need to normalise the scores.

The optimal variances calculated during hyperparameter selection (section 5.2) were: prior 0.528; C&K 0.328; PolarityClues 0.317; SentiWS 0.446; and SentiSpin 0.609. These values correlate with our intuition: C&K and PolarityClues have been hand-crafted, and have smaller error variances; SentiWS was manually finalised, and has a larger error; while finally SentiSpin was automatically generated, and has the largest error of all, larger in fact than the variance in the prior. We would expect the polarity values from a hand-crafted source to be more accurate, and this appears to be justified by our analysis.

6.2 Experimental Setup

The MLSA data (see section 3.5) consists of discrete polarity judgements - a word is positive, negative, or neutral, but nothing in between.[8] To allow direct evaluation against such a resource, we need to discretise the continuous range of polarity values; i.e. if the polarity value is above some positive threshold, we judge it to be positive; if it is below a negative threshold, negative; and if it is between the two thresholds, neutral. To choose this threshold before evaluation, we calculated a Gaussian kernel density estimate of the polarity values in the entire lexicon, as shown in figure 1. There is a large density near 0, reflecting that the bulk of the vocabulary is not strongly polar; indeed, so that the density of polar items is clearly visible, we have chosen a scale that forces this bulk to go off the top of the chart. The high density stops at around ± 0.23, and we have accordingly set this as our threshold.

We compared the merged resource to each of the original lexicons, as well as a "majority vote" baseline which represents an alternative method to combine lexicons. This baseline involves considering the polarity judgements of each lexicon (*positive*, *negative*, or *neutral*), and taking the most common answer. To break ties, we took the first answer when consulting the lexicons in the following order, reflecting their reliability: C&K, PolarityClues, SentiWS, SentiSpin.

For the automatically derived resources, we can introduce a threshold as we did for SentiMerge. However, to make these baselines as competitive as possible, we optimised them on the test data, rather than choosing them in advance. They were chosen to maximise the macro-averaged f-score. For SentiWS, the threshold was 0, and for SentiSpin, 0.02.

Note that a perfect score would be impossible to achieve, since 31 lemmas were annotated with more than polarity type. These cases generally involve polysemous words which could be interpreted with different polarities depending on the context. Indeed, two words appeared with all three labels: *Spannung* (tension) and *Widerstand* (resistance). In a political context, interpreting *Widerstand* as positive or

[8] The annotation scheme also allows a further three labels: *intensifier*, *diminisher*, and *shifter*. While this information is useful, we treat these values as neutral in our evaluation, since we are only concerned with words that have an inherent positive or negative polarity.

Lexicon	Precision	Recall	F-score
C&K	0.754	0.733	0.743
PolarityClues	0.705	0.564	0.626
SentiWS	**0.803**	0.513	0.621
SentiSpin	0.557	0.668	0.607
majority vote	0.548	**0.898**	0.679
SentiMerge	0.708	0.815	**0.757**

Table 3: Performance on MLSA, macro-averaged

negative depends very much on whose side you support. In such cases, a greater context is necessary to decide on polarity, and a lexicon simply cannot suffice.

6.3 Evaluation on MLSA

We calculated precision, recall, and f-score (the harmonic mean of precision and recall) for both positive and negative polarity. We report the average of these two scores in 3. We can see that in terms of f-score, SentiMerge outperforms all four data sources, as well as the majority vote. In applications where either precision or recall is deemed to be more important, it would be possible to adjust the threshold accordingly. Indeed, by dropping the threshold to zero, we achieve recall of 0.894, competitive with the majority vote method; and by increasing the threshold to 0.4, we achieve precision of 0.755, competitive with the C&K lexicon. Furthermore, in this latter case, the f-score also increases to 0.760. We do not report this figure in the table above because it would not be possible to predict such a judicious choice of threshold without peeking at the test data. Nonetheless, this demonstrates that our method is robust to changes in parameter settings.

The majority vote method performs considerably worse than SentiMerge, at least in terms of f-score. Indeed, it actually performs worse than the C&K lexicon, with noticeably lower precision. This finding is consistent with the results of Raykar et al. (2010), who argue against using majority voting, and who also find that it performs poorly.

The C&K lexicon achieves almost the same level of performance as SentiMerge, so it is reasonable to ask if there is any point in building a merged lexicon at all. We believe there are two good reasons for doing this. Firstly, although the C&K lexicon may be the most accurate, it is also small, especially compared to SentiSpin. SentiMerge thus manages to exploit the complementary nature of the different lexicons, achieving the broad coverage of SentiSpin, but maintaining the precision of the C&K lexicon for the most important lexical items.

Secondly, SentiMerge can provide much more accurate values for polarity strength than any human-annotated resource can. As Clematide and Klenner (2010) show, inter-annotator agreement for polarity strength is low, even when agreement for polarity direction is high. Nonetheless, some notion of polarity strength can still be helpful in computational applications. To demonstrate this, we calculated the precision, recall, and f-scores again, but weighting each answer as a function of the distance from the estimated polarity strength to the threshold. With this weighted approach, we get a macro-averaged f-score of 0.852. This is considerably higher than the results given in table 3, which demonstrates that the polarity scores in SentiMerge are useful as a measure of classification certainty.

6.4 Manual Inspection

In cases where all sources agree on whether a word is positive or negative, our algorithm simply serves to assign a more accurate polarity strength. So, it is more interesting to consider those cases where the sources disagree on polarity direction. Out of the 1205 lexemes for which we have data from all four sources, only 22 differ between SentiMerge and the C&K lexicon, and only 16 differ between SentiMerge and PolarityClues. One example is *Beschwichtigung* (appeasement). Here we can see the problem with trying to assign a single numeric value to polarity - in a political context, *Beschwichtugung* could be interpreted either as positive, since it implies an attempt to ease tension; or as negative, since it could be viewed as a sign of weakness. Another example is *unantastbar*, which again can be interpreted positively or negatively.

The controversial words generally denote abstract notions, or have established metaphorical senses. In the authors' view, their polarity is heavily context-dependent, and a one-dimensional score is not sufficient to model their contibution to sentiment.

In fact, most of these words have been assigned very small polarity values in the combined lexicon, which reflects the conflicting evidence present in the various sources. Of the 22 items which differ in C&K, the one with the largest value in the combined lexicon is *dominieren*, which has been assigned a fairly negative combined score, but was rated positive (0.5) in C&K.

7 Distribution

We are making SentiMerge freely available for download. However, with the expanding number of language resources, it is becoming increasingly important to link resources together, as mentioned in section 2. For this reason, we are publishing our resource as part of the Linguistic Linked Open Data[9] initiative. In particular, we have decided to follow the specifications set forth by Buitelaar et al. (2013), who propose a representation for sentiment resources based on Lemon (McCrae et al., 2011) and Marl (Westerski et al., 2011). Lemon[10] is a model for resource description which builds on LMF (Lexical Markup Framework),[11] and facilitates combination of lexicons with ontologies. Marl is an an ontology language designed for sentiment analysis, which has been fully implemented.[12]

8 Future Work

To align the disparate sources, a simple linear rescaling was used. However, in principle any monotonic function could be considered. A more general function that would still be tractable could be $u_i \mapsto \lambda u_i^\alpha$.

Furthermore, the probabilistic model described in section 5.1 makes several simplifying assumptions, which could be weaked or modified. For instance, we have assumed a normal distribution, with zero mean, both for the prior distribution and for the error terms. The data is not perfectly modelled by a normal distribution, since there are very clear bounds on the polarity scores, and some of the data takes discrete values. Indeed, we can see in figure 1 that the data is not normally distributed. An alternative choice of distribution might yield better results.

More generally, our method can be applied to any context where there are multiple resources to be merged, as long as there is some real-valued property to be aligned.

9 Conclusion

We have described the merging of four sentiment lexicons into a single resource, which we have named SentiMerge. To demonstrate the utility of the combined lexicon, we set up a word-level sentiment classification task using the MLSA corpus, in which SentiMerge outperformed all four of the underlying resources, as well as a majority vote baseline. As a natural by-product of the merging process, we are also able to indirectly evaluate the quality of each resource, and the results match both intuition and the performance in the aformentioned classification task. The approach we have taken requires no parameter setting on the part of the researcher, so we believe that the same method can be applied to other settings where different language resources present conflicting information. This work helps to bridge the gap between resource creation efforts, which may overlap in scope, and NLP research, where researchers often want to use all available data. Furthermore, by grounding our work in a well-defined Bayesian framework, we leave scope for future improvements using more sophisticated probabilistic models. To allow the community at large to use and build on this work, we are making SentiMerge publically available for download, and are incorporating it into the Linguistic Linked Open Data initiative.

[9] http://linguistics.okfn.org/resources/llod

[10] http://lemon-model.net

[11] http://www.lexicalmarkupframework.org

[12] http://www.gsi.dit.upm.es/ontologies/marl

Acknowledgements

This work was co-financed by the European Commission, within the FP7 ICT project TrendMiner,[13] under contract number 287863. We would like to thank the authors of the all the resources mentioned in this paper for permission to use their data. We also thank the anonymous reviewers for their helpful comments.

References

Paul Buitelaar, Mihael Arcan, Carlos A Iglesias, J Fernando Sánchez-Rada, and Carlo Strapparava. 2013. Linguistic linked data for sentiment analysis. In *Proceedings of the 2nd Workshop on Linked Data in Linguistics*.

Simon Clematide and Manfred Klenner. 2010. Evaluation and extension of a polarity lexicon for German. In *Proceedings of the First Workshop on Computational Approaches to Subjectivity and Sentiment Analysis*, page 7.

Simon Clematide, Stefan Gindl, Manfred Klenner, Stefanos Petrakis, Robert Remus, Josef Ruppenhofer, Ulli Waltinger, and Michael Wiegand. 2012. MLSA – a multi-layered reference corpus for German sentiment analysis. pages 3551–3556. European Language Resources Association (ELRA).

Thierry Declerck and Hans-Ulrich Krieger. 2014. TMO – the federated ontology of the TrendMiner project. In *Proceedings of the 9th International Language Resources and Evaluation Conference (LREC 2014)*.

Judith Eckle-Kohler and Iryna Gurevych. 2013. The practitioner's cookbook for linked lexical resources.

Birgit Hamp and Helmut Feldweg. 1997. GermaNet – a lexical-semantic net for German. In *Proceedings of the ACL workshop Automatic Information Extraction and Building of Lexical Semantic Resources for NLP Applications*, pages 9–15. Association for Computational Linguistics.

John McCrae, Dennis Spohr, and Phillip Cimiano. 2011. Linking lexical resources and ontologies on the semantic web with lemon. In *Proceedings of the 8th Extended Semantic Web Conference*.

Bo Pang and Lillian Lee. 2008. Opinion mining and sentiment analysis. *Foundations and trends in information retrieval*.

Vikas C Raykar, Shipeng Yu, Linda H Zhao, Gerardo Hermosillo Valadez, Charles Florin, Luca Bogoni, and Linda Moy. 2010. Learning from crowds. *The Journal of Machine Learning Research*, 11:1297–1322.

Robert Remus, Uwe Quasthoff, and Gerhard Heyer. 2010. SentiWS – a publicly available German-language resource for sentiment analysis. In *Proceedings of the 7th International Language Resources and Evaluation Conference (LREC 2010)*.

Joseph L Schafer and John W Graham. 2002. Missing data: our view of the state of the art. *Psychological methods*, 7(2):147.

Philip J Stone, Dexter C Dunphy, and Marshall S Smith. 1966. The general inquirer: A computer approach to content analysis.

Hiroya Takamura, Takashi Inui, and Manabu Okumura. 2005. Extracting semantic orientations of words using spin model. In *Proceedings of the 43rd Annual Meeting of the Association for Computational Linguistics*. Association for Computational Linguistics.

Ulli Waltinger. 2010a. GermanPolarityClues: A lexical resource for German sentiment analysis. In *Proceedings of the 7th International Language Resources and Evaluation Conference (LREC 2010)*.

Ulli Waltinger. 2010b. Sentiment analysis reloaded - a comparative study on sentiment polarity identification combining machine learning and subjectivity features. In *Proceedings of the 6th International Conferenceon Web Information Systems and Technologies (WEBIST 2010)*. INSTICC Press.

Adam Westerski, Carlos A. Iglesias, and Fernando Tapia. 2011. Linked opinions: Describing sentiments on the structured web of data. In *Proceedings of the 4th International Workshop Social Data on the Web*.

Michael Wiegand. 2011. *Hybrid approaches for sentiment analysis*. PhD dissertation, Universität des Saarlandes.

Theresa Wilson, Janyce Wiebe, and Paul Hoffmann. 2005. Recognizing contextual polarity in phrase-level sentiment analysis. In *Proceedings of the conference on human language technology and empirical methods in natural language processing*, pages 347–354. Association for Computational Linguistics.

[13] `http://www.trendminer-project.eu`

Linguistically motivated Language Resources for Sentiment Analysis

Voula Giouli **Aggeliki Fotopoulou**
Institute for Language and Speech Processing, Athena RIC
{voula;afotop}@ilsp.athena-innovation.gr

Abstract

Computational approaches to sentiment analysis focus on the identification, extraction, summarization and visualization of emotion and opinion expressed in texts. These tasks require large-scale language resources (LRs) developed either manually or semi-automatically. Building them from scratch, however, is a laborious and costly task, and re-using and repurposing already existing ones is a solution to this bottleneck. We hereby present work aimed at the extension and enrichment of existing general-purpose LRs, namely a set of computational lexica, and their integration in a new emotion lexicon that would be applicable for a number of Natural Language Processing applications beyond mere syntactic parsing.

1 Introduction

The abundance of user-generated content over the web has brought about the shift of interest to the opinion and emotion expressed by people or groups of people with respect to a specific target entity, product, subject matter, etc. The task of sentiment analysis involves determining the so-called *private states* (beliefs, feelings, and speculations) expressed in a particular text or text segment as opposed to factual information. More precisely, it is focused on the following: (a) *identification of sentiment expressions* in textual data and their *classification* as appropriate, and (b) *recognition* of *participants* in the private state, as for example, the entities identified as the *Source* and *Target* of the emotion. More recently, aspect-based sentiment analysis has also been in the focus of research (Wilson, 2008).

Traditionally, classification of sentiment expressions is usually attempted in terms of the general notion of *polarity* defined as *positive, negative and neutral*. Traditional approaches to text classification based on stochastic methods are quite effective when applied for sentiment analysis yielding quite satisfactory results. However, certain applications require for more fine-grained classifications of sentiment i.e. the identification of emotional states such as *anger*, *sadness*, *surprise*, *satisfaction*, etc. in place of mere recognition of the polarity. Such applications might be the identification of certain emotions expressed by customers (i.e., satisfaction, or dissatisfaction) with respect to some product or service, or the analysis of emotions and feelings described by users in blogs, wikis, fora and social media (Klenner at al., 2009). In this respect, stochastic approaches fail to recognize multiple or even conflicting emotions expressed in a document or text segment. In these cases, linguistic (syntactic and semantic knowledge) is necessary in order to assess the overall polarity of a clause and or the feeling expressed in it.

The paper is organised as follows: In section 2 we present the aims and scope of the specific work; section 3 gives an overview of related work on affective LRs, whereas section 4 gives an account of the LRs developed within the framework of Lexicon – Grammar. Our efforts towards enriching the existing resources with semantic information and re-purposing them are presented in sections 5 and 6 respectively, while section 7 outlines our conclusions and prospects for future research.

2 Aims and scope

We present work aimed at extending, enriching and re-purposing existing LRs, the ultimate goal being

Proceedings of the Workshop on Lexical and Grammatical Resources for Language Processing, pages 39–45,
Coling 2014, Dublin, Ireland, August 24 2014.

their integration in a tool for sentiment analysis. In specific, a suite of computational lexica developed within the framework of Lexicon – Grammar (LG) and treating *verbal and nominal predicates* denoting emotion were used. These resources were initially constructed manually as a means to describe general language, and they bear rich linguistic information that would be otherwise difficult to encode in an automatic way, namely (a) subcategorisation information, (b) semantic and distributional properties, and (c) syntactic transformations of the predicates. Within the current work, semantic information that is meaningful for sentiment analysis was also added to lexicon entries. The final resource was then used to bootstrap a *grammar of emotions*. This grammar is a rule-based approach to sentiment analysis aimed at capturing and modeling linguistic knowledge that is necessary for the task at hand.

The work presented here was based on a previous study (Giouli et al., 2013), making further extensive use of the Hellenic National Corpus (HNC), a large reference corpus for the Greek language (Hatzigeorgiou et al, 2000). Additionally, a suite of specialized corpora that were developed to guide sentiment studies in multimodal (Mouka et al., 2012) and in textual (Giouli and Fotopoulou, 2013) data was used. Thus, the resulting *Greek Sentiment Corpus*, that amounts to c. ~250K tokens, comprises audiovisual material (movies dialogues), and texts selected manually from various sources over the web. More particularly, the online edition of two newspapers along with a news portal were searched on a daily basis for the identification and selection of commentaries dealing with a set of predefined topics; Greek blogs and fora were also used as sources for text collection. The aforementioned corpus was annotated at the sentence and phrase level for opinion and emotion, and was subsequently used to populate the sentiment lexicon under construction. Moreover, initial steps were made towards creating a rule-based system for the identification of sentiment expressions in texts and computing the overall phrase polarity in context on the basis of corpus evidence.

3 Related work

A number of large-scale lexica appropriate for sentiment analysis have been developed either manually or semi-automatically. These range from mere word lists to more elaborate resources. General Inquirer (Stone et al. 1966), the Subjectivity lexicon integrated in OpinionFinder (Wiebe et al., 2005), and SentiWordNet (Esuli and Sebastiani 2006) are examples of such affective lexica. On the other hand, WordNet-Affect (Strapparava and Valitutti 2004), an extension of WordNet Domains, is linguistically oriented as it comprises a subset of *synsets* that are suitable to represent affective concepts in correlation with *affective words*. A set of A-labels is used to mark concepts representing emotions or emotional states, moods, eliciting emotions situations, and emotional responses. Finally, EmotiNet (Balahur et al, 2011) is a knowledge base (KB) for representing and storing affective reaction to real-life contexts and action chains described in text.

From a purely linguistic perspective – yet with a view to Natural Language Processing - substantial work has been devoted to the semantic classification of verbal predicates denoting emotion in (Mathieu, 1999). In this work, verbs denoting emotional states and evaluative stances should also be classified according to the so-called *semantic field'*. Verbs were, thus, categorized into homogenous semantic classes which share common syntactic properties; this classification is claimed to facilitate semantic interpretation.

Statistical approaches to sentiment analysis feature a "bag-of-word" representation (Hu and Liu, 2004). Rule-based systems, on the other hand, exploit linguistic knowledge in the form of syntactic/lexical patterns for computing polarity in context. In most cases, negative particles and modality are reported as the most obvious shifters that affect sentiment polarity (Polanyi and Zaenen 2006, Jia *et al.* 2009, Wiegand *et al.* 2010, Benamara et al., 2012). Finally, compositionality features have been explored for the computation of multiple or conflicted sentiments on the basis of deep linguistic analysis (Moilanen and Pulman, 2007), (Neviarouskaya et al., 2009), (Klenner et al., 2009).

4 Lexicon – Grammar tables

4.1 Lexicon – Grammar framework

The Lexical Resources hereby exploited were initially constructed in accordance with the Lexicon-Grammar (LG) methodological framework (Gross 1975), (Gross 1981). Being a model of syntax limited to the *elementary sentences* of the form *Subject – Verb – Object*, the theory argues that the unit of meaning is located at the sentence rather than the word level. To this end, linguistic analysis consists in converting each elementary sentence to its predicate-argument structure. Additionally, main complements (subject, object) are separated from other complements (adjuncts) on the basis of formal criteria; adverbial complements (i.e., prepositional phrases) are considered as crucial arguments only in the case that they characterize certain verb frames:

(1) John removed the cups *from the table.*

To cater for a more fine-grained classification, and the creation of homogenous word classes, this formal syntactic definition is further coupled with *distributional properties associated with words*, i.e., types of prepositions, features attached to nouns in subject and complement positions, etc. A set of transformation rules, construed as equivalence relations between sentences, further generate equivalent structures. It becomes evident, therefore, that the resulting resources are rich in linguistic information (syntactic structure, distributional properties and permitted transformational rules), which is encoded formally in the so-called LG tables.

4.2 The Lexicon – Grammar of verb and noun predicates denoting emotion

Within the LG framework, 130 noun predicates denoting emotions (*Nsent*) in Modern Greek were selected and classified into 3 classes, according to their syntactic and distributional properties (Fotopoulou & al., 2008). The 1st class comprises nouns of interpersonal relations with an obligatory prepositional complement and a conversed construction, as for example *θαυμασμός (= admiration).* The 2nd class are indicative of an external cause including a non obligatory prepositional complement, as for example *φόβος (= fear).* The 3rd class without complements have a static character, as for example *ευτυχία (= happiness).* Identification of the specific light verbs (or support verbs, *Vsup*) they select for was also performed. Furthermore, their distributional properties and their co-occurrence with specific verbs expressing diverse modalities (aspect, intensity, control, manifestation or verbal expression) have also been encoded in a formal way. These properties reveal the restrictions nouns impose on the lexical choice of verbs.

Furthermore, 339 Greek verbal predicates denoting emotion (*Vsent*) have been selected from various sources (i.e. existing reference lexicographic works and corpora) and were subsequently classified in five LG tables. Classification was performed on the basis of the following axes: (i) syntactic information (i.e, subcategorisation information); (ii) selectional restrictions (+Hum/ -Hum) imposed over their Subject and Object complements; and (iii) transformation rules. More precisely, as far as syntactic structure is concerned, the predicates under consideration were identified to appear in both transitive and intransitive constructions being represented as *N0 V N1* and *N0 V* respectively. Certain verbs also allow for a prepositional phrase complement represented as *N0 V Prep N1*[1] configurations. A close inspection over the data revealed the relationship between the N0 or N1 complements that denote the *Experiencer* of the emotion (i.e., the entity feeling the emotion). In two of the resulting classes the *Experiencer* is projected as the structural Subject of the verb, whereas the *Theme* or *Stimulus* is projected as their structural object. Similarly, the remaining 3 classes realize the *Theme/Stimulus* as the subject and the *Experiencer* as their object, their distinguishing property being their participation in unaccusative and middle constructions, the latter being linked to the implicit presence of an Agent (middle) and the absence of an Agent (unaccusative). These properties have been checked for the whole range of lexical data based on both linguistic introspection and corpus evidence.

A number of Harrisian constructions and transformations (Harris, 1951; 1964; 1968) have been extensively utilized within the LG formalism to define syntactically related and semantically equivalent structures. Apart from passivisation and middle alternation constructions - also relevant to emotion predicates - the restructuring transformation has been accounted for (Guillet and Leclère, 1981):

(2) Ο Γιάννης θαυμάζει *τη Μαρία για το θάρρος της*.
The John admires the Maria for the courage-her.
John admires Maria for her courage.

[1] Adopting the LG notation, N0 denotes a Noun in *Subject* position of a given verb V, whereas, N1 denotes its *Object*.

(3) Ο Γιάννης θαυμάζει <u>*το θάρρος της Μαρίας*</u>.
The John admires the courage the Maria-of
John admires Maria's courage.

Moreover, each verbal predicate was also coupled with morphologically-related *adjectives* and *nouns*, and the alignment of semantically equivalent nominal, verbal and adjectival structures was performed thereof. A number of semantically equivalent paraphrases of the verbs with the morphologically related nouns and adjectives were also encoded in the tables.

Finally, following the same methodology, a set of 2,500 verbal multi-word expressions denoting emotions were identified from corpora and classified in 13 categories according to their syntactic structure. The final resource comprises a total of ~3000 entries, organized in 21 LG tables with lemmas inter-connected via the tables relative to verbs.

5 Semantic classification of emotion predicates

Semantic classification of the verbal predicates has also been performed on the basis of their underlying semantics. In this way, the syntactic and distributional properties encoded in the LG tables have been coupled with semantic information that defines an affective taxonomy. These properties were added as columns in the tables that describe the verb predicates. Our goal was to group together predicates that are synonyms or near synonyms and to create an affective taxonomy hierarchical organized. To this end, certain abstractions and generalizations were performed where necessary for defining classes of emotion types.

Initially, 59 classes of emotion-related-senses were identified. At the next stage, a number of iterations followed aimed at grouping together senses that are semantically related. This procedure resulted in the identification of a set of senses that may be used as taxonomy of emotions. Following practices adopted in similar endeavours (i.e., Mathieu, 1999), each class was further assigned a tag that uniquely identifies the respective class. The following classes (19 classes) were identified: *anger*, *fear*, *sadness*, *disgust*, *surprise*, *anticipation*, *acceptance*, *joy*, *love*, *hate*, *disappointment*, *indifference*, *shame*, *envy*, *jealousy*, *relaxedness*, *respect*, *resentment*, and *remorse*.

Next, each entry was further specified as regards the specific relation that holds between the entry and the emotion type it belongs to. A set of properties were then defined for which each entry was then examined, namely: *FeelEmotion*, *EmotionManifestation*, *Behaviour*, and *EntailsEmotion*.

At a more abstract level, entries were further assigned a value for the semantic property *polarity*. Following previous works (Mathieu and Fellbaum, 2010), the encoding caters for the *apriori polarity* of the emotion denoted which subsumes one of the following values: (a) *positive, i.e.* predicates which express a pleasant feeling; (b) *negative,* i.e., predicates which express an unpleasant feeling; (c) *neutral*, and (d) *ambiguous,* i.e., predicates expressing a feeling the polarity of which is *context-dependent* (e.g., surprise).

Moreover, to better account for the semantic distinction between near synonyms that occur within a class such as *φοβάμαι (= I am scared), πανικοβάλλομαι (=panic), etc.*, entries are further coupled with the feature *intensity* with possible values: *low, medium, high, uncertain*. Intensity was attributed to the lexical items on the basis of linguistic introspection and the definitions of lexical entries.

6 Transforming Lexicon-Grammar tables to a grammar of emotions

Being initially developed to serve as a means of linguistic description, this framework has, never-theless, been proved to be applicable for the construction of robust computational lexica. And although it has been claimed (Mathieu, 2008) that the information is not *directly* exploitable for NLP applications due to the fact that certain pieces of information are not formally encoded or are *implicit*, a number of works (Hathout and Namer 1998, Danlos and Sagot 2009) have successfully managed to reformat LG tables in efficient large-scale NLP lexica.

To this end, we have tried to exploit information available in the tables and make the mappings that are necessary for the task of sentiment recognition. On the one hand, subcategorisation information with respect to selectional restrictions imposed over the Subject and Object of the verbal predicates was exploited. Once a verbal predicate has been identified, the constituent either in Subject or Object position that is also assigned a (+Hum) property corresponds unambiguously to the *Experiencer* of the emotion depending on the class it belongs to (i.e., SubjectExperiencer or Object Experiencer). Similarly, the NP in *Object* position of verbs that pertain to the 2nd class *αγαπώ (=love)* corresponds to the *Target* of the emotion. All other constituents correspond to the *Trigger* or *Cause*.

On these grounds, initial steps towards building a rule-based component that identifies emotion verbal and nominal predicates in texts along with the participating entities, namely the *Experiencer* and *Target* of the emotion expressed have been performed. To this end, a library of *local grammars* (Constant, 2003) for emotion predicates has been constructed modeling structures in the annotated corpus. Local grammars (also referred to in the literature as *graphs*) are algebraic grammars formulated as combinations of sequences of grammatical symbols in the form of regular expressions that describe natural language. In this sense, they are a powerful tool to represent the majority of linguistic phenomena in an intuitive manner. Moreover, they are compiled into finite state transducers that transform input text by inserting or removing special markers. Rules are sequentially applied to the text using longest match. We made use of the UNITEX platform (Paumier, 2013) for creating the graphs and then compiling them into finite state transducers. UNITEX consists of three modules, namely, corpus handling, lexicon development and grammar development that are integrated into a single intuitive graphical user interface. Based on the Lexicon-Grammar tables developed for the verbal predicates (c.f. section 2 above), we initially created five parameterized graphs manually; these graphs depict the syntactic and semantic properties of the predicates. At the next stage, a set of graphs was constructed automatically using UNITEX, each one representing the syntactic and semantic properties of a given predicate.

It should be noted, however, that LG tables provide descriptions at an abstract level. To remedy this shortcoming, a number of graphs and sub-graphs describing a wide range of syntactic phenomena (noun phrase, coordination, modifiers, negation, and valency shifters) were constructed manually. The set of graphs comprises a grammar applied to the text as a cascade for the identification of the *emotive* predicate, being either verbal or nominal, its *polarity* and the participants of the emotion event that can be identified from the underlying structure – namely the *Experiencer* and the *Theme* and the *Cause*.

7 Conclusions and future work

We have described work aimed at enriching, re-purposing and re-using already available LRs for a new task, namely identification of emotion expressions in texts. The existing lexica carry rich linguistic information which has been mapped onto categories that are meaningful for the task. Our efforts have been oriented towards developing a rule-based system that efficiently will eventually recognise emotion expressions in texts and the participants in the emotion event.

Future work has been planned already, consisting of the exploitation of other properties that are encoded in the LG tables, as for example the restructuring property as a facet of the aspect-based sentiment analysis and the conversion of the enriched LG tables to a standardised lexical format. Finally, the validation of the final resource is due against the manually annotated corpus.

Acknowledgments

The research within the project *LangTERRA: Enhancing the Research Potential of ILSP/"Athena" R.C. in Language Technology in the European Research ERA* leading to these results has received funding from the European Union Seventh Framework Programme (FP7/2007-2013).

References

Alexandra Balahur and Jesús M. Hermida and Andrés Montoyo and Rafael Muñoz. 2011. EmotiNet: A Knowledge Base for Emotion Detection in Text Built on the Appraisal Theories. In R. Muñoz et al. (Eds.): *Natural Language Processing and Information Systems, Lecture Notes in Computer Science*, Volume 6716, Springer-Verlag Berlin Heidelberg 2011, pp 27-39.

Farah Benamara, Baptiste Chardon, Yannick Mathieu, Vladimir Popescu, and Nicholas Asher. 2012. How do Negation and Modality Impact on Opinions? In *Proceedings of the Workshop on Extra-Propositional Aspects of Meaning in Computational Linguistics, ExProM '12*, Jeju, Republic of Korea, 2012, pp 10–18.

Matthieu Constant. 2003. *Grammaires locales pour l'analyse automatique de textes : méthodes de construction et outils de gestion*. Thèse de doctorat, Université de Marne-la-Vallée.

Laurence Danlos and Benoît Sagot. 2009. Constructions pronominales dans Dicovalence et le lexique-grammaire: Integration dans le Lefff. Actes du 27e Colloque international sur le lexique et la grammaire.

Andrea Esuli and Fabrizio Sebastiani. 2006. SENTIWORDNET: A Publicly Available Lexical Resource for Opinion Mining, in *Proceedings of the 5th Conference on Language Resources and Evaluation (LREC 2006)*, Genova, Italy, pp 417-422.

Christiane Fellbaum. 1998. *WordNet: An Electronic Lexical Database*. Cambridge, MA: MIT Press.

Aggeliki Fotopoulou, Marianna Mini, Mavina Pantazara and Argiro Moustaki. 2008. La combinatoire lexicale des noms de sentiments en grec modern. In *Iva Novacova & Agnes Tutin (eds), Le lexique des émotions. ELLUG*, Grenoble.

Voula Giouli and Aggeliki Fotopoulou. 2012. Emotion verbs in Greek. From Lexicon-Grammar tables to multi-purpose syntactic and semantic lexica. In *Proceedings of the XV Euralex International Congress (EURALEX 2012)*. Oslo, Norway.

Voula Giouli and Aggeliki Fotopoulou. 2013. Developing Language Resources for Sentiment Analysis in Greek. In *Proceedings of the Workshop "The semantic domain of emotions: cross-domain and cross-lingual considerations. From words to phrases/text and beyond*". Workshop organized within the framework of the *International Conference in Greek Linguistics. ICGL*, Rhodes.

Voula Giouli, Aggeliki Fotopoulou, Effie Mouka, and Ioannis E. Saridakis. 2013. Annotating Sentiment Expressions for Lexical Resourcres. In Blumenthal, Peter, Novakova, Iva, Siepmann, Dirk (eds.), *Les émotions dans le discours. Emotions in discourse*. Frankfurt, Main et al.: Peter Lang.

Maurice Gross. 1975. *Méthodes en syntaxe. Régime des constructions complétives*. Hermann, Paris.

Maurice Gross. 1981. Les bases empiriques de la notion de prédicat sémantique. *Langages* 15, 7-52.

Allain Guillet and Christian Leclère. 1981. La restructuration du sujet. *Langages* 65. Paris, France.

Zelling S. Harris. 1951. *Methods in Structural Linguistics*. The University of Chicago Press, Chicago.

Zelling S. Harris. 1964. The Elementary Transformations. In *T.D.A.P. University of Pennsylvania* 54, Pennsylvania.

Zelling S. Harris. 1968. *Mathematical Structures of Language*. Wiley, New York.

Nabil Hathout and Fiammetta Namer. 1998. Automatic Construction and Validation of French Large Lexical Resources: Reuse of Verb Theoretical Linguistic Descriptions. In *Proceedings of the Language Resources and Evaluation Conference, Grenada, Spain.*

Nick Hatzigeorgiu, Maria Gavrilidou, Stelios Piperidis, George Carayannis, Anna Papakostopoulou, Anna Spiliotopoulou, Anna Vacalopoulou, Penny Labropoulou, Elena Mantzari, Harris Papageorgiou, and Iason Demiros. 2000. Design and Implementation of the Online ILSP Greek Corpus. In *Proceedings of the 2nd Language Resources and Evaluation Conference (LREC, 2000)*, Athens, Greece.

Lifeng Jia, Clement Yu and Weiyi Meng. 2009. The effect of Negation on Sentiment Analysis and Retrieval Effectiveness. In *Proceedings of the 18th ACM conference on Information and knowledge management*, Hong Kong, pp. 1827-1830.

Manfred Klenner, Stefanos Petrakis and Angela Fahrni. 2009. Robust Compositional Polarity Classification. In *Recent Advances in Natural Language Processing (RANLP)*, Borovets, Bulgaria

Yvette Yannick Mathieu. 1999. Un classement sémantique des verbes psychologiques. *Cahiers du C.I.EL*: pp.115-134

Yvette Yannick Mathieu. 2008. Navigation dans un texte à la recherche des sentiments. *Linguisticae Investigationes*. 31:2, pp. 313-322.

Yvette Yannick Mathieu and Christiane Fellbaum, 2010. Verbs of Emotion in French and English. *Emotion*, vol. 70, 2010.

Karo Moilanen and Stephen Pulman. 2007. Sentiment Composition. In *Proceedings of Recent Advances in Natural Language Processing (RANLP)*, Borovets, Bulgaria, 2007, pp 378–382.

Effie Mouka, Voula Giouli, Aggeliki Fotopoulou, and Ioannis E. Saridakis. 2012. Opinion and emotion in movies: a modular perspective to annotation. In *Proceedings of the 4th International Workshop on Corpora for Research on Emotion, Sentiment & Social Signals (ES^3 2012)*. Istanbul, Turkey.

Alena Neviarouskaya, Helmut Prendinger, and Mitsuru Ishizuka. 2009. Compositionality Principle in Recognition of Fine-Grained Emotions from Text. In *Proceedings of the International Conference on Weblogs and Social Media*, AAAI, San Jose, USA, May 2009, pp. 278–281

Sébastien Paumier. 2003. *UNITEX User Manual.*

Livia Polanyi and Annie Zaenen. 2006. Contextual Valence Shifters. In Shanahan, J., Qu, Y., and Wiebe, J. *Computing Attitude and Affect in Text: Theory and Applications*. Berlin: Springer, pp. 1-10.

Philip J. Stone and Earl B. Hunt. 1963. A computer approach to content analysis: studies using the General Inquirer system. In *Proceedings of the May 21-23, 1963, Spring Joint Computer Conference. Detroit, Michigan, pp. 241-256.*

Carlo Strapparava and Alessandro Valitutti. 2004. WordNet-Affect: an affective extension of WordNet. In *Proceedings of Language Resources and Evaluation Conference* (LREC 2004), pp. 1083-1086.

Theresa Wilson, Janyce Wiebe, and Paul Hoffmann. 2005. Recognizing Contextual Polarity in Phrase-Level Sentiment Analysis. *In Proceedings of HLT-EMNLP-2005.*

Teresa Wilson. 2008. Fine-grained Subjectivity and Sentiment Analysis: Recognizing the Intensity, Polarity, and Attitudes of Private States. University of Pittsburgh. Available at: http://mpqa.cs.pitt.edu/data/TAWilsonDissertationCh7Attitudes.pdf. [Accessed November 2011]

Michael Wiegand, Alexandra Balahur, Benjamin Roth, Dietrich Klakow and Andres Montoyo. 2010. A survey on the Role of Negation in Sentiment Analysis. In: *Proceedings of NeSp-NLP '10, pp. 60-68.*

Using Morphosemantic Information in Construction of a Pilot Lexical Semantic Resource for Turkish

Gözde Gül İşgüder-Şahin
Department of Computer Engineering
Istanbul Technical University
Istanbul, 34469, Turkey
isguderg@itu.edu.tr

Eşref Adalı
Department of Computer Engineering
Istanbul Technical University
Istanbul, 34469, Turkey
adali@itu.edu.tr

Abstract

Morphological units carry vast amount of semantic information for languages with rich inflectional and derivational morphology. In this paper we show how morphosemantic information available for morphologically rich languages can be used to reduce manual effort in creating semantic resources like PropBank and VerbNet; to increase performance of word sense disambiguation, semantic role labeling and related tasks. We test the consistency of these features in a pilot study for Turkish and show that; 1) Case markers are related with semantic roles and 2) Morphemes that change the valency of the verb follow a predictable pattern.

1 Introduction

In recent years considerable amount of research has been performed on extracting semantic information from sentences. Revealing such information is usually achieved by identifying the complements (arguments) of a predicate and assigning meaningful labels to them. Each label represents the argument's relation to its predicate and is referred to as a semantic role and this task is named as semantic role labeling (SRL). There exists some comprehensive semantically interpreted corpora such as FrameNet and PropBank. These corpora, annotated with semantic roles, help researchers to specify SRL as a task, furthermore are used as training and test data for supervised machine learning methods (Giuglea and Moschitti, 2006). These resources differ in type of semantic roles they use and type of additional information they provide.

FrameNet (FN) is a semantic network, built around the theory of **semantic frames**. This theory describes a type of event, relation, or entity with their participants which are called **frame elements (FEs)**. All predicates in same semantic frame share one set of FEs. A sample sentence annotated with FrameNet, VerbNet and PropBank conventions respectively, is given in Ex. 1. The predicate "buy" belongs to "Commerce buy", more generally "Commercial transaction" frame of FrameNet which contains "Buyer", "Goods" as core frame elements and "Seller" as a non-core frame element as in Ex. 1. FN also provides connections between semantic frames like inheritance, hierarchy and causativity. For example the frame "Commerce buy" is connected to "Importing" and "Shopping" frames with "used by" relation. Contrary to FN, **VerbNet (VN)** is a hierarchical verb lexicon, that contains categories of verbs based on Levin Verb classification (Schuler, 2006). The predicate "buy" is contained in "get-13.5.1" class of VN, among with the verbs "pick", "reserve" and "book". Members of same verb class share same set of semantic roles, referred to as **thematic roles**. In addition to thematic roles, verb classes are defined with different possible syntaxes for each class. One possible syntax for the class "get-13.5.1" is given in the second line of Ex. 1. Unlike FrameNet and VerbNet, **PropBank (PB)** (Palmer et al., 2005) does not make use of a reference ontology like semantic frames or verb classes. Instead semantic roles are numbered from Arg0 to Arg5 for the core arguments.

Ex. 1 $[\text{Jess}]_{\text{Buyer-Agent-Arg0}}$ bought $[\text{a coat}]_{\text{Goods-Theme-Arg1}}$ from $[\text{Abby}]_{\text{Seller-Source-Arg2}}$[1]
Syntax: Agent V Theme {From} Source

[1]In PropBank Arg0 is used for actor, agent, experiencer or cause of the event; Arg1 represents the patient, if the argument is affected by the action, and theme, if the argument is not structurally changed.

Proceedings of the Workshop on Lexical and Grammatical Resources for Language Processing, pages 46–54,
Coling 2014, Dublin, Ireland, August 24 2014.

There doesn't exist a VerbNet, PropBank or a similiar semantically interpretable resource for Turkish (except for WordNet (Bilgin et al., 2004)). Also, the only available morphologically and syntactically annotated treebank corpus: METU-Sabanci Dependency Treebank (Eryiğit et al., 2011), (Oflazer et al., 2003), (Atalay et al., 2003) has only about 5600 sentences, which has presumably a low coverage of Turkish verbs. VerbNet defines possible syntaxes for each class of verbs. However, due to free word order and excessive case marking system, syntactic information is already encoded with case markers in Turkish. Thus the structure of VerbNet does not fit well to the Turkish language. PropBank simplifies semantic roles, but defines neither relations between verbs nor all possible syntaxes for each verb. Moreover only Arg0 and Arg1 are associated with a specific semantic content, which reduces the consistency among labeled arguments. Due to lack of a large-scale treebank corpus, building a high coverage PropBank is currently not possible for Turkish. FrameNet defines richer relations between verbs, but the frame elements are extremely fine-grained and building such a comprehensive resource requires a great amount of manual work for which human resources are not currently available for Turkish.

In this paper, we discuss how the semantic information supplied by morphemes, named as morphosemantics, can be included in the construction of semantic resources for languages with less resources and rich morphologies, like Turkish. We try to show that we can decrease manual effort for building such banks and increase consistency and connectivity of the resource by exploiting derivational morphology of verbs; eliminate mapping costs by associating syntactic information with semantic roles and increase the performance of SRL and word sense disambiguation by directly using morphosemantic information supplied with inflectional morphology. Then, we perform a pilot study to build a lexical semantic resource that contains syntactic information as well as semantic information that is defined by semantic roles both in VerbNet and PropBank fashion, by exploiting morphological properties of Turkish language.

2 Related Work

In study by Agirre et al. (2006) and Aldezabal et al. (2010), the authors discuss the suitability of PropBank model for Basque verbs. In addition to semantic role information, the case markers that are related to these roles are also included in the verb frames. It is stated that including case markers in Basque PropBank as a morphosemantic feature is useful for automatic tagging of semantic roles for Basque language which has 11 case markers. Hawwari et al. (2013) present a pilot study for building Arabic Morphological Pattern Net, that aims at representing a direct relationship between morphological patterns and semantic roles for Arabic language. Authors experiment with 10 different patterns and 2100 verb frames and analyze the structure and behavior of these Arabic verbs. The authors state that the results encourage them for a more comprehensive study. The SRL system for Arabic (Diab et al., 2008) and the light-verb detection system for Hungarian (Vincze et al., 2013) also benefited from the relation between case markers and semantic roles.

Furthermore, there are studies on exploiting morphosemantics in WordNets for different languages. Fellbaum et al. (2007), manually inspects WordNet's verb-noun pairs to find one-to-one mapping between an affix and a semantic role for English language. For example the nouns derived from the verbs with the suffixes $-er$ and $-or$, like $invent\text{-}inventor$ usually results as the agents of the event. However, it is stated that only two thirds of the pairs with this pattern could be classified as agents of the events. More patterns are examined and the regularity of these patterns are shown to be low for English language. In another work (Bilgin et al., 2004), authors propose a methodology, on exploiting morphosemantic information in languages where the morphemes are more regular. They perform a case study on Turkish, and propose application areas both monolingually and multilingually, such as globally enriching WordNets and auto detecting errors in WordNets. In a similiar work (Mititelu, 2012), morphosemantic information is added to Romanian WordNet and the proposed application areas in Bilgin et al. (2004) are examined and shown to be feasible.

Previous studies based on building Basque PropBank focus on the building process of Basque PropBank, rather than analysis of the regularity of case markers and the relation between semantic roles and case markers. Furthermore, the study related to building Arabic Morphological Pattern Net, aims to build a seperate dataset and map it to other resources such as Arabic VerbNet, WordNet and PropBank. Word-

Net has rich cross-language morphosemantic links however it does not list all arguments of predicates, thus its structure is not convenient for NLP tasks like semantic role labeling. These studies either make use of case markers or derivational morphology of verbs, not both. Moreover, some of them requires extra mapping resources and some are diffucult to get utilized for semantic interpretation of sentences. Most important of all, none of the studies investigates Turkish language. To the best of our knowledge, this is the first attempt to build such a lexical semantic resource for Turkish and perform experiments on data to expose the relationship between semantic roles and morphemes known as case markers and valency changers in Turkish.

3 Morphosemantic Features

In morphologically rich languages, the meaning of a word is strongly determined by the morphemes that are attached to it. Some of these morphemes always add a predefined meaning while some differ, depending on the language. However, only regular features can be used for NLP tasks that require automatic semantic interpretation. Here, we determine two multilingual morphosemantic features: case markers and verb valency changing morphemes and analyze the regularity and usability of these features for Turkish.

3.1 Declension and Case Marking

Declension is a term used to express the inflection of nouns, pronouns, adjectives and articles for gender, number and case. It occurs in many languages such as Arabic, Basque, Sanskrit, Finnish, Hungarian, Latin, Russian and Turkish. In Table. 1, statistic performed by Iggesen (2013), shows that there are 86

Number of Cases vs Number of Languages

2 cases	3 cases	4 cases	5-7 cases	8-9 cases	10 or more cases
23 languages	9 languages	9 languages	39 languages	23 languages	24 languages

Table 1: Case marking across languages

languages with at least 5 case markings. An examplary morphological analysis for the Turkish word *evlerinde "in his houses"* is given in Ex. 2. In this analysis, *ev* is inflected with ler morpheme for plurality, i for third person singular and $(n)de$ for locative (LOC) case.[2]

Ex. 2	ev	(- ler)	(-i)	(-nde)
	ev +Noun+	Pl +	P3s +	LOC

Even though the languages differ, the same case markers are used to express similiar meanings with some variation. In order to exemplify this statement, sentences with similiar meanings and the same case markers are given in Table 2 for languages Turkish and Hungarian, which have rich case marking systems. Relation between semantic roles and case markers can assist researchers in solving some of the

	NOM	ACC	DAT	LOC	ABL
TR	**Ben** geldim. **I-NOM** come-PAST. **I** came.	Avcı **tavşan-ı** gördü. Hunter **the rabbit-ACC** see-PAST. The hunter saw **the rabbit**.	Jack **okul-a** gitti. Jack **school-DAT** go-PAST. Jack went **to school**.	**Ankara'da** oturuyorum. **Ankara-LOC** live-P1s-PRES. I live **in Ankara**.	**Annem-den** geldim. **Mother-ABL** come-P1s-PAST. I came **from my mother**.
HR	**Ági** jött. **Ági** come-PAST **Ági** came.	Látom a **hegy-et**. see-P1s **mountain-ACC**. I see **the mountain**.	**Ági-nak** adtam ezt a könyv-et. **Ági-DAT** give-P1s-PAST book-ACC. I gave this book **to Ági**.	**Budapest-ban** lakom. **Budapest-LOC** live-P1s-PRES. I live **in Budapest**.	**Ági-tól** jöttem. **Ági-ABL** come-P1s-PAST. I came **from Ági**.

Table 2: Case marking in Turkish and Hungarian

challenging problems in natural language processing. In languages where case markers exist, these

- can be used as features for Semantic Role Labeling,
- can supply prior information for disambiguating word senses,
- can be used in language generation as such: Once the predicate and the sense is determined, the arguments can directly be inflected with the case markers associated with their roles.

[2]Throughout the paper NOM is used as nominative, ACC as accusative, DAT as dative, LOC as locative, ABL as ablative, COM as comitative.

3.2 Valency Changing Morphemes

The valency of a verb can be defined as the verb's ability to govern a particular number of arguments of a particular type. "In Turkish, verb stems govern relatively stable valency patterns or prototypical argument frames" as stated by Haig (1998). Consider the root verb *giy "to wear"*. One can derive new verbs from the root *giy "to wear"* such as *giy-in "to get dressed"*, *giy-dir "to dress someone"* and *giy-il "to be worn"*. These verbs are referred to as verb stems and these special suffixes are referred to as valency changing morphemes. Some advantages of valency changing morphemes are

- They exist for many languages.
- They are regular, easy to model and morphological analyzers available for such languages can analyze the valency of the verb stem.
- They are directly related to the number and type of the arguments, which are important for SRL related tasks.

By modeling the semantic role transformation from verb root to verb stem, we can automatically identify argument configuration of a new verb stem given the correct morphological analysis. By doing so, framing only the verb roots can guarantee to have frames of all verb stems derived from that root. This quickens the process of building a semantic resource, as well as automatizing and reducing the human error. In this section we present a pilot study for some available valencies in Turkish language. For the sake of simplicity, instead of thematic roles, argument labeling in the PropBank fashion is used.

Reflexive

As the word suggests, in reflexive verbs, the action defined by the verb has its effect directly on the person/thing who does the action (Hengirmen, 2002). The reflexive suffix triggers the suppression of one of the arguments. In Fig. 1 observed argument shift and in Table 3 some interesting reflexive Turkish verbs are given like *besle "to feed"* and *besle-n "to eat - feed himself"*.

$[\text{Kaçağ-ı}]_{A1}$ sakla-dı-lar.	$[\text{Kaçak}]_{A0}$ sakla-**n**-dı.
convict-ACC hide-PAST	convict hide-**REFL**-PAST
$[\text{They}]_{A0}$ hid $[\text{the convict}]_{A1}$.	$[\text{The convict}]_{A0}$ hid(himself).

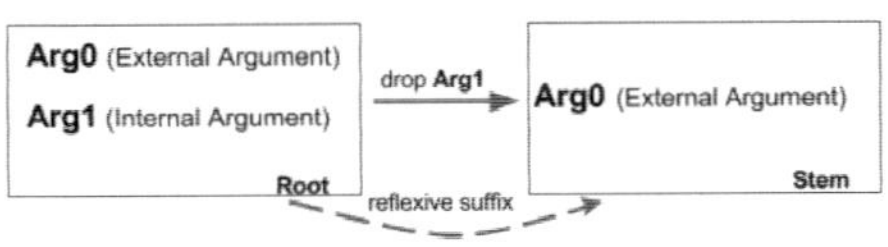

Figure 1: Argument transformation caused by reflexive suffix.

Root	Stem
giy (to wear)	giy-**in** (to get dressed)
hazırla (to prepare)	hazırla-**n** (to get ready)
koru (to protect)	koru-**n** (to protect himself)
öv (to praise)	öv-**ün** (to boast)
sakla (to hide)	sakla-**n** (to hide himself)
besle (to feed)	besle-**n** (to eat)

Table 3: Examples of reflexive verbs in Turkish

Reciprocal

Reciprocal verbs express actions done by more than one subject. The action may be done together or against each other. Reciprocal verbs may have a plural agent or two or more singular co-agents conjoined where one of them marked with COM case as shown in Fig 2. In both cases, the suppression of one of the arguments of the root verb is triggered. We have observed that the supressed argument may be in different roles (patient, theme, stimulus, experiencer, co-patient), but usually appears as Arg1 and rarely as Arg2. In Table 4, a small list of reciprocal verbs is given. Some semantic links are easy to see, whereas the link between *döv "to beat"* and *döv-üş "to fight"* is not that explicit.

$[\text{Oğlan}]_{A0}$ $[\text{kız-ı}]_{A1}$ öp-tü.	$[\text{Çift}]_{A0}$ öp-**üş**-tü.
boy girl-ACC kiss-PAST	couple kiss-**RECIP**-PAST
$[\text{The boy}]_{A0}$ kissed $[\text{the girl}]_{A1}$.	$[\text{They}]_{A0}$ kissed.

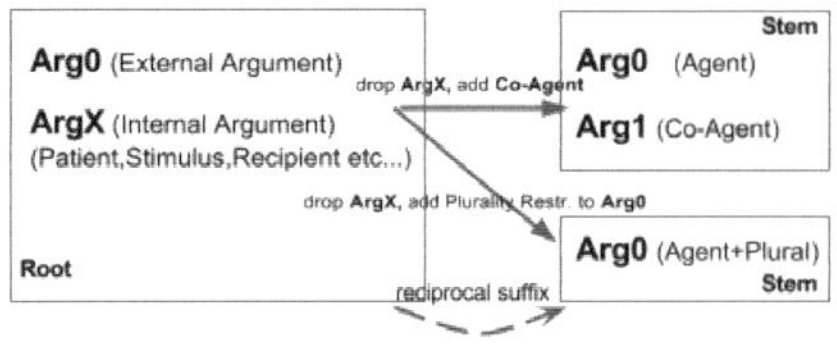

Figure 2: Argument transformation caused by reciprocal suffix.

Root	Stem	Meaning
küs (to offend)	küs-üş (to get cross)	with each other
öde (to pay)	öde-ş (to get even)	with each other
öp (to kiss)	öp-üş (to kiss)	with each other
sev (to love)	sev-iş (to make love)	with each other
döv (to beat)	döv-üş (to fight)	with each other
tanı (to know)	tanı-ş (to get to know)	each other

Table 4: Examples of reciprocal verbs

Causative

Causative category is the most common valence-changing category among Bybee's (1985) world-wide sample of 50 languages. Contrary to other morphemes, causative morpheme introduces of a new argument called causer to the valence pattern. In most of the languages, only intranstive verbs are causitivized (Haspelmath and Bardey, 1991). In this case, as shown in Fig. 3 the causee becomes the patient of the causation event. In other words, the central argument of the root verb, (Arg0 if exists, otherwise Arg1), is marked with ACC case and becomes an internal argument (usually Arg1) of the new causative verb. Some languages can have causatives from transitive verbs too, however the role and the mark of the causee may differ across languages. For the languages where the causee becomes an indirect object, like Turkish and Georgian, the central argument, Arg0 of the root verb, when transformed into a verb stem, receives the DAT case marker and serves as an indirect object (usually as Arg2), while Arg1 serves again as Arg1. This pattern for transitive verbs is given in Fig. 3. Some implicit relations exist in Table 5 such as *öl "to die"*, and cause someone to die *öl-dür "to kill"*. Transformation for intransitive verb *laugh* and transitive verb *wear*, is causitivized as follows:

[Kız]$_{A0}$ gül-üyor.	[Oğlan]$_{A0}$ [kız-ı]$_{A1}$ gül-**dür**-üyor.
girl laugh-PROG	boy girl-ACC gül-CAUS-PROG
[The girl]$_{A0}$ is laughing.	[The boy]$_{A0}$ is making [her]$_{A1}$ laugh.
[Kız]$_{A0}$ [mont-u-nu]$_{A1}$ giy-di.	[Oğlan]$_{A0}$ [kız-a]$_{A2}$ [mont-u-nu]$_{A1}$ giy-**dir**-di.
girl coat-POSS3S-ACC put+on-PAST	boy girl-DAT coat-POSS3S-ACC put+on-**CAUS**-PAST
[The girl]$_{A0}$ put on [her coat]$_{A1}$.	[The boy]$_{A0}$ had [the girl]$_{A2}$ put on [her coat]$_{A1}$.

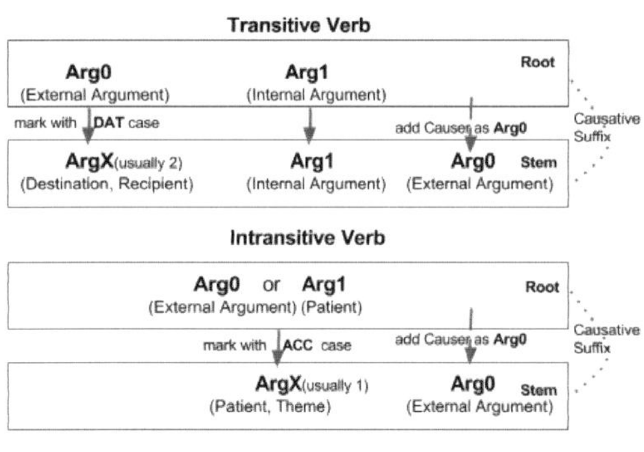

Figure 3: Argument transformation caused by causative suffix.

Root	Stem
ye (to eat)	ye-dir (to feed someone)
öl (to die)	öl-dür (to kill someone)
düş (to fall)	düş-ür (to drop sth.)
sür (to continue)	sür-dür (to resume)
oku (to read)	oku-t (to make someone read)
birleş (to join)	birleş-tir (to integrate)
yan (to get burnt)	yak (to set on fire)

Table 5: Examples of causative verbs

3.3 Application Areas

Semantic Role Labeling (SRL)

Semantic Role Labeling task is to identify the predicates and its arguments in the sentence, and then assign correct semantic roles to identified arguments. In Table 6, English sentences with different syntactic realizations and their translation into Turkish are given among with thematic roles annotated with

VN convention.[3] In the second column, all words written in bold represent the arguments in destination roles. English sentences can not decribe a common syntax for the destination role; different prepositions such as *into*, *at*, *onto* precedes the argument. However, in Turkish sentences they are always marked with dative case. Similiarly, in the last column of Table 6, source and initial location roles are emphasized. Again, it is hard to find a distinguishing feature that reveals these roles in English sentences. There may be different prepositions *out of*, *from* or no preposition at all, before the argument in one of these roles, but they are naturally marked with ablative case in Turkish sentences.

Lang	Destination	Source
#1.En	She$_{\text{Ag}}$ loaded boxes$_{\text{Th}}$ into the **wagon**$_{\text{Dest}}$.	He$_{\text{Ag}}$ backed out of the **trip**$_{\text{Sou}}$.
#1.Tr	Kutuları$_{\text{Th}}$ **vagon-a**$_{\text{Dest-DAT}}$ yükledi.	**Seyahat-ten**$_{\text{Sou-ABL}}$ vazgeçti.
#2.En	She$_{\text{Ag}}$ squirted water$_{\text{Th}}$ at **me**$_{\text{Dest}}$.	The convict$_{\text{Ag}}$ escaped **the prison**$_{\text{iniLoc}}$.
#2.Tr	**Ban-a**$_{\text{Dest-DAT}}$ su$_{\text{Th}}$ fışkırttı.	Mahkum$_{\text{Ag}}$ **hapis-ten**$_{\text{iniLoc-ABL}}$ kaçtı.
#3.En	Paint$_{\text{Th}}$ sprayed onto the **wall**$_{\text{Dest}}$.	He$_{\text{Ag}}$ came from **France**$_{\text{iniLoc}}$.
#3.Tr	**Duvar-a**$_{\text{Dest-DAT}}$ boya$_{\text{Th}}$ püskürtüldü.	**Fransa'dan**$_{\text{iniLoc-ABL}}$ geldi.

Table 6: Relation between case markers and semantic roles.

A subtask of automatic semantic role labeling is determining which features to extract from semantically annotated corpora. In recent studies, argument's relative position to predicate (before, after) and voice of the sentence (passive, active) were experimented as features for automatic SRL (Wu, 2013). However, there exist many features and finding the best features requires feature engineering and again extra time. These toy examples suggest that there may be a correlation between case markers and semantic roles. If that is the case, the SRL task can be reduced to predicate and argument identification task, since the labeling will be automatically or semi-automatically done by using case markers as features.

Word Sense Disambiguation

The task of finding the meaning of a word in the context in question is called word sense disambiguation. In Table 7 three senses of Turkish verb lemma *ayır* and their arguments with case markers are given. In the first sense, the arguments are marked with ACC and DAT, with ABL and NOM in the second and with ACC, ABL in the third. The second and the third senses are similiar. The action of reserving is usually performed on an indefinite object which usually appears in NOM form, where seperating is applied on a certain object that is usually marked with ACC case. After the arguments are identified, one can easily detect the sense of the verb "ayır" by looking at arguments' case markings.

	ayır.01 - To divide, split into pieces
#1.En	[He/she]$_{\text{Ag}}$ divided [the apple]$_{\text{Pat}}$ [into four]$_{\text{Dest}}$.
#1.Tr	[Elmay-**ı**]$_{\text{Pat-ACC}}$ [dörd-**e**]$_{\text{Dest-DAT}}$ **ayır**dı.
	ayır.02 - To keep, reserve (get-13.5.1)
#2.En	[I]$_{\text{Ag}}$ reserved [a table]$_{\text{Th}}$ [from the restaurant]$_{\text{Sou}}$.
#2.Tr	[Restoran-**dan**]$_{\text{Sou-ABL}}$ [masa]$_{\text{Th-NOM}}$ **ayır**dım.
	ayır.03 - To seperate (separate-23.1)
#3.En	[I]$_{\text{Ag}}$ separated [the yolk]$_{\text{Pat1}}$ [from the white]$_{\text{Pat2}}$.
#3.Tr	[Sarısın-**ı**]$_{\text{Pat1-ACC}}$ [beyazın-**dan**]$_{\text{Pat2-ABL}}$ **ayır**dım.

Table 7: Relation between case markers and word senses

4 Methodology

We have performed a feasibility study for using morphosemantic features in building a lexical semantic resource for Turkish. As discussed in Section 3.2, we assume we can automatically frame a verb (e.g $sakla - n(reflexive)$) that is derived with a regular valency changing morpheme (e.g. n), if the argument configuration of the root verb (e.g. $sakla$) is known. Hence, we have only framed root verbs. We have framed 233 root verbs and 452 verb senses. We have calculated the total number of valence changing morphemes as 425. This means 425 verbs can be automatically framed by applying the valency patterns to 233 root verbs. In this analysis we have only considered one sense of the verb since there may be cases where valency changing morpheme can not be applied to another sense of the verb. This can

[3]Throughout the paper Ag is used as agent, Th as theme, Dest as destination, Sou as source, Pat as Patient, IniLoc as initial location.

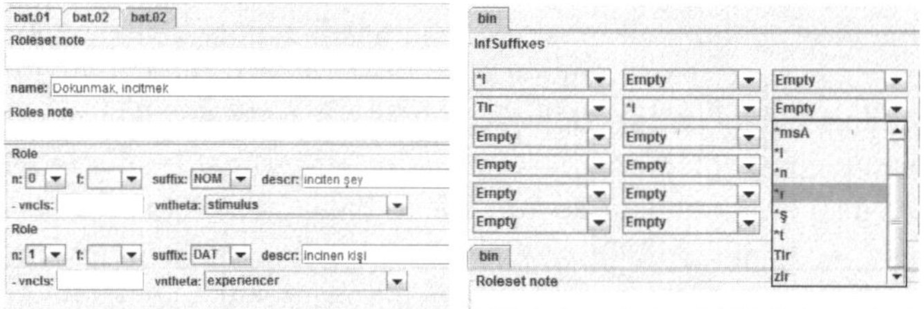

(a) Case marker info given in suffix list

(b) Verb derivational info as a drop down menu

Figure 4: Cornerstone Software Adjusted for Turkish

not be automatically determined. Moreover, a verb stem may have multiple senses. In that case automatically extracted argument transformation may be wrong, because the verb stem may have a completely different meaning.

Turkish is not among rich languages by means of computational resources as discussed before. Turkish Language Association (TDK) is a trustworthy source for lexical datasets and dictionaries. To run this pilot study, we have used the list of Turkish root verbs provided by TDK and the TNC corpus[4]. The interface built for searching the TNC corpus gives the possibility to see all sentences that were built with the verb the user is searching for (Aksan and Aksan, 2012). The senses of the verbs and case marking of their arguments are decided by manually investigating the sentences appear in search results of the TNC corpus. Then, the arguments of the predicates are labeled with VerbNet thematic roles and PropBank argument numbers, by checking the English equivalent of Turkish verb sense. This process is repeated for all verb senses.

For framing purposes, we have adjusted an already available open source software, cornerstone (Choi et al., 2010)[5]. To supply case marking information of the argument, a drop down menu containing six possible case markers in Turkish is added as shown in Fig 4a. Finally, another drop down menu that contains all possible suffixes that a Turkish verb can have is added, shown in Fig 4b. Theoretically, the number of possible derivations may be infinite for some Turkish verbs, due to its rich generative property. However, practically the average number of inflectional groups in a word is less than two (Oflazer et al., 2003). TDK provides a lexicon[6] for widely used verb stems derived from root verbs by a valency changing morpheme. To avoid framing a nonexisting verb, we have used a simple interface shown in Fig 4b to enter only the stems given by TDK. An example with the Turkish verb *bin "to ride"* is given in Fig 4b. The first line defines that one can generate a stem *bin-il "to be ridden by someone"* from the root *bin* by using the suffix *l*. Similiarly, second line illustrates a two layer derivational morphology, which can be interpreted as producing two verbs: *bin-dir "cause someone to ride something"* and *bin-dir-il "to be caused by someone to ride something"*.

5 Experiments and Results

In Table 8, number of co-occurences of each thematic role with each case marker are given. Since in PropBank only Arg0 and Arg1 have a certain semantic interpretation, we have used VerbNet thematic roles in our analysis. Some roles look highly related with a case marker, while some look arbitrary. Results can be interpreted in two ways: 1) If the semantic roles are known and case marker information is needed, Agent will be marked with NOM, Destination with DAT, Source with ABL and Recipient with DAT case with more than 0.98 probability, furthermore Patient and Theme can be restricted to NOM or ACC cases; 2) If case markers are known and semantic role information is needed, only restrictions and prior probabilities can be provided. Highest probabilities occur with COM-instrument, LOC-location, DAT-destination, ACC-Theme and NOM-Agent pairs. We have applied our proposed argument trans-

[4]TNC corpus is a balanced and a representative corpus of contemporary Turkish with 50 million words

[5]Cornerstone is also used for building English, Chinese and Hindi/Urdu PropBanks.

[6]This lexicon is not computationally available

	NOM	ACC	DAT	LOC	ABL	COM	Total	Explanation
Agent	318	0	1	0	0	0	319	Human or an animate subject that controls or initiates the action.
Patient	36	34	0	0	0	0	70	Participants that undergoe a state of change.
Theme	101	117	14	0	7	1	240	Participants in a location or experience a change of location
Beneficiary	1	2	5	0	0	0	8	Entity that benefits negatively or positively from the action.
Location	0	0	2	6	0	0	8	Place or path
Destination	1	0	66	0	0	0	67	End point or direction towards which the motion is directed.
Source	0	0	0	0	29	0	29	Start point of the motion.
Experiencer	13	5	4	0	0	0	22	Usually used for subjects of verbs of perception or psychology.
Stimulus	8	2	4	0	2	0	16	Objects that cause some response from Experiencer.
Instrument	0	0	0	0	0	10	10	Objects that come in contact with an object and cause a change.
Recipient	0	1	13	0	0	0	14	Animate or organization target of transfer.
Time	1	0	2	2	0	0	5	Time.
Topic	0	1	3	0	2	0	6	Theme of communication verbs.
Total	479	162	114	8	40	11	814	

Table 8: Results of Semantic roles - Case Marking

	#Intransitive	#Transitive	#Hold	#!Hold	Total
Reflexive	0	20	20	0	20
Reciprocal	8	18	26	0	26
Causative	26	11	37	0	37

Table 9: Results of Argument Transformation

formation on verbs with different valencies, and compared the argument configurations of the roots and stems. In Table 9, rows represent the valency changes applied to verb root, where Intransitive column contains the number of intransitive verbs that the pattern is applied to, and Transitive similiarly. The #Hold column shows the number of root verbs for which the proposed patterns hold, and #!Hold shows the number of times the pattern can not be observed. Reflexive pattern can only be applied to transitive verbs, while others can be applied to both. Experiments are done for reflexive, reciprocal and causative forms. Our preliminary results on a small set of root verbs show that proposed argument transformation can be seen as a regular transformation.

6 Conclusion and Future Work

In this study, we presented a pilot study for building a Turkish lexical semantic resource for 452 verb senses by making use of two morphosemantic features that appear to be useful for challenging NLP tasks. Our experimental results on 814 arguments showed that the first feature, case markers, are not arbitrarily linked with a semantic role. This brings us to a conclusion that they can be a distinguishing feature for SRL, word sense disambiguation and language generation tasks. We ran some experiments for the second feature, valency changing morphemes and observed that the transformation of the argument structures of root to stem follows a specific pattern, hence proposed transformation seems to be regular and predictable. The results suggest that argument configuration of the root verb may be enough to label any verb stem derived with valency changing morphemes. This gives us the ability to build a semantic resource in a shorter time and reduce the human error, as well as provide a direct relationship like "causativity", "reflexivity" and "reciprocity" between verbs except for some problematic cases explained in Sect. 5. To conclude, this study encourages us to continue using morphosemantic features and increase the size of this resource.

7 Acknowledgements

We thank Gülşen Eryiğit and our three anonymous reviewers for insightful comments and suggestions that helped us improve this work.

References

Eneko Agirre, Izaskun Aldezabal, Jone Etxeberria and Eli Pociello 2006. A Preliminary Study for Building the Basque PropBank. *In LREC 2006*, Genoa

Yeşim Aksan and Mustafa Aksan 2012. Construction of the Turkish National Corpus (TNC). *In LREC 2012*, İstanbul

Izaskun Aldezabal, María Jesús Aranzabe, Arantza Díaz de Ilarraza Sánchez and Ainara Estarrona. 2010. Building the Basque PropBank. *In LREC 2010*, Malta

Nart B. Atalay, Kemal Oflazer and Bilge Say. 2003. The Annotation Process in the Turkish Treebank. *In Proceedings of the EACL Workshop on Linguistically Interpreted Corpora. Budapest*

Orhan Bilgin, Özlem Çetinoğlu and Kemal Oflazer. 2004. Building a wordnet for Turkish. *Romanian Journal of Information Science and Technology*, 7.1-2 (2004): 163-172.

Orhan Bilgin, Özlem Çetinoğlu and Kemal Oflazer. 2004. Morphosemantic relations in and across Wordnets. *In Proceedings of the Global Wordnet Conference*, pp. 60-66. 2004.

Joan L. Bybee. 1985. *Morphology: A Study of the Relation between Meaning and Form. Typological Studies in Language 9 Amsterdam, Philadelphia: Benjamins*

Jinho D. Choi, Claire Bonial and Martha Palmer. 2010. Propbank Frameset Annotation Guidelines Using a Dedicated Editor, Cornerstone. *In LREC 10*, Malta

Mona Diab, Alessandro Moschitti and Daniele Pighin. 2008. Semantic Role Labeling Systems for Arabic Language using Kernel Methods *In Proceedings of the 46th Annual Meeting of the Association for Computational Linguistics: Human Language Technologies.*, 2008

Gülşen Eryiğit, Tugay İlbay and Ozan A. Can. 2011. Multiword Expressions in Statistical Dependency Parsing. *In Proceedings of the Workshop on Statistical Parsing of Morphologically-Rich Languages SPRML at IWPT*, Dublin

Christiane Fellbaum, Anne Osherson and Peter E Clark. 2007 Putting Semantics into WordNet's "Morphosemantic" Links. *Computing Reviews*, 24(11):503–512.

Ana-Maria Giuglea and Alessandro Moschitti. 2006. Semantic Role Labeling via FrameNet, VerbNet and PropBank. *In Proceedings of the 21st International Conference on Computational Linguistics*, pp. 929-936. 2006.

Geoffrey Haig. 1998. *Relative Constructions in Turkish. Otto Harrassowitz Verlag.*

Martin Haspelmath, Thomas M. Bardey 1991. *Valence change. HSK-Morphology. A Handbook on Inflection and Word Formation; ed. by G. Booij, C. Lehmann and J. Mugdan, MPI Leipzig, Universität Mainz*

Abdelati Hawwari, Wajdi Zaghouani, Tim O'Gorman, Ahmed Badran and Mona Diab. 2013. Building a lexical semantic resource for Arabic morphological Patterns. *In Communications, Signal Processing, and their Applications (ICCSPA)*

Mehmet Hengirmen. 2004. *Türkçe Dilbilgisi. Engin Yayınevi*

Oliver Iggesen 2013. *Number of cases. In World atlas of language structures online, ed. Matthew S. Dryer and Martin Haspelmath, Leipzig: Max Plank Institute for Evolutionary Anthropology Available online at http://wals.info/chapter/49*

Verginica B. Mititelu. 2012. Adding Morpho-semantic Relations to the Romanian Wordnet. *In LREC 2012*, İstanbul

Kemal Oflazer, Bilge Say, Dilek Z. Hakkani-Tür and Gökhan Tür. 2003. Building a Turkish Treebank. *Invited chapter in Building and Exploiting Syntactically annotated Corpora, Anne Abeille Editor, Kluwer Academic Publishers*

Martha Palmer, Paul Kingsbury and Daniel Gildea. 2005. The Proposition Bank: An Annotated Corpus of Semantic Roles. *In Computational Linguistics*, 31(1):71–106

Karin K. Schuler 2006. *VerbNet: A Broad-Coverage, Comprehensive Verb Lexicon* PhD diss., University of Pennsylvania

Veronika Vincze, István Nagy T. and János Zsibrita. 2013. Learning to detect english and hungarian light verb constructions. *ACM Trans. Speech Lang. Process.*, 10, 2, Article 6 (June 2013), 25 pages

Shumin Wu. 2013. Semantic Role Labeling Tutorial: Supervised Machine Learning methods. *In Conference of the North American Chapter of the Association for Computational Linguistics: Human Language Technologies*

Comparing Czech and English AMRs

Zdeňka Urešová Jan Hajič Ondřej Bojar
Charles University in Prague
Faculty of Mathematics and Physics
Institute of Formal and Applied Linguistics
Malostranské náměstí 25, 11800 Prague 1, Czech Republic
{uresova,hajic,bojar}@ufal.mff.cuni.cz

Abstract

This paper describes in detail the differences between Czech and English annotation using the Abstract Meaning Representation scheme, which stresses the use of ontologies (and semantically-oriented verbal lexicons) and relations based on meaning or ontological content rather than semantics or syntax. The basic "slogan" of the AMR specification clearly states that AMR is not an interlingua, yet it is expected that many relations as well as structures constructed from these relations will be similar or even identical across languages. In our study, we have investigated 100 sentences in English and their translations into Czech, annotated manually by AMRs, with the goal to describe the differences and if possible, to classify them into two main categories: those which are merely convention differences and thus can be unified by changing such conventions in the AMR annotation guidelines, and those which are so deeply rooted in the language structure that the level of abstraction which is inherent in the current AMR scheme does not allow for such unification.

1 Introduction

In this paper, we follow on a previous first exploratory investigation of differences in AMR annotation among different languages (Xue et al., 2014), which has classified the similarities and differences into four categories: (a) no difference, (b) local difference only (such as multiword expressions vs. single word terms), (c) reconcilable difference due to AMR conventions, and (d) deep differences which cannot be unified in the AMR guidelines. In this paper, we would like to elaborate especially on the (b) and (c) types, which have been only exemplified in the previous work. In this paper, we would like to not only go deeper, but also present quantitative comparison on 100 parallel sentences, for all the aforementioned categories and some of their subtypes.

We will first describe the basic principles of AMR annotation (Banarescu et al., 2013) (Sect. 2, building also on (Xue et al., 2014)), then present the data (parallel texts) which we have used for this study (Sect. 3), and describe the quantitative and qualitative comparison between AMR annotation of English and Czech (Sect. 4). In Sect. 5, we will summarize and discuss further work.

2 Abstract Meaning Representation (AMR)

Syntactic treebanks in several languages (Marcus et al., 1993; Hajič et al., 2003; Xue et al., 2005) and related annotated corpora such as PropBank (Palmer et al., 2005), Nombank (Meyers et al., 2004), TimeBank (Pustejovsky et al., 2003), FactBank (Saurí and Pustejovsky, 2009), and the Penn Discourse TreeBank (Prasad et al., 2008), coupled with machine learning techniques, have been used in many NLP tasks. These annotated resources enabled substantial amounts of research in different areas of semantic analysis. There had already been tremendous progress in syntactic parsing (Collins, 1999; Charniak, 2000; Petrov and Klein, 2007) and now in Semantic Role Labeling because of the existence of the PropBank (Gildea and Jurafsky, 2002; Pradhan et al., 2004; Xue and Palmer, 2004; Bohnet et al., 2013)

Proceedings of the Workshop on Lexical and Grammatical Resources for Language Processing, pages 55–64,
Coling 2014, Dublin, Ireland, August 24 2014.

and similar resources in other languages (Hajič et al., 2009), and TimeBank has fueled much research in the area of temporal analysis.

There have been efforts to create a unified representation which would cover at least a whole sentence, or even a continuous text (Hajič et al., 2003; Srikumar and Roth, 2013), and currently the Abstract Meaning Representation represents an attempt to provide a common ground for truly semantic and fully covering annotation representation.

An Abstract Meaning Representation is a rooted, directional and labeled graph that represents the meaning of a sentence and it abstracts away from such syntactic notions as word category (verbs and nouns), word order, morphological variation etc. Instead, it focuses on semantic *relations* between *concepts* and makes heavy use of predicate-argument structures as defined in PropBank (for English). As a result, the word order in the sentence is considered to be of little relevance to the meaning representation and is not necessarily maintained in the AMR. In addition, many function words (determiners, prepositions) that do not contribute to meaning and are not explicitly represented in AMR, except for the semantic relations they express. Readers are referred to Baranescu et al. (2013) for a complete description of AMR.[1]

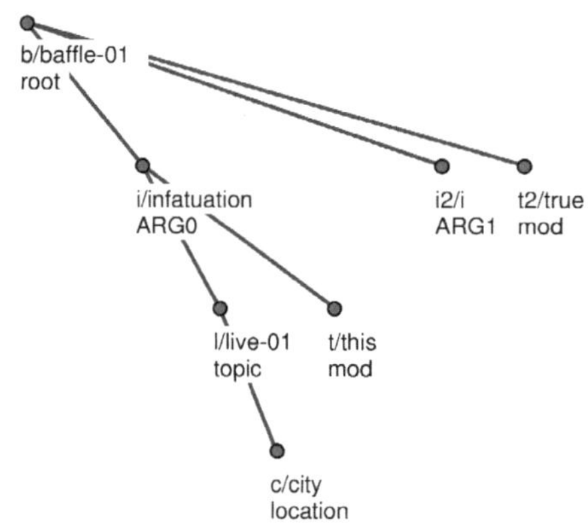

Figure 1: AMR annotation of the sentence *"This infatuation with city living truly baffles me."*

An example of an AMR-annotated sentence can be seen in Fig. 1. The predicate of the sentence (*baffle*) becomes the root of the annotation graph, with a reference to the correct sense `baffle-01` as found in PropBank frame files for `baffle`; PropBank frame files play the role of an ontology of events. Arguments of predicates, again as described in the PropBank frames, become the substitutes for roles of the "who did what to whom" interpretation - in the example sentence, *infatuation* - marked as `ARG0` - is the thing that baffles someone (the `ARG1`), i.e. *me* (the author of the text) in this case. This "baffling" is further modified by *"truly"*, and marked simply as a modifier, the semantics of which is fully represented by the word `true` itself. The agent (*infatuation*) has to be further restricted - it is the *"infatuation with city living"* which baffles the author - not just any infatuation. This is represented by the relation `topic` assigned to the edge between `infatuation` and `live-01` in the AMR graph, and the "living" (sense `live-01`) is further restricted by the `location` mentioned in the sentence, namely `city`. Finally, the modifier `this` is kept in, since it is needed for reference to previous text, where the "infatuation" has been first mentioned.

While the graphical representation in Fig. 1 is simplified in that it does not show the AMR's crucial `instance-of` relations explicitly as edges in the AMR graph, Fig. 2 shows the native underlying "bracketed" textual representation of the same tree, where the main nodes (i.e. those shown visibly in Fig. 1) are *mentions*, and the labels `baffle-01, true, live-01, city` etc. represent *links to external ontologies*. These links are currently represented only by these strings, or by links to PropBank

[1]This paragraph as well as the two preceding ones are taken over (and slightly adapted) from the introductory sections of a previous paper on this topic presented at LREC and co-authored by us (Xue et al., 2014); we share the same AMR formalism and data.

files for events. In the future, these links will be *wikified*, i.e. for concepts described in an external ontology, such as Wikipedia, they will be linked to it. The single- or two-letter "indexes" are in fact the labels (IDs) of the mentions, and they also serve for (co-)reference purposes; the slash ('/') is a shortcut for the `instance-of` relation.

```
(b / baffle-01
      :ARG0 (i / infatuation
            :topic (l / live-01
                  :location (c / city))
            :mod (t / this))
     :ARG1 (i2 / i)
     :mod (t2 / true))
```

Figure 2: Textual form of the AMR annotation of the sentence *"This infatuation with city living truly baffles me."*

In Czech, the event ontology has been approximated by the Czech valency dictionary, PDT-Vallex (Hajič et al., 2003), (Urešová, 2009), (Urešová and Pajas, 2009), (Urešová, 2006). No wikification of non-event nodes has been attempted yet; this is a continuing work, as it is for English.

3 The Data

We have drawn on a blog on Virginia road construction, taken from the WB part of the Penn Treebank. These sentences have already been annotated using AMRs, and also translated to Czech[2] and subsequently AMR-annotated. The English text has 1676 word and punctuation tokens (using the Penn Treebank style tokenization), and its annotated AMR representation contains 1231 nodes (not counting the `instance-of` nodes as separate nodes). The Czech version is a result of manually doubly-translated English original, which has been mutually checked and then one (slightly corrected) translation has been used for annotation. The Czech text has a total of 1563 tokens and its AMR representation contains 1215 nodes (again, not counting the `instance-of` nodes as separate nodes).

The data, once annotated, have been converted to a graph and in such a form presented to a linguist familiar with the AMR style annotation, to study and extract statistics for this comparison study. Fig. 3 shows such a side-by-side graphs for English and Czech AMR for the example parallel sentences.

4 The Comparison

4.1 Quantitative Comparison

In the first pass, we have concentrated on marking and counting the following phenomena:

- **structural identity**: sentences with identical structure have been marked as being structurally the same, even if some relation (edge) labels have been different
- **structural differences**: no. of structural differences have been noted in cases where one or more (sub)parts of the AMR graph differ between the two languages
- **local difference only**: out of the above, certain differences have been marked as "local only" - for example, if a multiword expression annotated as several nodes in one language corresponds to a single node in the other language
- **relation differences**: for each sentence, number of differences in relational labels has been counted
- **reference differences**: number of different references to an external ontology (or assumed differences in case no link to such an ontology was actually present in the annotation).

[2]...and Chinese, but that was not used for this study.

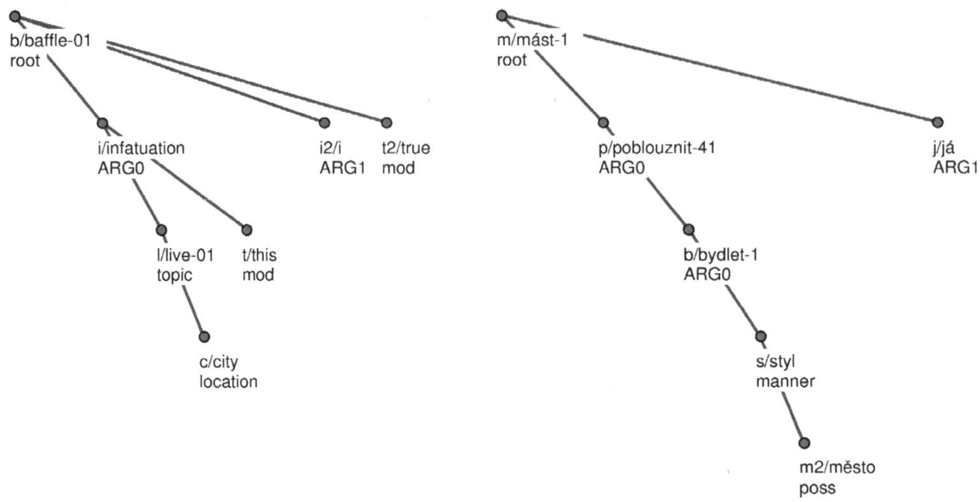

Figure 3: AMR annotation of the sentence *"This infatuation with city living truly baffles me."* and its translation to Czech (*"Tohle/this poblouznění/infatuation bydlením/living-INSTR v/in městském/city-like stylu/style mě/me pořád/still mate/baffles."*)

It is obvious that we could have observed also other types of differences, but at this point, we wanted to have at least an idea how many differences exist in our approx. 1500-token sample. The resulting figures are summarized in Table 1.[3]

Same structure	Different substructures	Local difference only	Relation differences	Reference differences
29 (sents)	193 (subgraphs)	92 (subgraphs)	331 (nodes)	37 (nodes)
of 100	of approx. 800[2]	of 193 (all diffs)	of 1215 Cz nodes	of 1215 Cz nodes
29 %	approx. 25 %[2]	47.7 %	27.2 %	3.0 %

Table 1: Number and percentages of differences in the annotated data

The number of truly identically annotated sentences (including relation labeling) was only four, two of which has been interjective "sentences" at the beginning of the document ("Braaawk!"). On the other hand, 18 additional sentences would be structurally identical (on top of the 29) if local differences were disregarded, bringing the (unlabeled sentence identity) total to 47, or almost half of the data (47=29+18).

4.2 Analysis of Differences

The main goal of this study is to analyze differences in the annotation for the two languages, Czech and English, and determine if a reconciliation of the annotation is possible or not (and for what reason it is / it is not). Based on the above quantitative analysis, we have concentrated on relation labeling differences due their high proportion, and on structural differences due to their heterogeneous nature. The differences in reference annotation are small, but this is due to the lack of full referential annotation (it has been done for events, but only assumed for other types of entities due to the lack of ontology, or better to say due to the lack of "wikification" annotation in both languages), rather than due to high agreement. We will come back to this once wikification of the annotation is finished.

[3]Structural differences are hard to quantify exactly, since the base is difficult to define; it is part of future work.

4.3 Differences in Relation Labeling

The differences in function labeling should be taken with a grain of salt. The crucial question is what should count as a difference in relation labeling if the structure differs - should this be automatically counted as a difference, or not at all? In the figures summarized in Table 1, we have taken a middle ground: if the structural difference implied a change in labeling by itself, we have not counted that difference in order not to "penalize" the sentence annotation twice.

More detailed inspection of relation labeling differences, which appear to be relatively frequent at more than 1/4th of all nodes in the annotation, revealed that the by far most frequent mismatch is caused by different argument labeling for events.[4] While for most purely transitive verbs there is a complete match, for most other there is a discrepancy due to the attempted semanticization of PDT-Vallex argument labels `ADDR` (addressee), `EFF` (effect) and `ORIG` (origin), while PropBank simply continues to number arguments of corresponding verbs consecutively (for example, *I thought there is.ARG1* ... vs. *Myslel/I-thought jsem, že/that tam/there je.ARG3←EFF/is ...*). The concept of "shifting" in PDT-Vallex, which compulsorily fills the first two arguments on syntactic grounds as `ACT(ARG0)` and `PAT(ARG1)` is another source of differences. Furthermore, PropBank leaves out `ARG0` e.g. for unaccusative verbs (for example *The window.ARG1 broke* vs. *Okno.ARG0←ACT/window se/itself rozbilo/broke.*). Finally, some differences are due to some arguments not being considered arguments at all in the other language, in which case some other AMR label is used instead (for example, *We could have spent 400M.ARG3 ... elsewhere* vs. ... *mohli/could utratit/spend 400M.extent ... jinde/elsewhere*).

These differences could possibly be consolidated (only) by carefully linking the two lexicons (with AMR guidelines intact). This is in fact being performed in another project (Sindlerova et al., 2014), but it is a daunting manual task, since the underlying theories behind PropBank and PDT-Vallex/EngVallex differ. However, one has to ask if it does make sense to do so, because with enough parallel data available, the mappings can be learned relatively easily: in most cases, no structural differences are involved and there will be a simple one-to-one mapping between the labels (conditioned on the particular verb sense).

4.4 Structural Differences

Local differences can be safely ignored, since they will be in most cases resolved during the assumed process of wikification, i.e., linking to an ontology concept. For example, the abbreviation *VDOT* (Virginia Department of Transportation), which has to be (and was) translated into Czech in an explanatory way (otherwise the sentence would become not quite understandable, if only because of the real-world context). Without wikification, it could not be linked as a whole, and thus a subgraph has been created with the AMR-appropriate internal semantic relations in the translation (e.g. *Virginia.location*, etc.).

Certain differences, albeit "localized" into a small subtree (or subgraph) corresponding to a single node or another small subtree (subgraph), cannot be resolved by wikification of a different event ontology (than PropBank or PDT-Vallex). For example, light verb constructions or even certain modal or aspectual constructions could have a single verb equivalent resulting in two node vs. single node annotation: *get close* vs. *přiblížit-se*, *make worse* vs. *zhoršit*, *take position (for sb)* vs. *zastávat-se* or *causing sprawl* vs. *roztahuje-se*.

Looking at the true structural differences, we have found that there are actually quite a few reasons for them to appear in the annotation. We will describe them in more detail below.

Non-literal translation is the primary reason for such differences.[5] For example, *destination* vs. *kam/where-to lidé/people jezdí/drive* (Fig. 4), or *job center* vs. *místo/place, kde/where pracuje/work hodně/many lidí/people*; these cases cannot be unified neither by changing the translation to a more literal one (because it would be strongly misleading in the given context, despite the fact that literal translation of both *destination* as well as *job center* does exist in Czech), neither by changing the guidelines, since the level of abstraction of AMR does not call for a unification of such concepts. Sometimes, non-literal

[4]The Czech PDT-Vallex argument labels have been mapped to PropBank labels as follows: ACT → ARG0, PAT → ARG1, ADDR → ARG2, EFF → ARG3 and ORIG → ARG4.

[5]This includes also cases of truly wrong translation, stemming of translator's misunderstanding of the facts behind the sentence. This has been found fairly often only after we studied the differences in depth, since a superficial reading and standard translation revision procedure did not help.

translation is forced upon the translation because no word-for-word translation exists, such as in *in the aggregate*, which has to be translated using an extra clause *z/from celkového/overall pohledu/view to/it je/is tak/so, že/that ...* (Fig. 5).

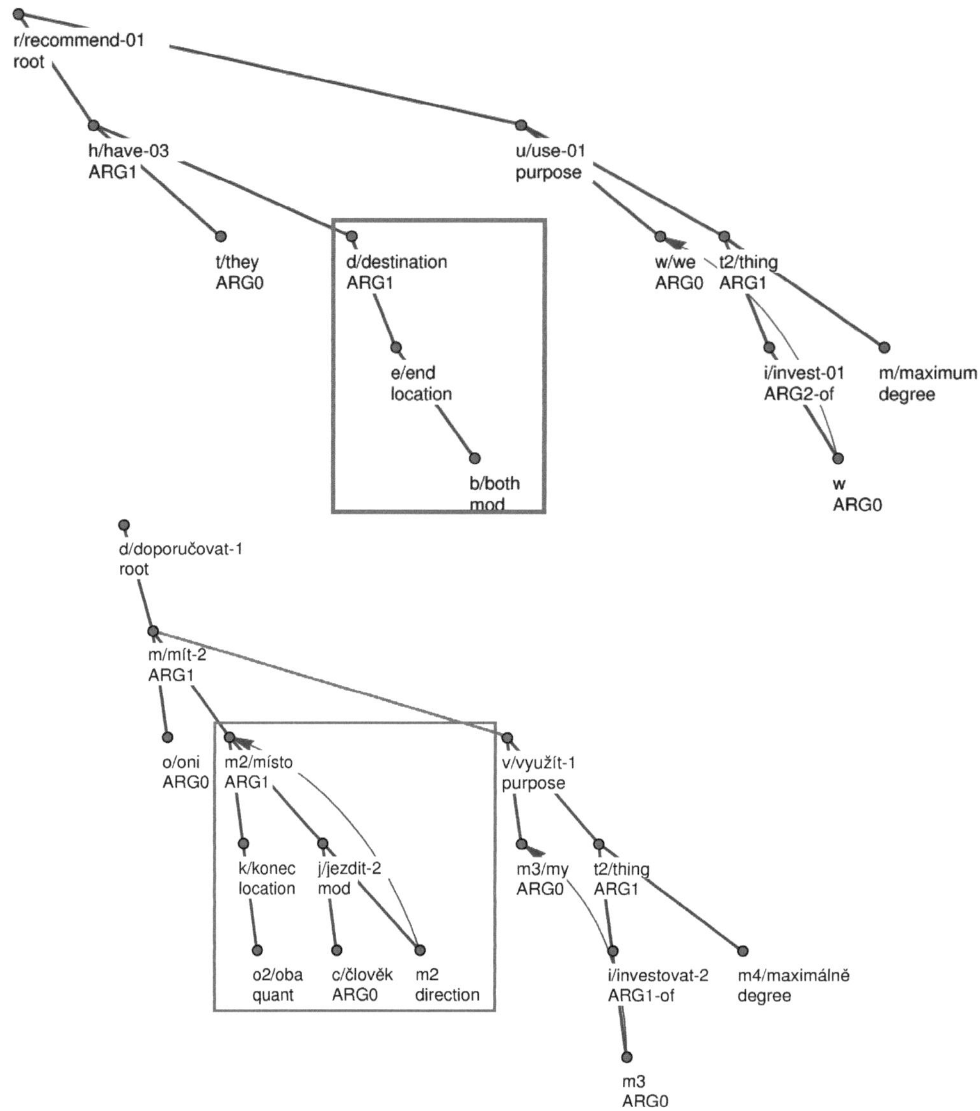

Figure 4: AMR structural difference: *destination* vs. *kam/where-to lidé/people jezdí/drive*

Phraseological differences and idioms form another large group of differences between the two languages. The possibility of changing the translation is even more remote than in the above case, even if we had the chance: the provided translation is actually the correct and perfect one. The reason for different annotation lies in the AMR scheme, which does not go that far to require "unified" annotation in such cases where the idiom or specific phrase cannot be linked to the external ontology as a single unit. For example, English "I don't see any point" is translated as "nemá/not-have smysl/purpose", and despite the fact that `have-purpose-91` is a specific event reference in English (and has been used in the annotation), the verb "see" still remains annotated as a separate event node, which is not the case in Czech, since no "seeing" is expressed in the sentence and it could hardly be asked for in the guidelines to be inserted. Similarly, *I commute back and forth* has been translated simply as *dojíždím/commute*, which is semantically perfectly equivalent but the *back and forth* has been kept in the English annotation, because

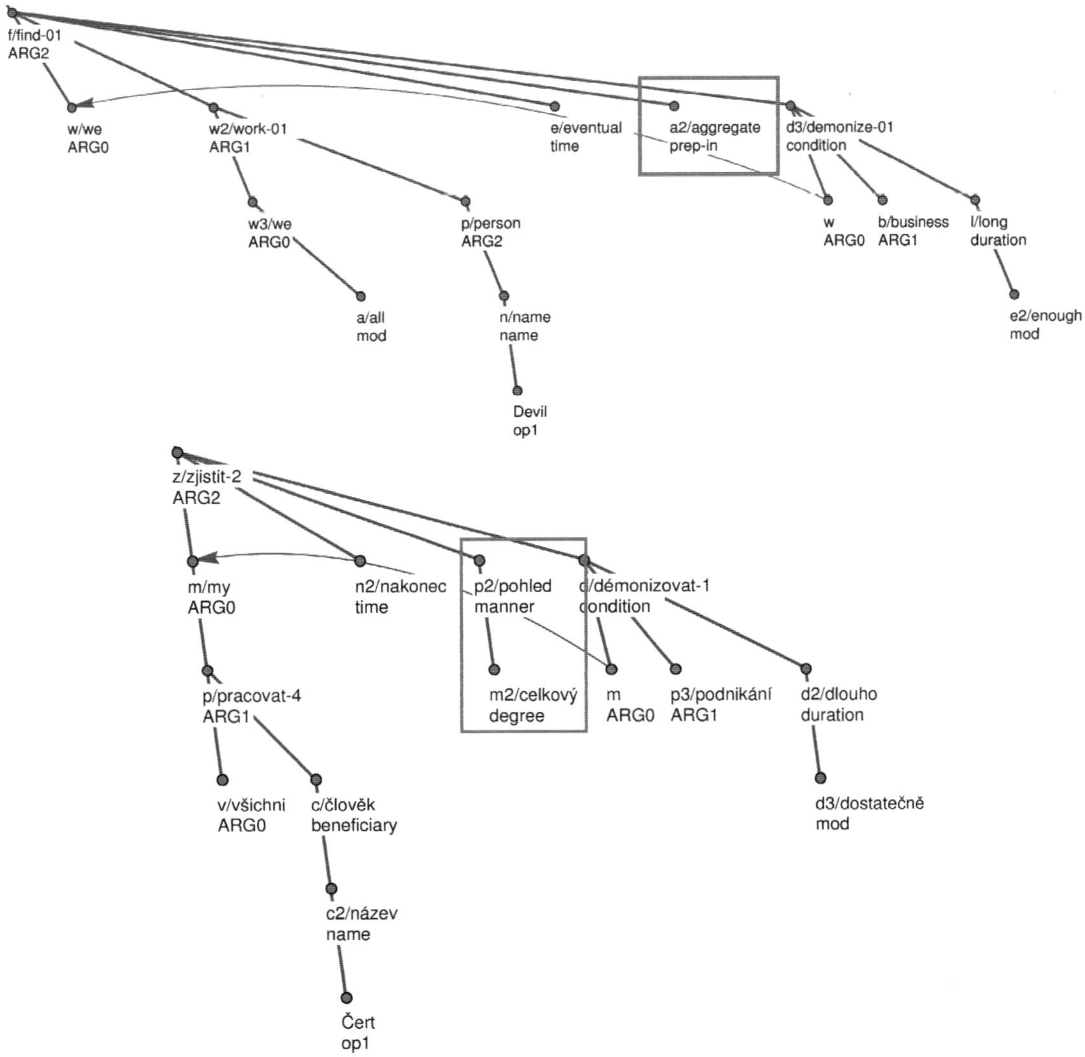

Figure 5: AMR structural difference: *in the aggregate* vs. *z/from celkového/overall pohledu/view to/it je/is tak/so, že/that ...*

deleting it was (probably) considered loss of information. It is only the confrontation with the translation to a different language when one realizes that with just a little more abstraction, the annotation could have been structurally the same (by keeping only the *commute* node in in the English annotation).[6]

Translation by interpretation is typically discouraged in translation school education, but sometimes it is necessary to use it for smooth understanding of the translated text. Often, such interpretation results in different AMR annotation. For example, *Virginia centrist* has been translated as *středový/centrist volič/voter [z/from Virginie/Virginia]*, because without the extra word *volič*, the literal translation of *centrist* would not be understandable correctly in this context (Fig. 6). Similarly, *a 55mph zone* vs. *zóna/zone s/with omezením/restriction na/to 55 mph* (added word *omezením/restriction*), or *traffic* vs. *dopravní/traffic zácpa/jam*.

Convention differences are inherent in many annotation schemes, and we have found them in AMR

[6]One could perhaps also argue that *adding* the equivalent of *back and forth* to the Czech translation would unify the translation, too; however, adding its literal equivalent in Czech *tam a zpět* would be considered superfluous and unnatural by Czech speakers.

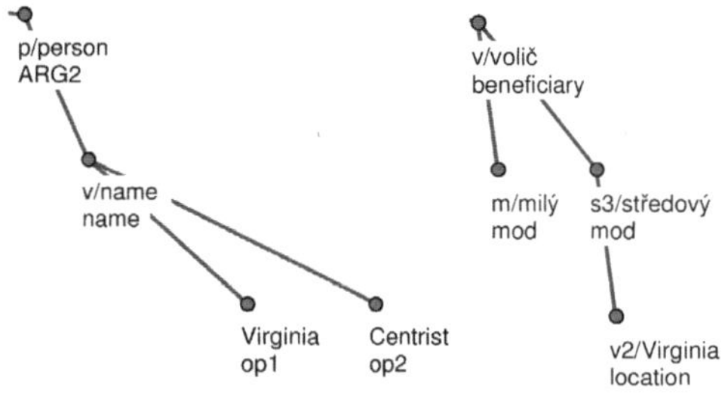

Figure 6: AMR structural difference: *Virginia Centrist* vs. *středový/centrist volič/voter [z/from Virginie/Virginia]*

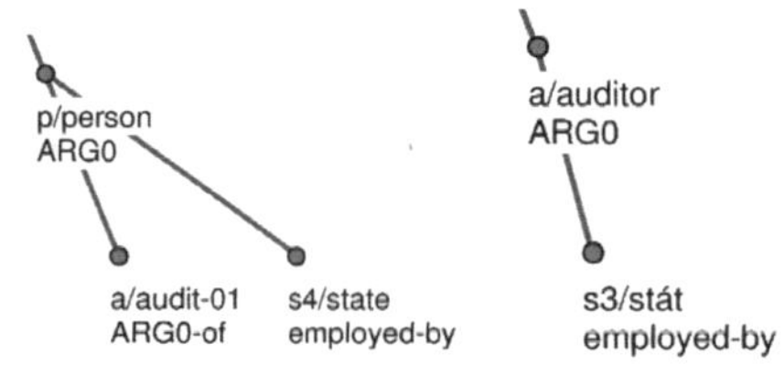

Figure 7: AMR convention difference: *auditor* as a single node vs. person, who audits

guidelines, too. Often, they were related to the use of `ARG-of` vs. keeping the nominalization as a single node. For example, for *auditor*, translated quite literally as *auditor* into Czech, has been annotated as "a person, who audits" in English while in the Czech AMR structure, there is a single node (Fig. 7) labeled as `auditor` (which undoubtedly will be correctly linked to some ontology entry after such linkage/wikification is complete). These differences might be harder to consolidate, since such conventions are very difficult to create proper guidelines for, especially across languages. No ontology (whether for events or objects) will be complete either (to base the decisions on a particular ontology content).

5 Conclusions and Future Work

We have investigated differences in the annotation of parallel texts using the Abstract Meaning Representation scheme, on approx. 1500 words of English-Czech corpus (100 sentences). We found and counted the number of identities and four types of differences (structural, structural local, relational, and referential), and exemplified them to see if a reconciliation (either by possibly changing the translation, the guidelines, or the annotation itself) is possible.

This is a work in progress. Substantial amount of work remains. We will have to use larger data, multiple annotation (interannotator agreement on English was relatively low and we expect to be the case on Czech, too, once two annotators start annotating the same sentences), and we would also have to actually suggest changes in the guidelines or their conventions, and to test them also on substantial amounts of data.

The immediate extension of this work will cover wikification, i.e. the linking of all nodes in the AMR representation of our dataset to some ontology: events are already covered, internally defined relations are already annotated, too (such as named entity types, dates, quantities, etc.), but external links remain to be added. We will not only use Wikipedia (as the term "wikification" might suggest), but we will extend this idea also to other sources, such as DBpedia or BabelNet, keeping all links in parallel if possible. This should allow for deep comparison of the two languages also content-wise. We should then be able to better answer the question of annotation unification which does depend on these links rather than on the annotation guidelines themselves.

Parallel AMR-annotated data will be used at the JHU 2014 Summer Workshop, where technology for AMR-based parsing, generation and possibly also MT will be developed, allowing also technological insight into the AMR scheme across languages.

Acknowledgements

This work was supported by the grant GP13-03351P of the Grant Agency of the Czech Republic, projects LH12093 and LM2010013 of the Ministry of Education, Youth and Sports of the Czech Republic, and the EU FP7 project 610516 "QTLeap". It has been using language resources distributed by the LINDAT/CLARIN[7] project of the Ministry of Education, Youth and Sports of the Czech Republic (project LM2010013).

[7] `http://lindat.cz`, resource used: `http://hdl.handle.net/11858/00-097C-0000-0023-4338-F`, also at `http://lindat.mff.cuni.cz/services/PDT-Vallex`

References

L. Banarescu, C. Bonial, S. Cai, M. Georgescu, K. Griffitt, U. Hermjakob, K. Knight, P. Koehn, M. Palmer, and N. Schneider. 2013. Abstract Meaning Representation for Sembanking. In *Proceedings of the 7th Linguistic Annotation Workshop*, Sophia, Bulgaria.

Bernd Bohnet, Joakim Nivre, Igor Boguslavsky, Richard Farkas, Filip Ginter, and Jan Hajič. 2013. Joint morphological and syntactic analysis for richly inflected languages. *Transactions of the Association for Computational Linguistics*, 1:415–428.

Eugene Charniak. 2000. A maximum-entropy-inspired parser. In *Proceedings of the 1st North American chapter of the Association for Computational Linguistics conference*, pages 132–139. Association for Computational Linguistics.

Michael Collins. 1999. *Head-driven Statistical Models for Natural Language Parsing*. Ph.D. thesis, University of Pennsylvania.

Daniel Gildea and Daniel Jurafsky. 2002. Automatic labeling of semantic roles. *Computational linguistics*, 28(3):245–288.

Jan Hajič, Jarmila Panevová, Zdeňka Urešová, Alevtina Bémová, Veronika Kolářová, and Petr Pajas. 2003. PDT-VALLEX: Creating a Large-coverage Valency Lexicon for Treebank Annotation. In *Proceedings of The Second Workshop on Treebanks and Linguistic Theories*, volume 9 of *Mathematical Modeling in Physics, Engineering and Cognitive Sciences*, pages 57–68. Växjö University Press, November 14–15, 2003.

Jan Hajič, Massimiliano Ciaramita, Richard Johansson, Daisuke Kawahara, Maria Martí, Lluís Màrquez, Adam Meyers, Joakim Nivre, Sebastian Padó, Jan Štěpánek, Pavel Straňák, Mihai Surdeanu, Nianwen Xue, and Yi Zhang. 2009. The CoNLL-2009 Shared Task: Syntactic and Semantic Dependencies in Multiple Languages. In Jan Hajič, editor, *Proceedings of the Thirteenth Conference on Computational Natural Language Learning (CoNLL): Shared Task*, pages 1–18, Boulder, CO, USA. Association for Computational Linguistics.

Jan Hajič, Alena Böhmová, Eva Hajicová, and Barbora Hladká. 2003. The Prague Dependency Treebank: A Three Level Annotation Scenario. In Anne Abeillé, editor, *Treebanks: Building and Using Annotated Corpora*. Kluwer Academic Publishers.

Mitchell P. Marcus, Beatrice Santorini, and Mary Ann Marcinkiewicz. 1993. Building a large annotated corpus of english: The penn treebank. *Computational Linguistics*, 19(2):313–330.

A. Meyers, R. Reeves, C. Macleod, R. Szekely, V. Zielinska, B. Young, and R. Grishman. 2004. The NomBank Project: An Interim Report. In *Proceedings of the NAACL/HLT Workshop on Frontiers in Corpus Annotation*, pages 24–31, Boston, Massachusetts.

Martha Palmer, Daniel Gildea, and Paul Kingsbury. 2005. The Proposition Bank: An annotated corpus of semantic roles. *Computational Linguistics*, 31(1):71–106.

Slav Petrov and Dan Klein. 2007. Improved inference for unlexicalized parsing. In *HLT-NAACL*, pages 404–411.

Sameer S Pradhan, Wayne Ward, Kadri Hacioglu, James H Martin, and Daniel Jurafsky. 2004. Shallow semantic parsing using support vector machines. In *HLT-NAACL*, pages 233–240.

Rashmi Prasad, Nikhil Dinesh, Alan Lee, Eleni Miltsakaki, Livio Robaldo, Aravind Joshi, and Bonnie Webber. 2008. The Penn Discourse Treebank 2.0. In *Proceedings of the 6th International Conference on Language Resources and Evaluation (LREC 2008)*, Marrakech, Morocco.

James Pustejovsky, Patrick Hanks, Roser Saurí, Andrew See, David Day, Lisa Ferro, Robert Gaizauskas, Marcia Lazo, Andrea Setzer, and Beth Sundheim. 2003. The TimeBank Corpus. *Corpus Linguistics*, pages 647–656.

Roser Saurí and James Pustejovsky. 2009. Factbank: a corpus annotated with event factuality. *Language resources and evaluation*, 43(3):227–268.

Jana Sindlerova, Zdenka Uresova, and Eva Fucikova. 2014. Resources in Conflict: A Bilingual Valency Lexicon vs. a Bilingual Treebank vs. a Linguistic Theory. In Nicoletta Calzolari (Conference Chair), Khalid Choukri, Thierry Declerck, Hrafn Loftsson, Bente Maegaard, Joseph Mariani, Asuncion Moreno, Jan Odijk, and Stelios Piperidis, editors, *Proceedings of the Ninth International Conference on Language Resources and Evaluation (LREC'14)*, pages 2490–2494, Reykjavik, Iceland, May 26-31. European Language Resources Association (ELRA).

Vivek Srikumar and Dan Roth. 2013. Modeling semantic relations expressed by prepositions. *Transactions of the Association for Computational Linguistics*, 1:231–242.

Zdeňka Urešová and Petr Pajas. 2009. Diatheses in the Czech Valency Lexicon PDT-Vallex. In Jana Levická and Radovan Garabík, editors, *Slovko 2009, NLP, Corpus Linguistics, Corpus Based Grammar Research*, pages 358–376, Bratislava, Slovakia. Jazykovedný ústav udovíta Štúra Slovenskej akadémie vied, Slovenská akadémia vied.

Zdeňka Urešová, 2006. *Verbal Valency in the Prague Dependency Treebank from the Annotator's Viewpoint*, pages 93–112. Veda, Bratislava, Bratislava, Slovensko.

Zdeňka Urešová. 2009. Building the PDT-VALLEX valency lexicon. In Catherine Smith Michaela Mahlberg, Victorina Gonzalez-Diaz, editor, *Proceedings of the Corpus Linguistics Conference)*, http://ucrel.lancs.ac.uk/publications/cl2009/100_FullPaper.doc, July 20-23. University of Liverpool, UK.

Nianwen Xue and Martha Palmer. 2004. Calibrating features for semantic role labeling. In *EMNLP*, pages 88–94.

Nianwen Xue, Fei Xia, Fu dong Chiou, and Martha Palmer. 2005. The Penn Chinese TreeBank: Phrase Structure Annotation of a Large Corpus. *Natural Language Engineering*, 11(2):207–238.

Nianwen Xue, Ondrej Bojar, Jan Hajic, Martha Palmer, Zdenka Uresova, and Xiuhong Zhang. 2014. Not an Interlingua, But Close: Comparison of English AMRs to Chinese and Czech. In Nicoletta Calzolari (Conference Chair), Khalid Choukri, Thierry Declerck, Hrafn Loftsson, Bente Maegaard, Joseph Mariani, Asuncion Moreno, Jan Odijk, and Stelios Piperidis, editors, *Proceedings of the Ninth International Conference on Language Resources and Evaluation (LREC'14)*, pages 1765–1772, Reykjavik, Iceland, May 26-31. European Language Resources Association (ELRA).

Acquisition and enrichment of morphological and morphosemantic knowledge from the French Wiktionary

Nabil Hathout   Franck Sajous   Basilio Calderone
CLLE-ERSS (CNRS & Université de Toulouse 2)

Abstract

We present two approaches to automatically acquire morphologically related words from Wiktionary. Starting with related words explicitly mentioned in the dictionary, we propose a method based on orthographic similarity to detect new derived words from the entries' definitions with an overall accuracy of 93.5%. Using word pairs from the initial lexicon as patterns of formal analogies to filter new derived words enables us to rise the accuracy up to 99%, while extending the lexicon's size by 56%. In a last experiment, we show that it is possible to semantically type the morphological definitions, focusing on the detection of process nominals.

1 Introduction

Around the 1980s the computational exploitation of machine-readable dictionaries (MRDs) for the automatic acquisition of lexical and semantic information enjoyed a great favor in NLP (Calzolari et al., 1973; Chodorow et al., 1985). MRDs' definitions provided robust and structured knowledge from which semantic relations were automatically extracted for linguistic studies (Markowitz et al., 1986) and linguistic resources development (Calzolari, 1988). Today the scenario has changed as corpora have become the main source for semantic knowledge acquisition. However, dictionaries are regaining some interest thanks to the availability of public domain dictionaries, especially Wiktionary.

In the present work, we describe a method to create a morphosemantic and morphological French lexicon from Wiktionary's definitions. This type of large coverage resource is not available for almost all languages, with the exception of the CELEX database (Baayen et al., 1995) for English, German and Dutch, a paid resource distributed by the LDC.

The paper is organized as follows. Section 2 reports related work on semantic and morphological acquisition from MRDs. In Section 3, we describe how we converted Wiktionnaire, the French language edition of Wiktionary, into a structured XML-tagged MRD which contains, among other things, definitions and morphological relations. In Section 4, we explain how we used Wiktionnaire's morphological sections to create a lexicon of morphologically related words. The notion of morphological definitions and their automatic identification are introduced in Section 5. In Section 6, we show how these definitions enable us to acquire new derived words and enrich the initial lexicon. Finally, Section 7 describes an experiment where we semantically typed process nouns definitions.

2 Related work

Semantic relations are usually acquired using corpora (Curran and Moens, 2002; van der Plas and Bouma, 2005; Heylen et al., 2008) but may also be acquired from MRDs. MRDs-based approaches are bound to the availability of such resources. However, for some languages including French, no such resource exists. Recent years have seen the development of large resources built automatically by aggregating and/or translating data originating from different sources. For example, Sagot and Fišer (2008) have built WOLF, *"a free French Wordnet"* and Navigli and Ponzetto (2010) BabelNet, a large multilingual semantic network. Such resources tend to favor coverage over reliability and may contain errors and

Proceedings of the Workshop on Lexical and Grammatical Resources for Language Processing, pages 65–74,
Coling 2014, Dublin, Ireland, August 24 2014.

inaccuracy, or be incomplete. Pierrel (2013), while criticizing these resources, describes the digitization process of the *Trésor de la Langue Française*, a large printed French dictionary. The first impulse of this long-course reverse-engineering project is described in (Dendien, 1994) and resulted in the *TLFi*, a fine-grained XML-structured dictionary. Pierrel advocates mutualization, recommends resources sharing and underlines how the use of the TLFi would be relevant for NLP. Though we totally agree on this assertion, we deplore that the resource, being only available for manual use and not for download, prevents its use for NLP.

Crowdsourcing has recently renewed the field of lexical resources development. For example Lafourcade (2007) designed JeuxDeMots, a *game with a purpose*, to collect a great number of relations between words. Other works use the content of wikis produced by crowds of contributors. Initially in the shadow of Wikipedia, the use of Wiktionary tends to grow in NLP studies since its exploitation by Zesch et al. (2008). Its potential as an electronic lexicon was first studied by Navarro et al. (2009) for English and French. The authors leverage the dictionary to build a synonymy network and perform random walks to find missing links. Other works tackled data extraction: Anton Pérez et al. (2011) for instance, describe the integration of the Portuguese Wiktionary and Onto.PT; Sérasset (2012) built Dbnary, a multilingual network containing "easily extractable" entries. If the assessment of Wiktionary's quality from a lexicographic point of view has not been done yet, Zesch and Gurevych (2010) have shown that lexical resources built by crowds lead to results comparable to those obtained with resources designed by professionals, when used to compute semantic relatedness of words. In Sajous et al. (2013a), we created an inflectional and phonological lexicon from Wiktionary and showed that its quality is comparable to those of reference lexicons, while the coverage is much wider.

Comparatively little effort has been reported in literature on the exploitation of semantic relations to automatically identify morphological relations. Schone and Jurafsky (2000) learn morphology with a method based on semantic similarity extracted by latent semantic analysis. Baroni et al. (2002) combine orthographic (string edit distances) and semantic similarity (words' contextual information) in order to discover morphologically related words. Along the same line, Zweigenbaum and Grabar (2003) acquire semantic information from a medical corpus and use it to detect morphologically derived words. More recently, Hathout (2008) uses the TLFi to discover morphologically related words by combining orthographic and semantic similarity with formal analogy.

I another work, Pentheroudakis and Vanderwende (1993) present a method to automatically extract morphological relations from the definitions of MRDs. The authors automatically identify classes of morphologically related words by comparing the semantic information in the entry of the derivative with the information stored in the candidate base form. This effort shows the crucial importance and the potential of the MRDs' definitions to acquire and discover morphological relationships of derived words.

3 Turning the French Wiktionary into a Machine-Readable Dictionary

As mentioned is section 2, the quality of collaboratively constructed resources has already been assessed and we will not debate further the legitimacy of leveraging crowdsourced data for NLP purpose. We give below a brief description of Wiktionary[1] and of the process of converting it into a structured resource.

Wiktionary is divided in language editions. Each language edition is regularly released as a so-called *XML dump*.[2] The "XML" mention is somewhat misleading because it suggests that XML markups encode the articles' microstructure whereas only the macrostructure (articles' boundaries and titles) is marked by XML tags. Remaining information is encoded in *wikicode*, an underspecified format used by the *MediaWiki* content-management system. As explained by Sajous et al. (2013b) and Sérasset (2012), this loose encoding format makes it difficult to extract consistent data. One can choose to either restrict the extraction to prototypical articles or design a fine-grained parser that collects the maximum of the available information. The former goal is relatively easily feasible but leads to a resource containing only a small subset of Wiktionary's entries. Our belief is that the tedious engineering work of handling all

[1] For further details, read Zesch et al. (2008) and Sajous et al. (2013b).

[2] The dump used in this work is `https://dumps.wikimedia.org/frwiktionary/20140226/frwiktionary-20140226-pages-articles.xml.bz2`

```
== {{langue|fr}} ==
=== {{S|nom|fr}} ===
{{fr-rég|kurs}}
'''course''' {{pron|kurs|fr}} {{f}}
# [[action|Action]] de [[courir]], [[mouvement]] de celui qui [[court]].
#* ''[...], il n'est de bruit qu'un ver qui taraude incessamment les boiseries et dans le plafond,
la '''course''' d'un rongeur.'' {{source|{{w|Jean Rogissart}}, ''Passantes d'Octobre'', 1958}}
# {{sport|nocat=1}} Toute [[épreuve]] [[sportif|sportive]] où la [[vitesse]] est en jeu.
#* ''Nos pères étaient donc plus sages que nous lorsqu'ils repoussaient l'idée des '''courses'''.
# {{vieilli|fr}} [[actes|Actes]] d'[[hostilité]] que l'on faisait [[courir|en courant]] les mers
ou [[entrer|en entrant]] dans le [[pays]] [[ennemi]].
{{usage}} On dit maintenant [[incursion]], [[reconnaissance]], [[pointe]], etc.
#* ''Pendant les guerres de la révolution, Chausey, trop exposé aux '''courses''' des corsaires
de Jersey, resta inhabité.''
# {{figuré|fr}} [[marche|Marche]], [[progrès]] [[rapide]] d'une personne ou d'une chose.
#* ''Rien ne peut arrêter ce conquérant, ce fléau dans sa '''course'''.''

==== {{S|dérivés}} ====
* [[courser]]
* [[coursier]]
```

Figure 1: Wikicode extract of the noun *course*

wikicode particularities is valuable. In our case, it enabled us to design an unprecedented large copylefted lexicon that has no equivalent for French.

The basic unit of Wiktionary's articles is the word form: several words from different languages having the same word form occur in the same page (at the same URL). In such a page, a given language section may be divided in several parts of speech which may in turn split into several homonyms subsections. In the French Wiktionary, the *course* entry, for example, describes both the French and English lexemes. The French section splits into a noun section (*une course* 'a run; a race') and a section related to the inflected forms of the verb *courser* 'to pursue'. The noun section distinguishes 11 senses that all have definitions illustrated by examples. An extract of the noun section's wikicode is depicted in Figure 1. As can be seen, some wiki conventions are recurrent (e.g. double-brackets mark hyperlinks) and are easy to handle. Handling dynamic templates (marked by curly brackets) is more tricky. In definitions, they mark notes related to particular domains, registers, usages, geographic areas, languages, etc. In Figure 1, the pattern `{{sport}}` indicates that the second sense relates to the domain of sport ; the pattern `{{vieilli|fr}}` in the following definition denotes a dated usage ; the pattern `{{figuré|fr}}` in the last definition indicates a figurative one. We inventoried about 6,000 such templates and their aliases: for example, 4 patterns (abbreviated or full form, with or without ligature) signal the domain of enology: `{{œnologie|fr}}`, `{{oenologie|fr}}`, `{{œnol|fr}}` and `{{oenol|fr}}`. Unfortunately, the existence of such patterns does not prevent a contributor to directly write domain name in the page: several versions of "hardcoded domains" may be found, e.g. `(oenologie)` or `(œnologie)`.

Inventorying all these variations enabled us: 1) to remove them from the definitions' text and 2) to mark them in a formal way. Thus, one can decide to remove or keep, on demand, entries that are marked as rare or dated, build a sublexicon of a given domain, remove diatopic variations or investigate only these forms (e.g. words that are used only in Quebec), etc.

The variations observed in the definitions also occur in phonemic transcriptions, inflectional features, semantic relations, etc. We focus here only on the information used in sections 6 and 7: definitions and morphological relations. However, we parsed Wiktionnaire's full content and extracted all kind of available information, handling the numerous variations that we observed to convert the online dictionary into a structured resource, that we called GLAWI.[3] It contains more than 1.4 million inflected forms (about 190,000 lemmas) with their definitions, examples, lexicosemantic relations and translations, derived terms and phonemic transcriptions. A shortened extract resulting from the conversion of the noun section of *course* is depicted in Figure 2. As can be seen, GLAWI includes both XML structured data and the initial corresponding wikicode. This version of the resource is intended to remain close to the Wiktionnaire's content, whereas other lexicons focused on a particular aspect will be released. Our aim is to provide ready-to-use lexicons resulting from different post-processing of GLAWI. Post-processing

[3]Resulting from the unification of GLÀFF and an updated version of WiktionaryX, GLAWI stands for *"GLÀFF and WiktionaryX"*. This resource is freely available at `http://redac.univ-tlse2.fr/lexicons/glawi.html`.

```xml
<pos type="nom" inlflected="0">
  <grammaticalInfo gender="f" number="s"/>
  <inflections>
    <infl form="courses" pos="Ncfp" lemma="course" prons="kuʁs"/>
  </inflections>
  <pron>kuʁs</pron>
  <definitions>
    <definition>
      <gloss>
        <txt>Action de courir, mouvement de celui qui court.</txt>
        <wiki>[[action|Action]] de [[courir]], [[mouvement]] de celui qui [[court]].</wiki>
      </gloss>
      <example>
        <wiki>''[…], il n'est de bruit qu'un ver qui taraude incessamment les boiseries et dans le plafond,
        la '''course''' d'un rongeur.'' {{source|{{w|Jean Rogissart}}, ''Passantes d'Octobre'', 1958}}</wiki>
        <txt>[…], il n'est de bruit qu'un ver qui taraude incessamment les boiseries et dans le plafond,
        la course d'un rongeur.</txt>
      </example>
    </definition>
    <definition>
      <gloss>
        <domain value="sport"/>
        <wiki>{{sport|nocat=1}} Toute [[épreuve]] [[sportif|sportive]] où la [[vitesse]] est en jeu.</wiki>
        <txt>Toute épreuve sportive où la vitesse est en jeu.</txt>
      </gloss>
      <example>
        <wiki>''Nos pères étaient donc plus sages que nous lorsqu'ils repoussaient l'idée des
        '''courses'''.'' {{source|J. Déhès, ''[[s:Essai sur l'amélioration des races chevalines de la
        France|Essai sur l'amélioration des races chevalines de la France]]'', 1868}}</wiki>
        <txt>Nos pères étaient donc plus sages que nous lorsqu'ils repoussaient l'idée des courses.</txt>
      </example>
    </definition>
    <subsection type="dérivés">
      <item>courser</item>
      <item>coursier</item>
    </subsection>
</pos>
```


Figure 2: Extract of the noun subsection of *course* converted into a workable format

steps will consist in 1) selecting information relevant to a particular need (e.g. phonemic transcriptions, semantic relations, etc.) and 2) detecting inconsistencies and correcting them. The initial GLAWI resource, containing all the initial information, will also be released so that anyone can apply additional post-processings. GLAWI unburdens such users from the efforts of parsing the wikicode.

Articles from Wiktionnaire may contain morphologically derived terms. Figures 1 and 2 show that *course* produces the derived verb *courser* and noun *coursier* 'courier'. Such derivational relations are collected from Wiktionnaire and included in GLAWI. We show below how we leverage this information, in addition to GLAWI's definitions, to acquire morphological and morphosemantic knowledge.

4 Acquisition of morphological relations from GLAWI morphological subsections

We first extracted from GLAWI the list of the lexeme headwords that have typographically simple written forms (only letters) and that belong to the major POS: noun, verb, adjective, and adverb. This list (GLAWI-HW) contains 152,567 entries: 79,961 nouns, 22,646 verbs, 47,181 adjective and 2,779 adverbs). In what follows, we only consider these words.

Then we created a morphological lexicon extracted from the morphological subsections[4] of GLAWI (hereafter GMS). The lexicon consists of all pairs of words (w_1, w_2), where w_1 and w_2 belong to GLAWI-HW and where w_2 is listed in one of the morphological subsections of the article of w_1 or vice versa. GMS contains 97,058 pairs. The extraction of this lexicon from GLAWI was very simple, all the variability in Wiktionnaire's lexicographic descriptions being supported by our parser (see Section 3).

The remainder of the paper presents two methods for extending GMS. In a first experiment, we complement this lexicon with new pairs acquired from GLAWI's definitions. In a second one, we show how some of GMS's morphological pairs can be classified with respect to a given semantic class.

[4]The morphological subsections appear under 4 headings in Wiktionnaire: *apparentés*; *apparentés étymologiques*; *composés*; *dérivés*.

w1	w2	w1	w2
bisannuel_A	an_N	républicain_N	république_N
compilation_N	compilateur_A	similaire_A	dissimilitude_N
foudroyeur_A	foudre_N	tabasser_V	tabassage_N
militance_N	militer_V	taxidermie_N	taxidermiser_V
presse_N	pression_N	volcan_N	volcanique_A

Figure 3: Excerpt of GMS lexicon. Letters following the underscore indicate the grammatical category.

5 Morphological definitions

Basically, a dictionary definition is a pair composed of a word and a gloss of its meaning. In the following, we will use the terms **definiendum** for the defined word, **definiens** for the defining gloss and the notation *definiendum* = *definiens*. The definition articulates a number of lexical semantic relations between the definiendum and some words of the definiens as in (1) where *chair* is a hyponym of *furniture*, is the holonym of *seat*, *legs*, *back* and *arm rests* and is also the typical instrument of *sit on*. Some of the relations are made explicit by lexical markers as *used to* or *comprising*.

(1) chair$_N$ = An item of **furniture** used to **sit on** or in comprising a **seat**, **legs**, **back**, and sometimes **arm rests**, for use by one person.

Martin (1983) uses these relations to characterize the definitions. In his typology, definitions as in (2) are considered to be (morphological) derivational because the definiendum is defined with respect to a morphologically related word. In these definitions, the lexical semantic relation only involves two words that are morphologically related. Being members of the same derivational family, the orthographic representations of these words show some degree of similarity that can help us identify the morphological definitions. In (2) for example, the written forms *nitrificateur* 'nitrifying' and *nitrification* 'nitrification' share a 10 letters prefix and only differ by 3 letters. This strong similarity is a reliable indicator of their morphologically relatedness (Hathout, 2011b). Building on this observation, a definition is likely to be morphological if its definiens contains a word which is orthographically similar to the definiendum.

(2) nitrificateur$_A$ = Qui produit, qui favorise la **nitrification**.
'nitrifying' 'that produces, that favors nitrification'

We used Proxinette, a measure of morphological similarity defined in (Hathout, 2008), to identify the morphological definitions. Proxinette is designed to reduce the search space for derivational analogies. The reduction is obtained by bringing closer the words that belong to the same derivational families and series, since it is precisely within these paradigms that an entry is likely to form analogies (Hathout, 2011a). Proxinette describes the lexemes by all the n-grams of characters that appear in their inflected forms in order to catch the inflectional stem allomorphy because it tends to also show up in derivation (Bonami et al., 2009). The n-grams have an additional tag that indicates if they occur at the beginning, at the end or in the middle of the word. This information is described by adding a # at the beginning and end of the written forms. For example, in Figure 4, *localisation* 'localization', *localiser* 'localize; locate' and *focalisation* 'focalization' share the `ions#` ending because it occurs in their inflected forms *localisations* (plural), *localisions* (1st person plural, indicative, imperfect) and *focalisations* (plural). n-grams of size 1 and 2 are ignored because they occur in too many words and are not discriminant enough. Proxinette builds a bipartite graph with the words of the lexicon on one side and the features (n-grams) that characterize them on the other. Each word is linked to all its features and each feature is connected to the words that own it (see Figure 4). The graph is weighted so that the sum of weights of the outgoing edges of each node is equal to 1. Morphological similarity is estimated by simulating the spreading of an activation. For a given entry, an activation is initiated at the node that represents it. This activation is then propagated towards the features of the entry. In a second step, the activations in the feature nodes are propagated towards the words that possess them. The words which obtain the highest activations are the most similar to the entry. The edge weights and the way the graph is traversed brings closer the words that share the largest number of common features and the most specific ones (i.e. the less frequent).

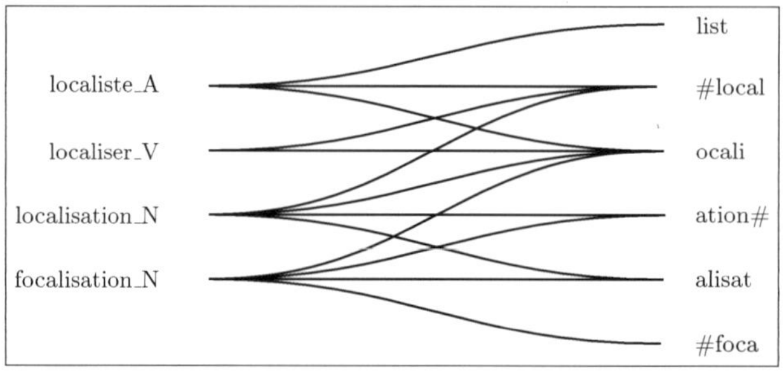

Figure 4: Excerpt of Proxinette bipartite graph. The graph is symmetric.

écholocalisation_N **relocalisation_N** **radiolocalisation_N** **géolocalisation_N** glocalisation_N **délocalisation_N** **antidélocalisation_A** **localisateur_N** **localisateur_A** vocalisation_N focalisation_N **localiser_V** **localisable_A** **délocalisateur_N** **localisé_A** **localiste_N** **localiste_A** **localisme_N** tropicalisation_N

Figure 5: The most similar words to the noun *localisation*. Words in boldface belong to the derivational family of *localisation*. Words in light type belong to its derivational series.

We applied Proxinette to GLAWI-HW and calculated for each of them a neighborhood consisting of the 100 most similar words. Figure 5 shows an excerpt of the neighborhood of the noun *localisation*. The occurrence of the verb *localiser* in this list enables us to identify the morphological definition (3).

(3) localisation$_N$ = Action de **localiser**, de se **localiser**.
'localization' 'the act of localizing, of locating'

The two experiments we conducted use the same data, namely the morphological definitions of GLAWI. These definitions are selected as follows:

1. We extracted all GLAWI definition glosses (definientia) with their entries and POS (definienda).

2. We syntactically parsed the definientia with the Talismane dependency parser (Urieli, 2013). Figure 6 presents the dependencies syntactic trees for the definientia in (4).

3. We tagged as morphological all definitions where, in the parsed definiens, at least one lemma (henceforth referred to as morphosemantic head) occurs in the definiendum neighborhood. For example, in (4), both definitions are tagged as morphological because *arrêter* occurs in the neighborhood of *arrêt*, and *découronner* and *couronne* occur in that of *découronnement*.

(4) a. arrêt$_N$ = Action de la main pour arrêter le cheval.
'stop' 'action of the hand to stop the horse'

b. découronnement$_N$ = L'action de découronner, d'enlever la couronne.
'uncrowning' 'the act of uncrowning, of removing the crown'

Morphosemantic heads may be the derivational base of the definiendum like *découronner*, a more distant ancestor like *couronne* or a "sibling" like in (2) where *nitrification* is a derivative of the definiendum base *nitrifier* 'nitrify'.

Figure 6: POS-tags and syntactic dependencies of the definientia of (4).

6 Acquisition of morphological relations from GLAWI morphological definitions

We extracted from GLAWI's morphological definitions the pairs of words (w_1, w_2) where w_1 is the definiendum and w_2 the definiens morphosemantic heads (or one of its morphosemantic head if it has many). After symmetrization, we obtained a lexicon (hereafter GMD) of 107,628 pairs. 32,256 of them belongs to GMS. A manual check of the 75,372 remaining pairs would enable its addition to GMS.

GMD additional pairs have been evaluated by three judges in two steps. The judges were instructed to set aside the orthographic variants as *desperado_N* / *despérado_N*. We first randomly selected 100 pairs and had them checked by three judges in order to estimate the inter-annotator agreement. The average F-measure of the agreement is 0.97 ; Fleiss's kappa is 0.65. The judges then checked 100 randomly selected pairs each. 9 out of the 300 pairs were variants and 19 errors were found in the 291 remaining ones which results in an overall accuracy of 93.5%. This method would lead to an increase of GMS by more than 70,000 pairs.

The general quality of these acquired pairs can be significantly increased by formal analogy filtering. The idea is to use analogy as a proxy to find pairs of words that are in the same morphological relation. GMS pairs being provided by Wiktionary contributors, we consider them as correct and use them as analogical patterns to filter out the pairs acquired from the morphological definitions. By formal analogy, we mean an analogy between the orthographic representations. For instance, the GMD pair *citrique_A*:*citron_N* form an analogy with *électrique_A*:*électron_N*. The latter being correct, we can assume that the former is correct too.

(5) a. citrique_A : citron_N = électrique_A : électron_N

b. fragmentation_N : défragmenter_V = concentration_N : déconcentrer_V

Analogies between strings are called formal analogies (Lepage, 2003; Stroppa and Yvon, 2005). One way to check a formal analogy is to find a decomposition (or factorization) of the four strings such that the differences between the first two are identical to the ones between the second two. In the analogy in (5a), the ending `ique` is replaced by `on` and the POS `A` by `N` in both pairs. We applied analogical filtering to GMS and GMD pairs. 86,228 pairs in GMD form at least one analogy with a pair in GMS; 53,972 of them do not occur in GMS. 300 of these pairs have been checked by three judges. They only found 3 variants and one error. The obtained accuracy is therefore over 99% (see Table 1).[5]

	initial		analogical	
	pairs	accuracy	pairs	accuracy
GMS	97,058	–	–	–
GMD	107,628	95.4%	86,228	99.8%
GMD \ GMS	75,372	93.5%	53,972	99.7%

Table 1: Summary of the quantitative results

GMD morphological relations will not be included into GLAWI. GMS and GMD are made available as separate resources on the GLAWI web page.

7 Semantic typing of the morphological definitions

The next experiment aims to demonstrate that morphological definitions could easily and quite accurately be typed semantically. We focus on a particular semantic type, namely definitions of process nominals such as (6) because they can be evaluated with respect to the Verbaction database (Hathout and Tanguy, 2002). Deverbal nominals have been extensively studied in linguistics (Pustejovsky, 1995) and used in a number of tools for various tasks. One of their distinctive feature is that they almost have the same meaning as their base verb. For instance, in (7) the noun and verb phrases are paraphrases of one another. Verbaction contains 9,393 verb-noun pairs where the noun is morphologically related to the verb and can be used to express the act denoted by the verb (e.g. *verrouiller*:*verrouillage*).[6] It has been

[5] Unfortunately, these results could not have been compared with those of Pentheroudakis and Vanderwende (1993) because their system makes use of a number of lexical and semantic resources that are not available for French. However, a comparison with Baroni et al. (2002) is underway although their method is corpus-based (and not MRD-based).

[6] Verbaction is freely available at: `http://redac.univ-tlse2.fr/lexiques/verbaction.html`.

used in syntactic dependency parsing by Bourigault (2007), in the construction of the French TimeBank by Bittar et al. (2011), in question answering systems by Bernhard et al. (2011), etc.

(6) verrouillage$_N$ = Action de verrouiller.
'locking' 'the act of locking.'

(7) nous **vérouillons la porte** rapidement 'we quickly lock the gate'
le **verrouillage de la porte** est rapide 'gate locking is quick'

In our experiment, we used the linear SVM classifier *liblinear* of Fan et al. (2008) to assign a semantic type to the definitions that have a nominal definiendum and where the morphosemantic head of the definiens is a verb as in (4) or (6). Verbaction was used to select a corpus of 1,198 of such definitions. Three judges annotated them. 608 definientia were tagged as processive and 590 ones as non processive. We then divided the corpus into a test set made up of 100 processive and 100 non processive definitions and a training set consisting of the remaining definientia.

The classifier is trained to recognize that the definientia in (4) express the same semantic relation between the morphosemantic head of the definiens and the definiendum. We use the method proposed by (Hathout, 2008) to capture this semantic similarity. Definientia are described by a large number of redundant features based on lemmata, POSs and syntactic dependencies. The features are n-grams calculated from Talismane parses (see figure 6). They are defined as follows:

1. We first collect all the paths that go from one word in the definiens to the syntactic root (e.g. [*arrêter*, *pour*, *action*] is a path that starts at *arrêter* in (4a)).

2. We extract all the n-grams of consecutive nodes in these paths.

3. Each n-gram yields 3 features: the sequence of the node's lemmata, the sequence of the nodes POS, and the sequence of syntactic dependency relations.

We obtained an accuracy of 97% for the semantic typing of the 200 definientia of the test set. The most immediate application of the classifier is the enrichment of Verbaction. Running the classifier on all the definitions with a nominal definiendum and a verbal morphosemantic head will provide us with new couples that could be added to the database. The classifier could also help us type process nouns that are not morphologically derived such as *audition* 'hearing' which is defined with respect to the verb *entendre* 'hear'. Similar typing could be performed for other semantic types such as agent nouns (in *-eur* or *-ant*), change of state verbs (in *-iser* or *-ifier*) or adjectives expressing possibility (in *-able*), etc. The experiment also shows that morphological definitions are well suited for semantic analysis because they express regular semantic relationship between pairs of words that are distinguished by their orthographic similarity.

8 Conclusion

In this paper, we have presented GLAWI, an XML machine-readable dictionary created from Wiktionnaire, the French edition of the Wiktionary project. We then showed that GLAWI was well suited for conducting computational morphology experiments. GLAWI contains morphological subsections which provide a significant number of valid and varied morphological relations. In addition, morphological relations can also be acquired from GLAWI morphological definitions. We presented a method to identify these definitions and the words in relation with a fairly good accuracy. We then used formal analogy to filter out almost all the erroneous pairs acquired from morphological definitions. In a second experiment, we demonstrate how to assign the morphological definitions to semantic types with a high accuracy.

This work opens several research avenues leading to a formal representation of the different form and meaning relations that underlie derivational morphology. The next move will be to organize the morphological relations into a graph similar to Démonette (Hathout and Namer, 2014) and identify the paradigms which structure them. We also plan to apply the semantic classification to other semantic types which could ultimately enable us to explore the intricate interplay between form and meaning.

References

Leticia Anton Pérez, Hugo Gonçalo Oliveira, and Paulo Gomes. 2011. Extracting Lexical-Semantic Knowledge from the Portuguese Wiktionary. In *Proceedings of the 15th Portuguese Conference on Artificial Intelligence*, EPIA 2011, pages 703–717, Lisbon, Portugal.

Rolf Harald Baayen, Richard Piepenbrock, and Leon Gulikers. 1995. The CELEX lexical database (release 2). CD-ROM. Linguistic Data Consortium, Philadelphia, PA.

Marco Baroni, Johannes Matiasek, and Harald Trost. 2002. Unsupervised discovery of morphologically related words based on orthographic and semantic similarity. In *Proceedings of the Workshop on Morphological and Phonological Learning of ACL-2002*, pages 48–57, Philadelphia, PA, USA.

Delphine Bernhard, Bruno Cartoni, and Delphine Tribout. 2011. A Task-Based Evaluation of French Morphological Resources and Tools. *Linguistic Issues in Language Technology*, 5(2).

André Bittar, Pascal Amsili, Pascal Denis, et al. 2011. French TimeBank: un corpus de référence sur la temporalité en français. In *Actes de la 18e Conférence Annuelle sur le Traitement Automatique des Langues Naturelles (TALN-2011)*, volume 1, pages 259–270, Montpellier, France.

Olivier Bonami, Gilles Boyé, and Françoise Kerleroux. 2009. L'allomorphie radicale et la relation flexion-construction. In Bernard Fradin, Françoise Kerleroux, and Marc Plénat, editors, *Aperçus de morphologie du français*, pages 103–125. Presses universitaires de Vincennes, Saint-Denis.

Didier Bourigault. 2007. *Un analyseur syntaxique opérationnel : SYNTEX.* Habilitation à diriger des recherches, Université Toulouse II-Le Mirail, Toulouse.

Nicoletta Calzolari, Laura Pecchia, and Antonio Zampolli. 1973. Working on the Italian Machine Dictionary: A Semantic Approach. In *Proceedings of the 5th Conference on Computational Linguistics - Volume 2*, pages 49–52, Stroudsburg, PA, USA.

Nicoletta Calzolari. 1988. The dictionary and the thesaurus can be combined. In Martha Evens, editor, *Relational Models of the Lexicon*, pages 75–96. Cambridge University Press.

Martin S. Chodorow, Roy J. Byrd, and George E. Heidorn. 1985. Extracting semantic hierarchies from a large on-line dictionary. In *Proceedings of the 23rd Annual Meeting on Association for Computational Linguistics*, ACL '85, pages 299–304, Stroudsburg, PA, USA.

James R. Curran and Marc Moens. 2002. Improvements in Automatic Thesaurus Extraction. In *Proceedings of the ACL Workshop on Unsupervised Lexical Acquisition*, pages 59–66, Philadelphia, USA.

Jacques Dendien. 1994. Le projet d'informatisation du TLF. In Éveline Martin, editor, *Les textes et l'informatique*, chapter 3, pages 31–63. Didier Érudition, Paris, France.

Rong-En Fan, Kai-Wei Chang, Cho-Jui Hsieh, Xiang-Rui Wang, and Chih-Jen Lin. 2008. Liblinear: A library for large linear classification. *The Journal of Machine Learning Research*, 9:1871–1874.

Nabil Hathout and Fiammetta Namer. 2014. La base lexicale démonette : entre sémantique constructionnelle et morphologie dérivationnelle. In *Actes de la 21e conférence annuelle sur le traitement automatique des langues naturelles (TALN-2014)*, Marseille, France.

Nabil Hathout and Ludovic Tanguy. 2002. Webaffix : Finding and validating morphological links on the WWW. In *Proceedings of the Third International Conference on Language Resources and Evaluation*, pages 1799–1804, Las Palmas de Gran Canaria, Spain.

Nabil Hathout. 2008. Acquisition of the morphological structure of the lexicon based on lexical similarity and formal analogy. In *Proceedings of the Coling workshop Textgraphs-3*, pages 1–8, Manchester, England.

Nabil Hathout. 2011a. Morphonette: a paradigm-based morphological network. *Lingue e linguaggio*, 2011(2):243–262.

Nabil Hathout. 2011b. Une approche topologique de la construction des mots : propositions théoriques et application à la préfixation en *anti-*. In *Des unités morphologiques au lexique* (Roché et al., 2011), pages 251–318.

Kris Heylen, Yves Peirsman, Dirk Geeraerts, and Dirk Speelman. 2008. Modelling Word Similarity: an Evaluation of Automatic Synonymy Extraction Algorithms. In *Proceedings of the Sixth International Language Resources and Evaluation (LREC'08)*, Marrakech, Morocco.

Mathieu Lafourcade. 2007. Making People Play for Lexical Acquisition with the JeuxDeMots prototype. In *SNLP'07: 7th International Symposium on Natural Language Processing*, Pattaya, Thailand.

Yves Lepage. 2003. *De l'analogie rendant compte de la commutation en linguistique*. Habilitation à diriger des recherches, Université Joseph Fourier, Grenoble.

Judith Markowitz, Thomas Ahlswede, and Martha Evens. 1986. Semantically significant patterns in dictionary definitions. In *Proceedings of the 24th Annual Meeting on Association for Computational Linguistics*, pages 112–119, Stroudsburg, PA, USA.

Robert Martin. 1983. *Pour une logique du sens*. Linguistique nouvelle. Presses universitaires de France, Paris.

Emmanuel Navarro, Franck Sajous, Bruno Gaume, Laurent Prévot, ShuKai Hsieh, Ivy Kuo, Pierre Magistry, and Chu-Ren Huang. 2009. Wiktionary and NLP: Improving synonymy networks. In *Proceedings of the 2009 ACL-IJCNLP Workshop on The People's Web Meets NLP: Collaboratively Constructed Semantic Resources*, pages 19–27, Singapore.

Roberto Navigli and Simone Paolo Ponzetto. 2010. BabelNet: Building a Very Large Multilingual Semantic Network. In *Proceedings of ACL'2010*, pages 216–225, Uppsala, Sweden.

Joseph Pentheroudakis and Lucy Vanderwende. 1993. Automatically identifying morphological relations in machine-readable dictionaries. In *Proceedings of the Ninth Annual Conference of the UW Centre for the New OED and Text Research*, pages 114–131.

Jean-Marie Pierrel. 2013. Structuration et usage de ressources lexicales institutionnelles sur le français. *Linguisticae investigationes Supplementa*, pages 119–152.

James Pustejovsky. 1995. *The Generative Lexicon*. MIT Press, Cambridge, MA.

Michel Roché, Gilles Boyé, Nabil Hathout, Stéphanie Lignon, and Marc Plénat. 2011. *Des unités morphologiques au lexique*. Hermès Science-Lavoisier, Paris.

Benoît Sagot and Darja Fišer. 2008. Building a Free French Wordnet from Multilingual Resources. In *Proceedings of OntoLex 2008*, Marrakech, Morocco.

Franck Sajous, Nabil Hathout, and Basilio Calderone. 2013a. GLÀFF, un Gros Lexique À tout Faire du Français. In *Actes de la 20e conférence sur le Traitement Automatique des Langues Naturelles (TALN'2013)*, pages 285–298, Les Sables d'Olonne, France.

Franck Sajous, Emmanuel Navarro, Bruno Gaume, Laurent Prévot, and Yannick Chudy. 2013b. Semi-automatic enrichment of crowdsourced synonymy networks: the WISIGOTH system applied to Wiktionary. *Language Resources and Evaluation*, 47(1):63–96.

Patrick Schone and Daniel S. Jurafsky. 2000. Knowledge-free induction of morphology using latent semantic analysis. In *Proceedings of the Conference on Natural Language Learning 2000 (CoNLL-2000)*, pages 67–72, Lisbon, Portugal.

Gilles Sérasset. 2012. Dbnary: Wiktionary as a LMF based Multilingual RDF network. In *Proceedings of the Eigth International Conference on Language Resources and Evaluation (LREC 2012)*, Istanbul, Turkey.

Nicolas Stroppa and François Yvon. 2005. An analogical learner for morphological analysis. In *Procs. of the 9th Conference on Computational Natural Language Learning (CoNLL-2005)*, pages 120–127, Ann Arbor, MI.

Assaf Urieli. 2013. *Robust French syntax analysis: reconciling statistical methods and linguistic knowledge in the Talismane toolkit*. Thèse de doctorat, Université de Toulouse-Le Mirail.

Lonneke van der Plas and Gosse Bouma. 2005. Syntactic Contexts for Finding Semantically Related Words. In Ton van der Wouden, Michaela Poß, Hilke Reckman, and Crit Cremers, editors, *Computational Linguistics in the Netherlands 2004: Selected papers from the fifteenth CLIN meeting*, volume 4 of *LOT Occasional Series*. Utrecht University.

Torsten Zesch and Iryna Gurevych. 2010. Wisdom of Crowds versus Wisdom of Linguists - Measuring the Semantic Relatedness of Words. *Journal of Natural Language Engineering.*, 16(01):25–59.

Torsten Zesch, Christof Müller, and Iryna Gurevych. 2008. Extracting Lexical Semantic Knowledge from Wikipedia and Wiktionary. In *Proceedings of the Sixth International Conference on Language Resources and Evaluation (LREC 2008)*, Marrakech, Morocco.

Pierre Zweigenbaum and Natalia Grabar. 2003. Learning derived words from medical corpora. In *9th Conference on Artificial Intelligence in Medicine Europe*, pages 189–198.

Annotation and Classification of Light Verbs and Light Verb Variations in Mandarin Chinese

Jingxia Lin[1] **Hongzhi Xu**[2] **Menghan Jiang**[2] **Chu-Ren Huang**[2]

[1]Nanyang Technological University
[2]Department of CBS, The Hong Kong Polytechnic University
jingxialin@ntu.edu.sg, hongz.xu@gmail.com,
menghan.jiang@connect.polyu.hk, churen.huang@polyu.edu.hk

Abstract

Light verbs pose an a challenge in linguistics because of its syntactic and semantic versatility and its unique distribution different from regular verbs with higher semantic content and selectional resrictions. Due to its light grammatical content, earlier natural language processing studies typically put light verbs in a stop word list and ignore them. Recently, however, classification and identification of light verbs and light verb construction have become a focus of study in computational linguistics, especially in the context of multi-word expression, information retrieval, disambiguation, and parsing. Past linguistic and computational studies on light verbs had very different foci. Linguistic studies tend to focus on the status of light verbs and its various selectional constraints. While NLP studies have focused on light verbs in the context of either a multi-word expression (MWE) or a construction to be identified, classified, or translated, trying to overcome the apparent poverty of semantic content of light verbs. There has been nearly no work attempting to bridge these two lines of research. This paper takes this challenge by proposing a corpus-bases study which classifies and captures syntactic-semantic difference among all light verbs. In this study, we first incorporate results from past linguistic studies to create annotated light verb corpora with syntactic-semantics features. We next adopt a statistic method for automatic identification of light verbs based on this annotated corpora. Our results show that a language resource based methodology optimally incorporating linguistic information can resolve challenges posed by light verbs in NLP.

1 Introduction

Identification of Light Verb Construction (LVC) plays an important role and poses a special challenge in many Natural Language Processing (NLP) applications, e.g. information retrieval and machine translation. In addition to addressing issues related to LVC as a contributing factor to errors for various applications, a few computational linguistics studies have targeted LVC in English specifically (e.g., Tu and Roth, 2011; Nagy et al., 2013). To the best of our knowledge, however, there has been no computational linguistic study dealing with LVCs in Chinese specifically. It is important to know that, due to their lack of semantic content, light verbs can behave rather idiosyncratically in each language. Chinese LVC, in particular, has the characteristic that allows many different light verbs to share similar usage and be interchangeable in some context. We should also note that light verbs in Chinese can take both verbs, deverabal nouns, and eventive nouns, while the morphological status of these categories are typically unmarked, Hence, it is often difficult to differentiate a light verb from its non-light verb uses without careful analysis of the data.

It has been observed that some Chinese light verbs can be used interchangeably but will have different selectional restrictions in some (and generally more limited) contexts. For example, the five light verbs *congshi*, *gao*, *jiayi*, *jinxing*, *zuo* (these words originally meant ‘engage’, ‘do’, ‘inflict’, ‘proceed’, ‘do’ respectively) can all take *yanjiu* ‘to do research’ as their complement and form a LVC. However, only the light verbs *gao* and *jinxing* can take *bisai* ‘to play games’ as complements, whereas the other light verbs *congshi*, *jiayi*, and *zuo* cannot. Since light verbs are often interchangeable yet

Proceedings of the Workshop on Lexical and Grammatical Resources for Language Processing, pages 75–82, Coling 2014, Dublin, Ireland, August 24 2014.

each also has its own selectional restrictions, it makes the identification of light verbs themselves both a challenging and necessary task. It is also observed that this kind of selectional versatility actually led to variations among different variants of Mandarin Chinese, such as Mainland and Taiwan. The versatility of Chinese light verbs makes the identification of LVCs more complicated than English.

Therefore, to study the differences among different light verbs and different variants of Chinese is important but challenging in both linguistic studies and computational applications. With annotated data from comparable corpora of Mainland and Taiwan Mandarin Chinese, this paper proposes both statistical and machine learning approaches to differentiate five most frequently used light verbs in both variants based on their syntactic and semantic features. The experimental results of our approach show that we can reliably differentiate different light verbs from each other in each variety of Mandarin Chinese.

There are several contributions in our work. Firstly, rather than focusing on only two light verbs *jiayi* and *jinxing* as in previous linguistic studies, we extended the study to more light verbs that are frequently used in Chinese. Actually, we will show that although *jiayi* and *jinxing* were often discussed in a pair in previous literature, the two are quite different from each other. Secondly, we show that statistical analysis and machine learning approaches are effective to identify the differences of light verbs and the variations demonstrated by the same light verb in different variants of Chinese. Thirdly, we provide a corpus that covers all typical uses of Chinese light verbs. Finally, the feature set we used in our study could be potentially used in the identification of Chinese LVCs in NLP applications.

This paper is organized as follows. Section 2 describes the data and annotation of the data. In Section 3, we conducted both statistical and machine learning methodologies to classify the five light verbs in both Mainland and Taiwan Mandarin. We discussed the implications and applications of our methodologies and the findings of our study in Section 4. Section 5 presents the conclusion and our future work.

2 Corpus Annotation

2.1 Data Collection

The data for this study is extracted from Annotated Chinese Gigaword corpus (Huang, 2009) which was collected and available from LDC and contains over 1.1 billion Chinese words, with 700 million characters from Taiwan Central News Agency and 400 million characters from Mainland Xinhua News Agency.

The light verbs to be studied are *congshi*, *gao*, *jiayi*, *jinxing*, *zuo*; these five are among the most frequently used light verbs in Chinese (Diao, 2004). 400 sentences are randomly selected for each light verb, half from the Mainland Gigaword subcorpus and the other from the Taiwan Gigaword subcorpus, which resulted in 2,000 sentences in total. The selection follows the principle that it could cover the different uses of each light verb.

2.2 Feature Annotation

Previous studies (Zhu, 1985; Zhou, 1987; Cai, 1982; Huang et al., 1995; Huang et al., 2013, among others) have proposed several syntactic and semantic features to identify the similarities and differences among light verbs, especially between the two most typical ones, i.e. *jinxing* (originally 'proceed') and *jiayi* (originally 'inflict'). For example, *jinxing* can take aspectual markers like *zhe* 'progressive marker', *le* 'aspect marker', and *guo* 'experiential aspect marker' while *jiayi* cannot (Zhou, 1987); *congshi* can take nominal phrases such as *disan chanye* 'the tertiary industry' as its complement while *jiayi* cannot. A few features are also found to be variant-specific; for example, Huang and Lin (2013) find that only the *congshi* in Taiwan, but not in Mainland Mandarin, can take informal and negative event complements like *xingjiaoyi* 'sexual trade'.

In our study, we selected 11 features which may help to differentiate different light verbs in each Mandarin variant as well as light verb variations among Mandarin variants, as in Table 1. All 2,000 examples collected for analysis were manually annotated based on the 11 features. The annotator is a trained expert on Chinese linguistics. Any ambiguous cases were discussed with another two experts in order to reach an agreement.

Feature ID	Explanation	Values (example)
1. OTHERLV	Whether a light verb co-occurs with another light verbs	Yes (***kaishi*** *jinxing taolun* Start proceed discuss 'start to discuss') No (*jinxing taolun* proceed discuss 'to discuss')
2. ASP	Whether a light verb is affixed with an aspectual marker (e.g., perfective *le*, durative *zhe*, experiential *guo*)	ASP.le (*jinxing-**le** zhandou* 'fighted') ASP.zhe (*jinxing-**zhe** zhandou* 'is fighting') ASP.guo (*jinxing-**guo** zhandou* 'fighted') ASP.none (*jinxing zhandou* 'fight')
3. EVECOMP	Event complement of a light verb is in subject position	Yes (***bisai*** *zai xuexiao jinxing* game at school proceed 'The game was held at the school') No (*zai xuexiao jinxing* ***bisai*** at school proceed game 'the game was held at the school')
4. POS	The part-of-speech of the complement taken by a light verb	Noun (*jinxing* ***zhanzheng*** proceed fight 'to fight') Verb (*jinxing* ***zhandou*** proceed fight 'to fight')
5. ARGSTR	The argument structure of the complement of a light verb, i.e. the number of arguments (subject and/or objects) that can be taken by the complement	One (*jinxing* ***zhandou*** proceed fight 'to fight') Two (*jinxing* ***piping*** proceed criticize 'to criticize') Zero (*jinxing* ***zhanzheng*** proceed fight 'to fight')
6. VOCOMP	Whether the complement of a light verb is in the V(erb)-O(bject) form	Yes (*jinxing* ***tou-piao*** proceed cast-ticket 'to vote') No (*jinxing* ***zhan-dou*** proceed fight-fight 'to fight')
7. DUREVT	Whether the event denoted by the complement of a light verb is durative	Yes (*jinxing* ***zhandou*** proceed fight-fight 'to fight') No (*jiayi* ***jujue*** inflict reject 'to reject')
8. FOREVT	Whether the event denoted by the complement of a light verb is formal or official	Yes (*jinxing* ***guoshi fangwen*** proceed state visit 'to pay a state visit') No (*zuo* ***xiao maimai*** do small business 'run a small business')
9. PSYEVT	Whether the event denoted by the complement of a light verb is mental or psychological activity	Yes (*jiayi* ***fanxing*** inflict retrospect 'to retrospect') No (*jiayi* ***diaocha*** inflict investigate 'to investigate')
10. INTEREVT	Whether the event denoted by the complement of a light verb involves interaction among participants	Yes (*jinxing* ***taolun*** proceed discuss 'to discuss') No (*jiayi* ***piping*** inflict criticize 'to criticize')
11. ACCOMPEVT	Whether the event denoted by the complement of a light verb is an accomplishment	Yes (*jinxing* ***jiejue*** proceed solve 'to solve') No (*jinxing* ***zhandou*** proceed fight-fight 'to fight')

Table 1: Features used to differentiate five Chinese light verbs.

3 Identification of light verbs based on annotated corpora

In this section, we adopted both statistical analysis and machine learning approaches to identify the five light verbs (*jiayi*, *jinxing*, *congshi*, *gao* and *zuo*) on the corpora with 2,000 annotated examples. The results of all approaches show that the five light verbs can be differentiated from each other in both Mainland and Taiwan Mandarin.

3.1 Identifying light verbs by statistical analysis

Both univariate analysis and multivariate analysis were used in our study for the identification. The tool we used is the Polytomous Package in R (Arppe, 2008).

3.1.1 Univariate analysis

Among the 11 independent features, one was found with only one level in both Mainland and Taiwan variants, i.e. all five light verbs in the two variants show the same preference over the features and thus excluded from the analysis. The feature is *OTHERLV* (all light verbs do not co-occur with another light verb in a sentence). Chi-squared tests were conducted for the significance of the co-occurrence of the remaining ten features with individual light verbs in both Mainland and Taiwan variants. The chisq.posthoc() function in the Polytoumous Package (Arppe, 2008) in R was used for the tests. The results are presented in Table 2, where the "+" and "-" signs indicate respectively a statistically significant overuse and underuse of a light verb with a feature, and "0" refers to a lack of statistical significance.

		Mainland Mandarin					Taiwan Mandarin				
Feature	N	*congshi*	*gao*	*jiayi*	*jinxing*	*zuo*	*congshi*	*gao*	*jiayi*	*jinxing*	*zuo*
POS.N	585	+	+	-	0	0	+	+	-	-	-
POS.V	1415	-	-	+	0	0	-	-	+	+	+
ARGSTR.one	376	0	-	-	0	+	+	-	-	+	0
ARGSTR.two	1039	-	0	+	0	-	-	-	+	-	+
ARGSTR.zero	585	+	+	-	0	0	+	+	-	-	-
VOCOMP.no	1939	0	0	0	0	0	0	0	+	-	0
VOCOMP.yes	61	0	0	0	0	0	0	0	-	+	0
EVECOMP.no	1919	+	-	+	-	-	+	0	+	-	0
EVECOMP.yes	81	-	+	-	+	+	-	0	-	+	0
ASP.guo	9	0	0	0	0	0	0	0	0	0	0
ASP.le	155	-	-	-	+	+	-	-	-	-	+
ASP.no	1835	+	+	+	-	-	+	+	+	+	-
ASP.zhe	1	0	0	0	+	0					
DUREVT.no	35	-	0	+	-	-	0	0	+	0	0
DUREVT.yes	1965	+	0	-	+	+	0	0	-	0	0
FOREVT.no	66	0	0	-	0	+	+	-	-	0	0
FOREVT.yes	1934	0	0	+	0	-	-	+	+	0	0
PSYEVT.no	1981	0	0	-	0	0	0	0	0	0	-
PSYEVT.yes	19	0	0	+	0	0	0	0	0	0	+
INTEREVT.no	1870	+	0	+	-	+	+	+	0	-	0
INTEREVT.yes	130	-	0	-	+	-	-	-	0	+	0
ACCOMPEVT.no	1904	+	+	-	+	+	+	+	-	+	0
ACCOMPEVT.yes	96	-	-	+	-	-	-	-	+	-	0

Table 2: Identifying light verbs in Mainland and Taiwan Mandarin via univariate analysis.

Table 2 suggests that in both Mainland and Taiwan Mandarin, each light verb shows significant preference for certain features, and thus can be distinguished from each other. For example, in Mainland Mandarin, although both *congshi* and *gao* show significant preference for the features *POS.N* and *ACCOMPEVT.no*, *congshi* differs from *gao* in that it also significantly prefers *DUREVT.yes* (taking complements denoting durative events, e.g., *yanjiu* 'to research'), *EVECOMP.no* (event complements do not occur in subject position), and *INTEREVT.no* (not taking complements denoting events involving interaction among participants, e.g., *taolun* 'to discuss'), whereas *gao* shows either a dispreference or no significant preference over these features. Take *gao* and *zuo* in Taiwan Mandarin as another example. While both light verbs literally means 'to do', there is no single feature preferred by both: *gao* prefers *POS.N*, *ARGSTR.zero*, *FOREVT.yes*, *INTEREVT.no*, *ACCOMPEVT.no*, whereas *zuo* shows significant preferences for *POS.V*, *ARGSTR.two*, *ASP.le*, and *PSYEVT.yes*.

3.1.2 Multivariate analysis

As shown in Table 2, in both Mainland and Taiwan Mandarin, some of the five light verbs share some features, which thus explains why sometimes they can be interchangeably used. This also indicates (a) that a particular feature is unlikely to be preferred by only one light verb and thus differentiates the verb from the others; (b) a certain context may allow the occurrence of more than one light verb. In this sense, a multivariate analysis was adopted to better classify the five light verbs in each variant. The multivariate analysis used in the current study is polytomous logistic regression (Arppe, 2008), and the tool we used is the Polytomous() function in the Polytoumous Package (Arppe, 2008) in R.

The results from the multivariate analysis were summarized in Table 3. The numbers shown in the table are the odds for the features in favor of or against the occurrence of each light verb: when the estimated odd is larger than 1, the chance of the occurrence of a light verb is significantly increased by the feature, e.g., the chance of Mainland *jiayi* occurring is significantly increased by *ARGSTRtwo* (76.47:1), followed by *ACCOMPEVTyes* (56:1), *VOCOMPyes* (23.54: 1), and *PSYEVTyes* (19.87: 1). When the estimated odd is smaller than 1, the chance of the occurrence of a light verb is significantly decreased by the feature, e.g., the chance of Mainland *jinxing* occurring is significantly decreased by *ACCOMPEVTyes* (0.1849: 1); in addition, "inf" and "1/inf" refer to odds larger than 10,000 and smaller than 1/10,000 respectively, whereas non-significant odds (p-value < 0.05) are given in parentheses.

	Mainland Mandarin					Taiwan Mandarin				
	congshi	*gao*	*jiayi*	*jinxing*	*zuo*	*congshi*	*gao*	*jiayi*	*jinxing*	*zuo*
(Intercept)	(1/Inf)	*0.02271*	(1/Inf)	(1/Inf)	(1/Inf)	(1/Inf)	(1/Inf)	(1/Inf)	(1/Inf)	(1/Inf)
ACCOMPEVTyes	(1/Inf)	*0.09863*	***56.25***	*0.1849*	(1/Inf)	(0.3419)	(1/Inf)	***11.33***	(0.1607)	*0.2272*
ARGSTRtwo	*0.2652*	***2.895***	***76.47***	(1.481)	*0.2177*	*0.1283*	(0.7613)	(Inf)	(0.7062)	(1.217)
ARGSTRzero	(1.097)	***3.584***	(1/Inf)	(1.179)	*0.245*	(0.6219)	***7.228***	(4.396)	*0.5393*	*0.2068*
ASPle	(0.7487)	(0.1767)	(0.8257)	(0.9196)	(1.853)	(1/Inf)	(1/Inf)	(0.3027)	(Inf)	***32.98***
ASPno	(Inf)	(1.499)	(Inf)	(0.2307)	(0.2389)	(0.9273)	(0.6967)	(Inf)	(Inf)	(0.2385)
ASPzhe	(1.603)	(1/Inf)	(0.4571)	(Inf)	(1/Inf)					
DUREVTyes	(Inf)	(2.958)	(1/Inf)	(Inf)	(Inf)	(Inf)	(Inf)	(1/Inf)	(0.9575)	(Inf)
EVECOMPyes	(1/Inf)	(1.726)	(1/Inf)	***3.975***	(1.772)	(1/Inf)	(0.8491)	(1/Inf)	***8.113***	(0.5019)
FOREVTyes	(2.744)	(1.227)	(Inf)	(0.7457)	*0.2679*	*0.0867*	(Inf)	(Inf)	(1.437)	(1.467)
INTEREVTyes	*0.03255*	(0.5281)	(0.5432)	***18.67***	*0.08902*	*0.1896*	(1/Inf)	(0.951)	***10.47***	(0.398)
PSYEVTyes	(1/Inf)	(1/Inf)	***19.87***	(1/Inf)	(0.9619)	(1/Inf)	(1/Inf)	(1.395)	(1/Inf)	(3.323)
VOCOMPyes	(0.1346)	(3.043)	***23.54***	(1.086)	(0.5344)	*0.18*	(2.35)	(Inf)	***3.161***	(0.5956)

Table 3: identifying light verbs in Mainland and Taiwan Mandarin via multivariate analysis.

As shown in Table 3, each of the light verbs in each Mandarin variant shows its favor and disfavor of certain features. Take Mainland Mandarin for example: although *congshi* has no feature significantly in its favor, but it is significantly disfavored by *ARGSTRtwo* (0.27:1) and *ITEREVTyes* (0.03:1); *gao* is disfavored by the aggregate of default variable values (0.02:1), and *ACCOMPEVTyes* (0.1:1), but is significantly favored by *ARGSTRtwo* and *ARGSTRzero*; the chance of *jiayi*'s ocucrrence is significantly increased by *ARGSTRtwo*(76.47:1), *ACCOMPEVTyes* (56.25:1), *VOCOMPyes* (23.54:1), and *PSYEVTyes* (19:87:1); *jinxing* has *INTEREVTyes* and *EVECOMPyes* in its favor, but *ACOMPEVTyes* in its disfavor; no feature is significantly in the favor of *zuo*, but this light verb is significantly disfavored by *ARGSTRtwo, ARGSTRzero, FOREVTyes* and *INTEREVTyes*.

The results in Table 3 also show that sometimes one key feature is able to identify two light verbs from each other, although not all five light verbs. Take Mainland Mandarin again for example. Most combinations of two light verbs from the five can be effectively differentiated by one feature. For instance, the feature *ARGSTRtwo* can differentiate *congshi/gao*, *congshi/jiayi*, *jiayi/zuo* and *gao/zuo*; the feature *INTEREVTyes* can differentiate *congshi/jinxing* and *jinxing/zuo*; the feature AC*COMPEVTyes* can differentiate the pairs *gao/jiayi* and *jinxing/jiayi*.

3.2 Identifying light verbs by classification

In this section, we resorted to machine learning technologies to study the same issue. Different classifiers were adopted to discriminate the five light verbs with the annotated corpora: ID3, Logistic Regression, Naïve Bayesian and SVM that are implemented in WEKA (Hall et al., 2009) and 10-fold cross validations were performed separately on the Taiwan and Mainland corpora.

The results were presented in Table 4. We can see that different classifiers provide similar results on both corpora, which means that the classification results are reliable and the features we annotated are effective in identifying the five light verbs. Overall, ID3 out-performs SVM slightly, with Logistic and NB not far behind. ID3 performs the best since the data is in low dimension. The detailed results including precision, recall and F-measure by ID3 on both corpora are shown in Table 5. The corresponding confusion matrixes are presented in Table 6. The confusion matrixes suggest two very important generalizations: (a) all five verbs can be classified with good confidence, and (b) the overall classification patterns of the Mainland and Taiwan Mandarin are very similar, which is consistent with the fact that Mainland and Taiwan Mandarin are two variants. However, we also observe that the confusion matrixes between various light verb pairs may differ between Mainland and Taiwan Chineses. This is the difference we would like to explore in the next section to propose a way to automatically predict these two variants. In addition, it is worth noting that all classifiers identify *jiayi* more effectively than other light verbs, which thus shows a potential different usage of *jiayi* from the others.

	ID3		Logistic		NB		SVM	
	TW	ML	TW	ML	TW	ML	TW	ML
jingxing	0.365	0.494	0.372	0.455	0.411	0.444	0.422	0.485
gao	0.612	0.391	0.609	0.364	0.598	0.377	0.575	0.354
zuo	0.571	0.566	0.568	0.582	0.525	0.576	0.574	0.561
jiayi	0.759	0.800	0.758	0.807	0.752	0.794	0.759	0.767
congshi	0.552	0.646	0.526	0.643	0.486	0.648	0.523	0.633
Average	0.574	0.585	0.567	0.576	0.555	0.573	0.571	0.565

Table 4: Result in F1-score of 10-fold cross validation of the classification of the five light verbs with different classifiers on the Taiwan (TW) and Mainland (ML) Corpora.

	Precision		Recall		F-Measure	
	TW	ML	TW	ML	TW	ML
jingxing	0.442	0.593	0.311	0.423	0.365	0.494
gao	0.681	0.449	0.557	0.347	0.612	0.391
zuo	0.610	0.570	0.537	0.562	0.571	0.566
jiayi	0.634	0.720	0.946	0.900	0.759	0.800
congshi	0.528	0.583	0.579	0.724	0.552	0.646
Average	0.580	0.586	0.588	0.599	0.574	0.585

Table 5: 10-fold cross validation result of ID3 algorithm on both corpora.

	jingxing		*gao*		*zuo*		*jiayi*		*congshi*	
	TW	ML	TW	ML	TW	ML	TW	ML	TW	ML
jingxing	**61**	**83**	15	27	36	40	38	11	46	35
gao	20	16	**113**	**70**	13	23	24	39	33	54
zuo	24	25	8	28	**108**	**118**	39	25	22	14
jiayi	5	11	0	6	5	6	**192**	**206**	1	0
congshi	28	5	30	25	15	20	10	5	**114**	**144**

Table 6: Confusion matrix of the classification with ID3 algorithm on both corpora.

3.3 Identifying light verbs by automatic clustering

We further used the clustering algorithm to test the differentiability of the five light verbs in both Mainland and Taiwan Mandarin. The results using the simple K-Means clustering algorithm on Taiwan and Mainland corpora are shown in Table 7. The results show that the light verb *jiayi* behaves quite differently from the other four light verbs in both Mainland and Taiwan corpora, which is similar to the analysis based on statistical methods in Section 3.1 and classification methods in Section 3.2. In both corpora, *jiayi* has a narrower usage than the other light verbs. Meanwhile, we can also find a cluster which is mainly formed by instances of *jiayi* from the Mainland corpus (i.e. cluster 0). After closer examination of the examples in this cluster, we found that it mainly includes sentences where *jiayi* takes complements denoting accomplishment events, e.g. *gaizheng* 'to correct' and *jiejue* 'to solve'. However, *jiayi* in Taiwan corpus mainly takes complements denoting activity events, and thus almost all instances of Taiwan *jiayi* are mixed with those of the other light verbs. Meanwhile, our results show a tendency that all other light verbs (*jinxing*, *congshi*, *zuo*, and *gao*) mostly take activity complements but fewer accomplishment complements in both Taiwan and Mainland corpora. More discussion on the light verb variations between Mainland and Taiwan Mandarin can be found in (Huang et al., 2014).

	Mainland						Taiwan				
	0	1	2	3	4		0	1	2	3	4
jinxing	2	32	110	23	37		30	10	77	20	64
gao	2	33	116	41	11		120	23	30	0	31
zuo	0	36	80	14	81		19	4	47	5	132
jiayi	68	0	161	0	0		0	0	1	6	196
congshi	0	67	66	21	46		90	20	68	0	22

Table 7: Clustering results on Mainland and Taiwan corpora.

4 Applications and Implications

4.1 Implications for Future Studies

In the study above, we were able to annotate a corpus with all the types of significant context and, based on this annotated corpus, we were able to use statistic model to differentiate the use of different light verbs in different contexts. Such a module of generic linguistic tools can have several potentially very useful applications. First, in translation, LVC is one of the most difficult constructions as there is less grammatical or contextual information to make the correct translation. Our approach is especially promising. As we encode contextual selection information for all light verbs, the same approach can be applied to the other languages in the target-source pair to produce optimal pair. Second, in information extraction, selection of different light verbs often conveys subtle difference in meanings. Our ability to differentiate similar light verbs in the same context could have great potential in extracting the subtle information change/increase in the same context. Lastly, in second language learning as well as error detection, light verbs have been one of the most challenging ones. Our studies can be readily applied to either error detection or second language learning environment to provide the correct context where a certain light very is preferred over another.

4.2 From light verb variations to variants for the same language

One of the biggest challenges in computational processing of languages is probably to identify newly emergent variants, such as the cross-strait variations of Mandarin Chinese. For these two variants, the most commonly cited ones were on lexical differences. Systematic grammatical differences were much more difficult to study and hence rarely reported (comp. Huang et al., 2009). As these are two newly divergent variants, their main grammars are almost all identical, except for some subtle differences, such as the selection between different light verbs and their complements. Our preliminary results of univariate and multivariate analysis can be found in Table 2 and 3. It shows not only the similarities/differences among the light verbs in each variety (e.g., both ML and TW *congshi* and *gao* show preferences over *POS.N*, whereas both ML and TW *jiayi* show dispreference), but also the similarities/differences of the corresponding light verbs in Mainland and Taiwan Mandarin. For instance, *jinxing* in TW tends to take VO compounds as its complements e.g., *jinxing toupiao* "cast a vote", which is consistent with the analysis in (Huang et al., 2013) (see more in Huang et al., 2014). But one thing should be pointed out is the difference is more between a significant and non-significant feature, rather than between a significant positive and significant negative feature.

5 Conclusion

In this paper, we addressed the issue of automatic classification of Chinese light verbs based on their usage distribution, based on an annotated corpus marking relevant contextual information for light verbs. We used both statistical methods and machine learning technologies to address this issue. It is found that our approaches are effective in identifying light verbs and their variations. The automatic generated semantic and syntactic features can also be used for future studies on other light verbs as well as other lexical categories. The result suggested that richly annotated language resources paired with appropriate tool can lead to effective general solution for some common issues faced by linguistics and natural language processing.

Acknowledgements

The work is supported by a General Research Fund (GRF) sponsored by the Research Grants Council (Project no. 543512) and NTU Grant NO. M4081117.100.500000.

Reference

Antti Arppe. 2008. Univariate, bivariate and multivariate methods in corpus-based lexicography - a study of synonymy. *Publications of the Department of General Linguistics*, University of Helsinki, volume 44.

Wenlan Cai. (1982). Issues on the complement of jinxing (“進行” 帶賓問題). *Chinese Language Learning (漢語學習)* (3), 7-11.

Yanbin Diao. 2004. *Research on Delexical Verb in Modern Chinese (現代漢語虛義動詞研究)*. Dalian: Liaoning Normal University Press.

Mark Hall, Eibe Frank, Geoffrey Holmes, Bernhard Pfahringer, Peter Reutemann and Ian H. Witten. 2009. The WEKA Data Mining Software: An Update. *SIGKDD Explorations*, 11(1):10-18.

Chu-ren Huang, Meili Yeh, and Li-ping Chang. 1995. *Two light verbs in Mandarin Chinese*. A corpus-based study of nominalization and verbal semantics. Proceedings of NACCL6, 1: 100-112.

Chu-Ren Huang. 2009. *Tagged Chinese Gigaword Version 2.0*. Philadelphia: Lexical Data Consortium, University of Pennsylvania. ISBN 1-58563-516-2

Chu-Ren Huang and Jingxia Lin. 2013. The ordering of Mandarin Chinese light verbs. In *Proceedings of the 13th Chinese Lexical Semantics Workshop*. D. Ji and G. Xiao (Eds.): CLSW 2012, LNAI 7717, pages 728-735. Heidelberg: Springer.

Chu-Ren Huang, Jingxia Lin, and Huarui Zhang. 2013. *World Chineses based on comparable corpus: The case of grammatical variations of jinxing*. 《澳门语言文化研究》, pages 397-414.

Chu-Ren Huang, Jingxia Lin, Menghan Jiang and Hongzhi Xu. 2014. Corpus-based Study and Identification of Mandarin Chinese Light Verb Variations. *COLING Workshop on Applying NLP Tools to Similar Languages, Varieties and Dialects*. Dublin, August 23.

István Nagy, Veronika Vincze, and Richárd Farkas. 2013. Full-coverage Identification of English Light Verb Constructions. *In Proceedings of the International Joint Conference on Natural Language Processing*, pages 329-337.

Yuancheng Tu and Dan Roth. 2011. Learning English light verb constructions: Contextual or statistical. In *Proceedings of the Workshop on Multiword Expressions: from Parsing and Generation to the Real World*. Association for Computational Linguistics.

Gang Zhou. 1987. *Subdivision of Dummy Verbs (形式動詞的次分類)*. Chinese Language Learning (漢語學習), volume 1, pages 11-14.

Dexi Zhu. (1985). *Dummy Verbs and NV in Modern Chinese (現代書面漢語里的虛化動詞和名動詞)*. Journal of Peking University (Humanities and Social Sciences) (北京大學學報(哲學社會科學版)), volume 5, pages 1-6.

Extended phraseological information in a valence dictionary for NLP applications

Adam Przepiórkowski, Elżbieta Hajnicz, Agnieszka Patejuk, Marcin Woliński
Institute of Computer Science, Polish Academy of Sciences
ul. Jana Kazimierza 5, 01-248 Warszawa
{adamp, hajnicz, aep, wolinski}@ipipan.waw.pl

Abstract

The aim of this paper is to propose a far-reaching extension of the phraseological component of a valence dictionary for Polish. The dictionary is the basis of two different parsers of Polish; its format has been designed so as to maximise the readability of the information it contains and its re-applicability. We believe that the extension proposed here follows this approach and, hence, may be an inspiration in the design of valence dictionaries for other languages.

1 Introduction

The starting point of the work reported here is Walenty, a valence dictionary for Polish described in Przepiórkowski et al. 2014 and available from `http://zil.ipipan.waw.pl/Walenty` (see §1.1). Walenty contains some valence schemata for verbal idioms; e.g., one of the schemata for KUĆ 'forge' says that it combines with a nominal subject, a nominal object and a prepositional phrase consisting of the preposition NA 'on' and the accusative singular form of the noun PAMIĘĆ 'memory' – this represents the idiom *ktoś kuje coś na pamięć* 'somebody rote learns something', lit. 'somebody forges something onto memory'. The current formalism handles various kinds of verbal phraseological constructions (cf. §1.2), but also has clear limitations. For example, in Polish one may welcome somebody "with arms wide open", and the current formalism makes it possible to express the "welcome with arms + *modifier*" part, but not the specifics of the allowed modifier, namely, that it is the adjective meaning "open", possibly itself modified by an intensifying adverb (cf. §1.3 for details).

The aim of this paper is to propose a new subformalism of Walenty for describing phraseological valence schemata (see §2). To the best of our knowledge, Walenty is already rather unique among valence dictionaries for various languages in paying so much attention to phraseological constructions (among its other rare or unique features), and at the same time it is practically employed in parsing by two different parsers of Polish (cf. §1.1). We believe that these traits make the current proposal to further extend the underlying formalism potentially interesting to the wider audience.

1.1 Walenty

Walenty is a valence dictionary which is meant to be both human- and machine-readable; in particular, it is being employed by two parsers of Polish, Świgra (an implementation of a Definite Clause Grammar description of fragments of Polish syntax; Woliński 2004) and POLFIE (an implementation of a Lexical Functional Grammar description of fragments of Polish; Patejuk and Przepiórkowski 2012). As these parsers are based on two rather different linguistic approaches, the valence dictionary must be sufficiently expressive to accommodate for the needs of both – and perhaps other to come.

Each verb is assigned a number of valence schemata[1] and each schema is a set of argument specifications. Walenty is explicit about what counts as an argument: if two morphosyntactically different phrases may occur coordinated in an argument position, they are taken to be different realisations of the same argument. This is exemplified in the following schema for TŁUMACZYĆ 'explain', as in *Musiałem im tłumaczyć najprostsze zasady i dlaczego trzeba je stosować* 'I had to explain them the most basic principles

[1] As long as the dictionary contains mostly morphosyntactic information, we avoid using the term *valence frame*.

Proceedings of the Workshop on Lexical and Grammatical Resources for Language Processing, pages 83–91,
Coling 2014, Dublin, Ireland, August 24 2014.

and why they should be adhered to' involving a coordinated phrase in the object position consisting of an NP (*najprostsze zasady* 'the most basic principles') and an interrogative clause (*dlaczego trzeba je stosować* 'why they should be adhered to'; marked here as `cp(int)`).

```
subj{np(str)} + obj{np(str); cp(int)} + {np(dat)}
```

There are three argument positions (separated by +) given in this schema: a subject, an object and an additional argument whose grammatical function is not specified but whose morphosyntactic realisation is described as a dative nominal phrase (`np(dat)`). The subject is also described as a nominal phrase (NP), but its case is specified as *structural*, i.e., potentially depending on the syntactic context. In Polish, such subjects are normally nominative, but – according to some approaches – they bear the accusative case when they are realised as numeral phrases of certain type. Similarly, the nominal realisation of the object is specified as structural, as it normally occurs in the accusative, unless it is in the scope of verbal negation, in which case it bears the genitive. Crucially, though, the object is specified here not just as an NP, but also alternatively as an interrogative (`int`) clausal argument (`cp`, for *complementiser phrase*). A parser may take this information into account and properly analyse a sentence with unlike coordination like the one involving TŁUMACZYĆ 'explain', given in the previous paragraph.

Other features of the formalism of Walenty worth mentioning here, and described in more detail in Przepiórkowski et al. 2014, are: the representation of control and raising (cf. Landau 2013 and references therein), specification of semantically defined arguments (e.g., locative, temporal and manner), with their possible morphosyntactic realisations defined externally (once for the whole dictionary), handling of various kinds of pronominal arguments, and other types of non-morphological case specifications (apart from the structural case). While there is no explicit semantic information in the dictionary at the moment (apart from such semantically defined arguments and control information), i.e., no subdivision of verbal lemmata into senses and no semantic role information, Walenty is currently being extended to include such a semantic layer.

1.2 Phraseology in Walenty

Two features of the Walenty formalism deal with multi-word expresssions. The simpler one is concerned with complex prepositions such as W KWESTII 'in (some) matter', NA TEMAT 'on (some) topic', Z POWODU 'because of' (lit. 'of reason'), etc. Unlike in case of usual prepositional phrases, parameterised with the preposition lemma and the grammatical case it governs (e.g., `prepnp(z,inst)` for a prepositional phrase headed by z 'with' and taking an instrumental NP), such complex prepositions seem to uniformly govern the genitive case, so explicit case information is not needed here. The following schema, for ROZPACZAĆ (*z powodu czegoś*) 'lament (because of something)', illustrates this type of arguments:

```
subj{np(str)} + {comprepnp(z powodu)}
```

Other, more clearly idiomatic arguments are currently specified as `fixed`, `lexnp` and `preplexnp`. Phrases of type `fixed` again have just one parameter: the exact orthographic realisation of the phrase; see the following schema for ZBIĆ 'beat' (as in *He beat them to a pulp*), with *na kwaśne jabłko* meaning literally 'into sour apple':

```
subj{np(str)} + obj{np(str)} + {fixed('na kwaśne jabłko')}
```

A more interesting type is `lexnp` with four parameters indicating the case of the NP, its grammatical number, the lemma of the head, and the modifiability pattern. The following schema for PŁYNĄĆ 'flow' (as in *Hot blood flows in his veins*), where the subject is a structurally-cased NP, as usual, but necessarily headed by KREW 'blood' in the singular, and the NP may contain modifiers (cf. `atr`), illustrates this:

```
subj{lexnp(str,sg,'krew',atr)} + {preplexnp(w,loc,pl,'żyła',ratr)}
```

The final lexical argument type is `preplexnp`, which contains an additional (initial) parameter, namely the preposition. In the above schema, the second argument is a PP headed by the preposition w 'in' combining with a locative NP in the plural. The NP must be headed by ŻYŁA 'vein' and must contain a possessive modifier (`ratr` stands for 'required attribute'). So this schema covers examples such as *Gorąca krew płynie w jego żyłach* 'Hot blood flows in his veins', but – correctly – not the non-phraseological *Gorąca krew płynie w żyłach* (no modifier of 'veins') or *Gorąca krew płynie w jego żyle* (singular 'vein').

The third possible value of the modifiability parameter is `natr`, for lexicalised arguments that cannot involve modification. The following schema for ZMARZNĄĆ 'get cold, freeze' handles the idiom *zmarznąć na kość* 'freeze to the marrow' (lit. 'freeze to (the) bone'); note that *kość* 'bone' cannot be modified here, as illustrated by the infelicitous *Zmarzł na gołą/twardą kość* '(He) froze to (the) naked/hard bone':

```
subj{np(str)} + {preplexnp(na,acc,sg,'kość',natr)}
```

Finally, `batr` ('bound attribute'), indicates that the NP must involve a possessive modifier meaning 'self' or '(one's) own', i.e., a form of either SWÓJ or WŁASNY. For example, ZOBACZYĆ 'see' is involved in an idiom meaning 'to see with one's own eyes', as in *Na własne oczy zobaczyłem jej uśmiech i to, że nie była wcale taka stara* 'With my own eyes I saw her smile and that she wasn't so old at all':[2]

```
subj{np(str)} + {np(str); ncp(str,że)} +
{preplexnp(na,acc,pl,'oko',batr)}
```

We will see below that a more expressive – and more general – scheme for the representation of phraseological valence is needed.

1.3 Limitations

A number of problems were identified with the formalism of Walenty as it was described in Przepiórkowski et al. 2014 and summarised above. To start with the simplest cases, it is a simplification to say that complex prepositions (`comprepnp` above) are internally unanalysable and always combine with genitive NPs. For example, while *z powodu* 'because of' cannot occur without any additional dependents, it is sufficient for the nominal form *powodu* 'reason' to be modified by an appropriate adjectival form for the whole expression to be complete, e.g., *z tego powodu* 'because of this', lit. 'of this reason', *z ważnego powodu* lit. 'of important reason', etc. This is not a general feature of such complex prepositions, though. For example, *w trakcie* 'during', lit. 'in (the) course', must combine with a genitive NP and the nominal form *trakcie* 'course' cannot be modified by an adjective (**w tym trakcie* lit. 'in this course').

Second, it is useful for parsers to have more grammatical information about lexically fixed arguments; for example, `fixed('na kwaśne jabłko')` clearly has the internal structure of a prepositional phrase.

Third, the current formalism allows for only two types of phraseological phrases to be specified in more detail: nominal (`lexnp`) and prepositional (`preplexnp`). While not so frequent, other kinds of idiomatic arguments also occur, including adjectival, adverbial and infinitival. For example, one of the idiomatic uses of MIEĆ 'have' is *mieć przechlapane* 'be in the doghouse, be in deep shit', lit. 'have (it) screwed', with an appropriate form of the adjective PRZECHLAPANY 'screwed'. Similarly, the verb DYSZEĆ 'pant' may be argued to optionally require the adverb LEDWO 'barely', as in *ledwo dyszeć* 'hardly breathe'. Also, KŁAŚĆ SIĘ 'lie down' typically occurs with the infinitival form of SPAĆ 'sleep'. The current formalism may describe such requirements only using the rather inflexible `fixed` notation.

Finally, and perhaps most importantly, modification possibilities within phraseological arguments are far richer than the four symbols `atr`, `natr`, `ratr` and `batr` could represent. One case in point is the idiom already mentioned in §1, namely, *witać kogoś z otwartymi ramionami* 'welcome somebody with open arms'. The best representation of the idiomatic argument realisation *z otwartymi ramionami* 'with open arms' is either `fixed('z otwartymi ramionami')` or `preplexnp(z,inst,pl,'ramię',atr)` or perhaps `preplexnp(z,inst,pl,'ramię',ratr)`. The first of these does not allow for any modification, so it does not cover *z szeroko otwartymi ramionami* 'with wide open arms', etc. The second mentions the possibility of modifiers of *ramionami* (which is the instrumental plural form of the noun RAMIĘ 'arm'), but does not constrain this possibility to (a class of) agreeing adjectives, so it would also cover the non-phraseological *z otwartymi ramionami Tomka* 'with Tomek's open arms', lit. 'with open

[2]The schema is split into two lines solely for typographic reasons.

arms Tomek.GEN'. Also, it makes such modification optional, while *witać kogoś z ramionami* 'welcome somebody with arms' is at best non-phraseological. Finally, the third possibility makes modification obligatory, but the current meaning of `ratr` is (for good reasons) constrained to possessive modifiers, so it again does not cover the case at hand, where adjectival modification is present.

2 Extended phraseological valence

One more objection against the current subformalism for phraseological arguments, apart from those adduced in the preceding subsection, is that it contains some *ad hoc* notation, whose meaning is not transparent. The best examples of this are `ratr` (a possessive modifier, not just any modifier) and `batr` (the modifier is a form of SWÓJ 'self's' or WŁASNY 'own'). In contrast, we propose a formalism which is not only more expressive, so as to deal with the limitations mentioned in §1.3, but also more transparent. As we will see below, the price to pay for this more expressive and principled formalism is that some argument specifications become more complex.

2.1 Categories of phraseological arguments

The first proposed generalisation is to replace category-specific symbols `lexnp` and `preplexnp` with the single `lex`, whose first parameter indicates the category of the phraseological argument. For example, the `lexnp(str,sg,'krew',atr)` specification given above could be replaced by `lex(np(str),sg,'krew',atr)`, and `preplexnp(w,loc,pl,'żyła',ratr)` – by `lex(prepnp(w,loc),pl,'żyła',ratr)`. Note that the first parameter of `lex` expresses more than just the grammatical category of the argument – it is the same specification of the morphosyntactic realisation – here, `np(str)` and `prepnp(w,loc)` – as used for non-phraseological arguments. Any (non-lexical, i.e., not `lex`, etc.) morphosyntactic specification used in Walenty could be used here, including also adjectival, adverbial and infinitival.

For example, for *mieć przechlapane* 'be in the doghouse, be in deep shit' mentioned above, where the adjective PRZECHLAPANY must occur in the singular neuter accusative and may be modified by an intensifying adverb (*mieć kompletnie przechlapane* lit. 'have (it) completely screwed'), the appropriate argument realisation could be described as: `lex(adjp(acc),n,sg,'przechlapany',atr)`. Similarly, the adverb *ledwo* 'barely' combining with forms of DYSZEĆ 'pant' could be described as `lex(advp(misc),'ledwo',natr)` (recycling the existing morphosyntactic specification `advp(misc)` for true adverbial phrases), and the infinitival form of SPAĆ 'sleep' co-occurring with KŁAŚĆ SIĘ 'lie down' – as `lex(infp(imperf),'spać',natr)` (again, reusing the standard notation for imperfective infinitival phrases, `infp(imperf)`).

2.2 Modification patterns

The most profound generalisation concerns, however, the specification of modification patterns within idiomatic arguments. We propose to retain three basic indicators, namely, `natr` (no modification possible), `atr` (modification possible) and `ratr` (modification required), but – in the case of the last two – additional information must be given specifying the kind of modification that is allowed or required. Additionally, `atr1` and `ratr1` are envisaged as variants of `atr` and `ratr` with the additional constraint that at most one such modifier may be present.[3]

For example, instead of `preplexnp(z,inst,pl,'ramię',ratr)` for *z otwartymi ramionami* 'with open arms', the following argument specification could be given, explicitly mentioning that the only possible modifier of *ramionami* 'arms' is an adjectival phrase (and not, say, a genitive modifier):[4]

```
{lex(prepnp(z,inst),pl,'ramię',ratr({adjp(agr)}))}
```

Note that morphosyntactic specifications of possible or required modifiers are enclosed in curly brackets, just as in case of direct arguments of verbs, and for the same reason: sometimes multiple morphosyntactic realisations are possible and may be coordinated, which indicates that they occupy the same syntactic position. An example of this is the expression *komuś cierpnie skóra na myśl o czymś* 'something makes

[3]In case of `ratr`, the obligatoriness of modifier together with this constraint mean that exactly one modifier must occur.

[4]The symbol `agr` indicates agreeing case here.

somebody's flesh creep', lit. 'somebody.DAT creeps skin.NOM on (the) thought.ACC about something.LOC'. The argument *na myśl o czymś* 'on (the) thought of something' may be realised in at least three ways: as a prepositional phrase as here (`prepnp(o,loc)`), as a finite clause introduced by the complementiser ŻE 'that' (`cp(że)`; e.g., *komuś cierpnie skóra na myśl, że (to się stało)* lit. 'somebody.DAT creeps skin.NOM on (the) thought.ACC that (this happened.REFL)'), or as a so-called correlative phrase which shares features of the first two realisations, e.g., *na myśl o tym, że (to się stało)* lit. 'on (the) thought about this.LOC that (this happened.REFL)' (`prepncp(o,loc,że)`). Such a disjunctively specified modification possibility may be expressed as follows (with the line broken for typographic reasons and indented for readability):

```
{lex(prepnp(na,acc),sg,'myśl',
      ratr({prepnp(o,loc);cp(że);prepncp(o,loc,że)}))}
```

This specification is still incomplete: the noun *myśl* may also be modified by an adjectival form, e.g., the adjectival pronoun *tę*, as in *skóra mi cierpnie na tę myśl* 'this thought makes my flesh creep', lit. 'skin.NOM me.DAT creeps on this.ACC thought.ACC'. This means that `adjp(agr)` must be added as a possible modifier type. But the status of this modifier type is different than the three modifier types given above: no two of these three phrases can co-occur unless they are coordinated, but any of them can co-occur (and cannot be coordinated) with `adjp(agr)`, e.g., *skóra mi cierpnie na samą myśl o tym* 'the sheer thought makes my flesh creep', lit. 'skin.NOM me.DAT creeps on sheer.ACC thought.ACC about this.LOC'. Hence, the two kinds of modification possibilities are analogous to two different arguments (here, actually, dependents) of a predicate occupying different syntactic positions, and the same notation could be used to specify them, with the + symbol:

```
{lex(prepnp(na,acc),sg,'myśl',
      ratr({prepnp(o,loc);cp(że);prepncp(o,loc,że)} + {adjp(agr)}))}
```

Such argument specifications involving `lex` may get even more complex due to the fact that `lex` may occur inside modification specifications of another `lex`, as in the following description of arguments such as *z otwartymi ramionami* 'with open arms', more accurate than the one given at the beginning of this subsection:

```
{lex(prepnp(z,inst),pl,'ramię',
      ratr({lex(adjp(agr),agr,agr,'otwarty',natr)}))}
```

Note that `lex(adjp(agr),agr,agr,'otwarty',natr)` replaces `adjp(agr)` within `ratr` and it specifies that not just any agreeing adjective phrase may modify the nominal form *rękami* 'arms', but only the simple adjective phrase consisting of an agreeing form of OTWARTY 'open' does.[5]

As discussed above, this is still not a complete description of the range of possibilities here, as the adjective *otwartymi* 'open' may itself be modified (contrary to the `natr` specification above), namely, by the adverb *szeroko* 'wide'. A closer approximation is given below:[6]

```
{lex(prepnp(z,inst),pl,'ramię',
      ratr({lex(adjp(agr),agr,agr,'otwarty',
                  atr({lex(advp(misc),'szeroko',natr)}))}))}
```

Note that this extension, with the possibility of `lex` recursion (of the centre-embedding type; Chomsky 1959), makes the language of schema specifications properly context-free.

2.3 Complex prepositions and fixed arguments

As noted in §1.3 above, the notation `comprep(...)` (e.g., `comprepnp(z powodu)`) is not sufficient to model various combinatory properties of complex prepositions: some of them (e.g., *z powodu* 'because of') may combine with a genitive NP or an agreeing adjective phrase, others (e.g., *w trakcie* 'during') may only co-occur with an NP, etc. We propose to reuse the `lex` notation to describe complex prepositions in a more satisfactory manner. For example, one of valence schemata of UMARTWIAĆ

[5]Recall that if `adjp(...)` is the first parameter of `lex`, the next two indicate gender and number, hence the two `agr`s after `adjp(agr)`.

[6]Sporadic examples of *z bardzo szeroko otwartymi ramionami* 'with arms very wide open' (note the additional *bardzo* 'very') may be found on the internet, but we draw the line here and do not model such occurrences.

SIĘ 'mortify oneself', which specifies such a `comprepnp(z powodu)` argument, could specify it the following way instead (with '_' indicating any number here):

```
{lex(prepnp(z,gen),_,'powód',ratr({np(gen);ncp(gen,że)}+{adjp(agr)}))}
```

In contrast, the requirement of *w trakcie* (where the noun must be in the singular and adjectival modification is not possible) could be spelled out this way:

```
{lex(prepnp(w,inst),sg,'trakt',ratr({np(gen);ncp(gen,że)}))}
```

As far as we can see, all complex prepositions could be described this way. On the other hand, there are cases of `fixed` arguments which could not be so described simply because they contain forms which cannot be specified with a reference to a lemma and morphosyntactic categories such as case or number. One example is the argument of the form `fixed('dęba')`, with the form *dęba* 'oak.GEN' of the noun DĄB 'oak', which co-occurs with forms STANĄĆ 'stand' in the idiomatic expression *stanąć dęba* 'rear' (of a horse), lit. 'stand oak'. However, since the form *dęba* is not used in contemporary Polish (the contemporary genitive of DĄB is *dębu*), this idiomatic argument cannot be expressed as `lex(np(gen),sg,'dąb',natr)`, as then parsers would try to analyse the non-phraseological (at best) sequence *stanąć dębu* as idiomatic. Instead, we propose to extend the `fixed` notation and add a parameter describing the general morphosyntax of such an argument, e.g., `fixed(np(gen),'dęba')`.

However, such `fixed` arguments with forms not attested in contemporary Polish are extremely rare and we envisage that almost all other specifications currently involving `fixed` can be translated into perhaps more precise specifications involving `lex`. For example, `fixed('na kwaśne jabłko')`, used in *zbić na kwaśne jabłko* 'beat into a pulp', literally meaning 'into sour apple', may be specified as follows:

```
{lex(prepnp(na,acc),sg,'jabłko',
     ratr({lex(adjp(agr),agr,agr,'kwaśny',natr)}))}
```

2.4 Syntactic sugar

There are two types of syntactic sugar that we would like to propose together with the above extensions. First of all, while it seems that the `comprepnp` notation for complex prepositions should be replaced by `lex`, we propose to leave such `comprepnp` specifications in the dictionary proper and define them in terms of `lex` specifications separately. The reason for this is that once a complex preposition occurs in the specification of a valence schema, it has the tendency to occur in many schemata; for example, `comprepnp(z powodu)` occurs in 126 schemata in the March 2014 version of Walenty. Replacing all these occurrences with the considerably more complex `lex` specification given above would diminish the readability of the dictionary. Instead, `comprepnp('z powodu')` (perhaps with inverted commas, to increase notational consistency) should be left in particular schemata and it should be defined in terms of `lex` once for the whole dictionary.[7]

The other kind of abbreviatory notation is best illustrated with idiomatic arguments which have so far required the `batr` modification indicator. Recall that `batr` means that a given noun may be modified by forms of either of the two adjectives meaning 'self's, own', i.e., forms of SWÓJ and WŁASNY. One example is the verb SPRÓBOWAĆ 'try', which may combine with the expression *swoich/własnych sił* 'one's power' rendering *spróbować swoich/własnych sił w czymś* 'try one's hand at sth', lit. 'try one's powers in something'. Given the notation introduced so far, this argument would have to be specified as follows:

```
{lex(np(gen),pl,'siła',ratr({lex(adjp(agr),agr,agr,'własny',natr)} +
                             {lex(adjp(agr),agr,agr,'swój',natr)}))}
```

This is not only hardly readable, but also misses the generalisation that the two possible modifiers are just the same kinds of adjectival phrases differing only in the lexical realisation of the adjective meaning 'self's, own'. We propose abbreviating such specifications as follows, with the use of `OR`:

```
{lex(np(gen),pl,'siła',
     ratr({lex(adjp(agr),agr,agr,OR('własny','swój'),natr)}))}
```

[7]This move would be analogous to specifying externally morphosyntactic realisations of semantically defined arguments such as `xp(locat)` or `xp(temp)` (see Przepiórkowski et al. 2014 for details).

While we could have reintroduced the `batr` notation to make this even more readable, this symbol is not used in Walenty uniformly, so it would make sense to replace it with more explicit notation involving `lex`. In particular, some argument specifications mentioning `batr` actually allow only for forms of WŁASNY, not SWÓJ. This is, e.g., the case with DORĘCZYĆ 'hand (over)', as in *doręczyć do rąk własnych* (but not *doręczyć do rąk swoich*) 'deliver as hand delivery', lit. 'hand to own hands', where the specification of the relevant argument in terms of `lex` explicitly mentions only one of these two adjectives:

```
{lex(prepnp(do,gen),pl,'ręka',
     ratr({lex(adjp(agr),agr,agr,'własny',natr)}))}
```

Note finally that this shorthand notation is useful not just in cases involving `batr` in the old formalism. One case in point is the expression *coś strzeliło komuś do głowy* 'something came over somebody', lit. 'something.NOM shot sombody.DAT to head.GEN', where the form of GŁOWA 'head' may be replaced by analogous forms of other nouns with the same meaning, including ŁEB and ŁEPETYNA, as specified below:[8]

```
{lex(prepnp(do,gen),sg,XOR('głowa','łeb','łepetyna'),atr({adjp(agr)}))}
```

3 Case study

In the current (as of the end of April 2014) version of Walenty, there are 7 complex prepositions used 691 times (in the schemata of 367 different verbs), 17 `fixed` phrases used 82 times (36 verbs), 177 `lexnp` phrases used 686 times (393 verbs) and 238 `preplexnp` phrases used 1133 times (496 verbs). The last two contain 1182 `natr` parameters, 217 `ratr` parameters, 40 `batr` parameters and 406 `atr` parameters. Summing up, there are 439 different lexicalisations used in 2567 schemata of 659 verbs. This means that the representation of idiomatic schemata is already non-negligible, and it is bound to increase, as more emphasis is put on such schemata in the current development of Walenty. Hence, the proposed changes – if adopted – will involve substantial interference into an existing resource, and may have a potentially adverse impact on the development of the lexicon, if the formalism proves to be too difficult for lexicographers. This section describes an experiment investigating this issue.

We selected 84 schemata of 36 verbs and asked two main lexicographers involved in the development of Walenty to rewrite these schemata using the proposed formalism. The schemata include 38 `fixed` arguments, 10 `comprepnp` arguments, 17 `lexnp` arguments and 28 `preplexnp` arguments. The last two contain 22 `natr` parameters, 6 `ratr` parameters, 4 `batr` parameters and 8 `atr` parameters. The schemata were selected manually, taking into account their frequency, diversity of types of lexicalisations and their parameters, as well as the expected difficulty of rewriting them. This is the reason for the over-representation of `fixed` phrases, which need to be completely reanalysed. We chose multiple schemata for the same verb, to give lexicographers the possibility to join them into a single schemata, given the more expressive new formalism. In particular, all 12 lexicalised schemata for the verb STAĆ 'stand' were selected for the experiment.

The two lexicographers worked on the textual format of the dictionary (cf. `http://zil.ipipan.waw.pl/Walenty`) without any support from a tool verifying the syntax of the schemata, etc. Correspondingly, when comparing their results, we ignored purely syntactic errors, including differences in bracketing etc., as such errors can be prevented by such a dedicated tool.

After ignoring such trivial differences, 34 of 84 schemata were found to be encoded differently by the two lexicographers. The differences included 3 cases of a wrong lemma, 5 cases of different values of grammatical categories of case, number, etc., and 7 differences concerning the introduction of new non-lexicalised arguments or merging schemata on the basis of the coordination criterion mentioned in §1.1. These differences are not directly connected with the proposed changes of the formalism for lexicalisations. Moreover, 9 differences concerned using `(r)atr` instead of `(r)atr1` (cf. §2.2) where a single realisation of a modifier is possible, as in the following (correct) argument specification for PRZEMARZNĄĆ 'freeze' surfacing in *przemarznąć do szpiku kości* 'freeze to the bone', lit. 'freeze to (the) marrow (of) bone(s)':

[8]This argument specification uses `XOR` instead of `OR` as only one of the lexemes meaning 'head' may be used at a time, unlike in the previous case, where forms of both SWÓJ and WŁASNY could be used simultaneously: *spróbować swoich własnych sił w czymś* lit. 'try one's own forces in something'.

```
{lex(prepnp(do,gen),sg,'szpik',ratr1({lex(np(gen),pl,'kość',natr)}))}
```

Since *kości* must appear exactly once, `ratr1` instead of `ratr` should be used here. Obviously, guidelines for lexicographers should emphasise this point.

Finally, 17 differences concerned core aspects of the new formalism, such as different modification patters (5), the lack of the morphosyntactic type for `fixed` (3) and an incorrect specification of the morphosyntactic type of `lex`, e.g., lack of aspect of `infp` (2). We judged 6 of them as considerably difficult cases of `fixed` lexicalisations, rewriting of which was not at all obvious. One such difficulty concerned an idiomatic use of WYJŚĆ 'exit' as in *ktoś wyszedł za kogoś za mąż* 'somebody married somebody else' (of a woman marrying a man, not the other way round), lit. 'somebody.NOM exited PREP[9] somebody.ACC PREP husband'. The problem lies in the *za mąż* 'PREP husband' part, where *mąż* could be analysed as the regular nominative, but then it would be unexpected that the preposition *za* occurs with a nominative noun (it normally combines with the accusative and the instrumental), or as an idiosyncratic accusative form only occurring in this idiom, similarly to *dęba* mentioned above occurring in *stanąć dęba* 'rear' – in this case the exceptional use of `fixed` would be justified, even though the use of `fixed` was explicitly discouraged in this experiment. The two specifications of the argument *za mąż* given by the two lexicographers are cited below[10].

```
{fixed(prepnp(za,acc),'za mąż')}
{lex(prepnp(za,nom),sg,'mąż',natr)}
```

In summary, we feel that the experiment showed that the new formalism is relatively clear and can be learnt by lexicographers, given some training. Support provided by a dedicated lexicographic tool should reduce the number of errors, especially syntactic inconsistencies. On the other hand, the experiment confirmed that some of the most difficult lexicalisations are those currently marked as `fixed`, and they clearly require special attention.

4 Discussion and conclusion

Many valence dictionaries mark some valence schemata as idiomatic – this is true, e.g., of the VALBU valence dictionary for German developed at the Institut für Deutsche Sprache (Schumacher et al. 2004; `http://hypermedia.ids-mannheim.de/evalbu/`), of the VALLEX dictionary of Czech developed at the Charles University in Prague (Lopatková et al. 2006; `http://ufal.mff.cuni.cz/vallex/`), as well as some previous valence dictionaries of Polish, including Polański 1980–1992 and the dictionary that was used to bootstrap the first version of Walenty, i.e., Świdziński 1998. However, we are not aware of another valence dictionary that would explicitly describe lexicalised arguments at the same level of detail as the version of Walenty presented in Przepiórkowski et al. 2014. Regardless of this level of detail, though, the formalism employed in that version suffers from a number of problems discussed in §1.3, limiting its ability to describe phraseological constructions precisely.

In this paper, we propose a far-reaching extension of the formalism of Walenty, making it possible to describe the syntactic structure of a lexicalised argument to any necessary depth. As noted in §2.2, the proposed extension makes the description language properly context-free, but this does not seem to be a problem for parsers employing the valence dictionary. On the contrary, as the parsers of Polish become more sophisticated and are developed with full semantic parsing in view, they need precise description of valence schemata that makes it possible to reliably distinguish idiomatic arguments from non-idiomatic compositional constructions.

The need for such deeper description of phraseological arguments in valence dictionaries has occasionally been expressed in the literature, e.g., by Žabokrtský (2005, 65–66, fn. 20), who notes that "[i]n case of multiword parts of phrasemes, the tree (and not only the sequence of forms) representing this part should be ideally captured in the lexicon...". This makes us hope that the current proposal will prove interesting also for the developers of valence lexica for languages other than Polish.

---

[9] The preposition ZA has a number of different uses and may be translated as 'behind', 'for', 'per', 'by', 'as', etc.

[10] Intuitively, the first representation seems appropriate to us, but we see no strong arguments supporting this intuition.

References

Noam Chomsky. 1959. On certain formal properties of grammars. *Information and Control* 2, 137–167.

Idan Landau. 2013. *Control in Generative Grammar: A Research Companion*. Cambridge: Cambridge University Press.

Markéta Lopatková, Zdeněk Žabokrtský, and Karolína Skwarska. 2006. Valency Lexicon of Czech Verbs: Alternation-Based Model. In *Proceedings of the Fifth International Conference on Language Resources and Evaluation, LREC 2006*, pages 1728–1733, ELRA, Genoa.

Agnieszka Patejuk and Adam Przepiórkowski. 2012. Towards an LFG parser for Polish: An exercise in parasitic grammar development. In *Proceedings of the Eighth International Conference on Language Resources and Evaluation, LREC 2012*, pages 3849–3852, ELRA, Istanbul, Turkey.

Kazimierz Polański (ed.). 1980–1992. *Słownik syntaktyczno-generatywny czasowników polskich*. Wrocław / Cracow: Zakład Narodowy im. Ossolińskich / Instytut Języka Polskiego PAN.

Adam Przepiórkowski, Elżbieta Hajnicz, Agnieszka Patejuk, Marcin Woliński, Filip Skwarski, and Marek Świdziński. 2014. Walenty: Towards a comprehensive valence dictionary of Polish. In Nicoletta Calzolari, Khalid Choukri, Thierry Declerck, Hrafn Loftsson, Bente Maegaard, Joseph Mariani, Asuncion Moreno, Jan Odijk and Stelios Piperidis (eds.), *Proceedings of the Ninth International Conference on Language Resources and Evaluation, LREC 2014*, pages 2785–2792, ELRA, Reykjavík, Iceland.

Helmut Schumacher, Jacqueline Kubczak, Renate Schmidt, and Vera de Ruiter. 2004. *VALBU – Valenzwörterbuch deutscher Verben*, volume 31 of *Studien zur deutschen Sprache. Forschungen des Instituts für Deutsche Sprache*. Tübingen: Narr.

Marek Świdziński. 1998. Syntactic Dictionary of Polish Verbs. Version 3a, unpublished manuscript, University of Warsaw.

Marcin Woliński. 2004. *Komputerowa weryfikacja gramatyki Świdzińskiego*. Ph.D. dissertation, Institute of Computer Science, Polish Academy of Sciences, Warsaw.

Zdeněk Žabokrtský. 2005. *Valency Lexicon of Czech Verbs*. Ph.D. dissertation, Charles University, Prague.

The fuzzy boundaries of operator verb and support verb constructions with *dar* "give" and *ter* "have" in Brazilian Portuguese

Amanda Rassi[1,2,3], **Cristina Santos-Turati**[1,2,3], **Jorge Baptista**[2,3], **Nuno Mamede**[3], **Oto Vale**[1]
{aprassi,mcturati,jbaptis}@ualg.pt, nuno.mamede@inesc-id.pt, otovale@ufscar.br
[1]UFSCar, Rodovia Washington Luís, km 235 - SP-310 São Carlos-SP, Brazil
[2]UAlg/CECL, Campus de Gambelas, 8005-139 Faro, Portugal
[3]INESC-ID Lisboa/L2F, Rua Alves Redol, n.º 9, 1000-029 Lisboa, Portugal

Abstract

This paper describes the fuzzy boundaries between support verb constructions (SVC) with *ter* "have" and *dar* "give" and causative operator verb (VopC) constructions involving these same verbs, in Brazilian Portuguese (BP), which form a complex set of relations: (i) both verbs are the support verb of the same noun (SVC); (ii) *dar* is the standard (active-like) SVC while *ter* is a converse (passive-like) SVC; and (iii) *dar* is a VopC, operating on a *ter* SVC. In this paper we have systematically studied these complex relations involving SVC and VopC for BP, which constitute a challenge to Natural Language Processing (NLP) systems, and have been often ignored in related work. The paper proposes a lexically-based strategy to implement SVC in a fully-fledged, rule-based parsing system, yielding an adequate semantic structure of the events (predicates) denoted by predicative nouns in SVC.

1 Introduction: basic concepts and a little history

The notion of support verb has been in use for a long time, under many different theoretical perspectives and various terminologies. In this paper, we adopt the Zellig S. Harris's (1991) transformational operator grammar framework. As early as 1964, Harris (1964, p.216-7) proposed the concept and named this particular type of construction as "U operator" nominalizations, linking sentences such as *He studies eclipes = He makes studies of eclipses*. It was, however, M. Gross (1981) who first provided the definition of support verb we will rely upon here. The support verb *make* (in the example above) can be seen as a sort of an auxiliary of the predicative noun *studies*, in charge of carrying the grammatical values of tense and person-number agreement that the noun is morphologically unable to express. In many cases, support verbs are practically devoid of meaning. For lack of space, we cannot detail further the properties of SVC, and only the briefest outline is provided here; a good overview can be found in (Gross, 1996; Gross, 1998; Lamiroy, 1998).

One of the most important theoretical contribution of the notion of support verb came from the fact that it provides a natural framework to adequately include in the kernel sentences of the language the large number of 'abstract' nouns, which do not have neither a verbal nor an adjectival counterpart; that is, they are *isolated* or *autonomous* nouns, lacking any nominalizations (in a synchronic perspective, at least). This phenomenon is particularly evident in Romance languages (French, Italian, Portuguese, Romanian and Spanish): FR: *Jean a fait grève* "Jean did strike"; IT: *Giovanni ha fatto sciopero "id."*; PT: *O João fez greve "id."*; RU: *Ioan a făcut grevă "id."*; SP: *Joan hizo huelga "id."*; cp. EN: **John did strike*, *John was on strike*).

Finally, nominal constructions are unlike any other predicative part-of-speech by the fact that predicative nouns can present more than one construction with different support verbs, while still expressing the same semantic predicate. Hence, for example, *greve* "strike" can have a SVC with both *fazer* "to make" (as above) and *estar em* "to be in": *O João está em greve* "João is on strike" (Ranchhod, 1990). Each SVC has its own specific properties, *e.g.* only SVC with *fazer* can undergo passive, while the general predicate remains the same.

Proceedings of the Workshop on Lexical and Grammatical Resources for Language Processing, pages 92–101, Coling 2014, Dublin, Ireland, August 24 2014.

In this paper, we also consider the concept of *operator verb* (*VopC*), introduced in the same paper (Gross, 1981, p. 23-39); two relatively clear situations were distinguished:

- a *causative operator verb* (*VopC*), which adds a new element to an elementary sentence; this element has an easily identifiable meaning: CAUSE; distributionally, this element suffers very loose constraints (and we define this as a *distributionally non constraint* position (*Nnr*)); if the base sentence under the operator is a support verb construction 1, the *VopC* may "absorb" the support verb and it may also introduce some formal changes in that sentence 1;

(1) *Isso* dá # *Max* tem (*fome* + *medo* + *sede*). [1] "This gives # Max has (hungry + fear + thirst)."

(2) *Isso* dá (*fome* + *medo* + *sede*) *em Max*. "This gives Max (hungry + fear + thirst)."

In (2), the support verb *ter* is absorbed under the operator *dar* and its subject becomes a dative, indirect complement, though the semantic roles of subject of *dar* (CAUSE) and of the subject of the predicative noun (EXPERIENCER), after this restructuring, remain the same.

- a *linking operator-verb* (*VopL*), which hardly modifies the meaning of the underlying sentence; it also adds an argument to the base sentence 1, but this is not a new one since it is bounded linked to a noun complement of the base sentence 1 (Ranchhod, 1990).

(3) *Max* tem # *Ana* está sob *o controle do Max*. "Max has # Ana is under Max's control."

(4) = Max_i tem *Ana sob o* (seu_i + **meu* + **teu*) *controle*. "Max_i has Ana under (his_i + *my + *your) control."

This paper reports an ongoing research to systematically classify the predicative nouns built with the support verbs *dar* and *ter* in Brazilian Portuguese (Rassi and Vale, 2013; Santos-Turati, 2012). Similar work has already been developed for the European variety (Vaza, 1988; Ranchhod, 1990; Baptista, 1997; Baptista, 2005). For many languages, including Portuguese, the studies on support verb constructions and causative constructions use a lexical approach, aiming at building dictionaries or lists of predicative nouns or at identifying those constructions (semi)automatically, *e.g.* for Portuguese (Hendrickx et al., 2010; Duran et al., 2011), for English (Grefenstette and Teufel, 1995), for German (Hanks et al., 2006; Storrer, 2007) and many other languages. As far as we could ascertain, no implementation of these SVC constructions has been made yet in NLP systems, particularly in parsers. Most systems considering these constructions just treat them as multiword expressions, ignoring their internal syntactic structure.

In this paper, we will show the complex set of relations involved in these SVC, where these verbs can function not only as support but also as operator verbs, thus rendering their description remarkably complex, particularly in view of Natural Language Processing. We aim at capturing the syntactic dependencies involved in these expressions, not as multiword, fixed strings, but as analyzable syntactic structures.

The paper is structured as follows: Next, Section 2 presents the current state of the collection and classification if these SVC in Brazilian Portuguese; Section 3 illustrates the syntactic-semantic relations between different constructions of *ter* and *dar*; Section 4 proposes a strategy for implementing the data in a rule-based parsing system; and, finally, Section 5 presents some concluding remarks and perspectives on future work.

2 Support verb constructions with *ter* "have" and *dar* "give"

The predicative nouns in this paper select the support verbs *dar* "give" and *ter* "have", and were retrieved from previous lists of predicative nouns in European Portuguese (Vaza, 1988; Baptista, 1997) and from the PLN.BR Full corpus (Bruckschein et al., 2008). This corpus contains 103,080 texts, with 29 million tokens, consisting of news pieces from *Folha de São Paulo*, a Brazilian newspaper (from 1994 to 2005). All these constructions were validated in real data, and in some cases also ressourcing to the web.

[1] In the examples, elements between brackets and separated by the '+' sign can all appear in that given syntactic slot. The symbol '#' delimits clauses, while the '*' mark signals the sentence as unacceptable. Correferent elements are linked by correference indexes $_i$. For clarity, all support verbs will be shown without italics in the examples. An approximate translation of Portuguese examples is provided, but its acceptability is irrelevant for the paper.

2.1 Nominal predicates with support verb *ter* "have"

We adopted several criteria that allowed us to constitute lexical-syntactic, relatively homogeneous, classes. These criteria were inspired in those taken from previous classifications, developed in the Lexicon-grammar framework of Maurice Gross (1975; 1988; 1996), for both Portuguese and other languages. The main classification criteria can be summarized as follows: (i) the number of arguments, considering constructions with a subject and one or two essential complements as arguments; (ii) the possibility of a noun admitting a sentential construction (in subject or complement position); (iii) the distributional nature of the arguments: if they are obligatorily human or allow for non-human nouns; (iv) the property of *symmetry* [2] between the arguments.

Following these criteria, we have so far classified around 1,000 nominal constructions from a list with 3,000 candidates of predicative nouns censed in the corpus (Santos-Turati, 2012). The already classified nominal predicates that select the support verb *ter* "have" in Brazilian Portuguese were divided into 9 classes (Table 1) [3].

Class	Structure	Example/Gloss	Count
TH1	*Nhum*$_0$ *ter Npred*	*Ana* tem *uma beleza impressionante* "Ana has an amazing beauty"	465
TNH1	*N-hum*$_0$ *ter Npred*	*A tinta* tem *um tom escuro* "The paint has a dark tone"	138
TR1	*N*$\pm$*hum*$_0$ *ter Npred*	*(Ana + a música)* tem *um ritmo contagiante* "(Ana + the music) has a contagious rhythm"	139
TH2	*Nhum*$_0$ *ter Npred Prep Nhum*$_1$	*Ana* tem *respeito por Max* "Ana has respect for Max"	111
TNH2	*N-hum*$_0$ *ter Npred Prep Nhum*$_1$	*O bombom* tem *gosto de avelã* "The bonbon has taste like hazelnut"	6
TR2	*N*$\pm$*hum*$_0$ *ter Npred Prep N-hum*$_1$	*(O carro + a cidade)* tem *um alto consumo de água* "(The car + the city) has a high consumption of water"	22
TS2	*Nhum*$_0$ *ter Npred Prep Nhum*$_1$ (Simetry)	*O patrão* tem *um acordo com o empregado* "The boss has an agreement with the employee"	38
TQF1	*QueF*$_0$ *ter Npred Prep N*$_1$	*Esse fato* tem *uma grande importância para Ana* "This fact has a great importance for Ana"	6
TQF2	*N*$_0$ *ter Npred Prep QueF*$_1$	*Ana* tem *medo de dirigir na estrada* "Ana has fear to drive on the road"	80
TOTAL			1,005

Table 1: SVC with support verb *ter* (Santos-Turati, 2012)

2.2 Nominal predicates with support verb *dar* "give"

The same criteria were also adopted for SVC with verb *dar* "give" (Rassi and Vale, 2013), though two differences were considered: (i) the constructions with a body-part noun (*Npc*) as argument were distinguished as a special class for their particular properties; and (ii), no symmetric constructions were found. We classified 900 support verb constructions with verb *dar* "give" in Brazilian Portuguese into 11 classes (Table 2).

3 Relations between *ter* "have" and *dar* "give"

First of all, it is necessary to distinguish three different kinds of relations established between verb *dar* and verb *ter* constructions. The first type of relation considers the verbs *dar* "give" and *ter* "have" as synonymous and classified as standard support verb constructions. The verb *dar* can replace the verb *ter* without any changes in the meaning of the sentence or in the selection restrictions of the arguments:

[2] The notion of symmetry in verbal constructions was initially presented by Borillo (1971) for French verbs - *Paul rencontre son frère* "Paul meets his brother" / *Paul et son frère se rencontrent* "Paul and his brother meet". In the case of the Portuguese nominal constructions, symmetry was presented in Ranchhod (1990) and Baptista (2005), who described the nominal predicates with the support verbs *estar com* and *ser de*, respectively.

[3] In Table 1 and Table 2, the left column shows the conventional codes for designating each class; and the second column represents its syntactic structure, indicated as follows: *Nhum* and *N-hum* for human and non-human noun respectively; $N\pm hum$ for both human or non-human noun; *Npc* for body-part noun; the indexes '$_0$' and '$_1$' indicate the subject and the complement position, respectively; *Npred* stand for the predicative noun; *Prep* for preposition; *QueF* for completive.

Class	Structure	Example/Gloss	Count
DH1	*Nhum*$_0$ *dar Npred*	*Ana* deu *uma pirueta* "Ana gave a pirouette"	133
DNH1	*N-hum*$_0$ *dar Npred*	*O balão* deu *um estouro* "The baloon gave a burst"	20
DR1	*N*$\pm$ *hum*$_0$ *dar Npred*	*(Max + O clima)* deu *uma refrescada* "(Max +The weather) gave a refreshed"	51
DH2	*Nhum*$_0$ *dar Npred Prep Nhum*$_1$	*Max* deu *um castigo para a Ana* "Max gave a punishment to Ana"	217
DNH2	*Nhum dar Npred Prep N-hum*$_1$	*Ana* deu *uma cozida nos legumes* "Ana gave a cooked in the vegetables"	137
DPC2	*Nhum*$_0$ *dar Npred Prep Npc*$_1$	*Max* deu *um tapa na cara da Ana* "Max gave a slap in Ana's face"	114
DQF2	*Nhum*$_0$ *dar Npred Prep QueF*$_1$	*Max* deu *um jeito de consertar o carro* "Max gave a way to fix the car"	52
DHR2	*Nhum*$_0$ *dar Npred Prep N*$\pm$ *hum*$_1$	*Ana* deu *destaque ao (Max + problema)* "Ana gave emphasis to (Max + the problem)"	60
DRH2	*N*$\pm$ *hum*$_0$ *dar Npred Prep Nhum*$_1$	*(Ana + O telhado)* deu *proteção ao Max* "(Ana + The roof) gave protection to Max"	32
DR2	*N*$\pm$ *hum*$_0$ *dar Npred Prep N-hum*$_1$	*(Ana+A lei)* deu *embasamento à teoria* "(Ana+The law) gave basis to the theory"	25
D3	*N*$_0$ *dar Npred Prep N*$_1$ *Prep N*$_2$	*Ana* deu *um apelido de macaco ao Max* "Ana gave the nickname monkey to Max"	59
TOTAL			900

Table 2: SVC with support verb *dar* (Rassi and Vale, 2013)

(5) *Ana* (deu + teve) *um* + *um(a)* (*birra* + *chilique* + *pirepaque* + *tremelique* + *troço*).
"Ana (gave + had) (a + an) (tantrum + hissy fit + outburst + shiver + thing)."

The second type of relation concerns the transformation named *Conversion* by G. Gross (1982; 1989), in which the predicative noun is maintained and their arguments change their relative position, without, however, changing their semantic roles. In these constructions, the sentence with AGENT subject is called the *standard* construction, while its equivalent sentence with the reversed argument order is called the *converse* construction. Usually, the support verbs of the standard and the converse construction are different, as it is also the preposition introducing the converse complement:

(6) *Ana deu algum apoio ao Max.* "Ana gave some support to Max."
[Conv.] = *Max* teve *algum apoio da Ana.* "Max had some support from Ana."

The third kind of relation linking the sentences with the verb *ter* and the verb *dar* is the causative operator construction (already mentioned in §1):

(7) *Isso* deu # *Ana* tem *coragem.* "This gave # Ana has courage."
= *Isso* deu *coragem à Ana.* "This gave courage to Ana."

These three types of relations are presented in the table below, with an example and the respective number of constructions in each type. From the intersection between the list of predicative nouns constructed with verb *ter* "have" and those with verb *dar* "give", we found 693 predicative nouns, distributed as shown in Table 3.

dar "give"	*ter* "have"	Example/Gloss	Count
SVCstandard	SVCstandard	*Ana* deu *um chilique* "Ana gave a hissy fit" *Ana* teve *um chilique* "Ana had a hissy fit"	35
SVCstandard	SVCconverse	*O policial* deu *uma multa ao Max* "The officer gave Max a fine" *Max* teve *uma multa* "Max had a fine"	72
VopCausative (VopC)	SVCstandard	*A flor* deu *alergia a Ana* "The flower gave allergy to Ana" *Ana* tem *alergia à flor* "Ana has an allergy"	586

Table 3: Comparative table with syntactic relations

3.1 Verbs *dar* and *ter* in standard SVC

Around 4.8% of the predicative nouns (35 constructions) accept both support verbs *dar* and *ter* in standard constructions, such as:

(8) *A empresa* (dá + tem) *atenção ao cliente.* "The company (gives + has) attention to the client."

(9) *O remédio* (dá + tem) *um efeito positivo no organismo.* "The medicine (gives + has) a positive effect on human body."

(10) *O resultado* (deu + teve) *um impacto significativo para o time.* "The result (gave + had) a significant impact to the team."

In Brazilian Portuguese, around 35 predicative nouns, such as *febre* "fever" and *dengue* "dengue", besides having both *dar* and *ter* as their support verb also allow *dar* as a causative operator on them (examples taken from the web):

[VopC]: *[Sua lição de casa:] água parada* dá *dengue.* "[...] still water gives (= causes) dengue."
[CVS_dar]: *Inclusive, a vizinha também* deu *dengue.* "Inclusive, the neighbour gave (= had) dengue."
[CVS_ter]: *O meu esposo já* teve *dengue.* "My husband already had dengue."

A few nouns (around 10), such as *amor* "love", *confiança* "trust" and *respeito* "respect", besides admitting the two support verbs in their basic construction, also admit *ter* in a converse construction:

(11) *O filho* dá *respeito à mãe.* "The son gives respect to the mother."
= *O filho* tem *respeito pela mãe.* "The son has respect for the mother."
[conv.] = *A mãe* tem *o respeito do filho.* "The mother has respect from her son."

3.2 Verb *dar* as standard SVC and *ter* as converse SVC

Around 10.4% of the predicative nouns (72 constructions) admit the verb *dar* in the standard construction and the verb *ter* in a converse construction, but not *ter* as a standard support. In Brazilian Portuguese, predicative nouns constructed with the support verb *dar* in a standard construction accept other converse verbs beyond the verb *ter* "have", such as *receber* "receive", *ganhar* "gain", *levar* "get" and *tomar* "take"[4].

(12) *Ana* deu *proteção ao Max.* "Ana gave protection to Max."
= *Max* (teve + recebeu) *a proteção da Ana.* "Max (had + received) the protection from Ana."

(13) *Ana* deu *uma ajuda ao Max.* "Ana gave a help to Max."
= *Max* (teve + ganhou) *uma ajuda da Ana.* "Max (had + gained) a help from Ana."

(14) *Ana* deu *uma resposta no Max.* "Ana gave an answer to Max."
= *Max* (teve + levou) *uma resposta da Ana.* "Max (had + got) an answer from Ana."

(15) *O policial* deu *uma multa ao Max.* "The officer gave a fine to Max."
= *Max* (teve + tomou) *uma multa do policial.* "Max (had + took) a fine from the officer."

3.3 Verb *dar* as *VopC* and *ter* as SVC

Around 84.8% (586 predicative nouns) of the elementary constructions with the support verb *ter* "have" also allow the causative operator verb *dar* "give"; some of these nouns constitute relatively homogenous semantic sets, *e.g.* the predicative nouns that express <feeling>, <sensation>, <emotion> or those that indicate <disease> (this semantic classification is just approximative):

[4]For European Portuguese equivalent converse constructions, see Baptista (1997); for a comparison between the two language variants, see Rassi *et al.* (2014).

(16) *Ana* tem *alegria*. "Ana has happiness."
(*Zé* + *A vinda do Zé* + *O fato de Zé ter voltado* + *Isso*) deu *alegria à Ana*.
"(Zé + Zé's coming + The fact of Zé has came + That) gave happiness to Ana."

(17) *Ana* tem *cólica*. "Ana has colic."
(*O chocolate* + *O fato de ter comido chocolate* + *Isso*) deu *cólica na Ana*.
"(The chocolat + The fact of she has eaten chocolat + That) gave a colic in Ana."

These predicative nouns allow a particular (impersonal?) construction with *dar*, in which the argument in subject position is not explicit, so the CAUSE element is also absent, and the sentence has the same overall meaning of the SVC with verb *ter* standard, but with an inchoative aspect; notice that the verb *dar* must be in the 3rd person singular, and it does not agree with the predicative noun:

(18) (Deu + *Deram) (*uma*) (*alegria* + *cólica*) *na Ana*. "Gives/gave (a) (hapiness + colic) in Ana."
= *Ana* teve (*uma*) (*alegria* + *cólica*). "Ana had (a) (hapiness + colic)."

(19) (Deu + ?*Deram) *umas* (*palpitações* + *cólicas*) *na Ana*. "Gives/gave some (palpitations + colics) in Ana."
= *Ana* teve *umas* (*palpitações* + *cólicas*). "Ana had some (palpitations + colics)."

3.4 Formalization into the Lexicon-Grammar

Because of the complex relations and the different syntactic status that the verbs *dar* and *ter* may show, these constructions are essentially determined by the lexicon, *i.e.*, they depend on the specific predicative noun. It is only natural that a lexically-based approach be taken in order to describe this properties, particularly in view of the implementation of such type of expressions in NLP systems. The Lexicon-Grammar framework constitutes such a methodological setting, as it presupposes the extensive and systematical survey and formal representation of the lexicon properties.

In the Lexicon-Grammar, a systematic description of linguistic phenomena is usually presented in the form of binary matrices: the lines contain the lexical entries while the columns represent syntactic-semantic properties of each entry. For example, for each predicative noun, distributional constraints on the arguments are represented; the elementary support verb and the main variants of this verb are encoded; the possibility of accepting conversion and the converse support verbs are explicitly provided; and all these syntactic-semantic informations are specified for each predicative noun. Besides its intrinsic linguistic interest, the main purpose for this formalization requirements is the application of the data in NLP. In the next section, we present a preliminary proposal for the implementation problems of these type of SVC in a rule-based parsing system of Portuguese.

4 Towards the implementation of SVC in a NLP system

Besides its linguistic interest, one of the goals of the formal representation of the lexical properties of predicative nouns and SVC into a Lexicon-Grammar such as described above (§3.4) is to allow for the implementation of these data in NLP systems. In this section an outline of the strategy adopted for its implementation specifically into a rule-based system, namely STRING (Mamede et al., 2012) [5], is presented. This is still an on-going work, so in the next lines we briefly sketch the system's architecture (§4.1.) and then (§4.2.) we present the strategy that we intend to implement for the adequate parsing of SVC with *ter* and *dar*, having in mind the complex structures and relations mentioned in §3.

4.1 STRING architecture

STRING is an NLP chain with a modular structure that executes all the basic processing tasks, namely: tokenization and text segmentation, part-of-speeh tagging, morphosyntactic disambiguation, shallow parsing (chuking) and deep parsing (dependency extraction). The parsing stage is performed by the rule-based parser XIP (Xerox Incremental Parser) (Mokhtar et al., 2002). XIP identifies the elementary

[5] http://string.l2f.inesc-id.pt/

constituents of a sentence, such as noun phrases (NP) or prepositional phrases (PP), and then these are structured by binary dependencies between them, corresponding to the syntactic relations, such as subject (SUBJ), direct complement (CDIR) or modifier (MOD). STRING also extracts Named Entities, performs time expressions identification and normalization, Anaphora Resolution and some Word-Sense disambiguation (WSD).

At the final stages of parsing, the system extracts the text events (or predicates) and their participants (arguments). The system currently extracts the EVENT structure for all full verbs and predicative nouns. In the case of verbs, it associates the events to their participants and circumstances, identifying their corresponding semantic roles (Talhadas, 2014), based on the sentence parse and the information available on the Portuguese full verbs Lexicon-Grammar (Baptista, 2012) [6]. Hence, for a sentence such as (20), the system parser extracts the event structure by way of the following dependencies:

(20) *Max costuma ler o jornal no café às sextas-feiras.* "Max uses to read the newspaper at the caffée on Fridays."

```
EVENT_AGENT(ler,Max)
EVENT_OBJECT(ler,jornal)
EVENT_LOC-PLACE(ler,café)
EVENT_TIME-FREQUENCY(ler,a_as sextas-feiras)
```

4.2 Strategy

In the case of a predicative noun in a SVC, one would want the predicative noun also to be captured as an EVENT, but *not* the support verb, since its role is basically that of an auxiliary of the noun. However, since the support verb conveys several important grammatical information, particularly the standard/converse orientation of the predicate[7], a SUPPORT dependency is first extracted, so in sentences such as in (21) one would get the dependency shown below:

(21) *Max* deu *um beijo na Ana.* "Max gave a kiss in Ana."

```
SUPPORT_STANDARD(beijo,deu)
```

To do so, one needs to provide the system with the information that *dar* is the (basic) standard support verb of the predicative noun *beijo* "kiss". It is also necessary to know that in this construction, the predicative noun is the direct complement (CDIR) of the support verb and that the dative complement can be introduced, in Brazilian Portuguese, by preposition *em* "in/on". The following rules illustrate (in a simplified way[8]) the functioning of the rule-based system:

```
if (CDIR(#1[lemma:dar],#2[lemma:beijo]) & ~SUPPORT(#2,#?))
   SUPPORT[vsup-standard](#1,#2)

if (SUPPORT(#1,?))
   EVENT[OTHER=+](#1).

if (SUPPORT[vsup-standard](#1[lemma:beijo],#2) &
   EVENT[other](#1) & SUBJ(#2,#3))
   EVENT[agent-generic=+](#1,#3).

if (SUPPORT[vsup-standard](#1[lemma:beijo],#2) & EVENT[other](#1) &
   ^MOD(#2,#3) & PREPD(#3,?[lemma:em]) )
   COMPL(#1,#3),
   EVENT[patient=+](#1,#3).
```

[6] This semantic role information is still not available for the predicative nouns, but it is currently being encoded.

[7] The support verb can convey aspectual, modal and even stylistic values, which are encoded in the lexicon and remain available in the system's output, even if not necessarily visible in the EVENT representation.

[8] The rule system should also take into account the distributional constraints on the argument slots, but, for simplicity, we dismissed it in this paper.

```
if (SUPPORT[vsup-standard](#1[lemma:beijo],#2) & EVENT[other](#1) &
   (^MOD[dat](#2,#3) || ^CLITIC(#2,#3[dat]) ) )
   CINDIR[dat=~](#1,#3),
   EVENT[patient=+](#1,#3).
```

The rules read as follows: First, a SUPPORT dependency with the feature _VSUP-STANDARD is extracted when the noun *beijo* "kiss" is the direct complement of the verb *dar* "give" (and no other support verb was extracted yet for that noun); based on this dependency, an EVENT (unary) dependency is extracted for the predicative noun; then, the subject of the standard support verb is assigned the agent semantic role (agent-generic in STRING's terminology); next, the prepositional phrase modifying (MOD) the support verb and introduced by preposition *em* "in" is converted into a complement (COMPL) of the predicative noun and assigned a semantic role of patient; a similar procedure is used for the dative complement, when reduced to a dative pronominal form, but in this case, instead of COMPL the CINDIR (indirect complement) dependency is used. All these rules are automatically produced for each predicative noun, from the information in the Lexicon-Grammar. The corresponding EVENT structure is represented below:

```
SUPPORT_VSUP-STANDARD(beijo,deu)
EVENT_AGENT(beijo,Max)
EVENT_PATIENT(beijo,Ana)
```

For the converse construction 4.2, while the EVENT structure remains the same, the SUPPORT dependency is:

(22) *Ana* ganhou *um beijo do Max.* "Ana got a kiss from Max."

```
SUPPORT_VSUP-CONVERSE(beijo,ganhou)
```

The converse construction entails the "swapping" of the arguments' syntactic function, while keeping their respective semantic roles. The detection of the converse construction triggers a set of rules that also swap the semantic roles associated to the predicative noun's syntactic slots. In the case where the same verb is both the standard and the converse support of a predicative noun, they are both extracted, at first, and then the presence of prepositional complements or the determiner of the noun can be used for disambiguation. This will be part of future work as, for the moment, whenever this happens, the converse construction is discarded. The assigning of semantic roles to the predicative noun's arguments is then made only once, and by general rules, both in the standard and in the converse constructions.

The situation is somewhat similar in the case of a causative-operator verb 4.2:

(23) *Essa notícia* deu *estresse no Max.* "This news gave stress in Max."

In this case, since the Lexicon-Grammar has encoded that the verb *dar* can be an operator on *ter*, and since the predicative noun *estresse* "stress" does not allow for *dar* to be its support, a general rule can apply, extracting the CAUSE relation expressed by the *VopC*, in a similar way as for the SUPPORT dependency. The EVENT structure is thus construed as shown below:

```
VOPC(estresse,deu)
EVENT(estresse,other)
EVENT_EXPERIENCER(estresse,Max)
EVENT_CAUSE(estresse,notícia)
```

However, when the same verb can be both a support and an operator verb, in the absence of tell-tale prepositional complements or other syntactic evidence, the detection of the adequate structure can not be done at this stage. We found only 35 predicative nouns which can be associated to the verb *dar* "give" with both categories, *i.e.* as a support and a *VopC*. It is also possible that both dependencies SUPPORT and CAUSE be extracted in order to disambiguate them at a later stage.

5 Conclusions and future work

In the near future, we intend to use the data encoded in the Lexicon-Grammar of these predicative nouns and build a SVC identification module for STRING. For the moment, the identification of all the syntactic phenomena, constituting as many different parsing cases as possible, is underway, in order to fully automatize the processing of converting the Lexicon-Grammar tables into the STRING, with XIP-compliant rules, in a similar way as it has already been done for the verbs (Baptista, 2012; Travanca, 2013; Talhadas, 2014). After implementing all the data in STRING we also intend to evaluate the system in order to check the extraction of the dependencies involving the support verbs and predicative nouns.

An important task ahead is the systematic comparison of the structures and properties here described against those of European Portuguese. First of all, the set of nouns available in each variant is not exactly the same, even if the concepts are shared; for example, *carona* in BP corresponds to the EP *boleia* "ride"; in other cases, the choice of the nominalization suffixes differ: in BP one uses the term *parada cardíaca*, while its equivalent in EP is *paragem cardíaca* "cardiac arrest". False-friends are also common: in BP, *chamada* "rebuke" is unrelated to EP *chamada* "phone call" (but, in this sense, it is also used in BP); the set of support verbs for each noun are different: as a synonym of *rebuke* we find the pair *dar-levar* (only in BP), while as equivalent to *phone call* the basic support verbs are *fazer-receber* (the same in BP and EP). Naturally, much in both variants is quite similar, though some patterns begin to emerge: the different choice of prepositions for the complement, mostly the alternation between *em* "in" in BP and *a* "to" in EP (both as dative complements); the choice of support verbs, with some being used for these predicative noun exclusively in BP (*ganhar* "gain" and *tomar* "take") or in EP (*pregar* "throw" and *apanhar* "take").

Acknowledgements

The authors would like to acknowledge the financial supports from Capes/PDSE under Processes BEX 12751/13-8 and BEX 6561/13-6 and also national funds through FCT – Fundação para a Ciência e a Tecnologia, under project PEst-OE/EEI/LA0021/2013. We would like to thank the comments of the anonymous reviewers, which helped to improve this paper.

References

Jorge Baptista. 1997. *Sermão, tareia* e *facada*. Uma classificação das construções conversas *dar-levar*. In *Seminários de Linguística*, volume 1, pages 5–37, Faro. Universidade do Algarve.

Jorge Baptista. 2005. *Sintaxe dos predicados nominais com SER DE*. Fundação Calouste Gulbenkian/Fundação para a Ciência e Tecnologia, Lisboa.

Jorge Baptista. 2012. A Lexicon-grammar of European Portuguese Verbs. In Jan Radimsky, editor, *Proceedings of the 31st International Conference on Lexis and Grammar*, volume 31, pages 10–16, Czech Republic, September. Università degli Studi di Salerno and University of South Bohemia in Nové Hrady.

Andrée Borillo. 1971. Remarques sur les verbes symétriques. *Langue Française*, (11):17–31.

Mírian Bruckschein, Fernando Muniz, José Guilherme Camargo Souza, Juliana Thiesen Fuchs, Kleber Infante, Marcelo Muniz, Patrícia Nunes Gonçalvez, Renata Vieira, and Sandra Maria Aluisio. 2008. Anotação linguística em XML do corpus PLN-BR. Série de relatórios do NILC, NILC- ICMC - USP.

Magali Sanches Duran, Carlos Ramisch, Sandra Maria Aluísio, and Aline Villavicencio. 2011. Identifying and analyzing Brazilian Portuguese complex predicates. In *Proceedings of the Workshop on Multiword Expressions: from Parsing and Generation to the Real World*, pages 74–82, Portland, USA.

Gregory Grefenstette and Simone Teufel. 1995. Corpus-based Method for Automatic Identification of Support Verbs for Nominalizations. *CoRR*, cmp-lg/9503010.

Maurice Gross. 1975. *Méthodes en syntaxe*. Hermann, Paris.

Maurice Gross. 1981. Les bases empiriques de la notion de prédicat sémantique. *Langages*, 63(3):7–52.

Gaston Gross. 1982. Un cas des constructions inverses: *donner* et *recevoir*. *Lingvisticae Investigationes*, 2:1–44.

Maurice Gross. 1988. Methods and tactics in the construction of a Lexicon-grammar. In The linguistic Society of Korea, editor, *Linguistics in the Morning Calm 2. Selected papers from SICOL-1986*, pages 177–197, Seoul. Hanshin Publishing Company.

Gaston Gross. 1989. *Les constructions converses du français*. Droz, Genebra.

Maurice Gross. 1996. Lexicon grammar. In K. Brown and J. Miller, editors, *Concise Encyclopedia of Syntactic Theories*, pages 244–259. Pergamon, Cambridge.

Maurice Gross. 1998. La fonction sémantique des verbes supports. In Béatrice Lamiroy, editor, *Travaux de Linguistique*, number 37, pages 25–46.

Patrick Hanks, Anne Urbschat, and Elke Gehweiler. 2006. German light verb constructions in corpora and dictionaries. *International Journal of Lexicography*, 19(4):439–457.

Zellig Harris. 1964. The Elementary Transformations. *Transformations and Discourse Analysis Papers*, (54):211–235.

Zellig Harris. 1991. *A Theory of Language and Information: A Mathematical Approach*. Clarendon Press, New York.

Iris Hendrickx, Amália Mendes, Sílvia Pereira, Anabela Gonçalves, and Inês Duarte. 2010. Complex predicates annotation in a corpus of Portuguese. in: Proceedings of the 4th ACL. In *Proceedings of the 4th ACL Linguistic Annotation Workshop*, pages 100–108, Uppsala, Sweden.

Béatrice Lamiroy. 1998. Le Lexique-grammaire: Essai de synthèse. In Béatrice Lamiroy, editor, *Travaux de Linguistique*, volume 37, pages 7–23.

Nuno Mamede, Jorge Baptista, Vera Cabarrão, and Cláudio Diniz. 2012. STRING: An hybrid statistical and rule-based natural language processing chain for Portuguese. In *International Conference on Computational Processing of Portuguese (Propor 2012)*, volume Demo Session, Coimbra, Portugal, April.

Salah Ait Mokhtar, Jean-Pierre Chanod, and Claude Roux. 2002. Robustness beyond shalowness: Incremental dependency parsing. *Natural Language Engineering*, pages 121–144.

Elisabete Ranchhod. 1990. *Sintaxe dos predicados nominais com Estar*. INIC - Instituto Nacional de Investigação Científica, Lisboa.

Amanda Rassi and Oto Vale. 2013. Predicative Nouns Suffixation associated to the verb *dar* (give) in Brazilian Portuguese. In Jorge Baptista and Mario Monteleone, editors, *Proceedings of the 32nd International Conference on Lexis and Grammar*, volume 32, pages 151–158, Faro, September. UAlg.

Amanda Rassi, Nathalia Perussi, Jorge Baptista, and Oto Vale. 2014. Estudo contrastivo sobre as construções conversas em PB e PE. In Cristina Fargetti, Odair Silva, Clotilde Murakawa, and Anise Ferreira, editors, *Anais do I CINELI - Congresso Internacional Estudos do Léxico e suas Interfaces*, volume 1, page (no prelo), Araraquara-SP, Maio. Universidade Estadual Paulista - UNESP.

Maria Cristina Andrade Santos-Turati. 2012. Descrição da estrutura argumental dos predicados nominais com o verbo-suporte *ter*. In *Seminário do GEL*, number 60, pages 20–21, São Paulo, Brasil. Grupo de Estudos Linguísticos do Estado de São Paulo - GEL.

Angelika Storrer. 2007. Corpus-based investigations on german support verb constructions. In Christiane Fellbaum, editor, *Collocations and Idioms: Linguistic, Lexicographic, and Computational Aspects*, pages 164–188. Continuum Press, London.

Rui Talhadas. 2014. Automatic Semantic Role Labeling for European Portuguese. Master's thesis, Universidade do Algarve, Faro.

Tiago Travanca. 2013. Verb Sense Disambiguation. Master's thesis, Instituto Superior Técnico, Universidade de Lisboa, June.

Aldina Vaza. 1988. Estruturas com nomes predicativos e o verbo-suporte *dar*. Master's thesis, Faculdade de Letras - Universidade de Lisboa.

Collaboratively Constructed Linguistic Resources for Language Variants and their Exploitation in NLP Applications – the case of Tunisian Arabic and the Social Media

Fatiha Sadat
University of Quebec in Montreal
201 President Kennedy, Montreal, QC, Canada
sadat.fatiha@uqam.ca

Fatma Mallek
University of Quebec in Montreal
201 President Kennedy, Montreal, QC, Canada
mallek.fatma@uqam.ca

Rahma Sellami
Sfax University, Sfax, Tunisia
rahma.sellami@fsegs.rnu.tn

Mohamed Mahdi Boudabous
Sfax University, Sfax, Tunisia
mehdiboudabous@gmail.com

Atefeh Farzindar
NLP Technologies Inc.
52 LeRoyer Street W, Montreal, Canada
farzindar@nlptechnologies.ca

Abstract

Modern Standard Arabic (MSA) is the formal language in most Arabic countries. Arabic Dialects (AD) or daily language differs from MSA especially in social media communication. However, most Arabic social media texts have mixed forms and many variations especially between MSA and AD. This paper aims to bridge the gap between MSA and AD by providing a framework for the translation of texts of social media. More precisely, this paper focuses on the Tunisian Dialect of Arabic (TAD) with an application on automatic machine translation for a social media text into MSA and any other target language. Linguistic tools such as a bilingual TAD-MSA lexicon and a set of grammatical mapping rules are collaboratively constructed and exploited in addition to a language model to produce MSA sentences of Tunisian dialectal sentences. This work is a first-step towards collaboratively constructed semantic and lexical resources for Arabic Social Media within the ASMAT (Arabic Social Media Analysis Tools) project.

1 Introduction

The explosive growth of social media has led to a wide range of new challenges for machine translation and language processing. The language used in social media occupies a new space between structured and unstructured media, formal and informal language, and dialect and standard usage. Yet these new platforms have given a digital voice to millions of user on the Internet, giving them the opportunity to communicate on the first truly global stage – the Internet (Colbath, 2012).

Social media poses three major computational challenges, dubbed by Gartner the 3Vs of big data: *volume, velocity, and variety*[1]. Natural Language Processing (NLP) methods, in particular, face further difficulties arising from the short, noisy, and strongly contextualised nature of social media. In order to address the 3Vs of social media, new language technologies have emerged, such as the identification and definition of users' language varieties and the translation to a different language, than the source.

[1] http://en.wikipedia.org/wiki/Big_data

Proceedings of the Workshop on Lexical and Grammatical Resources for Language Processing, pages 102–110,
Coling 2014, Dublin, Ireland, August 24 2014.

Furthermore, language in social media is very rich with linguistic innovations, morphology and lexical changes. People are not only socially connected across the world but also emotionally and linguistically (Sadat, 2013).

The importance of social media stems from the fact that the use of social networks has made everybody a potential author, which means that the language is now closer to the user than to any prescribed norms. Thus, considerable interest has recently been focused on the analysis of social media in order to create or enrich NLP tools and applications. There are, however, still many challenges to be faced depending on the used language and its variants.

This paper deal with Arabic language and its variants for the analysis of social media and the collaborative construction of linguistic tools, such as lexical dictionaries and grammars and their exploitation in NLP applications, such as translation technologies.

Basically, Arabic is considered as morphologically rich and complex language, which presents significant challenges for NLP and its applications. It is the official language in 22 countries spoken by more than 350 million people around the world[2]. Moreover, Arabic language exists in a state of diglossia where the standard form of the language, Modern Standard Arabic (MSA) and the regional dialects (AD) live side-by-side and are closely related (Elfardy and Diab, 2013). Arabic has more than 22 variants, refereed a as dialects; some countries share the same dialects, while many dialects may exist alongside MSA within the same Arab country. Arabic Dialects (AD) or daily language differs from MSA especially in social media communication. However, most Arabic social media texts have mixed forms and many variations especially between MSA and AD.

This paper describes our efforts to create linguistic resources and translation tool for TDA to MSA. First, a bilingual TDA-MSA lexicon and a set of TDA mapping rules for the social media context are collaboratively constructed. Second, these tools are exploited in addition to a language model extracted from MSA corpus, to produce MSA sentences of the Tunisian dialectal sentences of social media. The rule-based translation system can be coupled with a statistical machine translation system from MSA into any language, example French or English to provide a translation from TDA to French or English of original Tunisian dialectal sentences of social media.

This paper is organized as follows. In Section 2, we present some related works to this research. Section 3 discusses the Tunisian Dialect of Arabic (TDA) and its challenges in social media context. In Section 4, we present the collaboratively construct linguistic tools for the social media. Section 5 presents some evaluations of the combined TDA-MSA rule-based translation and disambiguation system. Section 6 concludes this paper and gives some future extensions.

2 Related Work

There have been several works on Arabic NLP. However, most traditional techniques have focused on MSA, since it is understood across a wide spectrum of audience in the Arab world and is widely used in the spoken and written media. Few works relate the processing of dialectal Arabic that is different from processing MSA. First, dialects leverage different subsets of MSA vocabulary, introduce different new vocabulary that are more based on the geographical location and culture, exhibit distinct grammatical rules, and adds new morphologies to the words. The gap between MSA and Arabic dialects has affected morphology, word order, and vocabulary (Kirchhoff and Vergyri, 2004). Almeman and Lee (2013) have shown in their work that only 10% of words (uni-gram) share between MSA and dialects. Second, one of the challenges for Arabic NLP applications is the mixture usage of both AD and MSA within the same text in social media context. Recently, research groups have started focusing on dialects. For instance, Columbia University provides a morphological analyzer (MAGEAD) for Levantine verbs and assumes the input is non-noisy and purely Levantine (Habash and Rambow, 2006b).

Given that DA and MSA do not have much in terms of parallel corpora, rule-based methods to translate DA-to-MSA or other methods to collect word-pair lists have been explored. Abo Bakr et al. (2008) introduced a hybrid approach to translate a sentence from Egyptian Arabic into MSA. This hybrid system consists of a statistical system for tokenizing and tagging, and a rule-based system for the construction of diacritized MSA sentences. Al-Sabbagh and Girju (2010) described an approach of

---

[2] http://en.wikipedia.org/wiki/Geographic_distribution_of_Arabic#Population

mining the web to build a DA-to-MSA lexicon. Salloum and Habash (2012) developed Elissa, a dialectal to standard Arabic tool that employs a rule-based translation approach and relies on morphological analysis, morphological transfer rules and dictionaries in addition to language models to produce MSA paraphrases of dialectal sentences.

Using closely related languages has been shown to improve MT quality when resources are limited. In the context of Arabic dialect translation, Sawaf (2010) built a hybrid MT system that uses both statistical and rule-based approaches for DA-to-English MT. In his approach, DA (but not TDA) is normalized into MSA by performing a combination of character- and morpheme-level mappings. They then translated the normalized source to English using a hybrid MT or alternatively a Statistical MT system.

Very few researches were reported on Tunisian variant of Arabic or any other Maghrebi variant. Hamdi et al. (2013) presented a translation system between MSA TDA verbal forms. Their approach relies on modeling the translation process over the deep morphological representations of roots and patterns, commonly used to model Semitic morphology. The reported results are aat 80% recall in the TDA into MSA and 84% recall in the opposite direction. However, the translation process was highly ambiguous, and a contextual disambiguation process was therefore necessary for such a process to be of practical use. Boudjelbene et al. (2013a, 2013b) described a method for building a bilingual dictionary using explicit knowledge about the relation between TDA and MSA and presented an automatic process for creating Tunisian Dialect corpora. However, their work focused on verbs mainly in order to adapt MAGEAD morphological analyser and generator of arabic dialect to TDA (Hamdi et al., 2013). Also, they developed a tool that generates TDA corpora and enrich semi-automatically the dictionaries they built. Experiments in progress showed that the integration of translated data improves lexical coverage and the perplexity of language models significantly. Their research was very pertinent for TDA but did not consider the mixture form of social media corpora.

Shaalan (2010) presented a rule-based approach for Arabic NLP and developed a transfer-based machine translation system of English noun phrase to Arabic. Their research showed that a rapid development of rule-based systems is feasible, especially in the absence of linguistic resources and the difficulties faced in adapting tools from other languages due to peculiarities an the nature of Arabic language.

In real-life practise, a company named Qordoba[3] launched social media translation service for Arabic in general. However, no demonstration or freely available version was found online. Furthermore, a new Twitter service automatically translates tweets from some Arabic language variants to English. However, this translation tool is not 100% accurate[4].

3 The Tunisian Dialect of Arabic and its Challenges in Social Media

Tunisian, or Tunisian Arabic[5] (TDA) is a Maghrebi dialect of the Arabic language, spoken by some 11 million people in coastal Tunisia. It is usually known by its own speakers as Derja, which means dialect, to distinguish it from Standard Arabic, or as *Tunsi*, which means Tunisian. In the interior of the country it merges, as part of a dialect continuum, into Algerian Arabic and Libyan Arabic.

The morphology, syntax, pronunciation and vocabulary of Tunisian Arabic are quite different from Standard or Classical Arabic. TDA, like other Maghrebi dialects, has a vocabulary mostly Arabic, with significant Berber substrates, and many words and loanwords borrowed from Berber, French, Turkish, Italian and Spanish. Derja is mutually spoken and understood in the Maghreb countries, especially Morocco, Algeria and Tunisia, but hard to understand for middle eastern Arabic speakers. It continues to evolve by integrating new French or English words, notably in technical fields, or by replacing old French and Spanish ones with Standard Arabic words within some circles. Moreover, Tunisian is also closely related to Maltese, which is not considered to be a dialect of Arabic for sociolinguistic reasons.

An exemple is the following sentences in Tunisian Dialect of Arabic (TDA) in social media, as presented in Figure 1. The underlined words (also in red) cannot be analyzable by MSA morphological analyzers, and thus need their own TDA analysis. Moreover, there are some words (in blue) expressed

---

[3] http://www.wamda.com/2013/06/qordoba-launches-new-social-media-translation-service
[4] http://www.neurope.eu/article/twitter-launches-arabic-translation-service
[5] http://en.wikipedia.org/wiki/Tunisian_Arabic

in languages other than Arabic, French in this case. At least three morphological tools are needed for this short text that is very common in social media.

It is often assumed that for the country in question, users of social media will use mostly if not always, the native language. However, this isn't always the case. Languages will be mixed up with up to three languages in a single "tweet" or blog. A Tunisian user of social media can involve the following languages or their variants: 1) native tongue (Arabic dialect), 2) MSA (example for greetings), 3) English and 4) the Colonial country's language, which is French in our case. In the case of Tunisian, French words/numbers may be used that sound like an Arabic word. An accurate machine translation for social media should manage this level of complexity, especially when ones add numerical characters and an ever-changing Lexicon of words.

سلام عليكم
ليوم ريت حاجة هبلتني ، نرفزتني و حشمتني في نفس الوقت
كنت في أحد الأسواق و معيا أجانب ، و بحكم قرب أحد المدارس من السوق كان هناك الكثير من الأطفال ؛ حتى لهنا لباس...
أنا تلهيت 5 دق و إذا بالصغار دايرين بالسياح و مادين يداهم و يقولو un dinar SVP
أي كيما نحكيلكم ، حتى حد في دنيا ما ينجم يحس شنيا حسيت أنا وقتها ، تقول واحد صب عليا سطل ماء بارد ، بارد بارشا...

Figure 1. Example of Social media text including a mixture of MSA, TDA and French language

4 Collaboratively Constructed Linguistic Tools for TDA

This section describes our effort in collaboratively constructing some linguitic tools that help translate Tunisian text of social media into MSA and other target languages considering MSA as a pivot language. Among these tools, a bilingual TDA-MSA lexicon and a set of mapping rules that will be integrated in the rule-based translation system (TDA-into-MSA). Furthermore, a language Modeling of MSA will help disambiguate the many translation hypothesis and thus select the best phrasal translation in MSA.


```
<?xml version="1.0" encoding="UTF-8"?>
<lexiques>
<lexique num_l="1" dt="اثنين اثنين اثنين زوز ثنين ثنين ثنن" msa="إثنان" />
<lexique num_l="2" dt="أكحل اكحل " msa=" أسود " />
<lexique num_l="3" dt="لكحل لكحل " msa=" الأسود " />
<lexique num_l="4" dt="كحل كحل " msa="سود سودا" />
<lexique num_l="5" dt="لكحل لكحل " msa="السود السودا" />
<lexique num_l="6" dt="كحلة كحلة " msa="سوداء سوداء" />
<lexique num_l="7" dt="أزرق فاروزي أزرق فاروزي" msa="أزرق" />
<lexique num_l="8" dt="فاروزية زرقة فاروزية زرقة" msa="زرقاء" />
<lexique num_l="9" dt="كيفاش كيفاه كيفاش كيفاه" msa="كيف" />
<lexique num_l="10" dt="علاش علاة لواش لواة لاش لاة لين لين علاش علاه لواش لواه لاش لاش لين" msa=
"لماذا" />
<lexique num_l="11" dt="آش_باش شنوا آش إشنوة واشي شنهو شنهي شنو شنو شنوا اش شنوة اشنوة
واشي شنهو اشي آشي" msa="ماذا" />
<lexique num_l="12" dt="فينو وينو فينو فينوا وينو وينوا" msa="أين_هو" />
<lexique num_l="13" dt="فينك وينك فينك وينك فينك وينك" msa="أين_انت" />
<lexique num_l="14" dt="هي_وين هي_فين فين_هي وين_هي وينهي وينهي فيني ويني فيني ويني فين
ويني فين" msa="أين_هي" />
<lexique num_l="15" dt="أنا_وين وين_أنا فين_أنا ويني_أنا فيني_أنا فيني ويني انا_فين فيني
فين_أنا فين" msa="أين_أنا" />
```


Figure 2. An example from the TDA-MSA lexicon database

4.1 The TDA-MSA Bilingual Lexicon

We have manually and collaboratively developed a bilingual TDA-MSA lexicon that contains around 1,600 source words in TDA and its corresponding translations in MSA, defined by a human expert. Furthermore, our research on some downloadded extracts from Tunisian blogs (around 6,000 words), showed a difference between verb morphology in TDA and that in MSA. We find that in TDA, the gender distinction is not marked. Similarly, we noticed the absence of the masculine and feminine dual in TDA.

In this phase, our aim was to build a bilingual lexicon of Tunisian nouns and verbs and their translations into MSA. Note that a term can be a noun, a verb, an adverb, etc. Furthermore, the most used imported words from other language than Arabic (Berbere, French, English, Turkish, Spanish, Maltese) and used in social media context were considered in this lexicon. These TDA-MSA couples are stored in an XML database. Figure 2 shows a bilingual TDA-MSA extract from the lexicon database, encoded in XML.

4.2 Grammatical Mapping Rules for TDA

Our second collaboratively constructed linguistic tool, consists on a set of mapping rules that were checked by human experts. This set consists of some rules applied on verbs transformation in TDA and their corresponding translation into MSA. In final, we have defined a set of 226 mapping rules from TDA into MSA on verbs transformation. Figure 3 shows an extract of the defined rules, encoded in XML. Figure 4 shows an example of a verb in TDA and its translation ito MSA using rule number 171 of the collaboratively built set of mapping rules.

4.3 Automatic Rule-based TDA-MSA Machine Translation

We have developed a rule-based translation system that is able to translate any social media text in TDA into MSA. This rule-based translation system can be coupled with any statistical machine translation system from MSA to another language to provide a translation of original Tunisian dialectal sentences of social media from TDA to that other language.

Figure 5 shows the different steps used in the translation of any social media text from TDA into MSA. First, for each word in the TDA social media text, we proceed by searching in the TDA-MSA lexicon database for the corresponding translation of the TDA word. Mostly, TDA nouns and imported words from other languages than Arabic were included in the lexicon. Second, we proceed by searching in the database of mapping rules for the source verb in TDA and its corresponding MSA translation, as shown in Figure 4. Last, both word-by-word translation candidates are extracted from the lexicons and using the set of mapping rules; thus considered as translation hypothesis.


```xml
<?xml version="1.0" encoding="UTF-8"?>
<lexiques>
<lexique num_r="1" prefixe="ما" proclitique="ت" postfixe="ش" nprefixe="لا" nproclitique=
"ت" npostfixe="" />
<lexique num_r="2" prefixe="ما" proclitique="ت" postfixe="ش" nprefixe="لا" nproclitique=
"ت" npostfixe="ي"/>
<lexique num_r="3" prefixe="ما" proclitique="ت" postfixe="ش" nprefixe="لا" nproclitique=
"ت" npostfixe="وا"/>
<lexique num_r="4" prefixe="ما" proclitique="ت" postfixe="وش" nprefixe="لا" nproclitique=
"ت" npostfixe="ا"/>
<lexique num_r="5" prefixe="ما" proclitique="ت" postfixe="وش" nprefixe="لا" nproclitique=
"ن" npostfixe="ن"/>
<lexique num_r="6" prefixe="" proclitique="ت" postfixe="وا" nprefixe="" nproclitique="ت"
 npostfixe="ون"/>
<lexique num_r="7" prefixe="" proclitique="ت" postfixe="وا" nprefixe="" nproclitique="ت"
 npostfixe="وا"/>
<lexique num_r="8" prefixe="" proclitique="ت" postfixe="وا" nprefixe="" nproclitique="ت"
 npostfixe="ان"/>
<lexique num_r="9" prefixe="" proclitique="ت" postfixe="وا" nprefixe="" nproclitique="ت"
 npostfixe="ا"/>
<lexique num_r="10" prefixe="" proclitique="ت" postfixe="وا" nprefixe="" nproclitique=
"ت" npostfixe="ن"/>
```


Figure 3. An example of some mapping rules from TDA to MSA

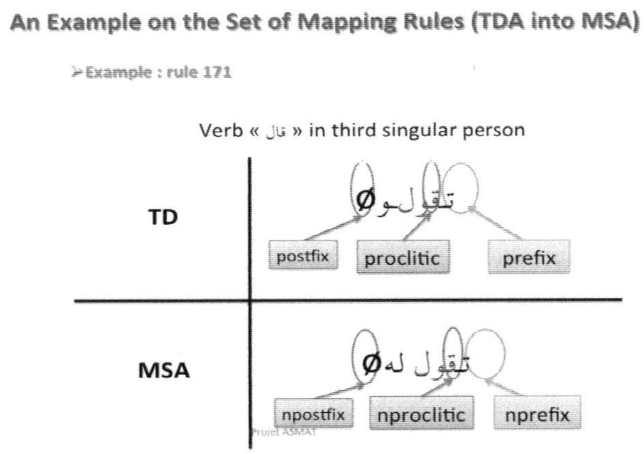

Figure 4. An example of the application of rule 171 for a verb in TDA and its translation into MSA

4.4 Language Modeling

The rule-based translation system is based on a word-by-word translation using the bilingual lexicon and the set of mapping rules. Thus, most of the time, one TDA sentence will have more than one possible translation. The language modeling (LM) of the target language (MSA) combined to the previous rule-based translation system will help disambiguate and select the best translation hypothesis in MSA.

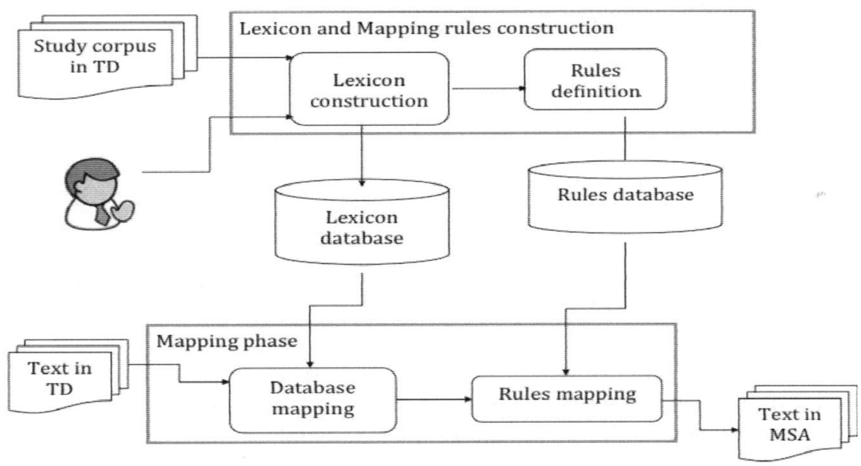

Figure 5. The rule-based translation approach for an automatic mapping from TDA to MSA

5 Evaluations

We have carried out some experiments and evaluations on the accuracy of the translation of TDA social media texts into MSA.

First, we collected manually a TDA corpus consisting of 6,000 words from some Tunisian forums and blogs. This corpus is very heterogeneous and multilingual, as many words are not in TDA but in MSA, French, English and sometimes using a certain style and form of social media, example using tweeter or SMS slangs). An extract of this corpus is presented in Figure 1.

For evaluation purposes, we considered a reference set of 50 phrases in TDA, translated manually into MSA. We also considered these 50 TDA phrases as the test set. Thus, we applied the proposed rule-based approach on this test set.

In order to combine adequately the rule-based translation approach to the language modeling (in MSA), we considered using the United Nation Arabic corpus to train a trigram language model. This training corpus contains around 50M words after cleaning the Latin content.

A preprocessing step is very crucial to any Arabic language processing. We considered tokenizing the MSA words using the D3 (Habash and Sadat, 2006a) scheme to overcome all problems of agglutination. The D3 scheme splits off clitics as follows: the class of conjunction clitics (w+ and f+), the class of particles (l+, k+, b+ and s+), the definite article (Al+) and all pronominal enclitics. These preprocessing are applied for both the hypothesis translation sentences and the training corpus, both in MSA. In addition to this preprocessing step, manual cleaning the MSA corpus of Latin contents was required. Thus, a trigram language model was implemented using the SRILM toolkit (Stolcke, 2002) on this training MSA corpus.

Next, we extracted all possible trigrams from the preprocessed MSA hypotheses translations and we computed the probability that these trigrams extracted appear in the MSA corpus based on the language model. A probability for each hypothesis translation is computed based on a trigram language model (LM). The hypothesis translation that has the highest probability is considered as the best translation.

Evaluations of the best translation sentence from TDA to MSA against the reference sentence in MSA were completed using the BLEU metric for automatic machine translation (Papineni et al., 2002). Our experiment produced a score of 14.32 BLEU. This low score could be related to our rule-based translation approach that is word-based and to the high number of unknown words in our source test file in other language variants than TDA. Adopting a phrasal translation and solving the problem of unknown words should be more effective.

Unfortunately, we could not found an available TDA-MSA test and reference files to conduct better evaluations in machine translation and social media context.

6 Conclusion and Future Work

Social media has become a key communication tool for people around the world. Building any NLP tool for texts extracted from social media is very challenging and daunting task and always be limited by the rapid changes in the social media. Considering an Arabic social media text is much more challenging because of the dominant use of English, French and other languages which intend to bring more problems to solve.

This paper presents our effort to create linguistic resources such as a bilingual lexicon, a set of grammatical mapping rule and a ruel-based translation and disambiguation system for the translation of any social media text from TDA into MSA. A language modeling of MSA is used in the disambiguation phase and the selection of the best translation phrase.

As for future work, we intend to enlarge the set of words in the TDA-MSA lexicon as well as the set of mapping rules. We intend to develop more grammatical rules for not only verbs but also adjectives and nouns. Furthermore, it would be interesting to build a parallel or comparable TDA-MSA corpus by selecting the most pertinent sources of social media and mining the web. A phrase-based statistical machine translation can be built using this parallel/comparable corpus and coupled to the rule-based translation system.

What we presented in this draft is a research on exploiting social media corpora for Arabic in order to analyze them and exploit them for NLP applications, such as machine translation within the scope of the ASMAT project.

Reference

Hitham Abo-Bakr, Khaled Shaalan, and Ibrahim Ziedan. 2008. A Hybrid Approach for Converting Written Egyptian Colloquial Dialect into Discretized Arabic. *Proceedings of the 6th International Conference on Informatics and Systems* 2008. Cairo University.

Rania Al-Sabbagh and Roxana Girju. 2010. Mining the Web for the Induction of a Dialectical Arabic Lexicon. *Proceedings of the 7th International Conference on Language Resources and Evaluation* LREC 2010. Valletta, Malta, May 19-21, 2010.

Khalid Almeman and Mark Lee. 2013. Automatic Building of Arabic Multi Dialect Text Corpora by Bootstrapping Dialect Words. *In Communications, Signal Processing, and their Applications* ICCSPA 2013. Sharjah, UAE, Feb.12-14, 2013.

Rahma Boujelbane, Mariem Ellouze Khemekhem, Siwar BenAyed, and Lamia Hadrich Belguith. 2013. Building Bilingual Lexicon to Create Dialect Tunisian Corpora and Adapt Language Model. *Proceedings of the 2nd Workshop on Hybrid Approaches to Translation,* ACL 2013. Sofia, Bulgaria.

Rahma Boujelbane, Mariem Ellouze Khemekhem, and Lamia Hadrich Belguith. 2013. Mapping Rules for Building a Tunisian Dialect Lexicon and Generating Corpora. *Proceedings of the International Joint Conference on Natural Language Processing*. Nagoya, Japan.

David Chiang, Mona Diab, Nizar Habash, Owen Rambow, and Safiullah Shareef. 2006. Parsing Arabic Dialects. *Proceedings of the European Chapter of ACL* EACL 2006.

Sean Colbath. 2012. Language and Translation Challenges in Social Media. *Proceedings of AMTA 2012, Government presentations*. Submitted by Raytheon BBN Technologies. Oct. 28th to Nov. 1st, 2012. San Diego, USA.

Mona Diab and Nizar Habash. 2007. Arabic Dialect Processing Tutorial. *Proceedings of HLT-NAACL, Tutorial Abstracts* 2007: 5-6.

Heba Elfardy and Mona Diab. 2013. Sentence-Level Dialect Identification in Arabic. *Proceedings of the 51st Annual Meeting of the Association for Computational Linguistics,* ACL 2013, Sofia, Bulgaria. 2013.

Nizar Habash and Fatiha Sadat. 2006. Arabic Pre-processing Schemes for Statistical Machine Translation. *Proceedings of the Human Language Technology Conference of the NAACL.* Companion volume: 49–52. New York City, USA.

Nizar Habash and Owen Rambow. 2006. MAGEAD: A Morphological Analyzer and Generator for the Arabic Dialects. *Proceedings of the 21st International Conference on Computational Linguistics and 44st Annual Meeting of the Association for Computational Linguistics*: 681–688, Sydney, Australia.

Ahmed Hamdi, Rahma Boujelbane, Nizar Habash, and Alexis Nasr. 2013. The Effects of Factorizing Root and Pattern Mapping in Bidirectional Tunisian - Standard Arabic Machine Translation. *Proceedings of MT Summit* 2013, Nice, France.

Ahmed Hamdi, Rahma Boujelbane, Nizar Habash, and Alexis Nasr. 2013. Un Système de Traduction de Verbes entre Arabe Standard et Arabe Dialectal par Analyse Morphologique Profonde. *Proceedings of TALN* 2013, Nantes, France.

Hanaa Kilany, Hassan. Gadalla, Howaida Arram, Ashraf Yacoub, Alaa El-Habashi, and Cynthia McLemore. 2002. Egyptian Colloquial Arabic Lexicon. *LDC catalog number LDC99L22.*

Katrin Kirchhoff, Jeff Bilmes, Sourin Das, Nicolae Duta, Melissa Egan, Gang Ji, Feng He, John Henderson, Daben Liu, Mohamed Noamany, Pat Schone, Richard Schwartz, and Dimitra Vergyri. 2003. Novel Approaches to Arabic Speech Recognition: Report from the 2002 Johns Hopkins Summer Workshop. *Proceedings of IEEE International Conference on Acoustics, Speech, and Signal Processing.* Hong Kong, China.

Katrin Kirchhoff and Dimitra Vergyri. 2004. Cross-dialectal Acoustic Data Sharing for Arabic Speech Recognition. *Proceedings of the International Conference on Acoustics, Speech, and Signal Processing*, 2004.

Kishore Papineni, Salim Roukos, Todd Ward, and Wei J. Zhu. 2002. BLEU: a Method for Automatic Evaluation of Machine Translation. *Proceedings of the 40th Annual Meeting of the Association for Computational Linguistics*: 311–318. Philadelphia, USA.

Fatiha Sadat. 2013. Arabic social media analysis for the construction and the enrichment of NLP tools. *In Corpus Linguistics* 2013. Lancaster University, UK. Jul. 22-26, 2013.

Hassan Sajjad, Kareem Darwish and Yonatan Belinkov. 2013. Translating Dialectal Arabic to English. *Proceedings of the 51st Annual Meeting of the Association for Computational Linguistics*: 1–6. Sofia, Bulgaria, Aug. 4-9 2013.

Wael Salloum and Nizar Habash. 2011. Dialectal to Standard Arabic Paraphrasing to Improve Arabic-English Statistical Machine Translation. *Proceedings of the First Workshop on Algorithms and Resources for Modelling of Dialects and Language Varieties*. Edinburgh, Scotland.

Wael Salloum and Nizar Habash. 2012. Elissa: A Dialectal to Standard Machine Translation System. *Proceedings of Coling 2012*: Demonstration Papers: 385-392, Mumbai, India.

Hassan Sawaf. 2010. Arabic Dialect Handling in Hybrid Machine Translation. *Proceedings of the Conference of the Association for Machine Translation in the Americas* AMTA 2010. Denver, Colorado.

Khaled Shaalan. 2010. Rule-based Approach in Arabic Natural Language Processing. *International Journal on Information and Communication Technologies*, 3(3).

Andreas Stolcke. 2002. SRILM—An Extensible Language Modeling Toolkit. *Proceedings of ICSLP*, 2002.

Rabih Zbib, Erika Malchiodi, Jacob Devlin, David Stallard, Spyros Matsoukas, Richard Schwartz, John Makhoul, Omar F. Zaidan, and Chris Callison-Burch. 2012. Machine translation of Arabic Dialects. *Proceedings of the 2012 Conference of the North American Chapter of the Association for Computational Linguistics*: Human Language Technologies, Montreal, Canada.

A Database of Paradigmatic Semantic Relation Pairs for German Nouns, Verbs, and Adjectives

Silke Scheible and Sabine Schulte im Walde
Institut für Maschinelle Sprachverarbeitung
Universität Stuttgart
{scheible,schulte}@ims.uni-stuttgart.de

Abstract

A new collection of semantically related word pairs in German is presented, which was compiled via human judgement experiments and comprises (i) a representative selection of target lexical units balanced for semantic category, polysemy, and corpus frequency, (ii) a set of human-generated semantically related word pairs based on the target units, and (iii) a subset of the generated word pairs rated for their relation strength, including positive and negative relation evidence. We address the three paradigmatic relations *antonymy, hypernymy* and *synonymy*, and systematically work across the three word classes of adjectives, nouns, and verbs.

A series of quantitative and qualitative analyses demonstrates that (i) antonyms are more canonical than hypernyms and synonyms, (ii) relations are more or less natural with regard to the specific word classes, (iii) antonymy is clearly distinguishable from hypernymy and synonymy, but hypernymy and synonymy are often confused. We anticipate that our new collection of semantic relation pairs will not only be of considerable use in computational areas in which semantic relations play a role, but also in studies in theoretical linguistics and psycholinguistics.

1 Introduction

This paper describes the collection of a database of paradigmatically related word pairs in German which was compiled via human judgement experiments hosted on Amazon Mechanical Turk. While paradigmatic relations (such as synonymy, antonymy, hypernymy, and hyponymy) have been extensively researched in theoretical linguistics and psycholinguistics, they are still notoriously difficult to identify and distinguish computationally, because their distributions in text tend to be very similar. For example, in *The boy/girl/person loves/hates the cat*, the nominal co-hyponyms *boy, girl* and their hypernym *person* as well as the verbal antonyms *love* and *hate* occur in identical contexts, respectively. A dataset of paradigmatic relation pairs would thus represent a valuable test-bed for research on semantic relatedness.

For the compilation of the relation dataset we aimed for a sufficiently large amount of human-labelled data, which may both serve as seeds for a computational approach, and provide a gold-standard for evaluating the resulting computational models. This paper describes our efforts to create such a ***paradigmatic relation dataset in a two-step process***, making use of two types of human-generated data: (1) human suggestions of semantically related word pairs, and (2) human ratings of semantic relations between word pairs. Furthermore, we are the first to ***explicitly work across word classes (covering adjective, noun and verb targets)***, and to ***incorporate semantic classes, corpus frequency and polysemy as balancing criteria into target selection***. The resulting dataset[1] consists of three parts:

1. A representative selection of target lexical units drawn from GermaNet, a broad-coverage lexical-semantic net for German, using a principled sampling technique and taking into account the three major word classes adjectives, nouns, and verbs, which are balanced according to semantic category, polysemy, and type frequency.
2. A set of human-generated semantically related word pairs, based on the target lexical units.
3. A subset of semantically related word pairs, rated for the strength of the relation between them.

[1]The dataset is available from http://www.ims.uni-stuttgart.de/data/sem-rel-database.

Proceedings of the Workshop on Lexical and Grammatical Resources for Language Processing, pages 111–119,
Coling 2014, Dublin, Ireland, August 24 2014.

We anticipate that our new collection of semantic relation pairs will not only be of considerable use in computational areas in which semantic relations play a role (such as Distributional Semantics, Natural Language Understanding/Generation, and Opinion Mining), but also in studies in theoretical linguistics and psycholinguistics. In addition, our dataset may be of major interest for research groups working on automatic measures of semantic relatedness, as it allows a principled evaluation of such tools. Finally, since the target lexical units are drawn from the GermaNet database, our results will be directly relevant for assessing, developing, and maintaining this resource.

2 Related work

Over the years a number of datasets have been made available for studying and evaluating semantic relatedness. For English, Rubenstein and Goodenough (1965) obtained similarity judgements from 51 subjects on 65 noun pairs, a seminal study which was later replicated by Miller and Charles (1991), and Resnik (1995). Finkelstein et al. (2002) created a set of 353 English noun-noun pairs rated by 16 subjects according to their semantic relatedness on a scale from 0 to 10. For German, Gurevych (2005) replicated Rubenstein and Goodenough's experiments by translating the original 65 word pairs into German. In later work, she used the same experimental setup to increase the number of word pairs to 350 (Gurevych, 2006).

The dataset most similar to ours is *BLESS* (Baroni and Lenci, 2011), a freely available dataset that includes 200 distinct English concrete nouns as target concepts, equally divided between living and non-living entities, and grouped into 17 broad classes such as *bird, fruit*. For each target concept, BLESS contains several relata, connected to it through a semantic relation (hypernymy, co-hyponymy, meronymy, attribute, event), or through a null-relation. BLESS thus includes two paradigmatic relations (hypernymy, co-hyponymy) but does not focus on paradigmatic relations. Furthermore, it is restricted to concrete nouns, rather than working across word classes.

3 Paradigmatic relations

The focus of this work is on semantic relatedness, and in particular on paradigmatic semantic relations. This section discusses the theoretical background of the notion of *paradigmatic semantic relations*. The term **paradigmatic** goes back to de Saussure (1916), who introduced a distinction between linguistic elements based on their position relative to each other. This distinction derives from the linear nature of linguistic elements, which is reflected in the fact that speech sounds follow each other in time. Saussure refers to successive linguistic elements that combine with each other as 'syntagma', and thus the relation between these elements is called 'syntagmatic'. On the other hand, elements that can be found in the same position in a syntagma, and which could be substituted for each other, are in a 'paradigmatic' relationship. While syntagmatic and paradigmatic relations can hold between a variety of linguistic units (such as morphemes, phonemes, clauses, or sentences), the focus of this research is on the relations between words.

Many studies in computational linguistics work on the assumption that paradigmatic semantic relations hold between words. As will become apparent in the course of this work, it is necessary to move beyond these definitions for an appropriate investigation of paradigmatic semantic relations. According to Cruse (1986), sense is defined as "the meaning aspect of a lexical unit", and he states that "semantic relations" hold between lexical units, not between lexemes.

The goal of this work is to create a database of semantic relations for German adjectives, nouns and verbs, focussing on the three types of paradigmatic relations referred to as *sense-relations* by Lyons (1968) and Lyons (1977): synonymy, antonymy, and hypernymy.

4 Experimental setup

Our aim was to collect semantically related word pairs for the paradigmatic relations antonymy, synonymy, and hypernymy for the three word classes nouns, verbs, and adjectives. For this purpose we implemented two experiments involving human participants. Starting with a set of target words, in the first experiment participants were asked to propose suitable antonyms, synonyms and hypernyms for each of the targets. For example, for the target verb *befehlen* ('to command'), participants proposed antonyms such as *gehorchen* ('to obey'), synonyms such as *anordnen* ('to order'), and hypernyms such as *sagen* ('to say').

In the second experiment, participants were asked to rate the strength of a given semantic relation with respect to a word pair on a 6-point scale. For example, workers would be presented with a pair "*wild – free*" and asked to rate the strength of antonymy between the two words. All word pairs were assessed with respect to all three relation types.

Both experiments will be described in further detail in Sections 5 and 6. The current section aims to provide an overview of GermaNet, a lexical-semantic word net for German, from which the set of target words was drawn (4.1). We then describe the selection of target words from GermaNet, which used a stratified sampling approach (4.2). Finally, we introduce the platform used to implement the experiments, Amazon Mechanical Turk (4.3).

4.1 Target source: GermaNet

GermaNet is a lexical-semantic word net that aims to relate German nouns, verbs, and adjectives semantically. GermaNet has been modelled along the lines of the Princeton WordNet for English (Miller et al., 1990; Fellbaum, 1998) and shares its general design principles (Hamp and Feldweg, 1997; Kunze and Wagner, 1999; Lemnitzer and Kunze, 2007). For example, lexical units denoting the same concept are grouped into synonym sets ('synsets'). These are in turn interlinked via conceptual-semantic relations (such as hypernymy) and lexical relations (such as antonymy). For each of the major word classes, the databases further take a number of semantic categories into consideration, expressed via top-level nodes in the semantic network (such as 'Artefakt/artifact', 'Geschehen/event', 'Gefühl/feeling'). However, in contrast to WordNet, GermaNet also includes so-called 'artificial concepts' to fill lexical gaps and thus enhance network connectivity, and to avoid unsuitable co-hyponymy (e.g. by providing missing hypernyms or hyponyms). GermaNet also differs from WordNet in the way in which it handles part of speech. For example, while WordNet employs a clustering approach to structuring adjectives, GermaNet uses a hierarchical structure similar to the one employed for the noun and verb hierarchies. Finally, the latest releases of WordNet and GermaNet also differ in size: While WordNet 3.0 contains at total of 117,659 synsets and 155,287 lexical units, the respective numbers for GermaNet 6.0 are considerably lower, with 69,594 synsets and 93,407 lexical units.

Since GermaNet is the largest database of its kind for German, and as it encodes all types of relations that are of interest for us (synonymy, antonymy, and hypernymy), it represents a suitable starting point for our purposes.

4.2 Target selection

The purpose of collecting the set of targets was to acquire a broad range of lexical items which could be used as input for generating semantically related word pairs (cf. Section 5). Relying on GermaNet version 6.0 and the respective *JAVA API*, we used a stratified sampling technique to randomly select 99 nouns, 99 adjectives and 99 verbs from the GermaNet files. The random selection was balanced for

1. the ***size of the semantic classes***,[2] accounting for the 16 semantic adjective classes and the 23 semantic classes for both nouns and verbs, as represented by the file organisation;
2. ***three polysemy classes*** according to the number of GermaNet senses:
   I) monosemous, II) two senses and III) more than two senses;
3. ***three frequency classes*** according to type frequency in the German web corpus *SdeWaC* (Faaß and Eckart, 2013), which contains approx. 880 million words:
   I) *low* (200–2,999), II) *mid* (3,000–9,999) and III) *high* ($\geq$10,000).

The total number of 99 targets per word class resulted from distinguishing 3 sense classes and 3 frequency classes, $3 \times 3 = 9$ categories, and selecting 11 instances from each category, in proportion to the semantic class sizes.

[2]For example, if an adjective GermaNet class contained 996 word types, and the total number of adjectives over all semantic classes was 8,582, and with 99 stimuli collected in total, we randomly selected $99 * 996/8,582 = 11$ adjectives from this class.

4.3 Experimental platform: Mechanical Turk

The experiments described below were implemented in Amazon Mechanical Turk (AMT)[3], a web-based crowdsourcing platform which allows simple tasks (so-called HITs) to be performed by a large number of people in return for a small payment. In our first experiment, human associations were collected for different semantic relation types, where AMT workers were asked to propose suitable synonyms, antonyms, and hypernyms for each of the targets. The second experiment was based on a subset of the generated synonym/antonym/hypernym pairs and asked the workers to rate each pair for the strength of antonymy, synonymy, and hypernymy between them, on a scale between 1 (minimum strength) and 6 (maximum strength). To control for non-native speakers of German and spammers, each batch of HITs included two examples of 'non-words' (invented words following German morphotactics such as *Blapselheit*, *gekortiert*) in a random position. If participants did not recognise the invented words, we excluded all their ratings from consideration. While we encouraged workers to complete all HITs in a given batch, we also accepted a smaller number of submitted HITs, as long as the workers had a good overall feedback score.

5 Generation experiment

5.1 Method

The goal of the generation experiment was to collect human associations for the semantic relation types antonymy, hypernymy, and synonymy. For each of our 3×99 adjective, noun, and verb targets, we asked 10 participants to propose a suitable synonym, antonym, and hypernym. Targets were bundled randomly in 9 batches per word class, each including 9 targets plus two invented words. The experiment consisted of separate runs for each relation type to avoid confusion between them, with participants first generating synonyms, then antonyms, and finally hypernyms for the targets, resulting in 3 word classes $\times$ 99 targets $\times$ 3 relations $\times$ 10 participants $= 8,910$ target–response pairs.

5.2 Results and discussion

(a) Total number of responses:

Table 1 illustrates how the number of generated word pairs distributes across word classes and relations. The total number per class and relation is 990 tokens (99 targets $\times$ 10 participants). From the maximum number of generated pairs, a total of 131 types (211 tokens) were discarded because the participants provided no response. These cases had been accepted via AMT nevertheless because the participants were approved workers and we assumed that the empty responses showed the difficulty of specific word–relation constellations, see below. For example, six out of ten participants failed to provide a synonym for the adjective *bundesrepublikanisch* 'federal republic'.

	ANT		HYP		SYN		*all*	
	types	tokens	types	tokens	types	tokens	types	tokens
ADJ	524	990	676	990	597	990	1,797	2,970
NOUN	708	990	701	990	621	990	2,030	2,970
VERB	636	990	662	990	620	990	1,918	2,970
all	1,868	2,970	2,039	2,970	1,838	2,970	5,745	8,910

Table 1: Number of generated relation pairs across word classes.

(b) Number of ambiguous responses:

An interesting case is provided by pairs that were generated with regard to different relations but for the same target word. Table 2 lists the number of types of such ambiguous pairs, and the intersection of the tokens. For example, if five participants generated a pair with regard to a target and relation x, and two participants generated the same pair with regard to relation y, the intersection is 2. The intersection

[3]https://www.mturk.com

is more indicative of ambiguity here, because in most cases of ambiguity the intersection is only 1, which might as well be the result of an erroneously generated pair (e.g., because the participant did not pay attention to the task), rather than genuine ambiguity. Examples of ambiguous responses with an intersection > 1 are *Gegenargument–Argument* 'counter argument – argument', which was provided five times as an antonymy pair and twice as a hypernymy pair; *freudlos–traurig* 'joyless – sad', which was provided four times as a synonymy pair and five times as a hypernymy pair; and *beseitigen–entfernen* 'eliminate – remove', which was provided five times as a synonymy pair and five times as a hypernymy pair.

	ANT+HYP		ANT+SYN		HYP+SYN		ANT+HYP+SYN	
	types	tokens	types	tokens	types	tokens	types	tokens
ADJ	6	6	4	4	195	342	2	2
NOUN	15	16	17	17	93	117	5	6
VERB	4	4	8	8	182	290	5	6
all	25	26	29	29	470	749	12	14

Table 2: Number of ambiguous relation pairs across word classes.

The ambiguities in Table 2 indicate that humans are quite clear about what distinguishes antonyms from synonyms, and what distinguishes antonyms from hypernyms. On the other hand, the line dividing hypernymy and synonymy is less clear, and the large amount of confusion between the two relations lends support to theories claiming that hypernymy should be considered a type of synonymy, and that real synonymy does not exist in natural languages for economical reasons. Furthermore, the confusion is most obvious for adjectives and verbs, for which the relation is considered less natural than for nouns, cf. Miller and Fellbaum (1991).

(c) Number of (different) responses across word classes and relations:

An analysis of the number of different antonyms, hypernyms and synonyms generated for a given target shows no noticeable difference at first glance: on average, 6.04 different antonyms were generated for the targets, while the number is minimally higher for synonyms with 6.08 different responses on average; hypernyms received considerably more (6.78) different responses on average. However, the distribution of the numbers of different antonym, hypernym, and synonym responses across the targets shows that the antonymy generation task results in more targets with a small number of different responses compared to the synonymy and the hypernym task (Figure 1): there are 10 targets for which all ten participants generated the same antonym (x = *number of different responses* = 1), such as *dunkel–hell* 'dark – light' and *verbieten–erlauben* 'to forbid – to allow', while there are 17 targets where they generated exactly two (x=2), and 29 targets where they suggested three different antonyms (x=3). In contrast, for hypernymy and synonymy, there are 0/3 targets where all participants agreed on the same response, and there are only 5/10 targets where they generated exactly two, and 8/21 targets where they generated only three different hypernyms/synonyms.

These results are in line with previous findings for English and Swedish by Paradis and Willners (2006) and Paradis et al. (2009), who argue against the strict contrast between 'direct' and 'indirect' antonyms which has been assumed in the literature (see, for example, Gross et al. (1989)) in favour of a scale of 'canonicity' where some word pairs are perceived as more antonymic than others. In particular, they propose that the weaker the degree of canonicity, the more different responses the target items will yield in an elicitation experiment. Similar to the current findings for German, they found that for English and Swedish there is a small core of highly opposable couplings which have been conventionalised as antonym pairs in text and discourse, while all other couplings form a scale from more to less strongly related. The ten targets for which all participants generated the same antonym response are thus likely to represent highly "canonical" pairings. The fact that the hypernymy and synonymy generation experiments results in fewer targets with only one or two different responses suggests that hypernymy and synonymy have a lower level of canonicity than antonymy.

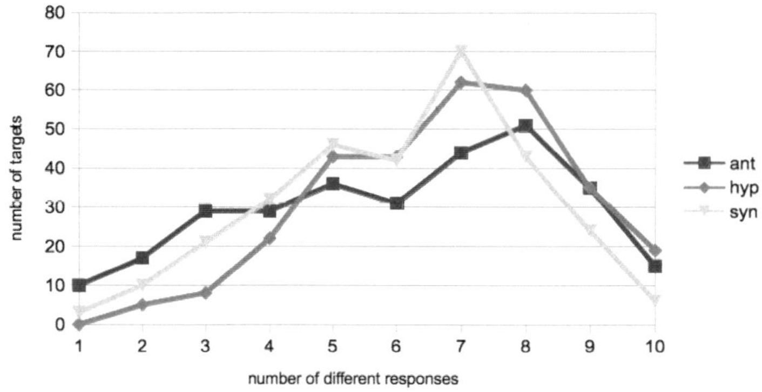

Figure 1: Number of targets plotted against the number of different responses.

Figure 2 demonstrates that the overall distributions of the frequency of responses are, however, very similar for antonyms, hypernyms and synonyms: between 72% and 77% of the responses were only given once, with the curves following a clear downward trend. Note that a strength of 10 in Figure 2 refers to the case of *one different response* (x=1) in Figure 1.

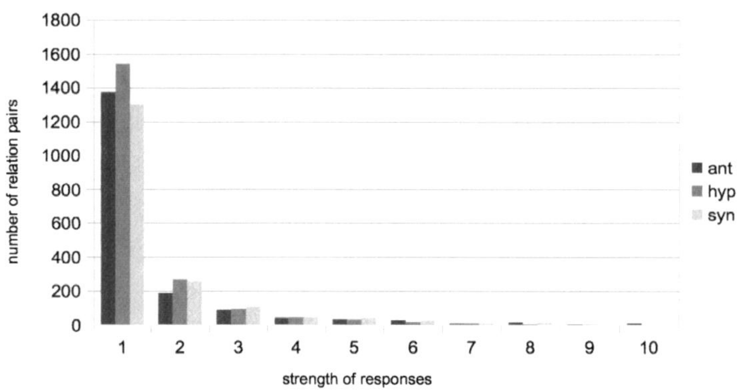

Figure 2: Response magnitude.

Finally, Figure 3 compares the number of blank responses (types and tokens) regarding antonyms, hypernyms and synonyms. Across word classes, 74/115 targets (types/tokens) received blank antonym responses, while only 25/34 targets received blank hypernym responses and only 32/62 targets received blank synonym responses. These numbers indicate that participants find it harder to come up with antonyms than hypernyms or synonyms. Breaking the proportions down by word class, Figure 3 demonstrates that in each case the number of missing antonyms (left panel: types; right panel: tokens) is larger than those of missing hypernyms/synonyms. Figure 3 also shows that the difficulty to provide relation pairs varies across word classes. While antonyms are the most difficult relation in general, there are more blank responses regarding adjectives and nouns, in comparison to verbs. Hypernymy seems similarly difficult across classes, and synonymy is more difficult for nouns than for adjectives or verbs.

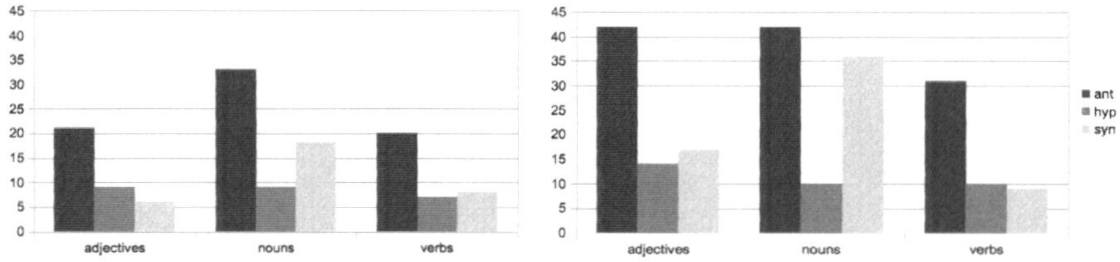

Figure 3: Blank responses (types and tokens).

(d) Comparison with GermaNet:

The results of the generation experiment can be used to extend and develop GermaNet, the resource the targets were drawn from: a large proportion of responses are not covered in GermaNet. Table 3 below shows for the three parts of speech and the three relation types how many responses were covered by both the generation experiment (EXP) and GermaNet (GN) (column 'Both'), how many of them only appear in the generation experiment (column 'EXP'), and how many are only listed in GermaNet ('GN'). Blank and multi-word responses in the experimental results were excluded from consideration. The comparison shows that the variety of semantic relation types in our experimental dataset is considerably larger than in GermaNet, while the overlap is marginal. Especially for antonyms, the coverage in GermaNet seems to be quite low, across word classes. For hypernymy and synonymy, the semantic relation types complement each other to a large extent, with each resource containing relations that are not part of the other resource. In sum, the tables confirm that extending GermaNet with our relation types should enrich the manual resource.

	ANT			HYP			SYN		
	Both	EXP	GN	Both	EXP	GN	Both	EXP	GN
ADJ	33	453	5	100	561	237	66	496	160
NOUN	3	633	2	108	561	393	59	516	150
VERB	10	542	2	132	507	260	40	554	109

Table 3: Relation coverage in Generation Experiment (EXP) and GermaNet (GN).

6 Rating experiment

6.1 Method

In the second experiment, Mechanical Turk workers were asked to rate the strength of a given semantic relation with respect to a word pair on a 6-point scale. The main purpose of this experiment was to identify and distinguish between "strong" and "weak" examples of a specific relation. The number of times a specific response was given in the generation experiment does not necessarily indicate the strength of the relation. This is especially true for responses that were suggested by only one or two participants, where it is difficult to tell if the response is an error, or if it relates to a idiosyncratic sense of the target word that the other participants did not think of in the first instance. Crucially, in the rating experiment all word pairs were assessed with respect to all three relation types, thus asking not only for positive but also negative evidence of semantic relation instances.

The set of word pairs used as input is a carefully selected subset of responses acquired in the generation experiment.[4] For each of the 99 targets and each of the semantic relations antonymy, synonymy, and hypernymy two responses were included (if available): the *response with the highest frequency* (random choice if several available), and a *response with a lower frequency* (2, if available, otherwise 1; random choice if several available). Multi-word responses and blanks were excluded from consideration. A manual post-processing step aimed to address the issue of duplicate pairs in the randomly generated dataset, where the same responses had been generated for two of the relations.

In theory, each target should have 6 associated pairs (2xANT, 2xHYP, 2xSYN). In practice, there are sometimes fewer than 6 pairs per target in the dataset, because (i) for some targets, only one response is available for a given relation (e.g., if all 10 participants provided the same response), or (ii) no valid response of the required frequency type is available. The resulting dataset includes 1,684 target-response pairs altogether, 546 of which are adjective pairs, 574 noun pairs, and 564 verb pairs. To avoid confusion, the ratings were collected in separate experimental settings, i.e., for each word class and each relation type, all generated pairs were first judged for their strength of one relation, and then for their strength of another relation.

[4]For time and money reasons, we could not collect the $8,910 \times 3 \times 10 = 267,300$ ratings for all responses.

6.2 Results and discussion

In the following, we present the results of the rating experiment in terms of mean rating scores for each word pair. The mean rating scores were calculated across all ten ratings per pair. The purpose of the analysis was to verify that the responses generated in the generation experiment are in fact perceived as examples of the given relation type by other raters. We thus looked at all responses for a given relation type in the data set and calculated the average value of all mean ratings for this relation type. For example, Figure 4 (left panel) shows that the responses generated as antonyms are clearly perceived as antonyms in the case of adjectives, with an average rating score of 4.95. Verb antonyms are also identified as such with a rating of 4.38. The situation for nouns, however, is less clear: an average rating of 3.70 is only minimally higher than the middle point of the rating scale (3.50). These findings support the common assumption that antonymy is a relation that applies well to adjectives and verbs, but less so to nouns. Responses generated as synonyms (plot omitted for space reasons), on the other hand, are identified as such for all three words classes, with average rating values of 4.78 for adjectives, 4.48 for nouns, and 4.66 for verbs.

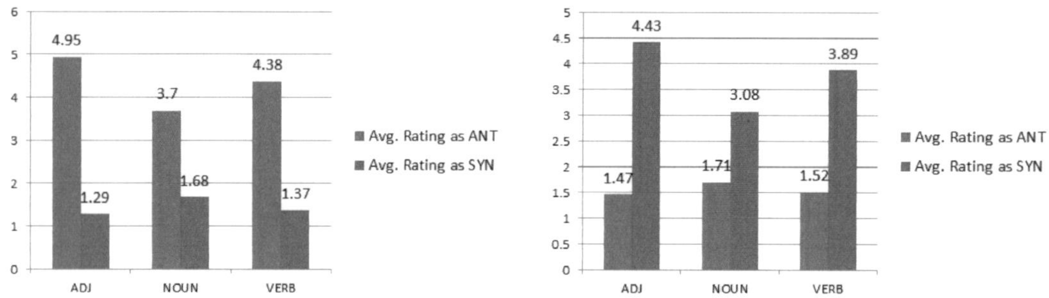

Figure 4: Average ratings of antonym/hypernym responses as ANT or SYN, across word classes.

Finally, Figure 4 (right panel) shows the average ratings as synonyms/antonyms for responses generated as hypernyms. The findings corroborate our analysis of synonym/hypernym confusion in Section 5: the distribution looks fairly similar to the one for synonyms, with low antonymy ratings, but an average synonymy rating of 4.43 for adjectives, 3.08 for nouns, and 3.89 for verbs. The results suggest that hypernymy is particularly difficult to distinguish from synonymy in the case of adjectives.

7 Conclusion

This article presented a new collection of semantically related word pairs in German which was compiled via human judgement experiments. The database consists of three parts:

1. A representative selection of target lexical units drawn from GermaNet, using a principled sampling technique and taking into account the three major word classes adjectives, nouns, and verbs, which are balanced according to semantic category, polysemy, and type frequency.
2. A set of 8,910 human-generated semantically related word pairs, based on the target lexical units.
3. A subset of 1,684 semantically related word pairs, rated for the strengths of relations.

To our knowledge, our dataset is the first that (i) focuses on multiple paradigmatic relations, (ii) systematically works across word classes, (iii) explicitly balances the targets according to semantic category, polysemy and type frequency, and (iv) explicitly provides positive and negative rating evidence. We described the generation and the rating experiments, and presented a series of quantitative and qualitative analyses. The analyses showed that (i) antonyms are more canonical than hypernyms and synonyms, (ii) relations are more or less natural with regard to the specific word classes, (iii) antonymy is clearly distinguishable from hypernymy and synonymy, and (iv) hypernymy and synonymy are often confused.

Acknowledgements

The research was funded by the DFG Sachbeihilfe SCHU-2580/2-1 (Silke Scheible) and the DFG Heisenberg Fellowship SCHU-2580/1-1 (Sabine Schulte im Walde).

References

Marco Baroni and Alessandro Lenci. 2011. How we BLESSed Distributional Semantic Evaluation. In *Proceedings of the EMNLP Workshop on Geometrical Models for Natural Language Semantics*, pages 1–10, Edinburgh, UK.

D. Allan Cruse. 1986. *Lexical Semantics*. Cambridge Textbooks in Linguistics. Cambridge University Press, Cambridge, UK.

Ferdinand de Saussure. 1916. *Cours de Linguistique Générale*. Payot.

Gertrud Faaß and Kerstin Eckart. 2013. SdeWaC – a Corpus of Parsable Sentences from the Web. In *Proceedings of the International Conference of the German Society for Computational Linguistics and Language Technology*, pages 61–68, Darmstadt, Germany.

Christiane Fellbaum, editor. 1998. *WordNet – An Electronic Lexical Database*. Language, Speech, and Communication. MIT Press, Cambridge, MA.

Lev Finkelstein, Evgeniy Gabrilovich, Yossi Matias, Ehud Rivlin, Zach Solan, Gadi Wolfman, and Eytan Ruppin. 2002. Placing Search in Context: The Concept Revisited. *ACM Transactions on Information Systems*, 20(1):116–131.

Derek Gross, Ute Fischer, and George A. Miller. 1989. Antonymy and the Representation of Adjectival Meanings. *Memory and Language*, 28(1):92–106.

Iryna Gurevych. 2005. Using the Structure of a Conceptual Network in Computing Semantic Relatedness. In *Proceedings of the 2nd International Joint Conference on Natural Language Processing*, pages 767–778, Jeju Island, Korea.

Iryna Gurevych. 2006. Thinking beyond the Nouns - Computing Semantic Relatedness across Parts of Speech. In *Sprachdokumentation & Sprachbeschreibung, 28. Jahrestagung der Deutschen Gesellschaft für Sprachwissenschaft*, Bielefeld, Germany.

Birgit Hamp and Helmut Feldweg. 1997. GermaNet – a Lexical-Semantic Net for German. In *Proceedings of the ACL Workshop on Automatic Information Extraction and Building Lexical Semantic Resources for NLP Applications*, pages 9–15, Madrid, Spain.

Claudia Kunze and Andreas Wagner. 1999. Integrating GermaNet into EuroWordNet, a Multilingual Lexical-Semantic Database. *Sprache und Datenverarbeitung*, 23(2):5–19.

Lothar Lemnitzer and Claudia Kunze. 2007. *Computerlexikographie*. Gunter Narr Verlag, Tübingen, Germany.

John Lyons. 1968. *Introduction to Theoretical Linguistics*. Cambridge University Press.

John Lyons. 1977. *Semantics*. Cambridge University Press.

George A. Miller and Walter G. Charles. 1991. Contextual Correlates of Semantic Similarity. *Language and Cognitive Processes*, 6(1):1–28.

George A. Miller and Christiane Fellbaum. 1991. Semantic Networks of English. *Cognition*, 41:197–229.

George A. Miller, Richard Beckwith, Christiane Fellbaum, Derek Gross, and Katherine J. Miller. 1990. Introduction to Wordnet: An On-line Lexical Database. *International Journal of Lexicography*, 3(4):235–244.

Carita Paradis and Caroline Willners. 2006. Antonymy and Negation: The Boundedness Hypothesis. *Journal of Pragmatics*, 38:1051–1080.

Carita Paradis, Caroline Willners, and Steven Jones. 2009. Good and Bad Opposites: Using Textual and Experimental Techniques to Measure Antonym Canonicity. *The Mental Lexicon*, 4(3):380–429.

Philip Resnik. 1995. Using Information Content to Evaluate Semantic Similarity in a Taxonomy. In *Proceedings of the 14th International Joint Conference on Artificial Intelligence*, pages 448–453, San Francisco, CA.

Herbert Rubenstein and John B. Goodenough. 1965. Contextual Correlates of Synonymy. *Communications of the ACM*, 8(10):627–633.

Improving the Precision of Synset Links Between Cornetto and Princeton WordNet

Leen Sevens **Vincent Vandeghinste** **Frank Van Eynde**
Centre for Computational Linguistics
KU Leuven
firstname@ccl.kuleuven.be

Abstract

Knowledge-based multilingual language processing benefits from having access to correctly established relations between semantic lexicons, such as the links between different WordNets. WordNet linking is a process that can be sped up by the use of computational techniques. Manual evaluations of the partly automatically established synonym set (synset) relations between Dutch and English in Cornetto, a Dutch lexical-semantic database associated with the EuroWordNet grid, have confronted us with a worrisome amount of erroneous links. By extracting translations from various bilingual resources and automatically assigning a confidence score to every pre-established link, we reduce the error rate of the existing equivalence relations between both languages' synsets (section 2). We will apply this technique to reuse the connection of Sclera and Beta pictograph sets and Cornetto synsets to Princeton WordNet and other WordNets, allowing us to further extend an existing Dutch text-to-pictograph translation tool to other languages (section 3).

1 Introduction

The connections between WordNets, large semantic databases grouping lexical units into synonym sets or synsets, are an important resource in knowledge-based multilingual language processing. EuroWordNet (Vossen, 1997) aims to build language-specific WordNets among the same lines as the original WordNet[1] (Miller et al., 1990), using Inter-Lingual-Indexes to weave a web of equivalence relations between the synsets contained within the databases. Cornetto[2] (Vossen et al., 2007), a Dutch lexical-semantic collection of data associated with the Dutch EuroWordNet[3], consists of more than 118 000 synsets. The equivalence relations establish connections between Dutch and English synsets in Princeton WordNet version 1.5 and 2.0. We update these links to Princeton WordNet version 3.0 by the mappings among WordNet versions made available by TALP-UPC [4]. The equivalence relations between Cornetto and Princeton have been established semi-automatically by Vossen et al. (1999). Manual coding was carried out for the 14 749 most important concepts in the database. These include the most frequent concepts, the concepts having a large amount of semantic relations and the concepts occupying a high position in the lexical hierarchy. Automatic linkage was done by mapping the bilingual Van Dale database[5] to WordNet 1.5. For every WordNet synset containing a dictionary's translation for a particular Dutch word, all its members were proposed as alternative translations. In the case of only one translation, the synset relation was instantly assumed correct, while multiple translations were weighted using several heuristics, such as measuring the conceptual distance in the WordNet hierarchy. We decided to verify the quality of these links and noticed that they were highly erroneous, making them not yet very reliable for multilingual processing.

[1] http://wordnet.princeton.edu
[2] http://tst-centrale.org/producten/lexica/cornetto/7-56
[3] http://www.illc.uva.nl/EuroWordNet
[4] http://www.talp.upc.edu
[5] http://www.vandale.be

Proceedings of the Workshop on Lexical and Grammatical Resources for Language Processing, pages 120–126,
Coling 2014, Dublin, Ireland, August 24 2014.

2 Improving the equivalence relations between Cornetto and Princeton WordNet

We manually evaluated the quality of the links between 300 randomly selected Cornetto synsets and their supposedly related Princeton synsets. A Cornetto synset is often linked to more than one Princeton synset. We found an erroneous link in 35.27% of the 998 equivalence relations we evaluated.

Each Cornetto synset has about 3.3 automatically derived English equivalents, allowing to roughly compare our evaluation to an initial quality check of the equivalence relations performed by Vossen et al. (1999). They note that, in the case of synsets with three to nine translations, the percentages of correct automatically derived equivalents went down to 65% and 49% for nouns and verbs respectively. Our manual evaluations are in line with these results, showing that only 64.73% of all the connections in our sample are correct. An example of where it goes wrong is the Cornetto synset for the animal *tor "beetle"*, which is not only appropriately linked to correct synsets (such as *beetle* and *bug*), but also mistakenly to the Princeton synset for the computational *glitch*. This flaw is most probably caused by the presence of the synonym *bug*, which is a commonly used word for errors in computer programs. Examples like these are omnipresent in our data[6] and led us to conclude that the synset links between Cornetto and Princeton WordNet definitely could be improved.

We build a bilingual dictionary for Dutch and English and use these translations as an automatic indicator of the quality of equivalence relations. In order to create a huge list of translations we merge several translation word lists, removing double entries. Some are manually compiled dictionaries, while others are automatically derived word lists from parallel corpora: we extracted the 1-word phrases from the phrase tables built with Moses (Koehn et al., 2007) based on the GIZA++ word alignments (Och and Ney, 2003). Table 1 gives an overview.

This resulted in a coverage of 52.18% (43 970 out of 84 264) of the equivalence relations for which translation information was available in order to possibly confirm the relation.

Translation dictionary	Reference	Method of compilation	Nr of word pairs
Wiktionary	www.wiktionary.org	Manual	23,575
FreeDict	www.freedict.com	Manual	49,493
Europarl	(Koehn, 2005)	Automatic	2,970,501
Opus	(Tiedemann, 2009)	Automatic	6,223,539
Sclera translations	www.pictoselector.eu	Manual	12,381

Table 1: The used translation sources

Figure 1 visualizes how we used the bilingual dictionaries to automatically evaluate the quality of the pre-established links between Cornetto and Princeton WordNet. We retrieve all the lemmas of the lexical units that were contained within a synset S_i (in our example, *snoepgoed "confectionary"* and *snoep "candy"* extracted from S_1). Each of these lemmas is looked up in the bilingual dictionary, resulting in a *dictionary words list* of English translations.[7] This list is used to estimate the correctness of the equivalence relation between the Cornetto and the Princeton synset.

We retrieve the *lexical units list* from the English synset T_j (in our example *candy* and *confect* extracted from T_1). We count the number of words in the *lexical units list* also appearing in the *dictionary words list* (the overlap being represented as the multiset Q). Translations appearing more than once are given more importance. For example, *candy* occurs twice, putting our overlap counter on 2. This overlap is normalized. In the example it is divided by 3 (*confect* + *candy* + *candy*, as the double count is taken into account), leaving us with a score of 66.67%. For the *gloss words list* we remove the stop words[8] and make an analogous calculation. In our example, *sweet* is counted twice (the overlap being represented as the multiset R) and this number is divided by the total number of gloss words available (again taking

[6] Other examples: *nederig "humble"* was linked to the synset for *flexible* (as a synonym for *elastic*), *waterachtig "aquatic"* was linked to the synsets for *grey* and *mousy*, *rocker* (*hardrocker*) was linked to the synset for *rocking chair*, etc.

[7] Note that this list can contain doubles (such as *candy* and *delicacy*), as these translations would provide additional evidence to our scoring algorithm. It is therefore not the case that the dictionary words list represents a *set*. It represents a *multiset*.

[8] http://norm.al/2009/04/14/list-of-english-stop-words

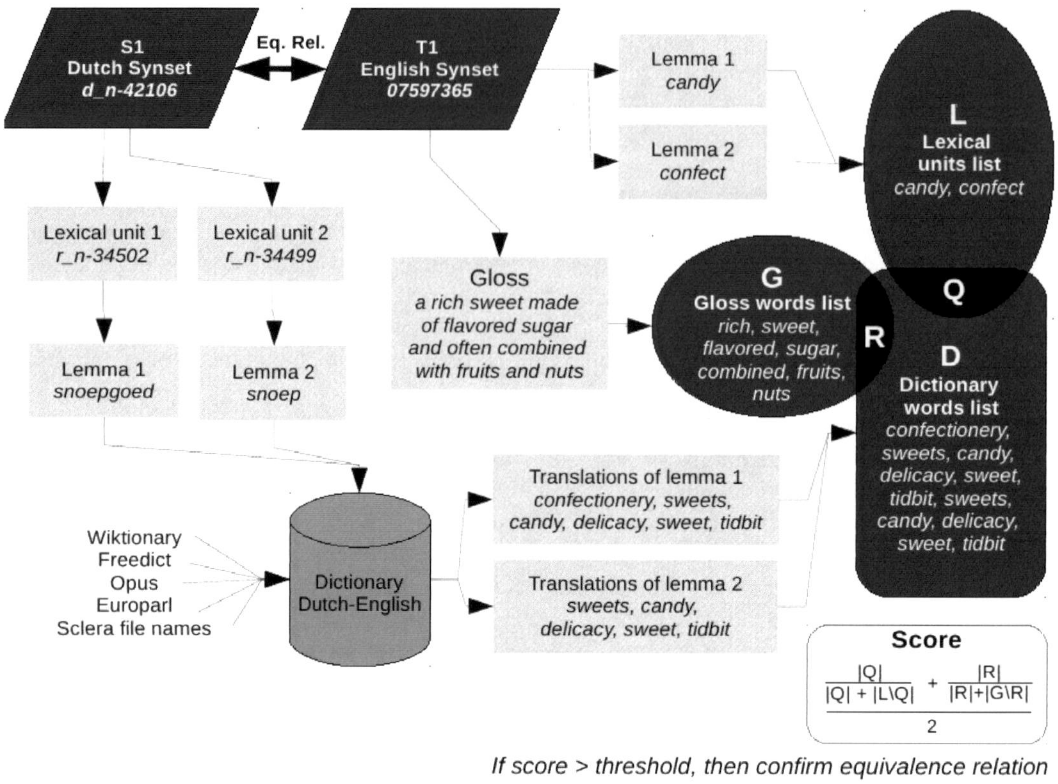

$$\frac{\frac{|Q|}{|Q| + |L\backslash Q|} + \frac{|R|}{|R|+|G\backslash R|}}{2}$$

Figure 1: The scoring mechanism with examples

into account the double count). Averaging this score of 25% with our first result, we obtain a confidence score of 45.83% for this equivalence relation. We calculated this confidence score for every equivalence relation in Cornetto.

We checked whether the automatic scoring algorithm (section 2) (dis)agreed with the manual judgements in order to determine a satisfactory threshold value for the acceptance of synset links. Evaluation results are shown in figure 2. While the precision (the proportion of accurate links that the system got right) went slightly up as our criterium for link acceptance became stricter, the recall (the proportion of correct links that the system retrieved) quickly made a rather deep dive. The F-score reveals that the best trade-off is reached when synset links getting a score of 0% are rejected, retaining any link with a higher confidence score. The results in Table 3 shows that we were able to reduce the error rate to 21.09%, which is a relative improvement of 40.20% over the baseline.

3 Improving the equivalence relations in the context of text-to-pictograph translation

Being able to use the currently available technological tools is becoming an increasingly important factor in today's society. *Augmentative and Alternative Communication* (AAC) refers to the whole of communication methods which aim to assist people that are suffering from cognitive disabilities, helping them to become more socially active in various domains of daily life. Text-to-pictograph translation is a particular form of AAC technology that enables linguistically-impaired people to use the Internet independently.

Filtering away erroneous synset links in Cornetto has proven to be a useful way to improve the quality of a text-to-pictograph translation tool. Vandeghinste and Schuurman (2014) have connected pictograph sets to Cornetto synsets to enable text-to-pictograph translation. Equivalence relations are important to allow reusing these connections in order to link pictographs to synsets for other languages than Dutch.

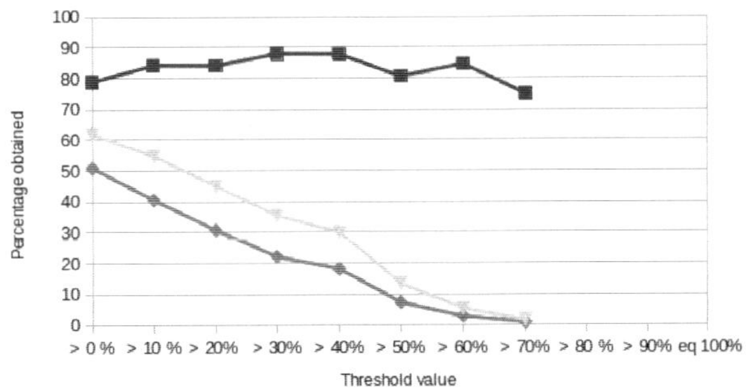

Figure 2: Precision (top line), recall (bottom line) and F-score (middle line) for different threshold values of link acceptance.

Vandeghinste and Schuurman (2014) released *Sclera2Cornetto*, a resource linking Sclera[9] pictographs to Cornetto synsets. Currently, over 13 000 Sclera pictographs are made available online, 5 710 of which have been manually linked to Cornetto synsets. We want to build a text-to-pictograph conversion with English and Spanish as source languages, reusing the Sclera2Cornetto data.

By improving Cornetto's pre-established equivalence relations with Princeton synsets, we can connect the Sclera pictographs with Princeton WordNet for English. The latter, in turn, will then be used as the intermediate step in our process of assigning pictographs to Spanish synsets.

Manual evaluations were made for a randomly generated subset of the synsets that were previously used by Vandeghinste and Schuurman (2014) for assigning Sclera and Beta[10] pictographs to Cornetto. Beta pictographs are another pictograph set for which a link between the pictographs and Cornetto was provided by Vandeghinste (2014).

Table 2 presents the coverage of our bilingual dictionary for synsets being connected to Sclera and Beta pictographs, which is clearly higher than the coverage over all synsets.

	Covered	Total	Difference with All synsets
All synsets	43 970 (52.18%)	84 264	-
Sclera baseline	5 294 (88.80%)	5 962	36.62%
Beta synsets	3 409 (88.94%)	3 833	36.76%

Table 2: Dictionary Coverage for different sets of synsets

Table 3 shows that the error rate of Cornetto's equivalence relations on the Sclera and Beta subsets is much lower than the error rate on the whole set (section 2). We attribute this difference to the fact that Vossen et al. (1999) carried out manual coding for the most important concepts in the database (see section 1), as the Sclera and Beta pictographs tend to belong to this category. In these cases, every synset has between one and two automatically derived English equivalents on the average, allowing us to roughly compare with the initial quality check of the equivalence relations performed by Vossen et al. (1999) showing that, in the event of a Dutch synset having only one English equivalent, 86% of the nouns and 78% of the verbs were correctly linked, while the ones having two equivalents were appropriate in 68% and 71% of the cases respectively.

The F-score in Figure 3 reveals that the best trade-off between precision and recall is reached at the $> 0\%$ threshold value, improving the baseline precision for both Sclera and Beta. We now retrieve all English synsets for which a non-zero score was obtained in order to assign Sclera and Beta pictographs to Princeton WordNet.

[9] http://www.sclera.be

[10] http://www.betavzw.be

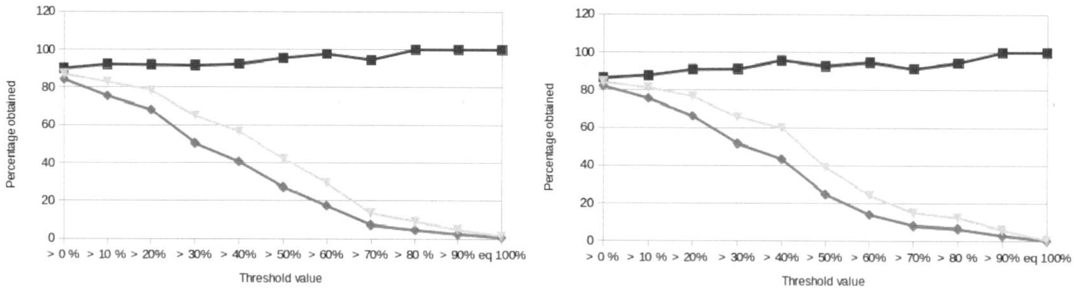

Figure 3: Precision (top line), recall (bottom line) and F-score (middle line) for Sclera and Beta synsets respectively, for different threshold values of link acceptance.

	Baseline	Current	Relative improvement
All	35.27%	21.09%	40.20%
Sclera	14.50%	9.95%	31.38%
Beta	15.77%	13.47%	14.58%

Table 3: The reduction in error rates of Cornetto's equivalence relations.

4 Related work

Using bilingual dictionaries to initiate or improve WordNet linkage has been applied elsewhere. Linking Chinese lemmata to English synsets (Huang et al., 2003) to create the Chinese WordNet is one such example. The 200 most frequent Chinese words and the 10 most frequent adjectives were taken as a starting set and found as translation equivalences for 496 English lemmata, making each Chinese lemma corresponding to 2.13 English synsets on average. Evaluations showed that 77% of the 496 equivalent pairs were synonymous. This accuracy rate dropped to 62.7% when the list of equivalence pairs was extended by including all WordNet synonyms. Sornlertlamvanich et al. (2008) assign synsets to bilingual dictionaries for Asian languages by considering English equivalents and lexical synonyms, listing all English translations and scoring synsets according to the amount of matching translations found, yielding an average accuracy rate of 49.4% for synset assignment to a Thai-English dictionary and an accuracy rate of 93.3% for synsets that are attributed the highest confidence score. Joshi et al. (2012) generate candidate synsets in English, starting with synsets in Hindi. For each Hindi synset, a bag of words is obtained by parsing its gloss, examples and synonyms. Using a bilingual dictionary, these Hindi words are translated to English. Various heuristics are used to calculate the intersection between the translated bag of words and the synset words, concepts or relations of the target language, such as finding the closest hyperonym synset (accuracy rate of 79.76%), the closest common synset word bag (accuracy rate of 74.48%) and the closest common concept word bag (accuracy rate of 55.20%). Finally, Soria et al. (2009) develop a mechanism for enriching monolingual lexicons with new semantic relations by relying on the use of Inter-Lingual-Indexes to link WordNets of different languages. However, the quality of these links is not evaluated.

5 Conclusions and future work

We have shown that a rather large reduction in error rates (a relative improvement of 40.20% on the whole set) concerning the equivalence relations between Cornetto and Princeton WordNet can be acquired by applying a scoring algorithm based on bilingual dictionaries. The method can be used to create new equivalence relations as well. Contrasting our results with related work shows that we reach at least the same level of correctness, although results are hard to compare because of conceptual differences between languages. An accuracy rate of 78.91% was obtained for the general set of Cornetto's equivalence relations, while its subset of Sclera and Beta synsets (denoting frequent concepts) acquired final precision rates of 90.05% and 86.53% respectively (compare with section 4).

One advantage of our method is that it could easily be reused to automatically build reliable links between Princeton WordNet and brand-new WordNets. Unsupervised clustering methods can provide us with synonym sets in the source language, after which the bilingual dictionary technique and the scoring algorithm can be applied in order to provide us with satisfactory equivalence relations between both languages. Semantic relations between synsets can then also be transferred from Princeton to the source language's WordNet.

Our improved links will be integrated in the next version of Cornetto. Future work will consist of scaling to other languages through other relations between WordNets.

6 Acknowledgements

We would like to thank Tom Vanallemeersch for providing us with the EuroParl and Opus alignment tables. We are also grateful to Martijn van der Kooij for sending us the mappings between the Dutch and English Sclera pictograph file names made in the Picto-selector project.

The research in this paper was partly funded by the support fund M.M. Delacroix under the Picto project, by the EU-CIP project Able-To-Include, and by the Program Advisory Committee of the Advanced Master of Artificial Intelligence of the University of Leuven.

References

Chu-Ren Huang, Elanna Tseng, Dylan Tsai and Brian Murphy. 2003. Cross-lingual Portability of Semantic relations: Bootstrapping Chinese WordNet with English WordNet Relations. *Languages and Linguistics*, 4(3): 509–532. Academia Sinica, Taipei.

Salil Joshi, Arindam Chatterjee, Arun Karthikeyan Karra and Pushpak Bhattacharyya. 2012. Eating Your Own Cooking: Automatically Linking Wordnet Synsets of Two Languages. *COLING (Demos)*: 239–246.

Philip Koehn. 2005. Europarl: A Parallel Corpus for Statistical Machine Translation. *Conference Proceedings: the tenth Machine Translation Summit*: 79–86. Phuket, Thailand.

Philip Koehn, Hieu Hoang, Alexandra Birch, Chris Callison-Burch, Marcello Federico, Nicola Bertoldi, Brooke Cowan, Wade Shen, Christine Moran, Richard Zens, Chris Dyer, Ondrej Bojar, Alexandra Constantin and Evan Herbst. 2007. Moses: Open Source Toolkit for Statistical Machine Translation *Annual Meeting of the Association for Computational Linguistics (ACL), demonstration session*. Prague, Czech Republic.

George A. Miller, Richard Beckwidth, Christiane Fellbaum, Derek Gross and Katherine Miller. 1990. Introduction to WordNet: An On-line Lexical Database. *International Journal of Lexicography*, 3(4): 235–244.

Franz Josef Och and Hermann Ney. 2003. A Systematic Comparison of Various Statistical Alignment Models. *Computational Linguistics*, 29(1): 19–51.

Claudia Soria, Monica Monachini, Francesca Bertagna, Nicoletta Calzolari, Chu-Ren Huang, Shu-Kai Hsieh, Andrea Marchetti and Maurizio Tesconi. 2009. Exploring Interoperability of Language Resources: the Case of Cross-lingual Semi-automatic Enrichment of Wordnets. In A. Witt, U. Heid, F. Sasaki and G. Sérasset (eds). *Special Issue on Interoperability of Multilingual Language Processing. Language Resources and Evaluation.*, 43(1): 87–96.

Virach Sornlertlamvanich, Thatsanee Charoenporn, Chumpol Mokarat, Hitoshi Isahara, Hammam Riza and Purev Jaimai. 2008. Synset Assignment for Bi-lingual Dictionary with Limited Resource. *Proceedings of the Third International Joint Conference on Natural Language Processing*: 673–678.

Jrg Tiedemann. 2009. News from OPUS – A Collection of Multilingual Parallel Corpora with Tools and Interfaces. In N. Nicolov and K. Bontcheva and G. Angelova and R. Mitkov (eds). *Recent Advances in Natural Language Processing*, Volume V. John Benjamins: Amsterdam/Philadelphia.

Vincent Vandeghinste. *Linking Pictographs to Synsets: Beta2Cornetto*. Technical report.

Vincent Vandeghinste and Ineke Schuurman. 2014. *Linking Pictographs to Synsets: Sclera2Cornetto*. LREC 2014. In press.

Piek Vossen. 1997. EuroWordNet: a multilingual database for information retrieval. *Proceedings of the DELOS workshop on Cross-language Information Retrieval*. Zurich.

Piek Vossen, Laura Bloksma, and Paul Boersma. 1999. The Dutch Wordnet. *EuroWordNet Paper*. University of Amsterdam, Amsterdam.

Piek Vossen, Katja Hofman, Maarten de Rijke, Erik Tjong Kim Sang and Koen Deschacht. 2007 The Cornetto Database: Architecture and User-Scenarios. *Proceedings of 7th Dutch-Belgian Information Retrieval Workshop DIR2007*. University of Leuven, Leuven.

Light verb constructions with 'do' and 'be' in Hindi: A TAG analysis

Ashwini Vaidya
University of Colorado
Boulder, CO
80309, USA
vaidyaa@colorado.edu

Owen Rambow
Columbia University
New York, NY
10115, USA
rambow@ccls.columbia.edu

Martha Palmer
University of Colorado
Boulder, CO
80309, USA
mpalmer@colorado.edu

Abstract

In this paper we present a Lexicalized Feature-based Tree-Adjoining Grammar analysis for a type of nominal predicate that occurs in combination with the light verbs "do" and "be" (Hindi *kar* and *ho* respectively). Light verb constructions are a challenge for computational grammars because they are a highly productive predicational strategy in Hindi. Such nominals have been discussed in the literature (Mohanan, 1997; Ahmed and Butt, 2011; Bhatt et al., 2013), but this work is a first attempt at a Tree-Adjoining Grammar (TAG) representation. We look at three possibilities for the design of elementary trees in TAG and explore one option in depth using Hindi data. In this analysis, the nominal is represented with all the arguments of the light verb construction, while the light verb adjoins into its elementary tree.

1 Introduction

Lexical resource development for computational analyses in Hindi must contend with a large number of light verb constructions. For instance, in the Hindi Treebank (Palmer et al., 2009), nearly 37% of the predicates have been annotated as light verb constructions. Hence, the combination of a noun with a light verb is a productive predicational strategy in Hindi. For example, the noun *yaad* 'memory' combines with *kar* 'do' to form *yaad kar* 'remember'.

In light verb constructions, the noun is a predicating element along with the light verb. The presence of two predicating elements representing a single meaning is a challenge for a linguistic theory that maps between syntax and semantics. Consequently, the argument structure representation for light verb constructions (LVC) has resulted in two opposing views in syntactic theory. One view supports a noun-centric analysis of the LVC, where the noun is represented with *all* the arguments of the LVC e.g. (Grimshaw and Mester, 1988; Kearns, 1988). The light verb's only role is to theta-mark the arguments of the LVC, without any semantic contribution. The second view proposes argument sharing between the noun and the light verb as they both contribute to the argument structure of the LVC (Butt, 1995; Ahmed et al., 2012). We refer to such analyses as verb-centric analyses.

Within the framework of this debate, we propose to use Lexicalized Feature-based Tree Adjoining Grammar, which is a variant of Tree Adjoining Grammar (TAG). TAG has been used to represent light verb constructions in French (Abeillé, 1988) and Korean (Han and Rambow, 2000). The primitive structures of TAG are its elementary trees, which encapsulate the syntactic and semantic arguments of its lexical anchor (for a light verb construction, the noun and light verb respectively will be the anchors). The association of a structural object with a linguistic anchor allows TAG to specify all the linguistic constraints associated with the anchor over a local domain. This is especially advantageous for composing the complex argument structure of a LVC. In comparison with other formalisms (e.g. context-free grammars), this property gives TAG an *extended domain of locality*.

Proceedings of the Workshop on Lexical and Grammatical Resources for Language Processing, pages 127–136,
Coling 2014, Dublin, Ireland, August 24 2014.

In this paper, we look at a particular group of nouns that occur with light verbs 'do' and 'be' (*kar* and *ho*) as part of a light verb construction. The same noun alternates with either light verb, resulting in a change in the argument structure of the verb. For example the noun *chorii* 'theft' can occur as either *chorii kar* 'theft do' or *chorii ho* 'theft happen'. There are nearly 265 nouns showing this alternation in the Hindi Treebank (Palmer et al., 2009)[1]. These constitute about 15% of the total light verb constructions in the Treebank. Note that other light verbs also occur in Hindi e.g. *de* 'give', *le* 'take' etc. but they are not part of this study.

Section 3 has some examples of these predicating nominals. Before this, Section 2 will introduce the TAG formalism. Section 4 describes the design of the elementary trees that are the basis of the analysis and in the final section we summarize our findings and make suggestions for future work.

2 Lexicalized Feature based Tree Adjoining Grammar

Tree-Adjoining Grammar (TAG) is a formal tree-rewriting system that is used to describe the syntax of natural languages (Joshi and Schabes, 1997). The basic structure of a TAG grammar is an elementary tree, which is a fragment of a phrase structure tree labelled with both terminal and non-terminal nodes. The elementary trees are combined by the operations of **substitution** (where a terminal node is replaced with a new tree) or **adjunction** (where an internal node is split to add a new tree).

The elementary trees in TAG can be enriched with feature structures (Vijay-Shanker and Joshi, 1988). These can capture linguistic descriptions in a more precise manner and also capture adjunction constraints. TAG with feature structures is also known as FTAG (Feature-structure based TAG). A TAG can also be lexicalized i.e., an elementary tree has a lexical item as one of its terminal nodes. Lexicalized TAG enhanced with feature structures is known as Lexicalized Feature-based Tree-Adjoining Grammar (LF-TAG). This has been used for developing computational grammars for English (XTAG-Group, 2001), French (Abeillé and Candito, 2000) and Korean (Han et al., 2000). In our analysis, we will also use LF-TAG, but we will refer to it as LTAG for convenience.

Figure 1 shows the basic steps for composing elementary trees containing feature structures. Each node has a top and a bottom feature structure. Features can be shared among nodes in an elementary tree. In the tree for the verb *running*, the variable $\boxed{1}$ is used to show that the verb must share the same features as the subject NP.

The tree for *running* is an **initial tree** with a single terminal for its argument noun phrase (NP). The tree for *is*, on the other hand, is a special type of elementary tree called the **auxiliary** tree. It has a foot node (marked with an asterisk), which is identical to its root node. The auxiliary tree will adjoin into the tree for *running* at the VP node only. The top and bottom feature structures for MODE at the VP node, have different values (*ind* and *ger*), and they cannot unify. This captures an adjunction constraint for *obligatory adjunction* and requires adjunction to take place at this node only.

During adjunction, the top of the root of the auxiliary tree (for *is*) will unify with the top of the adjunction site. The bottom of the foot of the auxiliary tree will unify with the bottom of the adjunction site. During substitution, the top node in the tree for *Jill* unifies with the node at NP.

This results in the second tree in Figure 1, post the operations of substitution and adjunction. In a final derivation step, top and bottom feature structures at each node will unify, to give the final derived tree with a single feature structure at each node. The resulting tree is called a *derived* tree, but another by-product of the TAG analysis is also the *derivation* tree. This tree has numbered node labels that record the history of composition of the elementary trees. For example, the tree for *Jill is running* can be seen in Figure 2. The root of this tree is labelled with *running*, which is an *initial* tree of the type *S*.

An important characteristic of lexicalized elementary trees is their correspondence with that lexical item's predicate-argument structure. This has sometimes been formalized as the PACP (Predicate-Argument Co-occurrence Principle) (Frank, 2002). The PACP restricts the structure of the elementary trees such that they may not be drawn arbitrarily. At the same time, lexicalized TAGs will often have the

[1]It is possible that many more nouns occur in this group, but all their alternations are not instantiated in the Treebank corpus.

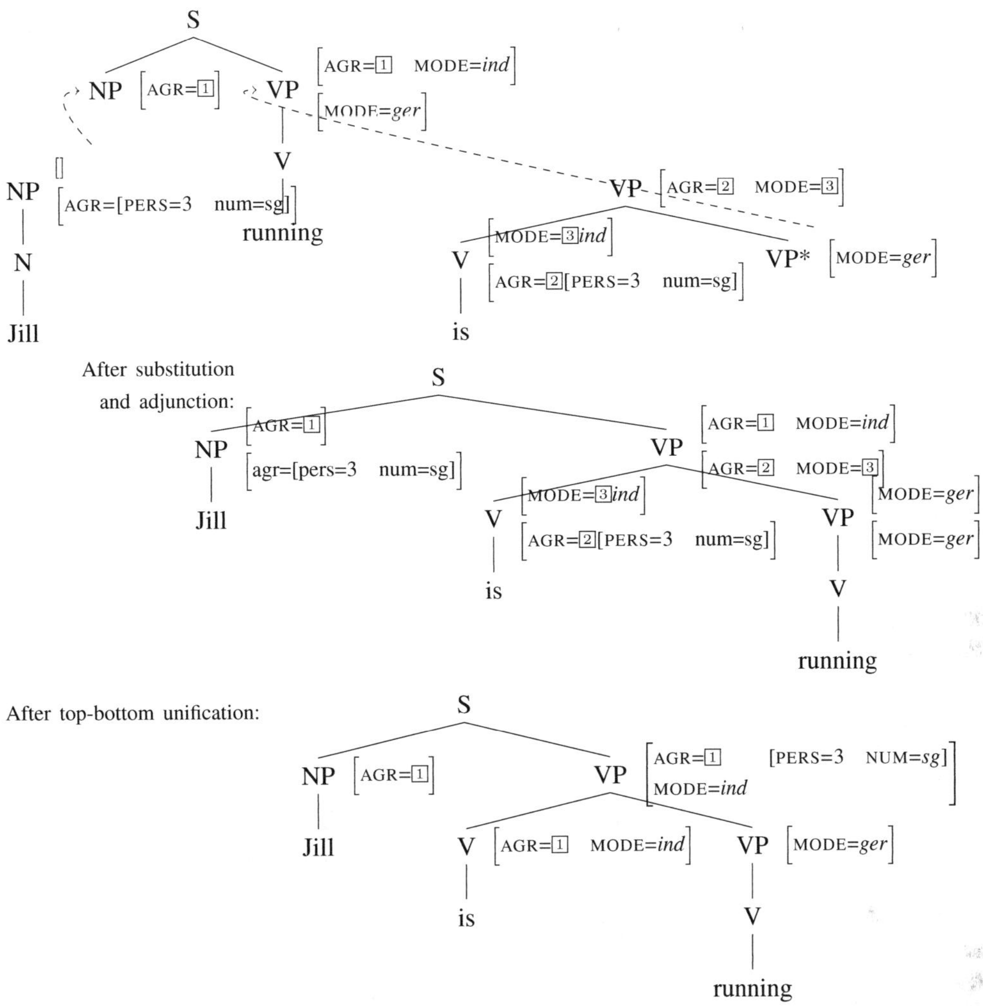

Figure 1: LTAG showing feature structures and constraints on adjunction (Example adapted from (Kallmeyer and Osswald, 2013))

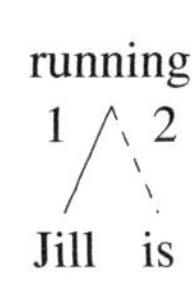

Figure 2: Derivation tree for 'Jill is running'. The dashed node indicates adjunction and the solid node indicates substitution

same lexical item realized as the anchor of varying syntactic realizations. For example a verb such as *run* will anchor a different elementary tree for its passive or interrogative variant.

3 Data

In this section, we introduce the nominal predicates that will be the focus of our LTAG analysis. Such nominals allow an agentive (ergative-marked[2]) subject with the light verb *kar* 'do'. In contrast, the same nominal does not have an agentive subject with *ho* 'be' (Ahmed and Butt, 2011). The alternation with *ho* 'be' has an intransitivizing effect. In (1) and (2), a change in the light verb results in the presence or absence of the agent argument. The nominal *chorii* is the same, but the LVC in (1) requires only a Theme argument, whereas (2) needs an Agent and a Theme.

(1) *gehene chorii hue.*
jewels.M theft.F be.Perf.MPl
'The jewels got stolen'

(2) *Ram-ne gehene chorii kiye.*
Ram-Erg jewels.M.Pl theft.F do.Perf.M.Pl
'Ram stole the jewels '

In English, a similar alternation structure may be found with light verbs in *bring to light* vs. *come to light* (Claridge, 2000). Here, two light verbs *bring* and *come* are used to express either a causative or inchoative reading. In the Hindi examples, the light verb *ho* 'be' and the light verb *kar* 'do' are used to express the inchoative vs. causative reading. In Persian, *kardan* 'make or do' and *ŝodan* 'become' are used in a manner similar (although not identical) to Hindi.

The noun *chorii* 'theft' belongs to a particular class of nouns where a change in the light verb does result in a change in the arguments, but the agent argument is always presupposed, irrespective of the light verb. For instance, the addition of a phrase such as *apne-aap* 'on its own' is semantically odd with example 1. This is because the event of 'theft' cannot occur without an agent, although it is unexpressed with the light verb *ho* 'be'. Contrast this with 4, where *apne-aap* is not odd and where the alternation with *kar* 'do' is not possible. The non-alternating noun *afsos* 'regret' occurs with an Experiencer subject, which can act spontaneously and hence allows the use of *apne-aap*.

(3) ??*aaj apne-aap gehene chorii hue*
today own-mine jewels.M theft.F be.Pres.MPl
'??Today the jewels got stolen by themselves '

(4) *aaj Ram-ko is baat-par apne-aap afsos huaa/*kiyaa.*
today Ram-Dat this issue-Loc own-mine regret.M be.Perf.M.Sg/*do.Perf.M.Sg
'Today Ram himself regretted this point/issue '

In order to model such nominals in TAG we have three options: first, a noun-centric analysis, where the nominal projects all the arguments of the LVC. In reference to the examples above, this would imply that the light verb *chorii* 'theft' would be represented by two trees– i.e., it would appear with two arguments with *kar* 'do' and only one with *ho* 'be'.

The second option is a verb-centric analysis, where the light verb *kar* 'do' would contribute the agentive argument, and *chorii* would contribute the object. The nominal's elementary tree would consist of only one argument, regardless of whether it combined with *kar* 'do' or *ho* 'be'. The third option is to

[2]Hindi is a split-ergative language, where ergative case on the subject is found only with transitive verbs in the perfective aspect. For non-perfective aspect, the subject is nominative.

represent the LVC *chorii kar* 'theft do; steal' as the anchor of a single elementary tree– a single multi-word expression. While the first two options are worth exploring, we discard the third option for two reasons: first, the LVC is highly productive in Hindi, which would imply that this would result in too many elementary trees in the grammar. Second, there is evidence that the LVC forms a phrasal category in the syntax (Mohanan, 1997; Davison, 2005). This means that individual components of the LVC may be moved away from each other, emphatic particles or negation may intervene and the noun component may be independently modified by an adjective. Therefore, the multi-word option would not be the best approach here. This is in contrast to previous TAG analyses for English LVCs where both nominal and verb are anchored in the same elementary tree (XTAG-Group, 2001).

Figure 3 shows the derivation trees (cf. Figure 2) for the three different analysis options as described above for the sentence *Ram ne gehene chorii kiye* 'Ram stole the jewels'. The LVC in question is *chorii kar* 'theft do'. The dashed line indicates adjunction into the elementary tree, whereas the solid line indicates substitution. In the noun-centric analysis, the light verb adjoins into the nominal's elementary tree and contributes no arguments of its own. For the verb-centric analysis, the light verb contributes the argument *Ram*, whereas the nominal contributes *jewels*. Finally, for the multi-word expression tree, *theft* and *do* are both anchors of the elementary tree.

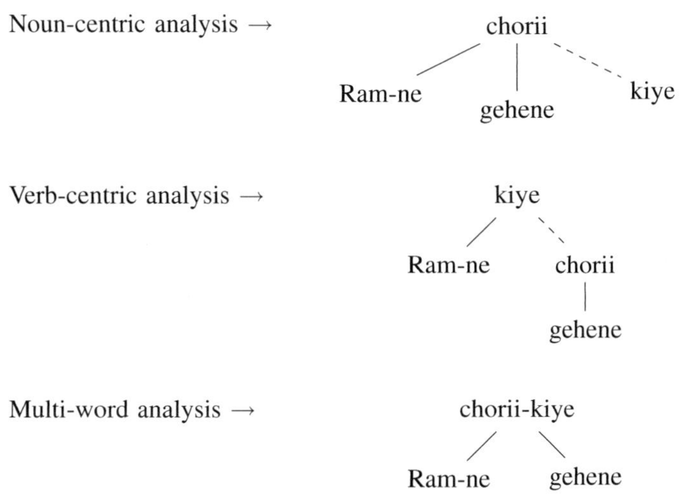

Figure 3: Derivation graphs showing three options for the analysis of *Ram ne gehene chorii kiye* 'Ram stole the jewels'. The LVC is *chorii kiye*.

In this paper we explore a noun-centric analysis of Hindi LVCs.[3]In the analysis that follows, we will describe two elementary trees for a noun like *chorii* i.e., when it combines with either *ho* 'be' or *kar* 'do'. Making the elementary structures richer and more complex increases ambiguity locally and we then have more descriptions for the same lexical item. But these structures also capture local dependencies i.e., the fact that the lexical item can appear in varying linguistic environments. Second, this is in keeping with the TAG notion of using complex elementary structures to capture linguistic properties and having very general operations (substitution and adjunction) to combine these structures. This has been used effectively in computational applications and is characterised by the slogan *complicate locally, simplify globally* (Bangalore and Joshi, 2010).

4 Analysis

In a noun-centric analysis, the light verb does not have arguments of its own. The full array of arguments for the light verb construction is instead represented in the nominal's tree. The light verb can only choose

[3]Based on the comments of the reviewers we are now considering a revision of the noun-centric analysis in this paper. It may seem that a verb-centric analysis may be more appropriate for Hindi LVCs. However, due to lack of space, we do not explore the second option fully in this paper and leave it to future work.

the semantic property of the nominal it may combine with (e.g., the light verb *ho* may combine only with nominals that have no agentive arguments). Other analyses e.g Ahmed et al. (2012) represent the light verb *kar* 'do' with arguments of its own. We discuss this in Section 5.

Our work follows Han and Rambow (2000)'s representation of Sino-Korean LVCs. This work has also proposed separate trees for the nominal and light verb. The elementary tree of the nominal is an an initial tree, and as it is considered the true predicate, it also chooses a syntactic structure that will realize all its arguments. The light verb on the other hand is represented as an auxiliary tree, therefore it is an adjunct to the nominal's basic structure. However, as it is a predicate, it is also a special type of auxiliary tree viz., a predicative auxiliary tree (Abeillé and Rambow, 2000).

The second feature of this analysis, also based on Han and Rambow (2000)'s work is the idea of the nominal as an underspecified base form. The nominal's elementary tree is not specified with respect to its category, rather, we use the label X, which projects to an XP. We also assume, following Han and Rambow that each node is specified with the feature `CAT` which has values like V or N, but the [`CAT=N`] feature on the noun is not realized unless the light verb composes with the elementary tree of the nominal. In addition, although the nominal is not a verb, it has the feature `TENSE=-` i.e., it is not tensed.

4.1 The light verb

In order to model the light verb *kar* 'do' in Example 2, we will construct an auxiliary tree with feature structures, anchored at *kar* 'do'. Figure 4 shows such an elementary tree. Note that this is a very different tree from 'full' *kar* 'do', which will have all its arguments. The light verb *kar* is inflected for person, number, and gender as well as tense and aspect. In this particular example, it is tensed, masculine, plural and has perfective aspect; therefore it appears as *kiye*. We assume that morphological analysis has already taken place in a separate module, such that the correct morphological surface form has been derived for 'do, masculine plural perfective'. In Figure 4, the XP_r (root) node and its right-branching daughters are [`CAT=V`] with linguistic information about gender, number, tense and aspect. The feature `AGT=+` at the top node implies that this auxiliary tree needs to unify with an initial tree that is also [`AGT=+`]. In contrast with *kar* 'do', the auxiliary tree of the light verb *ho* 'be' will have [`AGT=-`].

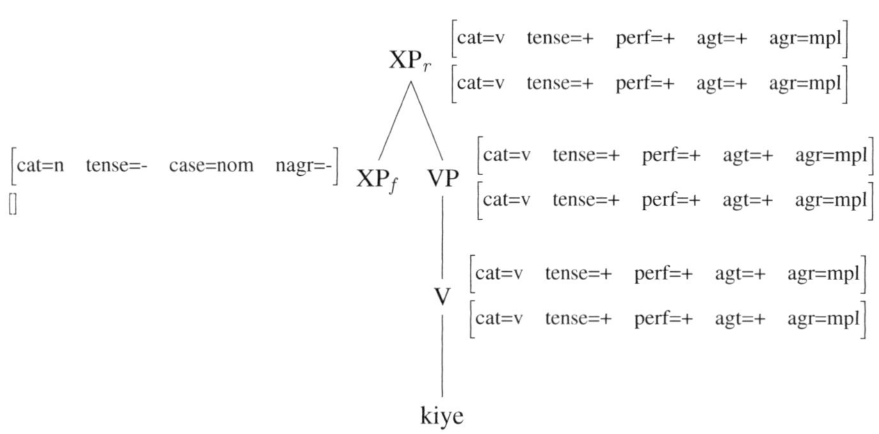

Figure 4: Elementary tree for light verb *kar* 'do' inflected as *kiye*'do.masc.pl.perf'

The XP_f (foot) node has [`TENSE=-`] and [`CAT=N`], which will enable it to adjoin into the elementary tree of a nominal. The `CASE` value is specified as `NOM` (nominative) as the light verb will assign nominative case to the noun. The `NAGR` feature is required when the light verb agrees in number and gender with the predicative nominal itself (Mohanan, 1997). As this will not occur in the examples we are working with, the value for `NAGR` is negative. For other 'standard' cases of agreement, the feature `AGR` is used (It is also useful to note that the verbal agreement rule in Hindi differs from English as the verb agrees with the highest nominative marked argument- and not necessarily the subject (Mohanan, 1995)).

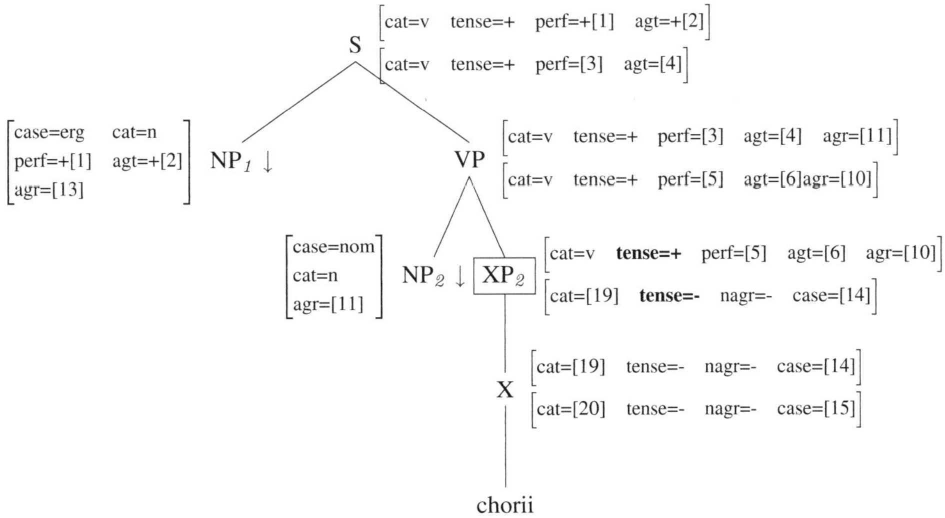

Figure 5: Tree for nominal *chorii* 'theft' -agentive, as seen in *Ram ne gehene chorii kiye* "Ram stole the jewels". The feature clash at XP_2 is marked with a box.

4.2 The nominal

In contrast to the impoverished argument structure of the light verb, the nominal in Figure 5 has the full array of arguments for *chorii* 'theft'. The tree is anchored by the lexical item *chorii* and the non terminals at NP_1 and NP_2 are marked with a ↓ for substitution with the actual lexical items.

The position of the arguments roughly follows the configuration described in Bhatt et al. (2013, p. 59) , where the first position is the ergative-marked argument and is found in a transitive sentence (but only if the property [PERF=+] is also present.)

The 'second' position is one where the object of the transitive verb is found. In Figure 5, this is represented as NP_2 and is the nominative marked argument. The elementary tree for the nominal is not complete, because of the feature clash at XP_2 between [TENSE=+] vs. [TENSE=−]. The feature clash represents an obligatory adjunction constraint which will require the light verb to adjoin at this node.

The first position in Figure 5 has the features for [PERF=+] and [AGT=+] as a consequence of having [CASE=ERG]. The agentive argument shares the values for PERF and AGT with the S node. This ensures that the light verb that adjoins into this tree will match the PERF and AGT values in NP_1. The argument in second position NP_2 will share its values for AGR with XP_2. At XP_2, the values for PERF, AGT and AGR should match with the root node of the light verb. Otherwise, adjunction will fail.

The light verb's tree as shown in Figure 4 will adjoin into the tree of the nominal. Post adjunction and substitution, we find a composed structure as seen in Figure 7.

The same noun *chorii* 'theft' may combine with the light verb *ho*. In that case, non-agentive *chorii* will choose an elementary tree such as Figure 6. This elementary tree appears without an agentive argument. Its single nominative Theme argument has moved to the first position at NP_1, leaving behind a co-indexed trace. Figure 6 shows that the site of adjunction into *chorii* 'theft' (non-agentive) is at XP_1. Adjunction cannot take place at XP_2 as the feature clash is higher up at XP_1. The single nominative argument of *chorii* (non-agentive) will move up to NP_1 in order to receive nominative case from the node CAT=V (Note that the node immediately above NP_2 has an underspecified CAT feature and this requires the argument to move to a higher position). The tree for non-agentive *chorii* will always combine with a light verb that is AGT=−. Its Theme argument will take nominative case irrespective of the tense-aspect value of the verb.

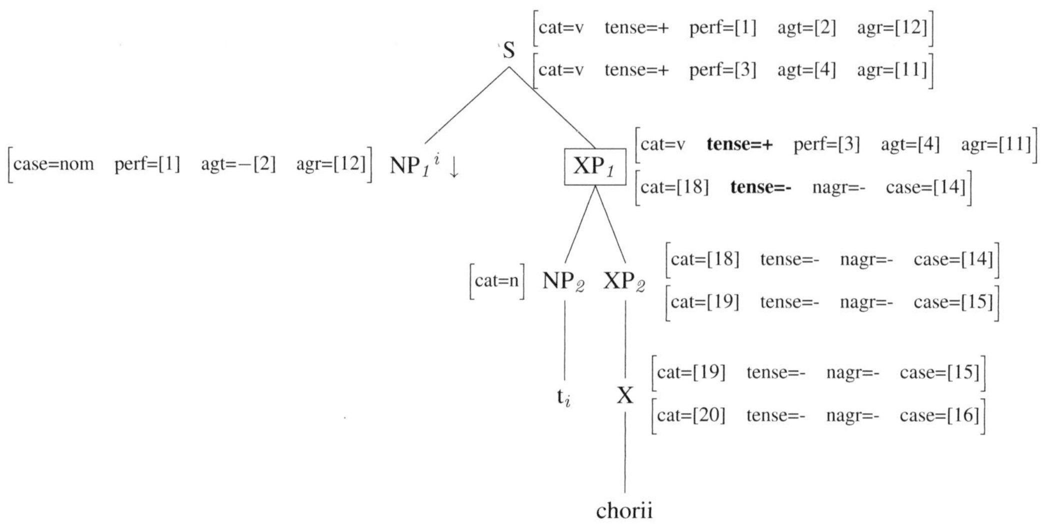

Figure 6: Tree for nominal *chorii* - non agentive as seen in *gehene chorii hue* 'The jewels were stolen'. The feature clash this time is higher in the tree at XP_1 and is marked with a box.

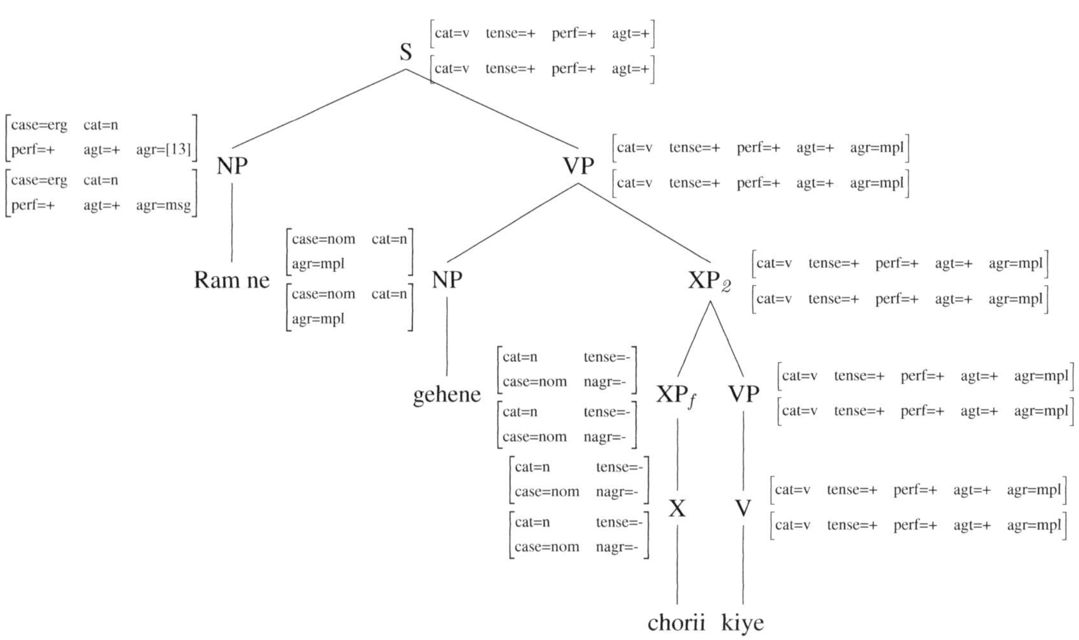

Figure 7: Post adjunction of the light verb's auxiliary tree into the initial tree *chorii* 'theft' at XP_2, we get the complete argument structure. Substitution at the nodes NP_1 and NP_2 gives us *Ram ne gehene chorii kiye* 'Ram stole the jewels'

5 Discussion

The elementary trees for *chorii* 'theft'–both agentive and non-agentive are able to capture its alternations with *kar* "do" and *ho* 'be'. This is in contrast to Ahmed et al. (2012)'s approach in an important way. They do not consider the nominal's alternation with the light verb *ho* "be" as a light verb construction. Instead, they maintain that it has a resultative reading and provide a different analysis within the Lexical Functional Grammar (LFG) framework. In fact, the alternation with *ho* "be" provides a useful lexical alternative to an alternative syntactic structure (such as a passive). The alternation of the light verb *ho* "be" and *kar* "do" is moreover a characteristic of a certain group of nominals only (not all can show this alternation e.g., *intizar* "waiting" cf. Ahmed and Butt (2011)). Therefore, we maintain that *chorii ho* "theft happen" is indeed a light verb construction.

Ahmed and Butt (2011)'s analysis looks at the noun and light verb as co-predicators i.e., it is a verb centric analysis. While this is different from the proposed analysis here, it is not impossible to construct elementary trees where the light verb's elementary tree consists of one argument i.e., the subject and the nominal (with its own argument) adjoins into it. The pros and cons of these two approaches need to be explored more thoroughly within the TAG framework and we leave this to future work.

While this work has examined one class of nominals that occur as part of light verb constructions, it does not complete the analysis of light verb constructions in Hindi. The behaviour of other nominal classes remains to be explored. There are also nominals that occur with light verbs other than *kar* 'do' and *ho* 'be'. Finally, while the work presented here is mainly theoretical, it is in keeping with recent proposals for extracting a Hindi TAG grammar from a phrase structure treebank (Bhatt et al., 2012; Mannem et al., 2009). The algorithm in Bhatt et al. (2012) relies on the annotated Hindi Dependency Treebank and proposes a rule extraction system for elementary trees. Therefore, the description of Hindi LVCs in TAG would be a useful addition to the implementation of a grammar extraction task.

Acknowledgements

The first author was supported by DAAD (Deutscher Akademischer Austausch Dienst) for a research stay at the University of Konstanz in 2013-14s. We are also thankful to Prof Miriam Butt for hosting the first author at the University of Konstanz. We would like to thank Bhuvana Narasimhan, Miriam Butt and the anonymous reviewers for their useful remarks on this paper. Any errors that remain are our own.

References

Anne Abeillé and Marie-Hélène Candito. 2000. FTAG: A Lexicalized Tree-Adjoining Grammar for French. In *Tree Adjoining Grammars: Formalisms, Linguistic Analysis and Processing*. CSLI Publications.

Anne Abeillé and Owen Rambow. 2000. Tree Adjoining Grammar: An Overview. In Anne Abeillé and Owen Rambow, editors, *Tree Adjoining Grammars: Formalisms, Linguistic Analysis and Processing*. CSLI Publications.

Anne Abeillé. 1988. Light verb constructions and Extraction out of NP in TAG. In Lynn MacLeod, Gary Larson, and Diane Brentari, editors, *Proceedings of the 24th Annual Meeting of the Chicago Linguistics Society*.

Tafseer Ahmed and Miriam Butt. 2011. Discovering Semantic Classes for Urdu N-V Complex Predicates. In *Proceedings of the International Conference on Computational Semantics (IWCS 2011), Oxford*.

Tafseer Ahmed, Miriam Butt, Annette Hautli, and Sebastian Sulger. 2012. A reference dependency bank for analyzing complex predicates. In *Proceedings of the Eight International Conference on Language Resources and Evaluation (LREC'12)*.

Srinivas Bangalore and Aravind Joshi. 2010. Introduction. In Srinivas Bangalore and Aravind Joshi, editors, *Supertagging: Using Complex Lexical Descriptions in Natural Language Processing*, pages 1–31. MIT Press, Cambridge.

Rajesh Bhatt, Owen Rambow, and Fei Xia. 2012. Creating a Tree Adjoining Grammar from a Multilayer Treebank. In *Proceedings of the 11th International Workshop on Tree Adjoining Grammars and Related Formalisms (TAG+11)*, pages 162–170.

Rajesh Bhatt, Annahita Farudi, and Owen Rambow. 2013. Hindi-Urdu Phrase Structure Annotation Guidelines. http://verbs.colorado.edu/hindiurdu/guidelines_docs/PhraseStructureguidelines.pdf, November.

Miriam Butt. 1995. *The Structure of Complex Predicates in Urdu*. CSLI Publications, Stanford.

Claudia Claridge. 2000. *Multi-word Verbs in Early Modern English: A Corpus-based Study*. Editions Rodopi B. V., Amsterdam-Atlanta edition.

Alice Davison. 2005. Phrasal predicates: How N combines with V in Hindi/Urdu. In Tanmoy Bhattacharya, editor, *Yearbook of South Asian Languages and Linguistics*, pages 83–116. Mouton de Gruyter.

Robert Frank. 2002. *Phrase Structure Composition and Syntactic Dependencies*. MIT Press, Cambridge.

Jane Grimshaw and Armin Mester. 1988. Light verbs and theta-marking. *Linguistic Inquiry*, 9(2):205–232.

Chung-hye Han and Owen Rambow. 2000. The Sino-Korean light verb construction and lexical argument structure. In *Proceedings of the Fifth International Workshop on Tree-Adjoining Grammars and Related Formalisms, TAG+5*.

Chung-hye Han, Juntae Yoon, Nari Kim, and Martha Palmer. 2000. A Feature based Lexicalized Tree Adjoining Grammar for Korean. Technical report, Institute for Research in Cognitive Science, University of Pennsylvania, http://www.cis.upenn.edu/~xtag/koreantag.

Aravind Joshi and Y. Schabes. 1997. Tree-adjoining grammars. In G. Rozenburg and A. Salomaa, editors, *Handbook of Formal Languages*, volume 3, pages 69–124. Springer.

Laura Kallmeyer and Rainer Osswald. 2013. Syntax-driven semantic frame composition in Lexicalized Tree Adjoining Grammars. *Journal of Language Modelling*, 1(2):267–330.

Kate Kearns. 1988. Light verbs in English. Manuscript, MIT (revised 2002).

Prashanth Mannem, Aswarth Abhilash, and Akshar Bharati. 2009. LTAG-spinal Treebank and Parser for Hindi. In *Proceedings of ICON-2009: 7th International Conference on Natural Language Processing*.

Tara Mohanan. 1995. Wordhood and Lexicality- Noun Incorporation in Hindi. *Natural Language and Linguistic Theory*, 13:75–134.

Tara Mohanan. 1997. Multidimensionality of representation- NV complex predicates in Hindi. In Alex Alsina, Joan Bresnan, and Peter Sells, editors, *Complex Predicates*. CSLI Publications, Stanford.

Martha Palmer, Rajesh Bhatt, Bhuvana Narasimhan, Owen Rambow, Dipti Misra Sharma, and Fei Xia. 2009. Hindi Syntax: Annotating Dependency, Lexical Predicate-Argument Structure, and Phrase Structure. In *Proceedings of ICON-2009: 7th International Conference on Natural Language Processing*, Hyderabad.

K. Vijay-Shanker and Aravind Joshi. 1988. Feature structure based Tree Adjoining Grammars. In *Proceedings of COLING 1988*.

The XTAG-Group. 2001. A Lexicalized Tree Adjoining Grammar for English. Technical report, IRCS, University of Pennsylvania.

The Lexicon-Grammar of Italian Idioms

Simonetta Vietri
Department of Political,
Social and Communication
Sciences
University of Salerno, Italy
vietri@unisa.it

Abstract

This paper presents the Lexicon-Grammar classification of Italian idioms that has been constructed on formal principles and, as such, can be exploited in information extraction. Among MWEs, idioms are those fixed constructions which are hard to automatically detect, given their syntactic flexibility and lexical variation. The syntactic properties of idioms have been formally represented and coded in binary matrixes according to the Lexicon-Grammar framework. The research takes into account idioms with ordinary verbs as well as support verb idiomatic constructions. The overall classification counts 7,000+ Italian idioms. In particular, two binary matrixes of two classes of idioms will be presented. The class **C1** refers to the Verb + Object constructions, whereas the class **EPC** refers to the prepositional constructions with the support verb *essere*. Pre-constructed lexical resources facilitate idioms retrieval both in the case of "hybrid" and "knowledge-based" approaches to Natural Language Processing.

1 Introduction

Idioms, and multi-word expressions in general, have always been "a pain in the neck", as Sag et al. (2001) state in the title of their paper. The formal representation and the construction of a computational linguistic model of idioms is not an easy task as shown by Gazdar et al. (1985), Pulman (1993), Abeillé (1995), Villavicencio et al. (2004), Muzny and Zettlemoyer (2013) to name a few of the many (computational) linguists who have carried out research on this topic.

It has always been pointed out that the main problem concerning the automatic analysis of idioms is the difficulty to disambiguate such constructions which are ambiguous by definition (Fothergill and Baldwin 2012, Li and Sporlender 2009, Fazly et al. 2009, McShane and Nirenburg 2014). However, given the flexibility of idioms, a more basic and still unsolved problem has to be taken into account: that is, the extraction and annotation of such constructions (Fellbaum 2011).

As Fazly et al. (2009, p. 61) point out "despite a great deal of research on the properties of idioms in the linguistics literature, there is not much agreement on which properties are characteristics of these expressions". The distinction drawn by Nunberg et al. (1994) between *idiomatic phrases* and *idiomatically combining expressions* has been adopted by most of the research on idioms. However, many problems still remain and they are due to two basic reasons. On one hand, idioms can be considered lexical units, given the fact that their "special meaning" is associated to a particular verb and one or more particular complements. On the other hand, idioms syntactically behave as non-idiomatic constructions. Passive is the syntactic construction more frequently analyzed by the linguistic research on idioms since it involves the occurrence of the fixed object to the left of the verb. However, idioms show a great deal of other syntactic constructions where the fixed object may not necessarily occur in postverbal position (see Vietri 2014, forthcoming).

It is for these peculiarities that idioms have also aroused the interest of the psycholinguistic researchers who have advanced several hypothesis on the processing of idioms (Swinney and Cutler,

Proceedings of the Workshop on Lexical and Grammatical Resources for Language Processing, pages 137–146,
Coling 2014, Dublin, Ireland, August 24 2014.

1979; Gibbs, 1995; Cacciari and Tabossi, 1988; Cutting and Bock, 1997; Sprenger et al., 2006).

The systematic description of French idiomatic and non-idiomatic constructions has been carried out by Gross (1982, 1988) and his colleagues (Leclère, 2002) on the basis of the formal principles of the Lexicon-Grammar methodology, as developed by Gross (1975, 1979). According to Gross, the basic syntactic unit is not the word but the simple or elementary sentence, and the Lexicon-Grammar of a language is organized into three main components: free sentences, frozen sentences (or idioms), support verbs sentences (Gross 1981, 1998). For each component, Gross and his colleagues built exhaustive classifications, systematically organized and represented by binary matrixes (named Lexicon-Grammar tables), where each syntactic and/or distributional property is marked "+" or "-" if accepted or not by a certain lexical unit. In the Lexicon-Grammar methodology, idiomatic and non-idiomatic constructions are built according to the same formal principles. The difference between these two types of constructions mainly concerns the distribution: idioms show a higher level of restricted distribution than non-idioms. The French Lexicon-Grammars are available at http://infolingu.univ-mlv.fr/english/.

A classification of English idioms and phrasal verbs has been carried out according to the same formal principles and criteria, respectively, by Freckleton (1985) and Machonis (1985). A Lexicon-Grammar of European Portuguese idioms has been built by Baptista (2005a, 2005b).

The Lexicon-Grammar classification of Italian idioms has been implemented on the basis of Gross' methodology. It includes more than 30 Lexicon-Grammar classes of idioms with ordinary verbs (sec. 2) and support verbs (sec. 3), for a total of more than 7,000 lexical entries[1]. The binary matrixes are created in Excel format.

2 The Lexicon-Grammar of Italian Idioms with Ordinary Verbs

The Lexicon-Grammar of idioms using ordinary verbs includes 12 classes for a total of 3,990 entries (sec. 2.1, Table 1). Each class of idioms contains those constructions which share the same definitional structure. In the Lexicon-Grammar framework, the definitional structure is identified on the basis of the arguments required by the operators (see Harris 1982). In the case of idioms, the operator consists of the Verb and the Fixed element(s), while the argument may be the subject and/or a free complement. This section shows only the main differences between the idioms' classes **C1** and **CAN**.

For example, idioms in (1) and (2) have two different definitional structures. On one hand, an idiom such as *tagliare la corda* in (1) is an operator that requires only one argument, i.e. the subject. On the other hand, an idiom such as *rompere le balle* in (2) is an operator that requires two arguments, the subject and the noun *Amy* within the prepositional complement. The prepositions *a* and *di* alternate and can be considered fixed:

1. *Amy ha tagliato la corda* "to sneak off"
   Amy-has-cut-the-rope
2. *Joe ha rotto le balle (a + di) Amy* "to annoy sb."
   Joe-has-broken-the-balls-(to + of)-Amy

Idioms such as (1) have been listed and analyzed in a class named **C1**, that counts about 1,200 entries. Furthermore, **C** indicates the "constrained" or "fixed" noun and **1** refers to its position in the sentence, in this case, the object position. These idioms have only one argument, that is the (non-fixed noun) in subject position. The definitional structure of the class **C1** is $\mathbf{N_0\ V\ C_1}$ where **N** indicates the free noun, **V** the verb and **C**, as previously stated, the fixed element. The subscripts **0** and **1** indicate the position of the noun within the sentence in a linear order, in this case, the subject and the object position.

Idioms such as (2) have been listed and analyzed in the class named **CAN**, that counts 320 entries. The definitional structure of this class is $\mathbf{N_0\ V\ C_1\ (a + di)\ N_2}$, since these idioms have two arguments,

[1] Vietri (1984) includes the very first classification of Italian idioms. Since then, the classification has been widely enriched, updated and completely re-examined. For a semantic study of Italian idioms, see Casadei (1996). A Lexicon-Grammar classification of Verb-particle constructions has been developed by Guglielmo (2013). From a different perspective, Masini (2005) provides a synchronic and diacronic analysis of Italian verb-particle constructions found in a corpus.

i.e. the subject $\mathbf{N_0}$ and the noun $\mathbf{N_2}$. The alternation of the prepositions *a* and *di* is represented between brackets, and the "+" sign indicates "either/or".

Each class, formally represented by a table in the form of a binary matrix, contains a specific number of idiomatic entries associated with a specific number of distributional and syntactic properties. In particular, each row of the matrix corresponds to an idiom, and each column to a property (or a construction). If the idiom accepts that particular property, a "+" sign is placed at the intersection between the row and the column; otherwise a "-" sign occurs.

As a sample of this type of lexical resource, I will give an excerpt of the class **C1** in Figure 1. The central non-numbered columns indicate the "part of speech" assigned to each lexical element that constitutes the idiomatic construction. In an idiom like *non alzare un dito* (lit. not lift a finger), the negation *non* is obligatory. On the other hand, the *si*-pronominal form is obligatory in idioms like *leccar<u>si</u> i baffi* (lit. lick-si the moustaches). The determiner can be Definite (Def), Indefinite (Ind), or null (Zero). As previously pointed out, **V** refers to the verb and **C** to the fixed noun.

The properties from [**1**] to [**3**] indicate the distribution of $\mathbf{N_0}$, i.e. the subject. It can be expressed by [± human] noun or a by a sentence [Ch F].

The distributional property [**4**] indicates if $\mathbf{C_1}$ is expressed by a body-part noun, whereas the morphological property [**5**] indicates if $\mathbf{C_1}$ can be in the plural form. Property [**4**] showed that 1,700+ idioms involve a body-part noun, at least the 24% of the overall classification. Property [**5**] is a useful piece of information because it refers to the possible variation of the fixed noun and, consequently, of the determiner.

[**1**] N_0 = + hum	[**2**] N_0 = - hum	[**3**] N_0 = Ch F	Neg	Pro	**V**	Def	Ind	Zero	$\mathbf{C_1}$	[**4**] C_1= body-part	[**5**] C_1= plural	[**6**] Unaccusative DET C_1 si V	[**7**] DET C_1 essere (V-PP + Adj)	[**8**] N_0 avere Det C_1 (V-PP + Adj)	[**9**] N_0 avere C da V-Inf	[**10**] Nominal = V-n di (Det+0) C_1	[**11**] VC Compound
+	-	-	-	-	allungare	il	-	-	muso	+	-	-	-	+	-	-	-
+	-	-	non	-	alzare	-	un	-	dito	+	-	-	-	-	-	-	-
+	-	-	-	-	alzare	la	-	-	testa	+	-	-	-	+	-	+	-
+	-	-	-	-	chiudere	il	-	-	capitolo	-	-	+	+	-	+	-	-
+	-	-	-	-	dipanare	la	una	-	matassa	-	-	+	+	-	+	-	-
+	-	-	-	-	incrociare	le	-	-	braccia	+	-	-	+	+	-	-	-
+	-	-	-	-	ingoiare	il	un	-	rospo	-	+	-	-	-	+	-	-
+	-	-	-	si	leccare	i	-	-	baffi	+	-	-	-	-	-	+	-
+	-	-	-	si	mangiare	il	-	-	fegato	+	-	-	-	-	-	-	-
+	-	-	-	si	mangiare	la	-	-	lingua	+	-	-	-	-	-	-	-
+	+	+	-	-	mostrare	la	-	-	corda	-	-	-	-	-	-	-	-
+	-	-	-	-	perdere	il	-	+	tempo	-	-	-	-	-	+	+	perditempo
+	-	-	-	-	rizzare	gli	-	-	orecchi	+	-	-	+	+	-	-	-
+	-	-	-	-	rompere	il	-	-	ghiaccio	-	-	+	+	-	-	-	-
+	-	-	-	-	scoprire	l'	-	-	acqua calda	-	-	-	-	-	-	+	-
+	-	-	-	-	scoprire	le	-	-	carte	-	-	-	+	+	+	-	-
+	-	-	-	-	scoprire	l'	-	-	America	-	-	-	-	-	-	+	-
+	-	-	-	-	tappare	il	un	-	buco	-	+	-	-	-	+	-	tappabuchi
+	-	-	-	-	vendere	-	-	-	fumo	-	-	-	-	-	+	-	vendifumo

Figure 1. The Class **C1**

The syntactic properties are numbered from **[6]** to **[10]**. In particular, **[6]** and **[7]** refer, respectively, to the unaccusative (3b) and the adjectival passive (3c) constructs in which some idioms may occur, as in the following:

3a.	*Liv ha dipanato la matassa* Liv-has-unraveled-the-skein	"to solve a problem"
3b.	*La matassa si è dipanata* The skein-si-is-unraveled	
3c.	*La matassa è dipanata* The-skein-is-unraveled	

Properties **[8]** and **[9]** indicate two more sentence structures in which idioms may occur. In particular, **[8]** refers to a sentence structure involving the verb *avere* ('to have') as in (4b):

4a.	*Gli operai incrociano le braccia* The-workers-cross-the-arms	"to go on strike"
4b.	*Gli operai hanno le braccia incrociate* The-workers-have-the-arms-crossed	

The syntactic property **[9]** indicates a particular structure where the verb is in the infinitive form and introduced by the preposition *da*, as in (5b):

5a.	*Joe ingoiò un rospo* Joe-swalled-a-toad	"to swallow a bitter pill"
5b.	*Joe ha un rospo da ingoiare* Joe-has-a-toad-to-swallow	

Notice that, in the constructions defined by properties **[6]-[9]**, $\mathbf{C_1}$ does not occur in its canonical position but to the left of the verb.

Property **[10]** concerns the possibility of having a nominalization, as in (6b). Finally, the morpho-syntactic property **[11]** shows the formation of a **VC** compound, as in (7b). The **VC** compound is explicitly indicated in the corresponding column.

6a.	*Joe ha alzato la testa* Joe-has-raised-the-head	"to rebel"
6b.	*L'alzata di testa (di + che ha fatto) Joe* The-raising-of-the-head (of + that-has-made)-Joe	
7a.	*Joe vende fumo* Joe-sells-smoke	"to be a snake oil salesman"
7b.	*Joe è un vendifumo* Joe-is-a-sell.smoke	

2.1 The Classes of Idioms with Ordinary Verbs

Table 1 contains all the classes of idioms with ordinary verbs. The first column indicates the name of the **L**exicon **G**rammar class, while the second column refers to the definitional structure of the idioms belonging to the corresponding class. The third column contains an idiomatic example for each class. Finally, the fourth column refers to the number of idioms listed in each class. The last class of Table 1, i.e. **PVCO,** contains those idioms where the fixed verb is followed by a comparative clause introduced by *come*[2].

The figures in the fourth column are to be taken as an approximate quantity, since this is an ongoing research. Therefore, the classes are subject to updating. Although approximate, the figures are an important piece of information because they show the idioms' distribution throughout the syntactic patterns.

[2] See also De Gioia (2001).

LG-class	*Sentence structure*	*Example*	N.
C0	C_0 V Ω	*il piatto piange*	80
C1	N_0 V C_1	*tirare le cuoia*	1,200
CAN	N_0 V C_1 (a + di) N_2	*rompere le scatole (a + di) N*	320
CDN	N_0 V C_1 di N_2	*non vedere l'ora di N*	90
CPN	N_0 V C_1 Prep N_2	*attaccare bottone con N*	550
CPC	N_0 V C_1 Prep C_2	*prendere lucciole per lanterne*	450
CPCPN	N_0 V C_1 Prep C_2 Prep N_3	*dire pane al pane a N*	20
NPC	N_0 V N_1 Prep C_2	*piantare N in asso*	350
PCPN	N_0 V Prep C_1 Prep N_2	*dare alla testa a N*	100
PC1	N_0 V Prep C_1	*parlare al muro*	600
PCPC	N_0 V Prep C_1 Prep C_2	*durare da Natale a Santo Stefano*	30
PVCO	N_0 V come C_1	*fumare come un turco*	200
			3,990

Table 1. Idioms with Ordinary Verbs

3 The Lexicon-Grammar of the Italian Idiomatic Support Verb Constructions

Idioms may be not only formed by an ordinary verb but also by support verbs, the most common of which are, in Italian, *avere* ('to have'), *essere* ('to be'), *fare* ('to make'). The main difference between support verbs (hereafter SV) and ordinary verbs constructions is linked to their meaning. That is, support verbs are semantically empty, while ordinary verbs are not. Therefore, support verbs are not predicates.

The idiomatic constructions formed by such verbs show a high degree of lexical and syntactic flexibility due to the semantic "emptiness" of the support verb. Such a flexibility of SV idioms is shown by (a) the alternation of support verbs with aspectual variants, (b) the production of causative constructions, (c) the deletion of the support verb itself that can trigger the formation of complex nominal groups and adverbials.

The Lexicon-Grammar of SV idioms (sec. 3.1, Table 2) includes 16 classes for a total of about 3,300 entries. I will present one of the classes defined by the general structure *N_0 essere Prep C* Ω, where it is the prepositional complement that is fixed and necessary to sub-categorize a possible further argument Ω, as in the following[3]:

8. *Nelly è al settimo cielo* "to be in seventh heaven"
   Nelly-is-at-the-seventh-sky
9. *Joe è ai ferri corti con Nelly* "to be at loggerheads with sb."
   Joe-is-at-the-short-irons-with-Nelly

In example (8), the fixed prepositional complement **PC** does not require a further argument besides the subject, whereas a free prepositional complement **PN** is required in the case of (9). Therefore, idioms like (8) and (9) have been listed in two different classes, respectively, **EPC** and **EPCPN**, where **E** indicates the verb *essere* ('to be'), **P** the preposition, **C** indicates the constrained noun, and **N** the free noun. Figure 2 is an excerpt of the class **EPC** which includes 500+ entries.

[3] The Lexicon-grammar of the French *être Prep* constructions has been built by Danlos (1988). The Portuguese constructions were analyzed by Ranchod (1983). A first classification of the Italian *essere Prep* constructions has been built by Vietri (1996). This early classification has been completely revised.

[1] N_0 = + hum	**[2]** N_0 = - hum	**[3]** N_0 = Che F	**V**	Prep	Prep-Det	$\mathbf{C_1}$	**[4]** C_1 = body-part	**[5]** Vsup = Stare	**[6]** Vsup = Restare-Rimanere	**[7]** Vsup = Diventare	**[8]** Vmt = Andare	**[9]** Vcaus = Mandare	**[10]** Vcaus = Mettere	**[11]** Vcaus = Ridurre	**[12]** Vop = Avere
+	+	-	essere	in	-	ballo	-	+	+	-	-	-	+	-	-
+	-	-	essere	in	-	bestia	-	+	+	-	+	+	-	-	-
-	+	-	essere	sotto	-	chiave	-	+	+	-	-	-	+	-	-
+	-	-	essere	-	sulla	corda	-	+	+	-	-	-	+	-	-
+	-	-	essere	-	alle	corde	-	+	+	-	-	-	+	-	-
-	+	-	essere	-	al	dente	+	-	+	-	-	-	-	-	-
+	-	-	essere	in	-	erba	-	-	+	+	-	-	-	-	-
+	+	-	essere	-	con i	fiocchi	-	-	+	+	-	-	-	-	-
+	-	-	essere	-	fuori dai	gangheri	-	+	+	-	+	+	-	-	-
+	-	-	essere	-	sul	lastrico	-	+	+	-	+	+	+	+	-
+	+	+	essere	fuori	-	luogo	-	-	+	-	-	-	-	-	-
+	-	-	essere	fuori	-	mano	+	+	+	-	-	-	-	-	-
+	+	-	essere	a	-	nudo	-	-	+	-	-	-	+	-	-
+	+	-	essere	sott'	-	occhio	+	+	+	-	-	-	-	-	+
-	+	-	essere	-	alle	porte	-	+	+	-	-	-	-	-	-
+	-	-	essere	-	sulle	spine	-	+	+	-	-	-	+	-	-
+	-	-	essere	-	al	tappeto	-	+	+	-	+	+	+	-	-
-	+	-	essere	-	sul	tappeto	-	+	+	-	-	-	+	-	-
+	-	-	essere	in	-	gamba	+	-	+	+	-	-	-	-	-
+	-	-	essere	-	al	verde	-	+	+	-	-	-	+	+	-

Figure 2. The class EPC

The distributional properties **[1]**-**[4]** have been previously illustrated (sec. 2, Figure 1). The properties from **[5]** to **[8]** indicate the possibility for the **EPC** constructions to occur with verbs other than *essere*. The verbs considered are *stare*[4], in **[5]**, *restare* and *rimanere* ('remain'), in **[6]**, *diventare* ('become, get') in **[7]**. The property **[8]** indicates that a construction with the verb of motion *andare* ('to go') may be acceptable.

However, the acceptability of all these constructions is lexically dependant, as in the following examples:

10. *Nelly (sta+ resta + *diventa + va) al settimo cielo* "to be in seventh heaven"
    Nelly-(stays + remains + *becomes + goes)-at-the-seventh-sky
11. *Joe (*sta + resta + diventa + *va) in gamba* "to be smart"
    Joe-(*stays + remains + becomes + *goes)-in-leg

EPC constructions can also enter complex sentence structures with causative verbs (see properties **[9]**--**[10]**) such as *mandare* ('send'), *mettere* ('to put'), *ridurre* ('make'), as in the following:

---

[4] I will literally translate this verb as "to stay". However, there is no equivalent in English since this verb is to be found in Romance languages like Italian, Portuguese and Spanish.

12. *Joe (mandò + *mise + *ridusse) Nelly al settimo cielo* "to be in seventh heaven"
Joe-(sent + *put + *reduced)-Nelly-at-the-seventh-sky

13. *Joe (mandò + mise + ridusse) Nelly sul lastrico* "to be on the skids"
Joe-(sent + put + reduced)-Nelly-on-the-pavement

Finally, property **[12]** indicates that the link operator (see Gross 1981) *avere* ('to have') may produce an acceptable sentence, as in (14b):

14a. *La situazione in Ukraina è sott'occhio* "to monitor N"
The-situation-in-Ukraine-is-under-eye

14b. *Obama ha sott'occhio la situazione in Ukraina*
Obama-has-under-eye-the-situation-in-Ukraine

3.1 The Classes of Idioms with Support Verbs

Table 2 lists only those classes of SV idioms containing at least 50 idiomatic entries[5]. As a general rule, the classes of idioms with the verb *essere* start with **E**, those ones with the verb *avere* start with **A**, and finally, those classes involving the verb *fare* start with **F**. The only exception is the class **PECO** which refers to the idioms of comparison where the verb *essere* is followed by a clause introduced by *come*[6].

LG class	**Sentence structure**	**Example**	**N.**
EPC	N_0 essere Prep C_1	*essere sulle spine*	530
EPCModif	N_0 essere Prep Adj C_1 N_0 essere Prep C_1 Adj	*essere di vecchio stampo* *essere in mani sicure*	130
EPCPN	N_0 essere Prep C_1 Prep N_2	*essere all'oscuro di N* *essere ai ferri corti con N*	140
EPCPC	N_0 essere Prep (C Prep C)$_1$	*essere nelle mani di Dio* *essere al passo con i tempi*	115
EAPC	N_0 essere Adj Prep C_1	*non essere dolce di sale*	100
PECO	N_0 essere Adj come C_1	*essere sordo come una campana*	360
AC	N avere C_1	*avere polso, avere (buon) occhio*	80
ACA	N avere C_1 Adj	*avere la memoria corta*	400
ACXC	N_0 avere C_1 Prep C_2 <=> C_1 di N_1 essere Prep C_2	*avere i nervi a fior di pelle* <=> *i nervi di N sono a fior di pelle*	180
ACPN	N_0 avere C_1 Prep N_2	*non avere la testa di N*	50
ACPC	N_0 avere C_1 Prep C_2	*avere il cervello tra le nuvole*	200
FC	N_0 fare C_1	*fare melina, fare lo gnorri*	300
FCPN	N_0 fare C_1 Prep N_2	*fare le bucce a, fare man bassa di N*	300
FCDC	N_0 fare (C di C)$_1$	*fare l'arte dei pazzi*	80
FCPC	N_0 fare C_1 Prep C_2	*fare un buco nell' acqua*	220
FPC(PN)	N_0 fare Prep C_1 (E + Prep N_2)	*fare sul serio, farsi in quattro per N*	50
Total			**3,235**

Table 2. Idioms with Support Verbs

[5] See Vietri (2014, forthcoming) for the complete classification.
[6] For the French classification of idiomatic comparisons see Gross (1984).

4 Annotating and Parsing Idioms

The Lexicon-Grammar classes of idioms can be exploited by the hybrid as well as the symbolic approach to Natural Language Processing. Some experimentation in this direction has already been carried out by Machonis (2011), who used NooJ to retrieve and disambiguate English phrasal verbs. NooJ is an NLP application developed by Silberztein (2003) that relies heavily on linguistic resources.

NooJ has been used to carry out experimentation on some of the Lexicon-Grammar classes of Italian idioms. The experimentation, still in progress, concerns the annotation and parsing of idioms. This application allows the construction of lexicons/dictionaries whose entries contain information such as the distributional and syntactic properties indicated in the Lexicon-Grammar classes. The Lexicon-Grammar classes of idioms can be converted in a NooJ dictionary of idioms. This dictionary, which contains thousands of entries, has to be linked to a grammar that describes the syntactic behaviour of idioms. By applying to a text such a dictionary/grammar pair, NooJ successfully annotates and parses idioms, also in case the constituents Verb + Fixed element(s) are discontinuous. An example of this is the sentence *John ha vuotato subito il sacco* (lit. John-has-immediately-emptied-the bag, "to spill the beans"), where the underlined adverb occurs between the verb and the fixed object.

However, the current NooJ version does not yet handle easily the syntactic flexibility and the lexical variation of idioms [7].

5 Conclusion

The Lexicon-Grammar classes of idioms are a manually-built linguistic resource that provides information about variation and flexibility of idioms. These classes, being formally coded, constitute an invaluable linguistic resource that can be used for research in (psycho)linguistics, and computational linguistics. The overall classification, as illustrated in Tables 1 and 2, outlines the syntactic patterns of the idiomatic constructions. This is a piece of information that can be regarded as the syntactic map of Italian idioms[8]. Furthermore, the lexico-syntactic information provided by the idioms' classes can also integrate the automatic Machine Translation evaluation methods[9].

The Lexicon-Grammar classes of idioms can be exploited by the hybrid as well as the symbolic approach to Natural Language Processing. Some experimentation in this direction has already been carried out by Machonis (2011) and by Vietri (2014, forthcoming). Both authors used the knowledge-based system NooJ. On the other hand, Baptista et al. (2014) used the Lexicon-Grammar classes of Portuguese idioms to test the hybrid system STRING.

Further experimentation will be conducted to evaluate the benefit of using the LG distributional and syntactic information in order to extract idioms from corpora. However, very huge corpora (consisting of documents in an informal language style) are needed, together with powerful tools able to perform complex searches on massive textual data.

References

Anne Abeillé. 1995. The Flexibility of French Idioms: a Representation with Lexicalized Tree Adjoining Grammar. In M. Everaert, E-J. van der Linden, A. Schenk, & R. Schreuder (Eds.), *Idioms: structural and psychological perspectives*. Hillsdale, NJ: Lawrence Erlbaum Associates: 15-41.

Jorge Baptista, Anabela Correia, and Graça Fernandes. 2005a. Léxico Gramática das Frases Fixas do Português Europeo», *Cadernos de Fraseoloxía Galega*, 7: 41-53.

Jorge Baptista, Anabela Correia, and Graça Fernandes. 2005b. Frozen Sentences of Portuguese: Formal Descriptions for NLP. Proceedings of the ACL workshop on Multiword Expressions: 72-79.

Jorge Baptista, Nuno Mamede, and Ilia Markov. 2014. Integrating a lexicon-grammar of verbal idioms in a Portuguese NLP system. COST Action IC1207 PARSEME meeting, 10-11 March 2014.

Cristina Cacciari, and Patrizia Tabossi. 1988. The comprehension of idioms. *Journal of Memory and Language*, 27: 668–683.

[7] Cignoni and Coffey (1998) provides the corpus-based results of the lexical variations of idioms.
[8] The complete Lexicon-Grammar classification of Italian idioms will be available at .unisa.it/docenti/simonettavietri/index.
[9] In this regard, see Giménez and Márquez (2010), Costa-jussà and Farrús (2013).

Federica Casadei. 1996. *Metafore ed espsressioni idiomatiche. Uno studio semantico sull'italiano*. Roma: Bulzoni.

Laura Cignoni, and Stephen Coffey. 1998. A corpus-based study of Italian idiomstic phrases: from citation forms to 'real-life' occurrences. *Euralex 1998 Proceedings*: 291-300.

Marta Ruiz Costa-jussà, and Mireia Farrús. 2013. Towards human linguistic machine translation evaluation. *Literary and Linguistic Computing*, Online publication date: 6-Dec-2013.

Cooper Cutting, and Kathryn Bock. 1997. That's the way the cookie bounces: Syntactic and semantic components of experimentally elicited idiom blends. *Memory and Cognition*, 25:57–71.

Laurence Danlos. 1988. Les phrases à verbe support être Prép. *Langages*, vol. 23, n. 90: 23-37.

Michele De Gioia. 2001. *Avverbi idiomatici dell'italiano. Analisi lessico-grammaticale*. Torino: L'Harmattan Italia.

Elisabete Ranchod. 1983. On the support verbs *ser* and *estar* in Portuguese. *Lingvisticae Investigationes*, VII(2): 317-353.

Afsaneh Fazly, Paul Cook, and Susanne Stevenson, S. (2009). Unsupervised Type and Token Identification of Idiomatic Expressions. *Computational Linguistics*, Vol. 35(1): 62-103.

Christiane Fellbaum. 2011. Idioms and Collocations. In C. Maienborn, K. von Heusinger, & P. Portner (Eds.), *Semantics. An International Handbook of Natural Language Meaning*. Vol. 1, Berlin/Boston: De Gruyter Mouton: 441-456.

Richard Fothergill, and Timothy Baldwin. 2012. Combining resources for MWE-token classification. In *Proceedings of the First Joint Conference on Lexical and Computational Semantics*: 100-104.

Peter Freckleton. 1985. Sentence idioms in English. Working Papers in Linguistics 11, University of Melbourne: 153-168.

Gerald Gazdar, Ewan Klein, Geoffrey Pullum, and Ivan Sag. 1985. *Generalized Phrase Structure Grammar*, Oxford: Basil Blackwell.

Raymond Gibbs. 1995. Idiomaticity and Human Cognition. In M. Everaert, E-J. van der Linden, A. Schenk, & R. Schreuder (Eds.), *Idioms: structural and psychological perspectives*. Hillsdale, NJ: Lawrence Erlbaum Associates: 97-116.

Jesùs Giménez, and Lluìs Màrquez. 2010. Linguistic mesures for automatic machine translation evaluation. *Machine Translation*, 24:209-240.

Maurice Gross. 1975. *Mèthodes en syntaxe*. Paris: Hermann.

Maurice Gross. 1979. On the failure of generative grammar. *Language,* 55(4): 859-885.

Maurice Gross. 1981. Les bases empiriques de la notion de prédicat semantique. *Langages*, 63, Paris: Larousse: 7-52.

Maurice Gross. 1982. Une classification des phrases "figées" du français. *Revue Québécoise de Linguistique* 11.2, Montréal: UQAM: 151-185.

Maurice Gross. 1984. Une famille d'adverbes figés: les constructions comparative en *comme*. *Revue Québécoise de Linguistique* 13.2:237-269

Maurice Gross. 1988. Les limites de la phrase figée. *Langages* 90, Paris: Larousse: 7-22.

Maurice Gross. 1998. La fonction sémantique des verbes supports. *Travaux de linguistique*, 37, Duculot: Louvain-la-Neuve: 25-46.

Daniela Guglielmo. 2013. Italian Verb-Adverbial Particle Constructions: Predicative Structures and Patterns of Variation. *Linguisticae Investigationes*, 36.2:229-243.

Zellig Harris. 1982. *A Grammar of English on Mathematical Principles*, New York: John Winsley and Sons.

Christian Leclère. 2002. Organization of the Lexicon-Grammar of French verbs. *Lingvisticæ Investigationes* XX(1): 29-48.

Linlin Li, and Caroline Sporleder. 2009. Classifier Combination for Contextual Idiom Detection Without Labelled Data. *Proceedings of the Conference on Empirical Methods in Natural Language Processing* (EMNLP 2009) Singapore: 315-323.

Peter Machonis. 1985. Transformations of verb phrase idioms: passivization, particle movement, dative shift. American Speech 60(4): 291-308.

Peter Machonis. 2011. Sorting Nooj out to take MWE's into account. In K. Vučković, B. Bekavac, & M. Silberztein (Eds.), *Automatic Processing of Various Levels of Linguistic Phenomena*. Newcastle upon Tyne: Cambridge Scholars Publishing: 152-165.

Francesca Masini. 2005. Multi-word Expressions between Syntax and the Lexicon: the Case of Italian Verb-particle Constructions.SKY Journal of Linguistics 18, pp. 145-173.

Marjorie McShane, and Sergei Nirenburg. 2014. The Idiom-reference Connection. *STEP '08 Proceedings of the 2008 Conference on Semantics in Text Processing*, ACL Stroudsburg, PA, USA: 165-177.

Grace Muzny, and Luke Zettlemoyer. 2013. Automatic Idiom Identification in Wiktionary. *Proceedings of the Conference on Empirical Methods in Natural language Processing* (EMNLP 2013), Seattle, Washington, USA: 1417-1421.

Geoffrey Nunberg, Ivan Sag, and Tom Wasow. 1994. Idioms. *Language*, Vol. 70, No. 3, 491-538.

Stephen Pulman. 1993. The recognition and Interpretation of idioms, Cacciari C. & Tabossi, P. (Eds.), *Idioms. Processing, Structure, and Interpretation*. New Jersey: Lawrence Erlbaum Associates: 249-270.

Ivan Sag, Timothy Baldwin, Francis Bond, Ann Copestake, and Dan Flickinger. 2001. Multiword Expressions: A Pain in the Neck for NLP. *Computational Linguistics and Intelligent Text Processing*. Berlin Heidelberg: Springer: 1-15.

Max Silberztein. 2003-. *NooJ Manual*. Available for download at: www.nooj4nlp.net.

Simone Sprenger, Willem Levelt, and Gerard Kempen. 2006. Lexical Access during the Production of Idiomatic Phrases. *Journal of Memory and Language*, 54: 161-184.

David Swinney, and Ann Cutler. 1979. The access and processing of idiomatic expressions. *Journal of Verbal Learning and Verbal Behavior*, 18: 523–534

Simonetta Vietri. 1984. *Lessico e sintassi delle espressioni idiomatiche. Una tipologia tassonomica in italiano e in inglese.* Napoli: Liguori.

Simonetta Vietri. 1996. The Syntax of the Italian verb 'essere Prep', *Lingvisticae Investigationes*, XX.2: 287-350.

Simonetta Vietri. 2014. *Idiomatic Constructions in Italian. A Lexicon-Grammar Approach*. Linguisticae Investigationes Supplementa, 31. Amsterdam & Philadelphia: John Benjamins (forthcoming).

Aline Villavicencio, Timothy Baldwin, T., and Benjamin Waldron. 2004. A Multilingual Database of idioms. *Proceedings of the Fourth International Conference on language Resources and Evaluation* (LREC 2004), Lisbon, Portugal: 1127-30.

Building a Semantic Transparency Dataset of Chinese Nominal Compounds: A Practice of Crowdsourcing Methodology

Shichang Wang, Chu-Ren Huang, Yao Yao, Angel Chan
Department of Chinese and Bilingual Studies
The Hong Kong Polytechnic University
Hung Hom, Kowloon, Hong Kong
shi-chang.wang@connect.polyu.hk
{churen.huang, y.yao, angel.ws.chan}@polyu.edu.hk

Abstract

This paper describes the work which aimed to create a semantic transparency dataset of Chinese nominal compounds (SemTransCNC 1.0) by crowdsourcing methodology. We firstly selected about 1,200 Chinese nominal compounds from a lexicon of modern Chinese and the Sinica Corpus. Then through a series of crowdsourcing experiments conducted on the Crowdflower platform, we successfully collected both overall semantic transparency and constituent semantic transparency data for each of them. According to our evaluation, the data quality is good. This work filled a gap in Chinese language resources and also practiced and explored the crowdsourcing methodology for linguistic experiment and language resource construction.

1 Introduction

The meaning of "马虎" (mǎhu, horse-tiger, 'careless') has nearly nothing to do with neither "马" (mǎ, 'horse') nor "虎" (hǔ, 'tiger'). However the meaning of "道路" (dàolù, road-way, 'road') is basically equal to "道" (dào, 'road') or "路" (lù, 'way'). And there are intermediate cases too, for instance, "江湖" (jiānghú, river-lake, 'all corners of the country'), its meaning is not equal to "江" (jiāng, 'river') plus "湖" (hú, 'lake'), but clear relatedness between them can be observed. This phenomenon is called semantic transparency of compounds. We distinguish between overall semantic transparency (OST) and constituent semantic transparency (CST). The semantic transparency of a compound, i.e., the overall semantic transparency, is the extent to which the compound retains its literal meaning in its actual meaning. The semantic transparency of a constituent of a compound, i.e., the constituent semantic transparency, is the extent to which the constituent retains its meaning in the actual meaning of the compound. Semantic similarity between the literal meaning and the actual meaning of a compound can be used to estimate the overall semantic transparency of a compound, for the more the literal meaning is retained in the actual meaning, the more similar they are. The same technique can be used to estimate constituent semantic transparency. Semantic transparency can be quantified; if we assign 0 to "fully opaque" and assign 1 to "fully transparent", then semantic transparency can be quantified as a closed interval $[0, 1]$.

The quantitative analysis of semantic transparency must be supported by semantic transparency datasets. In previous semantic transparency related studies on Chinese compounds, some researchers created some datasets to support their own studies. But this kind of datasets are usually relatively small and restrictive, so cannot be used widely, for example, (徐彩华 and 李镗, 2001; Myers et al., 2004; 干红梅, 2008; Mok, 2009), etc. Some datasets, although large enough and can be used in other studies, are not publicly accessible, for example, (王春茂 and 彭聃龄, 1999; 高兵 and 高峰强, 2005), etc. A large and publicly accessible semantic transparency dataset of Chinese compounds is still a gap in Chinese language resources.

Crowdsourcing, as an emerging method of data collection and resource construction (Snow et al., 2008; Callison-Burch and Dredze, 2010; Munro et al., 2010; Schnoebelen and Kuperman, 2010; Gurevych and Zesch, 2013; Wang et al., 2013) and an emerging method of behavioral experiment (Paolacci et al., 2010;

Proceedings of the Workshop on Lexical and Grammatical Resources for Language Processing, pages 147–156,
Coling 2014, Dublin, Ireland, August 24 2014.

Berinsky et al., 2011; Mason and Suri, 2012; Rand, 2012; Crump et al., 2013), is attracting more and more attention from the field of language study and language computing. As a method of data collection and resource construction, it has the advantages of high speed and low cost, etc. It can use redundancy to filter out noise in order to improve data quality; if used properly, it can produce expert-level data. As a method of experiment, besides the above advantages, it also has the following ones, (1) it is easier to obtain large samples, because the amount of potential participants is huge; (2) the diversity of participants is good, because the participants are from different places and have different backgrounds; (3) crowdsourcing environments are usually anonymous, so it is easier to collect certain sensitive data.

2 Method

2.1 Compound Selection

We use the following criteria to select compounds, (1) they are disyllabic nominal compounds; (2) each of them has the structure NN, AN, or VN; (3) they are composed of free morphemes; (4) they have mid-range word frequencies; and (5) they are used in both Mainland China and Taiwan. And we select compounds according to the following procedure:

(1) Extract monosyllabic nouns, adjectives and verbs mainly according to "The Dictionary of Contemporary Chinese (the 6th edition)" (现代汉语词典, 第 6 版), and thus we get three sets, a) the set of monosyllabic nouns, N; b) the set of monosyllabic adjectives, A; and c) the set of monosyllabic verbs, V.

(2) Extract the words of the structure NN, AN, or VN [1] from the "Lexicon of Common Words in Contemporary Chinese" (现代汉语常用词表). In this step, NN means both morphemes of the word appear in the set N; AN means the first morpheme appears in the set A and the second appears in the set N; VN means the first morpheme appears in the set V and the second appears in the set N. After this step, we get "word list 1".

(3) Extract the words which have mid-range frequencies [2] from the Sinica Corpus 4.0 (Chen et al., 1996). These words are represented in traditional Chinese characters. We convert them into simplified Chinese characters and only reserve the words which also appear in "word list 1". After this step, we get "word list 2".

(4) Manually verify "word list 2" to generate the final list. Things need to be verified include the following aspects. (a) Because in "word list 2" word structures are judged automatically, there are many errors, so we have to verify the correctness of the word structure judgments. (b) We have to make sure that the morphemes of each word are free morphemes. (c) We also need to delete some proper nouns.

The words we selected appear in both Sinica Corpus 4.0 and "Lexicon of Common Words in Contemporary Chinese". Since there is no completely reliable criterion to identify Chinese word, appearing in two lexicons ensures their word identity. This also ensures that they are used in both Mainland China and Taiwan, and further means they are quite possible to be shared in other Chinese language communities, for example Hong Kong, Macau, and Singapore, etc.

According to above criteria and procedure, we selected a total of 1,176 words. 664 (56.46%) of them have the structure NN; 322 (27.38%) have the structure AN; and 190 (16.16%) have the structure VN.

2.2 Experimental Design

Normally, a crowdsourcing experiment should be reasonably small in size. We randomly divide these 1,176 words into 21 groups, G_i $(i = 1, 2, 3, ..., 21)$; each group has 56 words.

[1] See 苑春法 and 黄昌宁 (1998), and Huang (1998) for relevant statistics.

[2] We use cumulative frequency feature to determine mid-range frequency. Sort the word frequency list of Sinica Corpus 4.0 descendingly; then calculate cumulative frequency word by word until each word corresponds with a cumulative frequency value; finally, plot a curve on a coordinate plane whose x-axis represents the ranks of words in the sorted list, and the y-axis represents cumulative frequency values. Very apparently, this curve can be divided into three successive phases; the words within each phase have similar word frequency features. According to this, we identify three word frequency categories, 5,163 high-frequency words (frequency range: $[182, 581823]$, cumulative frequency range: $[0\%, 80\%]$), 19,803 mid-range frequency words (frequency range: $[23, 181]$, cumulative frequency range: $(80\%, 93\%]$), and 177,496 low-frequency words (frequency range: $[1, 22]$, cumulative frequency range: $(93\%, 100\%]$). Sinica Corpus 4.0 contains about 11.2 million word tokens.

Questionnaires

We collect overall semantic transparency (OST) and constituent semantic transparency (CST) data of these words. In order to avoid interaction, we designed two kinds of questionnaires to collect OST data and CST data respectively. So G_i $(i = 1, 2, 3, ..., 21)$ has two questionnaires, one OST questionnaire for OST data collection and one CST questionnaire for CST data collection. Besides titles and instructions, each questionnaire has 3 sections. Section 1 is used to collect identity information includes gender, age, education and location. Section 2 contains four very simple questions about the Chinese language; the first two questions are open-ended Chinese character identification questions, the third question is a close-ended homophonic character identification question, and the fourth one is a close-ended antonymous character identification question; different questionnaires use different questions. Section 3 contains the questions for semantic transparency data collection. Suppose AB is a disyllabic nominal compound, we use the following question to collect its OST rating scores: "How is the sum of the meanings of A and B similar to the meaning of AB?" And use the following two questions to collect its CST rating scores of its two constituents: "How is the meaning of A when it is used alone similar to its meaning in AB?" and "How is the meaning of B when it is used alone similar to its meaning in AB?". 7-point scales are used in section 3; 1 means "not similar at all" and 7 means "almost the same".

In order to evaluate the data received in the experiments, we embedded some evaluation devices in the questionnaires. We mainly evaluated intra-group and inter-group consistency; and if the data have good intra-group and inter-group consistency, we can believe that the data quality is good. In each group we choose two words and make them appear twice, we call them intra-group repeated words and we can use them to evaluate the intra-group consistency. We insert into each group two same extra words, w_1"地步", w_2"高山", to evaluate the inter-group consistency.

Quality Control Measures

On a crowdsourcing platform like Crowdflower, the participants are anonymous, they may try to cheat and submit invalid data, and they may come from different countries and speak different languages rather than the required one. There may be spammers who continuously submit invalid data at very high speed and they may even bypass the quality control measures to cheat for money. In order to ensure that the participants are native Chinese speakers and to improve data quality, we use the following measures, (1) a participant must correctly answer the first two Chinese character identification questions in the section 2s of the questionnaires, and he/she must correctly answer at least one of the last two questions in these section 2s; (2) If a participant do not satisfy the above conditions, he/she will not see Section 3s; (3) each word stimulus in section 3s has an option which allows the participants to skip it in case he/she does not recognize that word; (4) all the questions in the questionnaires must be answered except the ones which allow to be skipped and are explicitly claimed to be skipped; (5) we wrote a monitor program to detect and resist spammers automatically; (6) after the experiment is finished, we will analyze the data and filter out invalid data, and we will discuss this in detail in section 3.

2.3 Experimental Platform and Procedure

We choose Crowdflower as our experimental platform, because according to our previous experiments, it is a feasible crowdsourcing platform to collect Chinese language data. We create one task for each questionnaire on the platform; there are 21 groups of word and each group has one OST questionnaire and one CST questionnaire, so there are a total of 42 tasks T_i^{ost}, T_i^{cst} $(i = 1, 2, 3, ..., 21)$. We publish these 42 tasks successively, and for each task we create a monitor program to detect and resist spammers. All of these tasks use the following parameters: (1) each task will collect 90 responses; (2) we pay 0.15USD for each response of OST questionnaire and pay 0.25USD for each response of CST questionnaire; (3) each worker account of Crowdflower can only submit one response for each questionnaire and each IP address can only submit one response for each questionnaire; (4) we only allow the workers from the following regions (according to IP addresses) to submit data: Mainland China, Hong Kong, Macau, Taiwan, Singapore, Malaysia, USA, UK, Canada, Australia, Germany, France, Italy, New Zealand, and Indonesia; and we can dynamically disable or enable certain regions on demand in order to ensure both data quality and quantity.

3 Data Refinement and Result Calculation

The OST dataset produced by the OST task T_i^{ost} ($i = 1, 2, 3, ..., 21$) is D_i^{ost}. The CST dataset produced by the CST task T_i^{cst} is D_i^{cst}. Each dataset contains 90 responses. Because of the nature of crowdsourcing environment, there are many invalid responses in each dataset; so firstly we need to filter them out in order to refine the data. A response is invalid if (1) its completion time is less than 135 seconds (for OST responses); its completion time is less than 250 seconds (for CST responses) [3]; or (2) it failed to correctly answer the first two questions of section 2s of the questionnaires; or (3) it wrongly answered the last two questions of section 2s of the questionnaires; or (4) it skipped one or more words in section 3s of the questionnaires; or (5) it used less than two numbers on the 7-point scales in section 3s of the questionnaires. The statistics of valid response are shown in Table 1.

The OST dataset D_i^{ost} ($i = 1, 2, 3, ..., 21$) contains n_i valid responses; it means word w in the OST dataset of the ith group has n_i OST rating scores; the arithmetic mean of these n_i OST rating scores is the OST result of word w. The CST results of the two constituents of word w are calculated using the same algorithm.

	OST		CST	
G_i	n	%	n	%
G_1	54	60	59	65.56
G_2	60	66.67	59	65.56
G_3	55	61.11	60	66.67
G_4	59	65.56	59	65.56
G_5	50	55.56	55	61.11
G_6	55	61.11	52	57.78
G_7	53	58.89	53	58.89
G_8	60	66.67	50	55.56
G_9	48	53.33	52	57.78
G_{10}	57	63.33	62	68.89
G_{11}	46	51.11	56	62.22
G_{12}	48	53.33	58	64.44
G_{13}	51	56.67	52	57.78
G_{14}	50	55.56	50	55.56
G_{15}	52	57.78	52	57.78
G_{16}	57	63.33	56	62.22
G_{17}	50	55.56	46	50.55
G_{18}	51	56.67	53	58.89
G_{19}	50	55.56	49	54.44
G_{20}	50	55.56	47	52.22
G_{21}	50	55.56	50	55.56
Max	60	66.67	62	68.89
Min	46	51.11	46	50.55
Median	51.5	57.22	53	58.89
Mean	52.67	58.52	53.81	59.76
SD	4.09	4.55	4.49	5.04

Table 1: The Amount of Valid Response in the OST and CST Datasets of Each Group

4 Evaluation

Three kinds of evaluation measures are used, (1) the intra-group consistency of the OST and CST results, (2) the inter-group consistency of the OST and CST results, and (3) the correlation between the OST and CST results.

[3]Each OST questionnaire has about 70 questions, and each CST questionnaire has about 130; in an OST or CST questionnaire, almost all the questions are the same except the stimuli words and can be instantly answered by intuition; note that a participant can take part in as many as 42 tasks; according to our test, if a participant is familiar with the tasks, he/she can answer each question in less than 2 seconds (less than 1 second to identify the stimulus word and another less than 1 second to rate it) without difficulty. $70 \times 2 = 140$ seconds, the expected time should be less than this, so we use 135 seconds as the temporal threshold for valid OST responses. The calculation of the temporal threshold for valid CST responses is similar, $130 \times 2 = 260$ seconds, the expected time should be less than this, so we use 250 seconds.

4.1 Intra-group Consistency

In each group G_i $(i = 1, 2, 3, ..., 21)$, we selected two words $w_{i,1}, w_{i,2}$ (intra-group repeated words) and made them appear twice between which there is enough distance; we can calculate the difference values between the results of the two appearances of these words.

Intra-group Consistency of OST Results

There are 21 groups and in each group there are two intra-group repeated words, so there are a total of 42 such words. Each intra-group repeated word appears twice, so we can obtain two OST results r_1, r_2. The difference value between the two results, $d = |r_1 - r_2|$, of each intra-group repeated word is calculated, so there are 42 difference values. Among them, the maximum value is 0.29; the minimum value is 0; the median is 0.1; their mean is 0.11; and their standard deviation is 0.08; all of these values are low and indicate that these OST datasets have good intra-group consistency (see Table 2).

Intra-group Consistency of CST Results

Each intra-group repeated word has two constituents, c_1, c_2, so each constituent gets two CST results, i.e., $r_{c1,1}, r_{c1,2}$ and $r_{c2,1}, r_{c2,2}$. We calculate the difference values for the two constituents, $d_1 = |r_{c1,1} - r_{c1,2}|$ and $d_2 = |r_{c2,1} - r_{c2,2}|$, and get 42 difference values of the first constituents and 42 difference values of the second constituents. Among the difference values of the first constituents, the maximum value is 0.27; the minimum value is 0; the median is 0.09; their mean is 0.1, and their standard deviation is 0.07; all of these values are low, this indicates that the CST results of the first constituents in the CST datasets of the 21 groups have good intra-group consistency. Among the difference values of the second constituents, the maximum value is 0.36; the minimum value is 0; the median is 0.07; their mean is 0.09, and their standard deviation is 0.09; all of these values are low; this indicates that the CST results of the second constituents in the CST datasets of the 21 groups have good intra-group consistency (see Table 3). So these 21 CST datasets have good intra-group consistency.

4.2 Inter-group Consistency

We inserted two inter-group repeated words, w_1"地步", w_2"高山", into all of these 21 groups G_i $(i = 1, 2, 3, ..., 21)$; we can evaluate the inter-group consistency by comparing their semantic transparency rating results in different groups. Since w_1, w_2 appear in all OST and CST questionnaires of 21 groups, we can obtain (1) 21 OST results of w_1, (2) 21 OST results of w_2, (3) 21 CST results of each of the two constituents $w_{1,c1}, w_{1,c2}$ of w_1, and (4) 21 CST results of each of the two constituents $w_{2,c1}, w_{2,c2}$ of w_2. Standard deviation can be used to measure difference, for example, the standard deviation of the 21 OST results of w_1 is 0.2; this value is small and indicates high consistency; because these 21 results are from the OST datasets of 21 groups respectively, so we can say that these 21 OST datasets have good inter-group consistency. The standard deviation of the 21 OST results of w_2 is 0.14; the standard deviation of 21 CST results of the first constituent of w_1 is 0.2, and that of the second is 0.18; the standard deviation of 21 CST results of the first constituent of w_2 is 0.15, and that of the second is 0.2; all of these values are small and all of them indicate good inter-group consistency (see Table 4).

4.3 Correlation between OST and CST Results

Each compound in the datasets has two constituents; both constituents affect the OST of the compound, but neither of them can solely determine the OST of the compound. So the mean of the two CST values of a compound is a fairly good estimation of its OST value. Therefore, if the datasets are reliable, in each group, we should observe strong correlation between the OST results and their corresponding means of the CST results. For each group, we calculate three Pearson product-moment correlation coefficients (r); r_1 is the r between the OST results and their corresponding CST results of the first constituents; r_2 is the r between the OST results and their corresponding CST results of the second constituents; and r_3 is the r between the OST results and their corresponding means of the CST results. The r_3 values of the 21 groups are all greater than 0.9 which indicates very strong correlation; among them, the maximum value is 0.96; the minimum value is 0.91; and their mean is 0.94 $(SD = 0.02)$; the r_1 and r_2 values are also

G_i	$w_{i,1/2}$	r_1	r_2	d
G_1	野狗	5.26	5.26	0
	关节	3.57	3.61	0.04
G_2	火灾	5.63	5.75	0.12
	耳光	2.68	2.9	0.22
G_3	笑脸	5.67	5.58	0.09
	神气	3.51	3.62	0.11
G_4	杂草	5.31	5.32	0.02
	死党	3.19	3.02	0.17
G_5	毒瘾	5.36	5.32	0.04
	水货	3.12	3.3	0.18
G_6	手掌	5.53	5.4	0.13
	火烧	5.25	4.96	0.29
G_7	低价	5.25	5.23	0.02
	黑洞	4.19	4.11	0.08
G_8	凉风	5.48	5.33	0.15
	风水	3.2	3.37	0.17
G_9	琴声	5.19	5.19	0
	手笔	3.69	3.75	0.06
G_{10}	白云	5.49	5.63	0.14
	风土	3.46	3.54	0.09
G_{11}	雨伞	5.48	5.39	0.09
	背心	3.26	3.24	0.02
G_{12}	灯塔	5.19	5.4	0.21
	脾气	3.6	3.54	0.06
G_{13}	狂风	5.47	5.39	0.08
	蓝本	3.37	3.41	0.04
G_{14}	高楼	5.54	5.52	0.02
	口角	3.46	3.56	0.1
G_{15}	泥土	5.54	5.37	0.17
	苦心	3.29	3.56	0.27
G_{16}	鲜花	5.49	5.53	0.04
	本分	3.82	4.07	0.25
G_{17}	店主	5.2	5.38	0.18
	香火	3.76	3.76	0
G_{18}	桃花	5.31	5.18	0.14
	色狼	3.41	3.25	0.16
G_{19}	钱包	5.22	5.28	0.06
	火气	4.04	3.88	0.16
G_{20}	河岸	5.28	5.18	0.1
	毛病	4.04	3.84	0.2
G_{21}	古城	5.06	5.02	0.04
	温床	3.8	4	0.2
			Max	0.29
			Min	0
			Median	0.1
			Mean	0.11
			SD	0.08

Table 2: The Intra-group Consistency of the OST Results of Each Group

reasonably high (see Table 5)[4]. The results support the reliability of these datasets.

5 Merging and Normalization

The evaluation results show that the collected data are generally reliable and have relatively high intra-group and inter-group consistency which further indicate that these datasets share similar scale and are basically comparable, so we can merge the 21 OST datasets into one big OST dataset D_{ost} and merge the 21 CST datasets into one big CST dataset D_{cst}. When we merge these datasets, we delete all the extra words which are used to evaluate the inter-group consistency; for the repeated words which are

[4]After merging and normalization (see Section 5), we calculated these three correlation coefficients between D_{ost} and D_{cst}, the results are $r_1 = 0.68$, $r_2 = 0.68$, $r_3 = 0.87$.

		c_1			c_2		
G_i	$w_{i,1/2}$	$r_{c1,1}$	$r_{c1,2}$	d_1	$r_{c2,1}$	$r_{c2,2}$	d_2
G_1	野狗	3.83	4.05	0.22	5.49	5.42	0.07
	关节	2.88	3.03	0.15	3.92	3.92	0
G_2	火灾	5.12	5.22	0.1	5.24	5.1	0.14
	耳光	4.27	4.27	0	2.19	2.51	0.32
G_3	笑脸	5.12	5.08	0.03	5.35	5.4	0.05
	神气	2.92	2.95	0.03	3.22	3.42	0.2
G_4	杂草	4.51	4.34	0.17	5.56	5.27	0.29
	死党	2.39	2.49	0.1	4.22	4.12	0.1
G_5	毒瘾	4.75	4.64	0.11	5.09	5.15	0.05
	水货	2.29	2.4	0.11	4.67	4.76	0.09
G_6	手掌	5.4	5.23	0.17	5.35	5.4	0.06
	火烧	5.08	5.02	0.06	5.38	5.46	0.08
G_7	低价	4.7	4.83	0.13	5.13	5.13	0
	黑洞	3.85	3.94	0.09	4.45	4.57	0.11
G_8	凉风	5.06	4.88	0.18	5.28	5.3	0.02
	风水	3.24	3.14	0.1	3.36	3.16	0.2
G_9	琴声	5	4.98	0.02	5	4.98	0.02
	手笔	3.63	3.71	0.08	3.71	3.83	0.12
G_{10}	白云	4.53	4.6	0.06	5.37	5.39	0.02
	风土	3.13	3.21	0.08	3.15	3.16	0.02
G_{11}	雨伞	4.45	4.55	0.11	5.36	5.55	0.2
	背心	3.8	3.79	0.02	2.64	3	0.36
G_{12}	灯塔	4.69	4.52	0.17	4.97	4.9	0.07
	脾气	3.03	3.21	0.17	3.28	3.4	0.12
G_{13}	狂风	4.15	4.19	0.04	5.15	5.27	0.12
	蓝本	2.52	2.79	0.27	3.44	3.42	0.02
G_{14}	高楼	4.42	4.36	0.06	5.14	5.12	0.02
	口角	3.56	3.5	0.06	3.08	3.06	0.02
G_{15}	泥土	5.08	5.02	0.06	5.06	5.13	0.08
	苦心	3.21	3	0.21	3.46	3.5	0.04
G_{16}	鲜花	4.34	4.34	0	5.11	5.09	0.02
	本分	3.8	3.63	0.18	3.32	3.38	0.05
G_{17}	店主	4.76	4.72	0.04	4.74	4.87	0.13
	香火	3.93	3.96	0.02	3.89	3.87	0.02
G_{18}	桃花	4.26	4.32	0.06	4.77	4.7	0.08
	色狼	3.4	3.36	0.04	2.74	2.68	0.06
G_{19}	钱包	4.63	4.61	0.02	4.57	4.49	0.08
	火气	3.55	3.29	0.27	3.53	3.41	0.12
G_{20}	河岸	4.98	4.91	0.06	5.15	5.17	0.02
	毛病	2.94	2.96	0.02	4.7	4.45	0.26
G_{21}	古城	4.68	4.56	0.12	5	4.98	0.02
	温床	3.68	3.88	0.2	3.66	3.6	0.06
			Max	0.27			0.36
			Min	0			0
			Median	0.09			0.07
			Mean	0.1			0.09
			SD	0.07			0.09

Table 3: The Intra-group Consistency of the CST Results of Each Group

used to evaluate the intra-group consistency, the final result of each of them is the mean of its two results. According to our definition, the range of semantic transparency value is $[0, 1]$, but the experimental results are obtained using 7-point scales, so we need to normalize these results in order to map them to the range $[0, 1]$. The normalized OST and CST results will be merged into D_{ost} and D_{cst} respectively. Assume that, in the dataset D_{ost}, the OST result of the ith $(i = 1, 2, 3, ..., 1176)$ word is S_i^w, and the normalized result is $S_i'^w$, then,

$$S_i'^w = \frac{S_i^w - 1}{6}$$

G_i	OST w_1	OST w_2	CST $w_{1,c1}$	CST $w_{1,c2}$	CST $w_{2,c1}$	CST $w_{2,c2}$
G_1	2.94	5.52	2.85	2.97	4.56	5.56
G_2	3.6	5.55	3.15	3.2	4.92	5.75
G_3	3.51	5.64	3.17	3.23	4.75	5.58
G_4	3.81	5.68	3.53	3.59	4.58	5.42
G_5	3.74	5.46	3.38	3.56	4.64	5.55
G_6	3.65	5.55	3.63	3.56	4.85	5.65
G_7	3.58	5.51	3.47	3.58	4.75	5.23
G_8	3.22	5.53	3.4	3.36	4.8	5.48
G_9	3.31	5.15	3.48	3.52	4.69	5.42
G_{10}	3.58	5.53	3.42	3.34	4.69	5.27
G_{11}	3.7	5.67	3.46	3.32	4.52	5.36
G_{12}	3.33	5.71	3.19	3.28	4.41	5.14
G_{13}	3.47	5.78	3.58	3.56	4.73	5.38
G_{14}	3.48	5.58	2.94	2.94	4.42	5.3
G_{15}	3.4	5.42	3.42	3.27	4.62	5.1
G_{16}	3.47	5.56	3.34	3.25	4.59	5.16
G_{17}	3.6	5.56	3.3	3.26	4.5	5.17
G_{18}	3.67	5.67	3.36	3.34	4.47	5
G_{19}	3.28	5.56	3.2	3.29	4.37	5.18
G_{20}	3.56	5.48	3.21	3.36	4.72	5.34
G_{21}	3.62	5.32	3.2	3.28	4.5	5.24
Max	3.81	5.78	3.63	3.59	4.92	5.75
Min	2.94	5.15	2.85	2.94	4.37	5
Median	3.56	5.55	3.36	3.32	4.62	5.34
Mean	3.5	5.54	3.32	3.34	4.62	5.35
SD	0.2	0.14	0.2	0.18	0.15	0.2

Table 4: The Inter-group Consistency of the OST and CST Results

And assume that, in the dataset D_{cst}, the CST result of the jth $(j = 1, 2)$ constituent of the ith word is $S^c_{i,j}$, and the normalized result is $S'^c_{i,j}$, then,

$$S'^c_{i,j} = \frac{S^c_{i,j} - 1}{6}$$

6 Distribution

Influenced by outliers and perhaps other factors, the OST and CST results cannot cover the whole range of the scale $[0, 1]$; both ends shrink towards the central point 0.5, and the shrinkage of each end is about 0.2; nevertheless, the results can still assign proper ranks of semantic transparency to the compounds and their constituents which are generally consistent with our intuitions. Among the normalized OST results, the maximum is 0.81; the minimum is 0.28; the median is 0.63; and their mean is 0.62 $(SD = 0.09)$. Among the normalized CST results of the first constituents (C1.CST results), the maximum is 0.77; the minimum is 0.19; the median is 0.57; and their mean is 0.56 $(SD = 0.09)$. And among the normalized CST results of the second constituents (C2.CST results), the maximum is 0.79; the minimum is 0.22; the median is 0.6; and their mean is 0.58 $(SD = 0.1)$. The distributions of OST, C1.CST, and C2.CST results are similar; all of them are negatively skewed (see Figure 1), and their estimated skewnesses are -0.66, -0.77, and -0.63 respectively. These distributions exhibit that more compounds and their constituents in our datasets have relatively high semantic transparency values.

7 Conclusion

This work created a dataset of semantic transparency of Chinese nominal compounds (SemTransCNC 1.0), which filled a gap in Chinese language resources. It contains the overall and constituent semantic transparency data of about 1,200 Chinese disyllabic nominal compounds and can support semantic transparency related studies of Chinese compounds, for example, theoretical, statistical, psycholinguistic, and

G_i	r_1	r_2	r_3
G_1	0.68	0.68	0.91
G_2	0.72	0.72	0.93
G_3	0.76	0.78	0.96
G_4	0.76	0.77	0.96
G_5	0.75	0.56	0.95
G_6	0.63	0.72	0.91
G_7	0.83	0.78	0.94
G_8	0.76	0.77	0.96
G_9	0.68	0.81	0.95
G_{10}	0.84	0.83	0.95
G_{11}	0.78	0.71	0.91
G_{12}	0.72	0.77	0.95
G_{13}	0.85	0.86	0.96
G_{14}	0.69	0.85	0.95
G_{15}	0.68	0.82	0.95
G_{16}	0.82	0.85	0.95
G_{17}	0.79	0.83	0.94
G_{18}	0.81	0.86	0.96
G_{19}	0.76	0.8	0.95
G_{20}	0.76	0.75	0.94
G_{21}	0.73	0.86	0.96
Max	0.85	0.86	0.96
Min	0.63	0.56	0.91
Median	0.76	0.78	0.95
Mean	0.75	0.78	0.94
SD	0.06	0.07	0.02

Table 5: The Correlation Coefficients between the OST and CST Results

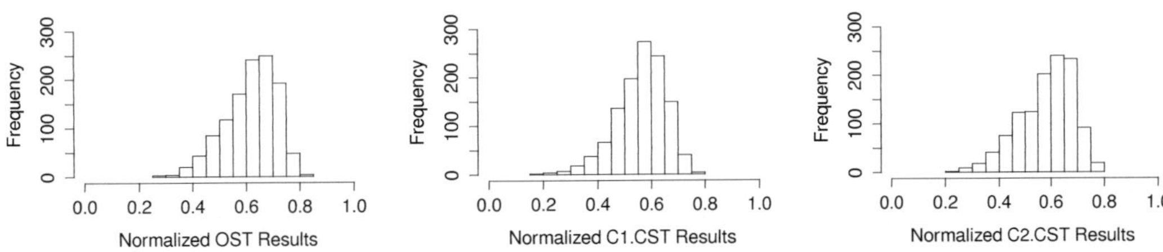

Figure 1: The Distributions of the Normalized OST and CST Results

computational studies, etc. And this work was also a successful practice of crowdsourcing method for linguistic experiment and language resource construction. Large scale language data collection experiments which require large amount of participants are usually very difficult to conduct in laboratories using the traditional paradigm. Crowdsourcing method enabled us to finish the data collection task within relatively short period of time and relatively low budget (1,000USD); during the process of the experiment, we needed not to organize and communicate with the participants, it saved a lot of time and energy. The participants are from all over the world, so it is better than traditional laboratory method in the aspect of participant diversity. The data collected have very good intra-group and inter-group consistency, the OST and CST data highly correlate with each other as expected, and the results are consistent with our intuitions: all of these indicate good data quality. The methods of questionnaire design, quality control, data refinement, evaluation, emerging, and normalization can be used in crowdsourcing practices of the same kind.

Acknowledgements

The work described in this paper was supported by grants from the Research Grants Council of the Hong Kong Special Administrative Region, China (Project No. 544011 & 543512).

References

Adam J Berinsky, Gregory A Huber, and Gabriel S Lenz. 2011. Using mechanical turk as a subject recruitment tool for experimental research. *Submitted for review*.

Chris Callison-Burch and Mark Dredze. 2010. Creating speech and language data with amazon's mechanical turk. In *Proceedings of the NAACL HLT 2010 Workshop on Creating Speech and Language Data with Amazon's Mechanical Turk*, pages 1–12. Association for Computational Linguistics.

Keh-Jiann Chen, Chu-Ren Huang, Li-Ping Chang, and Hui-Li Hsu. 1996. Sinica Corpus: Design Methodology for Balanced Corpora. In B.-S. Park and J.B. Kim, editors, *Proceeding of the 11th Pacific Asia Conference on Language, Information and Computation*, pages 167–176. Seoul:Kyung Hee University.

Matthew JC Crump, John V McDonnell, and Todd M Gureckis. 2013. Evaluating amazon's mechanical turk as a tool for experimental behavioral research. *PloS one*, 8(3):e57410.

Iryna Gurevych and Torsten Zesch. 2013. Collective intelligence and language resources: introduction to the special issue on collaboratively constructed language resources. *Language Resources and Evaluation*, 47(1):1–7.

Shuanfan Huang. 1998. Chinese as a headless language in compounding morphology. *New approaches to Chinese word formation: Morphology, phonology and the lexicon in modern and ancient Chinese*, pages 261–284.

Winter Mason and Siddharth Suri. 2012. Conducting behavioral research on amazon' s mechanical turk. *Behavior research methods*, 44(1):1–23.

Leh Woon Mok. 2009. Word-superiority effect as a function of semantic transparency of chinese bimorphemic compound words. *Language and Cognitive Processes*, 24(7-8):1039–1081.

Robert Munro, Steven Bethard, Victor Kuperman, Vicky Tzuyin Lai, Robin Melnick, Christopher Potts, Tyler Schnoebelen, and Harry Tily. 2010. Crowdsourcing and language studies: the new generation of linguistic data. In *Proceedings of the NAACL HLT 2010 Workshop on Creating Speech and Language Data with Amazon's Mechanical Turk*, pages 122–130. Association for Computational Linguistics.

James Myers, Bruce Derwing, and Gary Libben. 2004. The effect of priming direction on reading chinese compounds. *Mental Lexicon Working Papers*, 1:69–86.

Gabriele Paolacci, Jesse Chandler, and Panagiotis G Ipeirotis. 2010. Running experiments on amazon mechanical turk. *Judgment and Decision making*, 5(5):411–419.

David G Rand. 2012. The promise of mechanical turk: How online labor markets can help theorists run behavioral experiments. *Journal of theoretical biology*, 299:172–179.

Tyler Schnoebelen and Victor Kuperman. 2010. Using amazon mechanical turk for linguistic research. *Psihologija*, 43(4):441–464.

Rion Snow, Brendan O'Connor, Daniel Jurafsky, and Andrew Y Ng. 2008. Cheap and fast—but is it good?: evaluating non-expert annotations for natural language tasks. In *Proceedings of the conference on empirical methods in natural language processing*, pages 254–263. Association for Computational Linguistics.

Aobo Wang, Cong Duy Vu Hoang, and Min-Yen Kan. 2013. Perspectives on crowdsourcing annotations for natural language processing. *Language Resources and Evaluation*, 47:9–31.

干红梅. 2008. 语义透明度对中级汉语阅读中词汇学习的影响. *语言文字应用*, 1:82–90.

徐彩华 and 李镗. 2001. 语义透明度影响儿童词汇学习的实验研究. *语言文字应用*, 1:53–59.

王春茂 and 彭聃龄. 1999. 合成词加工中的词频, 词素频率及语义透明度. *心理学报*, 31(3):266–273.

苑春法 and 黄昌宁. 1998. 基于语素数据库的汉语语素及构词研究. *世界汉语教学*, 2(1):13.

高兵 and 高峰强. 2005. 汉语字词识别中词频和语义透明度的交互作用. *心理科学*, 28(6):1358–1360.

Annotate and Identify Modalities, Speech Acts and Finer-Grained Event Types in Chinese Text

Hongzhi Xu
Department of CBS
The Hong Kong Polytechnic University
hongz.xu@gmail.com

Chu-Ren Huang
Faculty of Humanities
The Hong Kong Polytechnic University
churenhuang@gmail.com

Abstract

Discriminating sentences that denote modalities and speech acts from the ones that describe or report events is a fundamental task for accurate event processing. However, little attention has been paid on this issue. No Chinese corpus is available by now with all different types of sentences annotated with their main functionalities in terms of modality, speech act or event. This paper describes a Chinese corpus with all the information annotated. Based on the five event types that are usually adopted in previous studies of event classification, namely state, activity, achievement, accomplishment and semelfactive, we further provide finer-grained categories, considering that each of the finer-grained event types has different semantic entailments. To differentiate them is useful for deep semantic processing and will thus benefit NLP applications such as question answering and machine translation, etc. We also provide experiments to show that the different types of sentences are differentiable with a promising performance.

1 Introduction

Event classification is a fundamental task for NLP applications, such as question answering and machine translation, which need deep understanding of the text. Previous work (Siegel, 1999; Siegel and McKeown, 2000; Palmer et al., 2007; Zarcone and Lenci, 2008; Cao et al., 2006; Zhu et al., 2000) aims to classify events into four categories, namely state, activity, accomplishment and achievement, i.e. Vendler's framework adopted from linguistic studies (Vendler, 1967; Smith, 1991). High performance was reported on the classification, however based on the assumption that all sentences describe an event, which is not case in real text. Modalities and speech acts are not considered and no finer-grained classification is proposed.

The aim for aspectual classification for a specific language is to build verb classes. In such framework, viewpoint aspect in terms of perfective vs. imperfective is not considered. For example, *he is eating a sandwich* and *he ate a sandwich* are all instances of accomplishment. However, we argue that this framework is not enough for more accurate event processing. It is obvious that the two sentences have different meanings and different consequences. The situation described by the first sentence is still going on at the speech time, while the second sentence implies that the event has finished. So, in the perspective of event processing, it is necessary and important to discriminate the two different aspects.

Another important issue is that not all sentences describe events. For example, Austin (1975) discriminated two different types of sentences: constative and performative. Sentences that report or describe events are in the first category. Sentences of the performative category mainly refer to speech (illocutionary) acts, actions that are done by speech. For example, by uttering the sentence *I declare that the new policy will take effect from now on*, the authorized speaker brings a new policy into effect. In this case, uttering the sentence itself is an event. Discriminating speech acts are especially useful in speech corpora, e.g. (Avila and Mello, 2013).

Modality is important due to its interaction with factuality and truth of the embedded propositions. For example, *he can eat two sandwiches* describes a dynamic modality about the subject's ability of eating.

Proceedings of the Workshop on Lexical and Grammatical Resources for Language Processing, pages 157–166,
Coling 2014, Dublin, Ireland, August 24 2014.

However, no eating event has actually happened. Modality has been considered in modeling speaker's opinions (Benamara et al., 2012), machine translation (Baker et al., 2012), etc.

Sauri et al. (2006; 2012) proposed a framework for modeling modalities. However, their definition of modality is a little different from that used by linguists. The main motivation of their work is to predict the factuality of a proposition. As a result, all factors that may affect the factuality of propositions are regarded as modalities. In our framework, we will adopt the definition in linguistic studies that modality expresses a speaker's belief or attitude on an embedded proposition (Palmer, 2001). Factuality is determined by many factors other than modalities. However, we don't want to mix all the factors together in linguistic perspective.

In this paper, we will describe a Chinese corpus in which different sentence types are discriminated. Finer-grained event types are also incorporated with a theory proposed in (Xu and Huang, 2013). The details of the framework will be discussed in the next section.

The remaining of the paper is organized as follows. Section 2 introduces the theoretical framework we shall adopt for our annotation. Section 3 describes a Chinese corpus we annotated with some statistical information. Section 4 describes a classification experiment based on the annotated corpus. Section 5 is the conclusion and our future work.

2 The Annotation Framework

In this section, we will give an introduction to the theoretical framework from a linguistic perspective. There are two main levels for the classification. Sentences are first discriminated according to their main functions, e.g. constative and performative (Austin, 1975). Constative sentences are further divided into modality which mainly expresses the addresser's propositional attitude and event which is a description or report of a real situation without the speaker's attitude. One basic assumption is that one sentence only has one main function in terms of expressing speaker's modality, speech act or describing an event. So, there is no overlap among the three types of sentences.

2.1 Modality

Sentences denoting modalities are different from the sentences reporting events in that the former only refers to a proposition upon which the speaker expresses his attitude its truth value, while the later is a fact without incorporating speakers' opinions but only speaker's perception. It is possible that speakers can make mistakes in their perceptions. However it is beyond the linguistic level and there is no way to predict the correctness based on the surface of the sentence. Thus, it is another issue out of the discussion of this paper. We adopt the modal theory by Palmer (2001). According to him, modality could be divided into epistemic, deontic and dynamic.

Epistemic modality expressed the speaker's opinion on the truth of the embedded proposition in terms of necessity and possibility. Informally, epistemic modality expresses what may be in the world. For example, *ta1 ken3ding4 zai4 ban4gong1shi4* "he must be in his office" describes an epistemic modality of the speaker that he is sure about the truth of the embedded proposition.

Deontic modality expresses what should be in the world, according to speaker's expectations, certain rules, laws and so on. For example, *ni3 bi4xu1 zun1shou3 gui1ze2* "You must obey the rules".

Dynamic modality describes the abilities of a subject, such as *ta1 hui4 you2you3* "he can swim", *wo3 de0 ban4gong1shi4 ke3yi3 kan4jian4 da4hai3* "you can see the ocean from my office".

Evaluation is also treated as a modality in our framework. Evaluation describes the speaker's opinion on a proposition. It is different from epistemic in that it suggests rather than makes judgment on the truth of a proposition. For example, *ta1 suan4shi4 shi4jie4shang4 zui4hao3 de0 ge1shou3 le0* "he should be the best singer in the world". Evaluative sentences only refer to those that contain explicit markers, e.g. *suan4shi4* "should be". The sentence *ta1 shi4 shi4jie4shang4 zui4hao3 de0 ge1shou3* "he is the best singer in the world" is not treated as evaluation. In this sense, evaluative is not equivalent to subjective.

Exclamation is treated as a subset of evaluation. Take *nian2qing1 ren2 a0 !* "Young people!" for example, it mostly expresses an implicit evaluation, e.g. only young people could do crazy things of some kind, based on which the exclamation is expressed by the speaker.

2.2 Speech act

For speech act (illocutionary act), we adopt the theory by Searle (1976), where five different categories are proposed, namely assertive, expressive, directive, commissive and declaration. In addition, we also put interrogative sentences under this category. Speech act sentences only refer to those sentences that are explicit utterances, e.g. the sentences quoted in text.

Assertive is to commit the speaker (in varying degrees) to something's being the case or the truth of the expressed proposition. For example, *wo3 zheng4ming2 ta1 shi4 xue2sheng1* "I certify that he is a student".

Expressive expresses the psychological state specified in the sincerity condition about a state of affairs specified in the propositional content. Verbs for expressive speech act includes *xie4xie4* "thank", *bao4qian4* "apologize", *huan1ying2* "welcome", *dui4bu4qi3* "sorry" etc. For example, *xie4xie4 bang1mang2* "Thanks for your help".

Directive is usually a command or requirement of the speaker to get the hearer to do something. For example, *ni3 guo4lai2 yi1xia4* "Come here please".

Commissive is to commit the speaker (in varying degrees) to some future course of action. For example, *wo3 hui4 bang1 ni3* "I shall help you".

Declaration is to bring about the correspondence between the propositional content and reality. Successful performance guarantees that the propositional content corresponds to the world. For example, *wo3 xuan1bu4 ben3 ci4 hui4yi4 zheng4shi4 kai1mu4* "The conference now start".

Interrogative is an illocutionary act of the speaker that requires the hearer to provided some information. For example, *ni3 jiao4 shen2me0 ming2zi4 ?* "What's your name?" and *ni3 qu4 ting1 na4 ge4 jiang3zuo4 ma0 ?* "Will you attend the speech?" Interrogative sentences are usually with a question mark "?". However, not all sentences with question mark are interrogative. For example, rhetorical questions usually don't need the answer from the hearer. Instead, it actually expresses the speaker's evaluation on a situation. For example, the sentence *wo3 zen3me0 ke3yi3 bu4 jin4xin1 zhao4gu4 ?* "How could I not take care of him carefully?" should be labelled as evaluative modality rather than interrogative speech act.

2.3 Events

Here, we describe a new framework by incorporating finer-grained event categories as described in (Xu and Huang, 2013). Each of the finer-grained categories corresponds to only one of the five coarse categories. So, it is an extension of and is compatible with the Vendler's framework.

2.3.1 Primitive Events

According to Xu and Huang (2013), there are three event primitives, namely static state (S), dynamic state (D), and change of state. Static state is equivalent to the previous notion *state*, which is a homogeneous process, where all subparts are of the same kind of event. Dynamic state refers to an ongoing dynamic process, e.g. running, eating etc., that is perceived like a state. Change of state is then defined as a change from one state, either static or dynamic, to another state.

Change of state actually refers to the previous notion *achievement*. Theoretically, there are four types of changes: static-static change (SS), static-dynamic change (SD), dynamic-static change (DS) and dynamic-dynamic change (DD). In detail, SD change is somewhat equivalent to inceptive achievement, and DS change is somewhat equivalent to terminative or completive achievement.

Event Type	Representation	Example	
Static State	—	ta1 hen3 gao1	*he is tall*
Dynamic State	~~~	ta1 zai4 pao3bu4	*he is running*
SS Change	—|—	ta1 bing4 le0	*he got ill*
SD Change	—|~~~	ta1 kai1shi3 pao3bu4 le0	*he started running*
DS Change	~~~|—	ta1 ting2zhi3 pao3bu4 le0	*he stopped running*
DD Change	~~~|~~~	dian4nao3 qi3dong4 hao3 le0	*the computer finished startup*

Table 1: Primitives of Events.

Table 1 shows the extended event primitives with some illustrative examples. We use '—' and '~~~' to denote static state and dynamic state respectively. ' | ' is used to denote a temporal boundary. In case of change of state, the temporal boundary overlap with the logical boundary, i.e. the change.

Negations usually denote static state. In Chinese, there are two negation adverbs, *bu4* "not" and *mei2you3* "not". However, they are different in that the former negates a generic event meaning that such event doesn't happen, while the latter negates the existence of an event instance. For example, *ta1 bu4 he1jiu3* "he doesn't drink" describes an attribute of the subject, which is intrinsically a static state. *ta1 mei2you3 he1jiu3* "he didn't drink" describes a fact that there is no event instance of his drinking, which is also a static state. Negation of a modality is still a modality. For example, *ta1 bu4 ke3neng2 zai4 ban4gong1shi4* "he cannot be in his office" still describes an epistemic modality.

2.3.2 Complex Events

Based on the primitives, we can compose complex events. Delimitative describes a temporal bounded static state that has a potential starting point and ending point, within which the static state holds, e.g. *ta1 bing4 le0 yi1 ge4 xing1qi1* "he was ill for one week". Process describes a temporal bounded dynamic state that has a potential starting point and ending point, within which the dynamic state holds, e.g. *ta1 pao3 le0 yi1 ge4 xiao3shi2* "he ran for one hour". Semelfactive is different from Process in that its durations is quite short and is usually perceived as instantaneous. In other words, the temporal boundaries of semelfactive is usually naturally determined. For example, *ta1 qiao1 le0 yi1 xia4 men2* "he knocked the door once". There is no way to length the duration of the knocking action. However, a series of iterative semelfactives could form dynamic process. For example, *ta1 qiao1 le0 yi1 ge4 xiao3shi2 de0 men2* "he knocked the door for an hour" gives a reading of iterative knocks.

For static state and dynamic state, we can only refer to their holding at a certain time point. In other words, delimitative and process describe the life cycle of a state. For example, *ta1 bing4 zhe0 ne0* "he is ill" and *ta1 wan3shang4 jiu3dian3 de0 shi2hou0 zai4 pao3bu4* "He was running at 9:00pm". It is also possible to claim that in a certain period, which for some reason became the focus of a conversation, a state holds. For example, *ta1 na4 liang3 tian1 dou1 bing4 zhe0* "he was ill in that two days" and *ta1 wan3shang4 jiu3dian3 dao4 shi2dian3 de0 shi2hou0 zai4 pao3bu4* "From 9:00pm to 10:00pm, he was running". In this case, they are also state rather than delimitative or process. The difference is that there is no information about the starts and the ends, while delimitative and process do.

Accomplishment is composed by a process with a final state. For example, *ta1 xie3 le0 yi1 feng1 xin4* "he wrote a letter" describes an accomplishment composed by a writing process with a final state, i.e. the existence of the letter. The final state of an accomplishment could also be dynamic. For example, *ta1 ba3 dian4nao3 qi3dong4 le0* "he started up the computer" describe an accomplishment with a dynamic final state, i.e. the normal working of computer.

Some Resultative Verb Compounds (RVCs) in Chinese can denote achievements. However, they are easy to be confused with accomplishment. Based on the representation, the difference of them is that accomplishment encodes the start of the dynamic process, while achievement doesn't. For example, *ta1 xie3 wan2 le0 na4 feng1 xin4* "He (write-)finished the letter" describes a DS change. To differentiate them, we can use the *yi3qian2* "before" test. As in this example, *ta1 xie3 wan2 na4 feng1 xin4 yi3 qian2* "before he finished the letter" refers to the period that includes the writing process. This means that

RVCs only focus on the final culminating point and are thus achievements. On the other hand, *ta1 xie3 na4 feng1 xin4 zhi1 qian2* "before he wrote the letter" refers to the period before the writing process. So, *ta1 xie3 le0 yi1 feng1 xin4* "he wrote a letter" is then an accomplishment.

There is a counterpart for accomplishment, which is composed by an instantaneous dynamic process (semelfactive) with a final state. RVCs can also denote instantaneous accomplishment. For example, *ta1 da3sui4 le0 yi1 ge4 bei1zi0* "he hit and broke a cup" is an accomplishment composed by a semelfactive hitting action with a final state, i.e. the broken of the cup. Similarly, the final state could also be dynamic. For example, in *ta1 tan2zhuan4 le0 yi1 ge4 shai3zi0* "He flicked and putted a spin on the dice", the predicate *tan2zhuan4* "flick-spin" is a compound that combines the predicate *tan2* "flick" and *zhuan4* "spin". The whole event is composed by a semelfactive flicking and a final dynamic state of the dice's spin.

Table 2 shows the seven event types with examples. Theoretically, there could be unlimited number of complex events. However, the notions listed here are important in that they are the lexicalized units which reflect the human's cognition of real world events. For the perspective of computational linguistics, discriminating all these linguistic events will be a fundamental step for deeper natural language understanding.

2.3.3 The Neutral Aspect

Some sentences don't include an explicit viewpoint aspect, e.g. without any aspectual markers. For example, *ta1 kan4 xiao3shuo1* "he read novel" can possibly denote different event types in different contexts. *yi3qian2, ta1 kan4 xiao3shuo1* "he read novel before" denotes an attribute of the subject that he reads novels, while *da4jia1 dou1 hen3mang2, xiao3hai2er0 xie3 zuo4ye4, ta1 kan4 xiao3shuo1* "Everyone is busy, children are doing homework, he is reading novels" describes a dynamic state. The aspects of these examples are given by the specified contexts. Such sentences are usually called with NEUTRAL aspect (Smith, 1991). In our framework, such sentences are ignored for now, unless the context can help the annotator to figure out the aspectual information.

<table>
<tr><td>Semelfactive</td><td>|˜|</td><td>ta1 qiao1 le0 qiao1 men2</td><td>"he knocked the door"</td></tr>
<tr><td>Delimitative</td><td>|—-|</td><td>ta1 bing4 le0 yi1 ge4 xing1qing1</td><td>"he was ill for one week"</td></tr>
<tr><td>Process</td><td>|~~~~|</td><td>ta1 pao3 le0 yi1 ge4 xiao3shi2</td><td>"he ran for an hour"</td></tr>
<tr><td>Instantaneous
Accomplishment</td><td>|˜|—
|˜|~~~</td><td>ta1 da3sui4 le0 bei1zi0
ta1 tan2zhuan4 le0 yi1 ge4 shai3zi0</td><td>"he broke the cup"
"He putted a spin on the dice"</td></tr>
<tr><td>Accomplishment</td><td>|~~~~|—
|~~~~|~~~</td><td>ta1 xie3 le0 yi1 feng1 xin4
ta1 ba3 dian4nao3 qi3dong4 le0</td><td>"he wrote a letter"
"he started up the computer"</td></tr>
</table>

Table 2: Complex event types that are composed by more than one primitives.

The overall hierarchy is shown in Figure 1. Some traditional notions are kept in use e.g. *accomplishment* and *achievement*. However, they now refer to event types rather than verb classes.

3 Annotating a Chinese Corpus

3.1 Data Selection

For annotation, we choose Sinica Treebank 3.0 (Huang et al., 2000), which contains more than 60,000 trees. Sinica Treebank is a subset of Sinica Corpus (Chen et al., 1996), which is a balanced corpus that contains different genres of materials, including news, novels and some transcripts of spoken Chinese. Sinica Treebank is annotated based on the Information-based Case Grammar (Chen and Huang, 1990). The annotated syntactic and semantic information is kept for further studies, e.g. feature evaluation and selection.

For annotation, we only select the sentences that are labeled as S and end with punctuation of period '。', exclamation '！', semicolon '；' and question mark '？'. After removing duplicate sentences, we get 5612 sentences Table 3 shows the detailed information of the raw corpus. There are 45728 tokens from 11681 types in the corpus. For the heads of the sentences, there are 2127 different verbs.

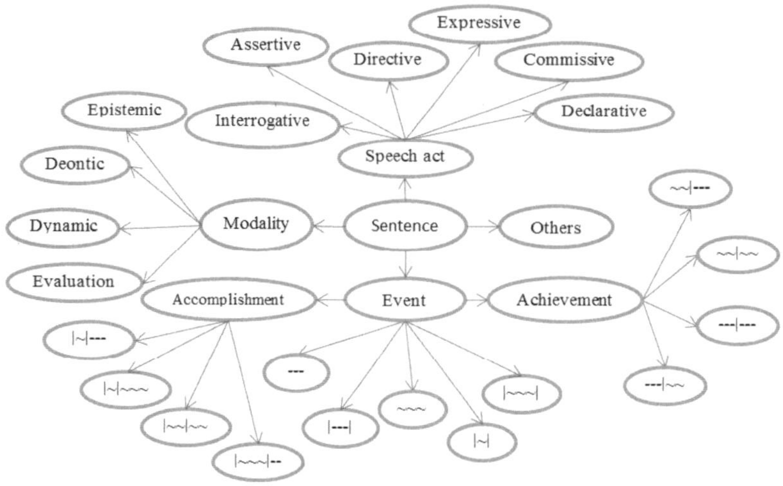

Figure 1: Sentence type hierarchy.

Sentences	Different Verbs	Different Words	Tokens	Characters
5612	2127	11681	45728	75960

Table 3: Distribution information of the corpus for annotation.

3.2 Annotation Result

Each sentence is labeled as one specific finer-grained category from the 23 categories described in Section 2. Whenever an example could not be decided by the annotator, it is discussed with another two linguistic experts to make the final decision. However, we also did agreement test, which will be discussed later.

Finally, we annotated 1044 instances in modality, 764 speech act instances and 3811 event instances. The distribution information is shown in Table 4. We can see that some event types, although theoretically exist, don' t encounter any examples, such as the instantaneous accomplishment with dynamic final state: |˜|˜˜˜.

Static state contains more than 40% instances. We think that it reflects the real distribution of event types as we don' t make any bias for selecting data. Static state can be further divided into several subcategories, e.g. attributive, relational, habitual, etc., which will be our future work.

<table>
<tr><th>Type</th><th>No.</th><th>Type</th><th>No.</th><th>Type</th><th>No.</th><th>Type</th><th>No.</th><th>Type</th><th>No.</th></tr>
<tr><td>Epistemic</td><td>303</td><td>Assertive</td><td>64</td><td>—</td><td>2475</td><td>—|—</td><td>471</td><td>|˜|—</td><td>257</td></tr>
<tr><td>Deontic</td><td>219</td><td>Expressive</td><td>13</td><td>˜˜˜</td><td>166</td><td></td><td></td><td>|˜|˜˜˜</td><td>0</td></tr>
<tr><td>Dynamic</td><td>111</td><td>Directive</td><td>65</td><td>|—|</td><td>6</td><td>—|˜˜˜</td><td>96</td><td>|˜˜˜|—</td><td>163</td></tr>
<tr><td>Evaluation</td><td>411</td><td>Commissive</td><td>58</td><td>|˜˜˜|</td><td>48</td><td>˜˜˜|—</td><td>79</td><td>|˜˜˜|˜˜˜</td><td>40</td></tr>
<tr><td>Interrogative</td><td>559</td><td>Declarative</td><td>2</td><td>|˜|</td><td>4</td><td>˜˜˜|˜˜˜</td><td>2</td><td></td><td></td></tr>
</table>

Table 4: Distribution of different event types in the annotated corpus.

Table 5 shows the number of the main verbs regarding how many event types they can denote excluding modality and speech act. We can see that more than 200 verbs correspond to more than one category. This shows that the verbs alone sometimes could not determine the event type.

No. of Event Types	1	2	3	4	5	6	7
No. of Verbs	1395	155	44	9	7	1	1

Table 5: Number of verbs with regard to how many event types they can denote.

	Accuracy	F1-Measure	Kappa
Annotator 1	0.862	0.762	0.837
Annotator 2	0.821	0.677	0.784
Annotator 1+2	0.842	0.716	0.811

Table 6: Annotation agreements between the main annotator and annotator1, annotator 2, annotator 1+2. Annotator 1+2 means the combination result of the two annotators, i.e. all the 2000 examples.

3.3 Agreement Evaluation

In order to test the reliability of the annotation, we randomly select 2000 examples from the corpus and let another two linguists annotate them. Each of the linguists annotate half of them. The annotation results are then compared with the main annotator. The agreements between the main annotator and the other two annotators in terms of accuracy, F1 measure and Kappa value are shown in Table 6. The F1 measures are calculated based on the assumption that the main annotator's result is the gold standard. The result shows a very high agreement which means that our new framework for event type classification is reliable and easy for annotation.

4 Automatic Classification of Chinese Sentences and Event Types

In this section, we conduct two classification experiments. The first is to discriminate the three sentence types regarding their main functions, speech act, modality and event. The second is the classification with the finer-grained categories. Before the experiments, we will first discuss the features that may help for the classification.

4.1 Features

As suggested in previous literatures (Siegel, 1999; Siegel and McKeown, 2000; Zhu et al., 2000; Cao et al., 2006), the following features are considered as important for event type classification.

Main verbs and their complements including argument structure are the most important indicators to an event type. Negation of the main verb is a strong indicator for static state, as discussed above.

Aspectual markers, 着 *zhe0* "ZHE", 了 *le0* "LE", 过 *guo4* "GUO" and some aspectual light verbs, e.g. 在 *zai4* "be doing", 开始 *kai1shi3* "start", 继续 *ji4xu4* "continue", 停止 *ting2zhi3* "stop", 完成 *wan2cheng2* "finish", are strong indicators for different event types.

Temporal adverbials are also important features, which could potentially disambiguate neutral sentences, e.g., *yi3qian2, ta1 kan4 xiao3shuo1* "he read novel before" as discussed above.

Frequency adverbs, such as 经常 *jing1chang2* "often", 偶尔 *ou3er3* "sometimes", etc., are indicators for habitual states. For example, *ta1 jing1chang2 qu4 he1jiu3* "he often goes for drinking" is a habitual state rather than a specific event.

Modalities could be expressed by auxiliaries, adverbs, sentence final particles etc. in Chinese. Adverbs that modify the main verb, such as 可能 *ke3neng2* "possibly", are important features for identifying modalities. Sentence final particles (SFP) and punctuation marks are also good indicators to evaluative modality.

Since we don't maintain a dictionary for the above indicators, we use a general feature set including the dependency structure and the combinations of the dependent constituents. We suggest that the above linguistic rules could be reflected by the dependency structures, which could be captured by the classifiers. Meanwhile, the experiment result here is only to serve as a baseline for future comparisons. In all, the features are listed in Table 7 with some examples.

ID	**Feature**	**Example**
f_1	Head	head:word:kan4, head:pos:verb, head:subj:word:ta1, head:subj:pos:pron, head:obj:xp:NP, head:obj:xp:noun-noun
f_2	Dependency	dep:word:ta1, dep:pos:pron, dep:word:bu4, dep:pos:adv, dep:word:xiao3shuo1, dep:pos:noun, dep:word:le0, dep:pos:particle,
f_3	COMB	subj:word:ta1-head:word:kan4-obj:xp:noun-noun, subj:pos:pron-head:pos:verb-obj:xp:NP,

Table 7: Feature template we use for our classification of event types. Feature examples are based on the sentence *ta1 (he) bu4 (not) kan4 (read) zhen1tan4 (detective) xiao3shuo1 (novel) le0 (LE)* "he doesn't read detective novels any more".

	f_1			$+f_2$			$+f_3$		
	Prec	Rec	F1	Prec	Rec	F1	Prec	Rec	F1
Event	0.709	0.939	0.807	0.853	0.969	0.908	0.833	0.974	0.898
Modality	0.395	0.124	0.189	0.731	0.473	0.574	0.744	0.431	0.545
SpeechAct	0.430	0.130	0.199	0.829	0.664	0.737	0.845	0.609	0.707
MacroAvg	0.511	0.398	0.399	0.804	0.702	0.740	0.807	0.671	0.717
Accuracy	0.679			0.836			0.824		

Table 8: Coarse level classification result.

4.2 Experimental Result

To give a real performance, the annotated syntactic and semantic information are not used. Instead, we use the Stanford word segmenter (Tseng et al., 2005) and Stanford parser (Chang et al., 2009) to get the syntactic structure of the sentences. All the experiment are results of 5-fold cross validation with a SVM classifier implemented in LibSVM (Chang and Lin, 2011).

The result of the coarse level classification for modality, event and speech act is shown in Table 8. We can see that the overall performance is reasonable. The F-Measure for modality is not as good as the others. This is due to the fact that the modal markers and operators are quite critical for identifying modalities, which may be sparse in our corpus. We suggest that maintaining a comprehensive dictionary of modal operators could benefit the identification of the modalities. We can also see that the feature set f_3 harms the performance, which is also caused by the feature sparseness problem.

For finer-grained classification, we use two different ways. The first way is to use a hierarchical classification scheme. An instance is first classified as event, modality or speech act. According to the result of the first round classification, the instance is put into the corresponding finer-grained model for further classification. The second way is to classify all instances all at once based on a model trained on all finer-grained categories.

Considering that some categories contain only few examples, which will provide unreliable evaluation of the performance, we combined accomplishments with static final state and dynamic state, so does for instantaneous accomplishment. We use '=' to denote a general state, which could be either static or dynamic. Static state and delimitative are combined together, while dynamic state, process and semelfactive are combined. Expressive, declarative and DD change are ignored in the experiments. The classification results with feature sets f_1 and f_2 are shown in Table 9. The hierarchical classification is slightly better than the all-at-once classification. Meanwhile, the accuracy for hierarchical classification is 0.621, which is much better than the predominant guess 0.443.

We should note that parsing accuracy will significantly affect the result of event type classification. This is true in the sense that the semantic content of words and their syntactic relations are all critical

<table>
<tr><th></th><th colspan="3">All-At-Once</th><th colspan="3">Hierarchical</th></tr>
<tr><th></th><th>Precision</th><th>Recall</th><th>F1</th><th>Precision</th><th>Recall</th><th>F1</th></tr>
<tr><td>—</td><td>0.609</td><td>0.952</td><td>0.743</td><td>0.627</td><td>0.938</td><td>0.751</td></tr>
<tr><td>~~~</td><td>0.840</td><td>0.078</td><td>0.142</td><td>0.830</td><td>0.069</td><td>0.127</td></tr>
<tr><td>—|—</td><td>0.454</td><td>0.384</td><td>0.415</td><td>0.473</td><td>0.418</td><td>0.443</td></tr>
<tr><td>—|~~~</td><td>0.583</td><td>0.083</td><td>0.142</td><td>0.537</td><td>0.104</td><td>0.173</td></tr>
<tr><td>~~~|—</td><td>0</td><td>0</td><td>0</td><td>0</td><td>0</td><td>0</td></tr>
<tr><td>|~~~~|===</td><td>0.438</td><td>0.084</td><td>0.140</td><td>0.394</td><td>0.108</td><td>0.168</td></tr>
<tr><td>|~|===</td><td>0.496</td><td>0.159</td><td>0.239</td><td>0.516</td><td>0.210</td><td>0.295</td></tr>
<tr><td>Epistemic</td><td>0.710</td><td>0.419</td><td>0.524</td><td>0.638</td><td>0.442</td><td>0.520</td></tr>
<tr><td>Deontic</td><td>0.629</td><td>0.360</td><td>0.455</td><td>0.573</td><td>0.383</td><td>0.457</td></tr>
<tr><td>Dynamic</td><td>0.388</td><td>0.233</td><td>0.290</td><td>0.391</td><td>0.287</td><td>0.330</td></tr>
<tr><td>Evaluation</td><td>0.592</td><td>0.319</td><td>0.412</td><td>0.523</td><td>0.302</td><td>0.382</td></tr>
<tr><td>Interrogative</td><td>0.844</td><td>0.789</td><td>0.815</td><td>0.818</td><td>0.789</td><td>0.803</td></tr>
<tr><td>Directive</td><td>0.692</td><td>0.309</td><td>0.418</td><td>0.695</td><td>0.354</td><td>0.458</td></tr>
<tr><td>Assertive</td><td>0</td><td>0</td><td>0</td><td>0.1</td><td>0.031</td><td>0.047</td></tr>
<tr><td>Commissive</td><td>0.83</td><td>0.277</td><td>0.409</td><td>0.713</td><td>0.155</td><td>0.246</td></tr>
<tr><td>MacroAvg</td><td>0.540</td><td>0.296</td><td>0.343</td><td>0.522</td><td>0.306</td><td>0.347</td></tr>
<tr><td>Accuracy</td><td>0.620</td><td></td><td></td><td>0.621</td><td></td><td></td></tr>
</table>

Table 9: 5-fold cross validation result of finer-grained classification with f_1 and f_2 features.

for the classification. Besides the parsing problem, there are other linguistic issues behind. Many modal operators could result in different modalities, such as 应该 *ying1gai1* “should”, 会 *hui4* “will/can/may”, 要 *yao4* “want/will/should/must” etc. Sometimes, it is hard to decide which meaning is correct in a context. There may be also other linguistic issues that we have not discovered yet. This corpus thus could be used for both linguistic study and computational applications, e.g. event processing.

5 Conclusion

In this paper, we present a Chinese corpus annotated with modalities, speech acts and finer-grained event types. We also provide experiments on classification in different levels of categories with a general feature set. The experimental result is acceptable concerning the difficult linguistic issues behind. In future, we would like to continue our research work on improving the corpus and exploring more semantic information including lexical semantic structures and lexical relations such as WordNet to improve the performance of the classification.

Acknowledgements

The work is supported by a General Research Fund (GRF) sponsored by the Research Grants Council (Project no. 543810 and 543512).

References

John Langshaw Austin. 1975. *How to do things with words: Second Edition*. Harvard University Press, Cambridge, MA.

Luciana Beatriz Avila and Heliana Mello. 2013. Challenges in modality annotation in a brazilian portuguese spontaneous speech corpus. *Proceedings of WAMM-IWCS2013*.

Kathryn Baker, Michael Bloodgood, Bonnie Dorr, Chris Callison-Burch, Nathaniel Filardo, Christine Piatko, Lori Levin, and Scott Miller. 2012. Use of modality and negation in semantically-informed syntactic mt. *Language in Society*, 38(2).

Farah Benamara, Baptiste Chardon, Yannick Mathieu, Vladimir Popescu, and Nicholas Asher. 2012. How do negation and modality impact on opinions? In *Proceedings of the Workshop on Extra-Propositional Aspects of Meaning in Computational Linguistics*, pages 10–18.

Defang Caò, Wenjie Li, Chunfa Yuan, and Kam-Fai Wong. 2006. Automatic chinese aspectual classification using linguistic indicators. *International Journal of Information Technology*, 12(4):99–109.

Chih-Chung Chang and Chih-Jen Lin. 2011. Libsvm: a library for support vector machines. *ACM Transactions on Intelligent Systems and Technology*, 2(3):1–27.

Pi-Chuan Chang, Huihsin Tseng, Dan Jurafsky, and Christopher D. Manning. 2009. Discriminative reordering with chinese grammatical relations features. In *Proceedings of the Third Workshop on Syntax and Structure in Statistical Translation*, pages 51–59.

Keh-Jiann Chen and Chu-Ren Huang. 1990. Information-based case grammar. In *Proceedings of the 13th conference on Computational linguistics*, pages 54–59.

Keh-Jiann Chen, Chu-Ren Huang, Li-Ping Chang, and Hui-Li Hsu. 1996. Sinica corpus: Design methodology for balanced corpora. In *Proceedings of Pacific Asia Conference on Language, Information and Computing (PACLIC)*, pages 167–176.

Chu-Ren Huang, Feng-Yi Chen, Keh-Jiann Chen, Zhao ming Gao, and Kuang-Yu Chen. 2000. Sinica treebank: design criteria, annotation guidelines, and on-line interface. In *Proceedings of the second workshop on Chinese language processing: held in conjunction with the 38th Annual Meeting of the Association for Computational Linguistics*, pages 29–37.

Alexis Palmer, Elias Ponvert, Jason Baldridge, and Carlota Smith. 2007. A sequencing model for situation entity classification. In *Proceedings of the 45th Annual Meeting of the Association of Computational Linguistics*, pages 896–903.

Frank Robert Palmer. 2001. *Mood and Modality*. Cambridge University Press, Cambridge.

Roser Sauri and James Pustejovsky. 2012. Are you sure that this happened? assessing the factuality degree of events in text. *Computational Linguistics*, 38(2):261–299.

Roser Sauri, Marc Verhagen, and James Pustejovsky. 2006. Annotating and recognizing event modality in text. In *Proceedings of 19th International FLAIRS Conference*, pages 333–338.

John R. Searle. 1976. A classification of illocutionary acts. *Language in Society*, 5(1):1–23.

Eric V. Siegel and Kathleen R. McKeown. 2000. Learning methods to combine linguistic indicators: Improving aspectual classification and revealing linguistic insights. *Computational Linguistics*, 26(4):595–628.

Eric V. Siegel. 1999. Corpus-based linguistic indicators for aspectual classification. In *Proceedings of the 37th annual meeting of the Association for Computational Linguistics on Computational Linguistics*, pages 112–119.

Carlotta Smith. 1991. *The Parameter of Aspect*. Kluwer Academic Publishers, Dordrecht.

Huihsin Tseng, Pichuan Chang, Galen Andrew, Daniel Jurafsky, and Christopher Manning. 2005. A conditional random field word segmenter for sighan bakeoff 2005. In *Proceedings of the Fourth SIGHAN Workshop on Chinese Language Processing*, volume 171.

Zeno Vendler, 1967. *Linguistics in Philosophy*, chapter Verbs and times, pages 97–121. Cornell University Press, Ithaca.

Hongzhi Xu and Chu-Ren Huang. 2013. Primitives of events and the semantic representation. In *Proceedings of the 6th International Conference on Generative Approaches to the Lexicon*, pages 54–61.

Alessandra Zarcone and Alessandro Lenci. 2008. Computational models for event type classification in context. In *Proceedings of the International Conference on Language Resource and Evaluation (LREC)*, pages 1232–1238.

Xiaodan Zhu, Chunfa Yuan, Kam-Fai Wong, and Wenjie Li. 2000. An algorithm for situation classification of chinese verbs. In *Proceedings of the second workshop on Chinese language processing: held in conjunction with the 38th Annual Meeting of the Association for Computational Linguistics*, volume 12, pages 140–145.

Author Index

Association for Computational Linguistics
209 N. Eighth Street
Stroudsburg, Pennsylvania 18360

CURRAN ASSOCIATES INC
proceedings.com